JUSTICE IN THE WORKPLACE:

Approaching Fairness in Human Resource Management

SERIES IN APPLIED PSYCHOLOGY

Edwin A. Fleishman, George Mason University
Series Editor

JUSTICE IN THE WORKPLACE:

Approaching Fairness in Human Resource Management

Edited by
RUSSELL CROPANZANO
Colorado State University

LAWRENCE ERLBAUM ASSOCIATES, PUBLISHERS
1993   Hillsdale, New Jersey   Hove and London

Lawrence Erlbaum Associates, Inc., Publishers
365 Broadway
Hillsdale, New Jersey 07642

Library of Congress Cataloging-in-Publication Data

Justice in the workplace : approaching fairness in human resource
    management / edited by Russell Cropanzano.
        p.   cm.
    Includes bibliographical references and index.
    ISBN 0-8058-1055-2
    1. Employee rights.   2. Justice.   3. Personnel management.
I. Cropanzano, Russell.
HF5549.5.E428J87   1992
658.3'15—dc20   91-44766
                                                       CIP

Printed in the United States of America
10   9   8   7   6   5   4   3   2

Contents

PART III: JUSTICE AT THE ORGANIZATIONAL AND
INTERORGANIZATIONAL LEVEL

Foreword

There is a compelling need for innovative approaches to the solution of many pressing problems involving human relationships in today's society. Such approaches are more likely to be successful when they are based on sound research and applications. This *Series in Applied Psychology* offers publications that emphasize state-of-the-art research and its application to important issues of human behavior in a variety of societal settings. The objective is to bridge both academic and applied interests.

Most fundamentally, people are the substance and building blocks of work organizations. An organization's successes are usually social successes, just as its failings tend to be social failings. Managers, as opposed to technicians, allocate the lion's share of their time to people: motivating them, rewarding them, coordinating them, and even removing them from their work units. The discipline of human resource management has a long history, coming of age as a set of sophisticated technical tools to help organizations deal with the ubiquitous concerns and complications involved in managing people. But, like all technical tools, human resource interventions ultimately stand and fall on the people who administer them, and, in turn, on the people whom they administer. Although technical competence may be necessary, it is not a sufficient condition for success. Human resource management must also attend to the concerns of the people being managed. It is here that research on organizational justice is so important. The justice perspective offers a complementary view of the human resource enterprise. It offers us a look at the organization from the vantage point of personal concerns, wants, and needs. As such, it holds out the promise of both more effective and more humane organizations.

The editor of this volume has been able to bring together, for the first time, concepts and issues related to justice in organizations. All of the authors in this book are interested in both human resource management and social justice. Although every one of the authors has arrived at a similar place, each has approached it from different directions. The editor and several contributors to this volume are long-standing students of justice and have contributed to the original conceptual spadework that taught us when, how, and why individuals perceive justice. Their chapters expand from this strong theoretical foundation. They have extended their work, encompassing human resource management under the rubric of social justice. Other authors have reached out from the opposite direction. Several of these chapters began as attempts to understand particular organizational interventions. How, for example, can we increase the effectiveness of compensations systems? Of customer service? Of employee grievance systems? Of workplace drug screening? In each case, an attention and concern for social justice provided at least some of the answers.

This collection of chapters then, is both comprehensive and diverse. It begins by laying out the theoretical basis of justice theory and then proceeds to apply these insights to a variety of human resource interventions. In each case, we have a better understanding and, perhaps, some ways to make work better for us all.

Edwin A. Fleishman, Editor
Series in Applied Psychology

INTRODUCING JUSTICE TO THE WORKPLACE

1 Injustice and Work Behavior: A Historical Review

Russell Cropanzano
Marjorie L. Randall
Colorado State University

In recent years many human resource interventions have been reexamined in light of organizational justice. One can see this trend manifested in many areas, including such things as performance evaluation (Greenberg, 1986; Folger, Konovsky, & Cropanzano, 1991, Folger & Lewis, chapter 5, this volume), drug testing (Konovsky & Cropanzano, 1991, chapter 9, this volume), layoffs (Brockner & Greenberg, 1990; Konovsky & Brockner, chapter 6, this volume), and pay satisfaction (Folger & Konovsky, 1989; Miceli, chapter 12, this volume). Each of these, along with a variety of justice-based interventions, is discussed in this volume. In each case we attempt to demonstrate how this work can guide managers in the administration of more effective personnel systems and also offer directions for additional research. Put very broadly, this volume is about the present and future of organizational justice, and it should be readily apparent that the present is broad and the future looks bright.

However, it is also important to realize that justice was not always a major issue for human resource managers. This is especially interesting in light of the fact that workers and their unions have long battled for what they feel to be just and humane working conditions (cf. Fantasia, 1988; Painter, 1987). Managers and researchers, however, were slower to realize the importance of due process and fair treatment. Given this, it seems prudent to include a chapter on the past, as a preamble to the present and the future. As we see later, an interest in justice did not evolve from some abstract academic theory, but from day-to-day reality of working organizations. This was evident at the outset.

Fairness first came to the attention of organization researchers almost by accident. During World War II, Stouffer, Suchman, DeVinney, Star, and Williams (1949) were conducting an extensive research program that examined various aspects of soldiers' adjustment to army life. As part of one particular project, Stouffer and his colleagues compared promotion satisfaction between officers in the army air corps and their counterparts in the military police. Promotions in the air corps were fast and steady, whereas officers in the police typically moved up the ranks slowly. Intuitively, it would have seemed reasonable to expect that the air corps would be more satisfied. After all, these individuals had much more of the desired outcome. In fact, the results showed the exact opposite. To the surprise of these researchers, military police offers were significantly more pleased with their opportunities for advancement.

Stouffer et al. reasoned that the differences in satisfaction were likely due to each group's particular frame of reference. Officers in the air corps saw their peers promoted rapidly and, by comparison, judged themselves to be unfairly treated. In the military police, on the other hand, men saw their peers promoted more slowly. Hence, by comparison, police officers saw themselves as fairly treated. Stouffer and his colleagues had realized an important point: Justice is defined in reference to some standard. Based on this assessment, the researchers coined the term relative deprivation (RD). The deprivation is relative in that it is compared to some reference point and is not an absolute or objective quantity. This straightforward idea became the basis for much of the subsequent research.

RELATIVE DEPRIVATION AS A FEELING AND AS A THEORY

As Crosby (1976) noted, since the initial work of Stouffer and his colleagues, RD has acquired two distinct meanings. First, it can refer "to the emotion one feels when making negatively discrepant comparisons" (Crosby, 1979, p. 88). Alternatively, RD also refers to a set of theories that articulate the comparisons that are likely to produce perceived injustice. Put more loosely, RD sometimes refers to an emotional outcome and sometimes refers to the various theories that explain how that outcome comes about. In any case, the fundamental principal underlying RD is that individuals make certain social comparisons. People experience injustice based on these judgments (Pettigrew, 1967).

Relative deprivation has proven to be an extremely useful construct. Over the years it has helped in understanding such things as urban violence (Gurr, 1968a, 1968b), racism (Sears & McConahay, 1970; Grindstaff, 1968), class discrimination (Runciman, 1966), and revolution (Gurr, 1970). Although all of this work is important, it is beyond the scope of this volume. Rather, we focus on the implications of justice for work behavior. Further, as becomes clear here, RD is not the only approach to understanding justice. As Greenberg (1987a) emphasized, more recent approaches do exist. However, these models have typically retained RD's central premise. That is, justice is defined relative to some referent standard. Put another way, the relative amount is of central importance in determining perceived fairness. Under the appropriate circumstances, people will happily accept meager rewards or complain bitterly about what appear to be extravagant rewards.

Organizations, if they do nothing else, provide individuals with a variety of outcomes and also offer a collection of other people to serve as possible frames of reference. As such, justice considerations are bound to have an important effect on organization life. Some of the early demonstrations of this focused on pay satisfaction (Patchen, 1961). In one study Lawler and Porter (1963) compared the pay satisfaction of first-line supervisors to that of more highly paid company presidents. Once more, in line with the justice perspective, the first-line supervisors reported higher pay satisfaction—even though they earned less money overall. Similar findings were also obtained by Smith, Kendall, and Hulin (1969). They found that job satisfaction was higher than would be expected in a poor factory but less than anticipated at a well-paying organization. The notion of comparative standards has received additional support in more recent field investigations (Berkowitz, Fraser, Treasure, & Cochran, 1987; Sweeney, McFarlin, & Inderrieden, 1990). It is now a generally accepted finding that pay amount and pay satisfaction are not highly correlated (Miceli and Lane, 1991). Once more we see a consistent theme: Individuals seem to be defining their outcomes in comparison to an available referent standard. So long as pay is not comparatively low, satisfaction can remain at reasonable levels (Lawler, 1971).

Similar findings were also obtained by researchers examining the satisfaction of various disadvantaged groups. For example, as Black Americans moved up the economic ladder, they were likely to become more displeased with the social status quo (Pettigrew, 1964, 1967, 1971). In related work on gender, Martin (1981) and Major (1987) each reviewed the types of referents that a female worker can utilize. As expected, both found that perceptions of injustice varied widely depending on the nature of the comparison. For example, Martin, Price, Bies, and Powers (1979) examined the standards used by secretaries. These individuals could compare themselves with either other secretaries or with company executives. As expected, even when pay level was held constant, individuals expressed more discontent when they used executives as a referent.

EQUITY THEORY

It was within this intellectual climate of relative deprivation and social comparison that Adams first devised Equity Theory (see Adams, 1965 and Adams & Freedman, 1976, for more complete reviews). Equity Theory incorporated the notion of social comparison into a quasi-mathematical formula. The essential idea was that when individuals work for an organization they present certain inputs (e.g., ability or job performance). Based on what they put in, people expect to get something out. So, for example, if an individual inputs high performance he or she might expect a high pay level. Adams (1965) expressed this as a ratio of outcomes over inputs. The difficult thing for workers is to determine when a given ratio is fair. Adams argued that individuals determine fairness by comparing their ratio to the ratio of some similar other. Put another way, this allows one to see if, given a certain level of inputs, he or she is getting a reasonable amount.

Equity Theory, like the relative deprivation approach, predicted that comparatively low rewards, and not their absolute level, would produce dissatisfaction. This discontent would then motivate individuals to take action that reduces the discrepancy between their ratio and the ratio of the comparison person. For example, one might reduce his or her inputs (perhaps by lowering performance levels) or, if possible, find a way to increase outcomes. However, Adams added an additional idea: It is also possible that an individual could perform a comparison and determine that he or she is getting relatively more outcomes than is a referent other. In this over-reward situation, an individual should not feel anger or resentment, but he or she may instead experience guilt, shame, or remorse. These emotions are also negative and therefore should motivate the individual to reduce the imbalance. Because individuals do not usually forego positive outcomes, people are generally likely to respond by increasing inputs. That is, they are expected to work harder.

These predictions were tested in a field experiment conducted by Adams (1963). In this study, individuals were made to believe that they were overpaid in either a flat salary or a piece-rate schedule. In accordance with predictions, overpaid and salaried individuals actually worked harder. However, the piece-rate individuals faced a dilemma. If they worked harder they earned more money and thereby accentuated the inequity. Their resolution was an interesting one. Once more, as expected, under a piece-rate payment schedule individuals completed fewer units of work (lower quantity), but they increased the quality.

Adams' predictions, although counterintuitive, were essentially supported. Equity Theory was not only able to explain much of the previous research, it was also able to make new and powerful predictions. Give this, it comes as no surprise that the model inspired a great deal of subsequent research. Most of this work was, in at least a general sense, supportive (cf. Greenberg, 1982; Adams & Freedman, 1976; Walster, Berscheid, & Walster, 1965).

CRITICS AND REFINEMENTS OF JUSTICE THEORY

A variety of authors raised concerns over the construct validity of Adams' inequity manipulation (e.g., Lawler, 1968; Prichard, 1969; Carrell & Dittrich, 1978; Schwab, 1980). To understand these concerns, one has to consider the manipulation of overequity used in the early research (e.g., Adams, 1963). In these studies individuals were made to feel overpaid by being bluntly told that they were unqualified for the job. This manipulation may well have threatened participants' self-esteem or job security. Hence, individuals were indeed motivated to work hard, but perceived injustice was not necessarily the reason why.

In response to these critiques, additional research was conducted using unconfounded induction procedures (Garland, 1973; Greenberg, 1988). In Greenberg's field experiment, for example, employees were randomly assigned to temporary offices. These were of high, equal, or low status. Consistent with Equity Theory, those assigned to higher status offices showed higher performance and those assigned to lower status offices showed lower performance. In another experiment, Greenberg and Ornstein (1983) assigned subjects either high or low status job titles. All individuals did the same work. Those with high status titles showed higher performance. Findings like these have led recent reviewers to conclude that Equity Theory has been generally supported (e.g., Greenberg, 1990a; Mowday, 1987).

Construct validity, however, is not the only problem that has plagued Equity Theory. The equity rule of fairness states that justice is based, at least partially, on individuals being rewarded based on what they contribute. In the workplace, for example, this could translate into higher pay for higher performers. However, other allocation systems are also available. Deutsch (1985), for example, noted that a desired outcome could be split evenly. This is termed an equality distribution. Similarly, outcomes could also be assigned to individuals based on individual necessity. This would be termed a need distribution.

Deutsch (1985) maintained that a variety of factors can influence one's choice of an allocation rule. For example, an equity rule is typically used by people from individualistic cultures, or when the emphasis is on maximizing group performance, or when the allocator is depressed. On the other hand, an equality rule is most likely to occur among individuals from collectivistic cultures, or when the emphasis is on maintaining group harmony, or when performance is largely determined by uncontrollable factors, or when the allocator is in a positive mood (Greenberg, 1983; Leung & Bond, 1984; Murphy-Berman, Berman, Singh, Pachauri, & Kumar, 1984; Sinclair & Mark, 1991). Of course, these approaches are not mutually exclusive. When making allocation decisions, individuals often combine rules (Elliot & Meeker, 1986). Although this work does not rule out Equity Theory, it does place boundary conditions around the model. Fortunately, more recent theory has articulated these boundaries in more detail. James (chapter 2, this volume) discusses this work at greater length.

A third problem involves the relationship between unfairness and behavioral outcomes. If justice is to have practical relevance it is important to show that it impacts something other than self-report measures. It needs to be demonstrated that justice affects other forms of behavior. This issue has typically been discussed in the context of conflict. Various researchers have maintained that, at least under some circumstances, injustice causes conflict (e.g., Crosby, 1976;

Mark & Folger, 1984). Martin, however, reviewed extensive evidence indicating that individuals often accept injustice without responding. Even when unfairly treated, Martin (1986) found that individuals were often hesitant to take action. In one role-playing study, for example, Martin, Brickman, and Murray (1984) found that the magnitude of underpayment was unrelated to subjects' reported tendency to engage in conflict. Given these findings, Martin et al. (1984) raised the possibility that the availability of "mobilization resources," or the means to successfully engage an authority figure, are more important than injustice per se (see also McCarthy & Zald, 1977).

Martin's concern has been addressed by recent research. Both laboratory (Cropanzano & Baron, in press) and field (Greenberg, 1990b) studies have shown that in many situations individuals will indeed take action to resolve a perceived inequity. Greenberg (chapter four, this volume) considers various types of human resource interventions. In each case he reviews considerable evidence that justice affects important work behaviors. Nevertheless, Martin's (1986) central concern remains an important one. One approach to addressing this problem involves articulating the circumstances under which underreward will, in fact, lead to perceived relative deprivation. It seems to be the case that a person experiencing an unfavorable comparison will not necessarily feel him or herself to be deprived. Although a variety of RD models exist (see Crosby, 1984, and Martin, 1981, for more extensive reviews), the two that have inspired the most organizational research have been proposed by Crosby (1976) and Folger (1986). These are discussed in more detail below.

After reviewing the relevant literature, Crosby (1976) noted that several components of relative deprivation were common to most models of injustice. Integrating the earlier frameworks of Adams (1965), Gurr (1970), and others, Crosby constructed a list of five preconditions that she believed were necessary for RD to occur. First, an individual must want an outcome X. Second, the individual must see a similar other possess X. Third, the individual must feel entitled to X. Fourth, the individual must not feel personally responsible for not having X. Fifth, the individual must feel that it is feasible to obtain X sometime in the future. The fifth precondition was derived after some controversy. In particular, Gurr (1970) posited that feasibility must be low for RD to occur. In any case, Crosby maintained that RD would occur when all five of these conditions were present.

An empirical test of Crosby's model produced equivocal results (Bernstein & Crosby, 1980). These authors noted that subjects reported RD even if they thought they were at least somewhat at fault. Furthermore, the feasibility findings were exactly opposite those predicted by Crosby (1976), but supporting Gurr (1970). In particular, Bernstein and Crosby found that feasibility had to be low for individuals to experience RD.

To account for these anomalous findings, Folger (1986) offered Referent Cognitions Theory (RCT) as an alternate model. According to RCT, an individual will not experience RD unless he or she can imagine a different, and more favorable, alternative. Consistent with the work reviewed earlier, Folger (1986) suggested that individuals experience RD after making a disadvantageous comparison. The standard utilized is referred to as the referent. A high referent exists when the alternative outcome is favorable. Referents can come from prior expectations, social standards, or simply from an individual's imagination. However, a high referent, in and of itself, is not sufficient to trigger RD. Rather, there must also be a low likelihood of receiving the outcome sometime in the future (Folger, Rosenfield, & Rheaume, 1983). A series of subsequent laboratory studies provided RCT with generally good empirical support (Folger, Rosenfield, Rheaume, & Martin, 1983; Folger, Rosenfield, & Robinson, 1983).

Despite these additions and elaborations, the justice perspective typified by relative deprivation and equity theory was still incomplete. In particular, this works focused only on the outcomes of an allocation decision. Such an approach was tantamount to saying that people are only concerned with what they get and that they otherwise do not particularly care how they are treated. Our everyday experience tells us that this is not the case. This was a major weakness in the early theories of justice and led to the development of procedural justice theories.

PROCEDURAL JUSTICE

Outcomes are not the only relevant issue to an individual; the way one is treated is equally important. Experience suggests that the favorability of a single outcome is less crucial when the underlying allocation process is fair, perhaps because we can feel confident that such a system will meet our needs in the future. This concern over process has been termed procedural fairness. Depending on our perceptions of procedural fairness, our response may be very different in one situation than in another. People who believe themselves to be victims of injustice may respond in very different ways, depending on their perceptions of how and why that injustice occurred. For example, an individual who believes he or she was denied a raise because of unfair discrimination on the part of management is likely to respond in a much more negative way than if he or she believed that it was because he or she did not meet minimum performance standards. Equity theory provides no way of predicting the individual's response. Because Equity Theory does not include procedures it does not allow for clear predictions (Folger, 1977; Folger & Greenberg, 1985; Greenberg, 1987a; Lind & Tyler, 1988). In other words, whereas the focus in Equity Theory is on what was decided, the focus in procedural justice is on how the decision was reached.

Perhaps the clearest way of illustrating the difference between the ideas of distributive and procedural justice is through the example of a courtroom trial (Lind & Tyler, 1988). The judge, who presides over the procedure of conducting the trial, is responsible for seeing that the trial is conducted fairly and according to prescribed policies. In contrast, the jury is responsible for deciding the verdict, or the "outcome," which will result from the "inputs," or the actions of the person on trial. Two separate kinds of justice are at work in this situation. If the defendant perceives the jury's verdict (the outcome) as being unfair, it is still possible to perceive the judge's conducting of the proceedings (the procedure) as being fair, or vice versa. In other words, the two aspects may be evaluated independently of one another (Tyler, 1984). Of course, it is hoped that both the distributive and procedural components of the situation will be fair.

Much of the research on procedural justice to date has been conducted outside of the organizational context. Some has focused on defendants' perceptions of courtroom fairness, as described previously. Tyler (1984) assessed perceptions of distributive fairness (whether or not the verdict was fair) and procedural justice (i.e., whether the procedures were administered impartially), and the subjects' attitudes toward judges and courts. Tyler found that perceptions of distributive justice were related to satisfaction with the verdict (the outcome), but that defendants' evaluation of the judicial system as a whole was predicted only by the fairness of the procedures. In cases in which a defendant received an unfavorable verdict but was fairly treated, the individual had an unfavorable opinion of the outcome, but not the court system that produced it. Such results could not have been predicted by equity theory.

Further research by Tyler (1987) examined individuals' support for and perceptions of the legitimacy of police officers and courts, and found factors relating to procedural justice (e.g., the opportunity to state their case prior to the decision) predicted these attitudes, which proved to be unrelated to the fairness of the outcome. Similar results have been found for the influence of perceptions of injustice on an individual's support for political candidates (Tyler, Rasinski, & McGraw, 1985). These perceptions were found to have greater influence than outcome-related concerns. And Barrett-Howard and Tyler (1986) examined the importance of procedural justice in allocation decisions, and found it to be equal in importance to distributive justice as a criterion in decisions concerning the allocation of scarce resources. Procedures were also found to be the primary determinants of the perception of overall fairness across a variety of situations, including certain social settings, and in the workplace.

The impetus behind research on procedural justice in organizational settings has largely been dissatisfaction with equity theory and distributional factors. For example, Dyer and Thirault (1976) evaluated the effectiveness of Lawler's (1971) model of pay satisfaction, which borrows heavily from equity theory. Dyer and Thirault pointed out that Lawler's model does not consider pay administration variables, which would influence the fairness of the system of reward distribution in an organization. For their study conducted among American and Canadian managers, Dyer and Thirault added 12 administrative-type items to their questionnaire, and found that these procedural variables significantly improved the fit of the model. This expanded model was also found by Weiner

(1980) to be more effective than the Lawler model for predicting consequences (turnover, absenteeism, and pro-union attitudes) of pay dissatisfaction. Recent work on pay system satisfaction is reviewed by Miceli (chapter 12, this volume).

Research on satisfaction with performance appraisal has also found a significant impact from procedural variables (Folger & Lewis, chapter 5, this volume). In a study conducted among employees of a large manufacturing firm, Landy, Barnes, and Murphy (1978) found that five items on the questionnaire predicted whether the performance evaluations were perceived as having been fair and accurate: (a) the opportunity for the subordinate to express his or her feelings, (b) the existence of a formal appraisal system, (c) supervisor's knowledge or the subordinate's performance, (d) frequency of evaluations, and (e) does the evaluation provide feedback that is related to job performance. All five of these are procedural items. A follow-up study (Landy, Barnes-Farrell, & Cleveland, 1980) found that the actual favorability of the evaluation (the outcome) was not related to perceptions of fairness and accuracy.

Greenberg (1986) asked managers to generate statements by responding to an open-ended questionnaire in which they described determinants of particularly fair and unfair performance evaluations. Using a Q-sort procedure, these responses were then categorized by other managers. This process yielded seven distinct determinants of fairness. In a factor analysis of the ratings of the perceived importance of these determinants, only two factors emerged, which together accounted for 94.7% of the variance. Five of the categories loaded on a procedural factor, and two on a distributive factor. In his discussion of the implications of his findings, Greenberg cautioned against neglecting either dimension. Distributive justice and procedural justice should be treated as separate and interacting, rather than competing constructs.

Perceived procedural justice has been shown to have an impact on employee attitudes toward both supervisors and the organization as a whole. In a study on reactions to pay raise decisions, Folger and Konovsky (1989) conducted a survey among manufacturing plant employees to determine the relative impact of fairness of outcomes (distributive justice) and fairness of procedures (procedural justice) on employee attitudes. In this study, procedural justice accounted for unique variance in two employee attitudes: trust in the supervisor and commitment to the organization. And in a study of workers in Great Britain, Cook and Wall (1980) found that trust in management to treat employees fairly was positively related to measures of identification, involvement, and loyalty. These findings are consistent with the notion that the perceived fairness of procedures influences our attitudes toward the overall system in ways that could not be predicted by outcomes alone.

In addition to measuring attitudes, research has been done that attempted to assess the effect of procedural justice on the intent to file a grievance (a retaliation). In a study by Greenberg (1987b), subjects received either high, medium, or low monetary outcomes as a result of a fair or unfair procedure. Subjects then completed a questionnaire containing items designed to measure perceptions of procedural fairness, liking for the experimenter, and so forth. In addition, subjects had an opportunity to tear off slips of paper containing what they believed to be a telephone number they could call to report unfair treatment in an experiment. The only subjects who showed this intent to retaliate were subjects who had received low outcomes as a result of unfair procedures. However, the exact relationships between specific practices and fairness perceptions in this study are difficult to determine because a compound operationalization of an unfair procedure was used; the procedure violated prevailing payment allocation practices and also failed to base allocations on accurate performance information.

Similar results were obtained in a field study by Fryxell and Gordon (1989). These researchers surveyed a group of unionized workers. They found that satisfaction with their union was most strongly predicted by the extent to which their grievance system supplied both distributive and procedural justice. Procedural justice has become a major concern in the design of conflict resolution systems (Brett, Goldberg, & Ury, 1990; Gordon & Fryxell, chapter 11, this volume).

In response to this evidence, relative deprivation theories have evolved to the point where they now attempt to incorporate notions of procedural justice, although some theoretical differences remain (Shapiro, chapter 3, this volume). Loosely speaking, unfair procedures have been proposed to have their effect because they have an "ought" quality about them. That is, not only has the individual failed to received a desired outcome (a distributive injustice), but from a moral point of view this failure should not have occurred. Put another way, the discrepant state was due to the disingenuous activity of another person.

Given this, theories of RD were modified to take procedures into account. Crosby (1984) has reduced her list of preconditions to only two: The individual must want the outcome and also feel deserving. Folger's (1986) RCT model has been similarly modified and has been tied more explicitly to procedural justice. Folger and his colleagues (Cropanzano & Folger, 1989; Folger & Martin, 1986), now maintain that perceived injustice occurs as the result of two judgments. First, an individual must ask him or herself if he or she would have received the desired outcome under different conditions. This is the outcome discrepancy or distributive justice part of the theory and is based on the referent comparison. Next the individual must also ask if he or she should have gotten the outcome in question. "Would" and "should" therefore become the two central questions linking procedural and distributive justice. This is much like Crosby's (1984) desirability (distributive) and deservingness (procedural) components.

INTERACTIONAL JUSTICE

A third type of justice was proposed by Bies and Moag (1986). These authors noted that to a large extent individuals make justice appraisals based on the quality of the interpersonal treatment they receive. Bies and Moag called this the "communication criteria of fairness" (p. 46). They referred to it as interactional justice and maintained that it could be distinguished from procedural justice, because procedures refer to the structural quality of the decision process, whereas interactional justice refers to a social exchange between two participants. Research on interactional justice is reviewed by Baron (chapter 7, this volume). Bies (1985) reported on research involving job applicants' perceptions of how fairly they were treated by organizations. He found four attributes of interpersonally fair procedures. These were termed truthfulness, respect, propriety of questions, and justification. The first three attributes deal with the nature of the communication while it is occurring. The last one has to do with removing any discontent following an unfair procedure.

The truthfulness attribute was further divided into two components: deception and candidness. In the first place, job candidates do not like being deceived. In Bies' study, deception was the most frequently cited reason for perceiving unfairness. However, to avoid an unfavorable reaction, organizations had to do more than not lie. Participants also expected to be treated in a forthright manner. Individuals do not like overly favorable "snow jobs". Rather, they preferred that organizations present them with a realistic and accurate description of the circumstances under which they would be working.

Bies' (1985) and Bies and Moag's (1986) second major attribute was rudeness. Put simply, individuals expect to be treated in a polite and respectful fashion. They do not respond favorably to insults or discourteous behavior. This is consistent with later work by Baron (1988, 1990) showing that critical feedback makes people angry and has negative effects on employee performance.

The third attribute of interactional fairness concerns the propriety of questions that the applicants are asked. Once more, this actually involved two components. For one thing, some questions are considered improper by their very nature. One example presented by Bies and Moag (1986) involves a female applicant who was asked personal questions about her future plans for having children. Other improper questions are those that involve prejudicial statements. For example, one Black candidate in Bies and Moag's study was questioned about his race.

Bies' (1985) final attribute, justification, comes into play following negative outcomes or unfair treatment. It may be possible to rectify an injustice with an adequate justification (Bies & Shapiro, 1988; Folger, Rosenfield, & Robinson, 1983). Bies (1987) argued that a sense of anger over injustice can be reduced or eliminated by providing the injured party with a social account (i.e., an explanation or an apology). Bies (1987) reviewed evidence to support this position.

In recent years some researchers have stopped separating procedural and interactional justice (Greenberg, chapter 4, this volume). The general perspective is that organizations should see justice in a broader social context (cf. James, chapter 2, this volume). Both the interpersonal treatment and the formal decision processes are attributes of this broader context. Despite their similarity, however, it is important to emphasize that both formal procedures and communication quality are important in predicting work outcomes (Konovsky & Brockner, chapter 6, this volume; Clemmer, chapter 9, this volume). Put simply, even if procedures and interpersonal treatment are parts of the same phenomenon, both may well be important for understanding organizational behavior.

JUSTICE IN THE WORKPLACE: IMPLICATIONS
FOR HUMAN RESOURCE MANAGEMENT

Although much of the original justice research came out of legal and social psychological traditions, over the last several years organizational scholars have applied these concepts to a growing number of human resource interventions. This development has been useful for both researchers and managers. From the research perspective, justice serves as a useful orientation that allows for a fuller understanding of workplace behavior. Many of the early ideas about justice have been modified and expanded in light of this new evidence. However, this work offers substantially more than an interesting academic exercise. From an applied perspective, the research provides many new recommendations for effectively administering personnel programs.

This volume details both the contributions and the potential contributions of justice theories to human resource management. The first four chapters, including this one, provide some general background, whereas later chapters are more focused and more applied. In chapter 2, James broadens the general overview provided in this chapter in consideration of cultural and social determinants of justice. In chapter 3 Shapiro reviews various theoretical perspectives to answer an important question: Why does procedural justice work? She reviews the available evidence and proposes a new theoretical model. In chapter 4 Greenberg explores the general issue of designing justice into personnel administration systems. He considers a series of human resource interventions that demonstrate the important role played by interpersonal fairness.

Chapter 5 examines the issue of due process in performance evaluations. Folger and Lewis begin by discussing the meaning of due process. They show that the concept has also appeared in both political science and law, but with somewhat different usages than the one currently popular in the organizational sciences. Folger and Lewis argue that the organizational behavior definition is somewhat limiting. They therefore apply the broader, legal usage to work settings. In doing so, the authors identify three core principals of organizational due process. They then analyze performance evaluation in light of these dimensions and note that self-appraisals can help ensure perceived fairness. Folger and Lewis conclude by reviewing a variety of additional reasons for including self-appraisals into performance evaluation.

Chapter 6 investigates the management of victim and survivor reactions to layoffs. Mary Konovsky and Joel Brockner maintain that previous research has emphasized either the layoff victim (the individuals who are terminated) or the layoff survivor (the individuals who remain with the organization). Using both distributive and procedural justice, the authors construct a model that is applicable to both victims and survivors. Research supporting the model is then reviewed. The authors offer managers a list of suggestions for minimizing the negative consequences of employee layoffs.

In chapter 7 Robert Baron discusses destructive feedback as a source of feelings of injustice. Baron reviews a program of research that applies interactional justice to employee feedback. He shows that much of the feedback given in organizations is destructive in nature (e.g., it is personal, general, and not task related). He reviews evidence that such unfair feedback has negative effects by lowering worker self-efficacy, lowering performance, and leading to unproductive ways of approaching conflicts. The author gives a series of recommendations for presenting constructive feedback. In addition, Baron also presents research indicating the best ways to alleviate the negative effects of destructive feedback.

Chapter 8 discusses the literature on drug-testing programs. Mary Konovsky and I note that both distributive and procedural justice are relevant to understanding workers' responses. Consistent with previous research, distributive justice is conceptualized as the ratio of employee inputs (e.g., job characteristics and type of drug used) to employee consequences (e.g., firing or rehabilitation). Both of these are important for understanding outcome fairness. Other evidence is reviewed indicating that procedures (e.g., right of appeal, random testing, union involvement in designing the program) are also important in determining perceived justice. Finally, we consider how distributive and procedural justice work together to make drug testing more or less acceptable to employees. We conclude by noting the characteristics of effective testing programs.

Chapter 9 examines justice in service encounters. Elizabeth Clemmer notes that the service sector has become an important component of the American economy. Despite this, little research exists on the determinants of customer satisfaction with service work. The author reviews empirical evidence examining consumer perceptions of fairness. Clemmer finds that distributive, procedural, and interactive justice all contribute to customer satisfaction. Based on this evidence, the author presents several principals of fair service work. In addition to these applied implications, Clemmer's chapter is also important for conceptual reasons, in that it demonstrates the role of justice in situations that do not involve a hierarchy of power.

In chapter 10, Maryalice Citera and Joan Rentsch review evidence indicating that most organizational mergers end in disappointment. Further, human resource issues are one reason commonly cited for this high failure rate. As with both grievance systems and layoffs, Citera and Rentsch note that merger research has contributed little to facilitate our conceptual understanding. The authors present a theory showing that procedural justice can be used to understand worker responses to mergers. They lay out a program of research for testing their theory, and conclude with a series of suggestions for managers.

In chapter 11, Gordon and Fryxell review the current literature on employee grievance systems. Taking an exchange perspective, the authors note the responsibilities and rights of both unions and management. They then extend their review to include non-union grievance systems. Following this overview, Gordon and Fryxell note the fragmentary nature of previous research. In order to remedy this problem, the authors use current procedural justice theory to develop a new conceptual framework. Evidence supporting this model is discussed at length.

Finally, in chapter 12, Marcia Miceli discusses pay satisfaction. She notes that although justice considerations are important determinants of compensation satisfaction, fairness has not been incorporated into a broad conceptual model along with other factors. Miceli remedies this problem by doing an extensive review of the literature. Out of this evidence, she constructs a new theoretical framework that specifies the role of justice. Data supportive of this view are presented, and the author makes suggestions for managers and future researchers.

As should be apparent from this review, the selection of chapters is quite broad. Each author examines a different research area and presents implications for managerial practice. In addition, many of the contributors also use justice theories to formulate new conceptual frameworks. Taken together, this volume should serve to demonstrate the richness and importance of justice research.

REFERENCES

Adams, J. S. (1963). Toward an understanding of inequity. *Journal of Abnormal and Social Psychology, 47*, 422–436.

Adams, J. S. (1965). Inequity in social exchange. In L. Berkowitz (Ed.), *Advances in experimental social psychology* (Vol. 2, pp. 267–299). New York: Academic Press.

Adams, J. S., & Freedman, S. (1976). Equity theory revisited: Comments and annotated bibliography. In L. Berkowitz (Ed.), *Advances in experimental social psychology* (Vol. 9, pp. 43–90). New York: Academic Press.

Baron, R. A. (1988). Negative effects of destructive criticism: Impact on conflict, self-efficacy, and task performance. *Journal of Applied Psychology, 73*, 199–207.

Baron, R. A. (1990). Countering the effects of destructive criticism: The relative efficacy of four potential interventions. *Journal of Applied Psychology, 75*, 235–245.

Barrett-Howard, E., & Tyler, T. R. (1986). Procedural justice as a criterion in allocation decisions. *Journal of Personality and Social Psychology, 50*, 296–305.

Berkowitz, L., Fraser, C., Treasure, F. P., & Cochran, S. (1987). Pay, equity, job gratifications, and comparisons in pay satisfaction. *Journal of Applied Psychology, 72*, 544–551.

Bernstein, M., & Crosby, F. (1980). An empirical examination of relative deprivation theory. *Journal of Experimental Social Psychology, 16*, 442–456.

Bies, R. J. (1985). *Individual reactions to corporate recruiting encounters: The importance of fairness.* Unpublished manuscript.

Bies, R. J. (1987). The predicament of injustice: The management of moral outrage. In L. L. Cummings & B. M. Staw (Eds.), *Research in organizational behavior* (Vol. 9, pp. 289–319). Greenwich, CT: JAI Press.

Bies, R. J., & Moag, J. S. (1986). Interactional justice: Communication criteria of fairness. In R. J. Lewicki, B. H. Sheppard, & M. Bazerman (Eds.), *Research on negotiation in organizations* (Vol. 1, pp. 43–55). Greenwich, CT: JAI Press.

Bies, R. J., & Shapiro, D. L. (1988). Voice and justification: Their influence on procedural and fairness judgments. *Academy of Management Journal, 31,* 676–685.

Brett, J. M., Goldberg, S. B., & Ury, W. L. (1990). Designing systems for resolving disputes in organizations. *American Psychologist, 45,* 162–170.

Brockner, J., & Greenberg, J. (1990). The impact of layoffs on survivors: An organizational justice perspective. In J. Carroll (Ed.)., *Advances in applied social psychology: Business settings* (pp. 45–75). Hillsdale, NJ: Lawrence Erlbaum Associates.

Carrell, M. R., & Dittrich, J. E. (1978). Equity theory: The recent literature, methodological considerations, and new directions. *Academy of Management Review, 3,* 202–210.

Cook, J., & Wall, T. (1980). New work attitude measures of trust, organizational commitment and personal need non-fulfillment. *Journal of Occupational Psychology, 53,* 39–52.

Cropanzano, R., & Baron, R. A. (in press). Injustice and organizational conflict: The moderating effect of power restoration. *International Journal of Conflict Management.*

Cropanzano, R., & Folger, R. (1989). Referent cognitions and task decision autonomy: Beyond equity theory. *Journal of Applied Psychology, 74,* 293–299.

Crosby, F. (1976). A model of egoistical relative deprivation. *Psychological Review, 83,* 85–113.

Crosby, F. (1984). Relative deprivation in organizational settings. In B. M. Staw & L. L. Cummings (Eds.), *Research in organizational behavior* (Vol. 6, pp. 51–93). Greenwich, CT: JAI Press.

Deutsch, M. (1985). *Distributive justice.* New Haven, CT: Yale University Press.

Dyer, L., & Thirault, R. (1976). The determinants of pay satisfaction. *Journal of Applied Psychology, 61,* 596–604.

Elliott, G. C., & Meeker, B. F. (1986). Achieving fairness in the face of competing concerns: The different effects of individual and group characteristics. *Journal of Personality and Social Psychology, 50,* 754–760.

Fantasia, R. (1988). *Cultures of solidarity: Consciousness, action, and contemporary American workers.* Berkeley, CA: University of California Press.

Folger, R. (1977). Distributive and procedural justice: combined impact of "voice" and improvement on experienced inequity. *Journal of Personality and Social Psychology, 35,* 108–119.

Folger, R. (1986). Rethinking equity theory: A referent cognitions model. In H. W. Bierhoff, R. L. Cohen, & J. Greenberg (Eds.), *Justice in social relations* (pp. 145–162). New York: Plenum.

Folger, R., & Greenberg, J. (1985). Procedural justice: An interpretive analysis of personnel systems. In K. Rowland & G. Ferris (Eds.), *Research in personnel and human resources management* (Vol. 3, pp. 141–183). Greenwich, CT: JAI Press.

Folger, R., & Konovsky, M. A. (1989). Effects of procedural and distributive justice on reactions to pay raise decisions. *Academy of Management Journal, 32,* 115–130.

Folger, R., Konovsky, M. A., & Cropanzano, R. (1992). A due process metaphor for performance appraisal. In B. M. Staw & L. L. Cummings (Eds.), *Research in organizational behavior* (Vol. 14, pp. 129–177). Greenwich, CT: JAI Press.

Folger, R., & Martin, C. (1986). Relative deprivation and referent cognitions: Distributive and procedural justice effects. *Journal of Experimental Social Psychology, 22,* 531–546.

Folger, R., Rosenfield, D., & Rheaume, K. (1983). Roleplaying effects of likelihood and referent outcomes on relative deprivation. *Representative Research in Social Psychology, 13,* 2–10.

Folger, R., Rosenfield, D., Rheaume, K., & Martin, C. (1983). Relative deprivation and referent cognitions. *Journal of Experimental Social Psychology, 19,* 172–184.

Folger, R., Rosenfield, D., & Robinson, T. (1983). Relative deprivation and procedural justifications. *Journal of Personality and Social Psychology, 45,* 268–273.

Fryxell, G. E., & Gordon, M. E. (1989). Workplace justice and job satisfaction as predictors of satisfaction with unions and management. *Academy of Management Journal, 32,* 851–866.

Garland, H. (1973). The effects of piece-rate underpayment and overpayment on job performance: A test of equity theory with a new induction procedure. *Journal of Applied Social Psychology, 3,* 325–334.

Greenberg, J. (1982). Approaching equity and avoiding inequity in groups and organizations. In J. Greenberg & R. L. Cohen (Eds.), *Equity and justice in social behavior* (pp. 389–435). New York: Academic Press.

Greenberg, J. (1983). Self-image vs. impression management in adherence to distributive justice standards: The influence of self-awareness and self-consciousness. *Journal of Personality and Social Psychology, 44,* 5–19.

Greenberg, J. (1986). Organizational performance appraisal procedures: What makes them fair? In R. J. Lewicki, B. H. Sheppard, & M. Bazerman (Eds.), *Research on negotiation in organizations* (Vol. 1, pp. 25–41). Greenwich, CT: JAI Press.

Greenberg, J. (1987a). A taxonomy of organizational justice theories. *Academy of Management Review, 12,* 9–22.

Greenberg, J. (1987b). Reactions to procedural injustice in payment distributions: do the means justify the ends? *Journal of Applied Psychology, 72,* 55–61.

Greenberg, J. (1988). Equity and workplace status: A field experiment. *Journal of Applied Psychology, 73,* 606–613.

Greenberg, J. (1990a). Organizational justice: Yesterday, today, and tomorrow. *Journal of Management, 16,* 399–432.

Greenberg, J. (1990b). Employee thefts as a reaction to underpayment inequity: The hidden cost of pay cuts. *Journal of Applied Psychology, 75,* 561–568.

Greenberg, J., & Ornstein, S. (1983). High status job titles as compensation for underpayment: A test of equity theory. *Journal of Applied Psychology, 68,* 285–296.

Grindstaff, C. F. (1968). The Negro, urbanization, and relative deprivation in the deep South. *Social Problems, 15,* 345–352.

Gurr, T. R. (1968a). A causal model of civil strife: A comparative analysis using new indices. *American Political Science Review, 62,* 1104–1124.

Gurr, T. R. (1968b). Urban disorder, perspectives from the comparative study of civil strife. In L. H. Masotti & D. R. Bowen (Eds.), *Riots and rebellion: Civil violence in the urban community.* Beverly Hills, CA: Sage.

Gurr, T. R. (1970). *Why men rebel.* Princeton, NJ: Princeton University Press.

Konovsky, M. A., & Cropanzano, R. (1991). Perceived fairness of employee drug testing as a predictor of employee attitudes and job performance. *Journal of Applied Psychology, 76,* 698–707.

Landy, F. J., Barnes, J. L., & Murphy, K. R. (1978). Correlates of perceived fairness and accuracy of performance evaluation. *Journal of Applied Psychology, 63,* 751–754.

Landy, F. J., Barnes-Farrell, J. L., & Cleveland, J. N. (1980). Perceived fairness and accuracy of performance evaluation: a follow-up. *Journal of Applied Psychology, 65,* 355–356.

Lawler, E. E. III. (1968). Equity theory as a predictor of productivity and work quality. *Psychological Bulletin, 70,* 596–610.

Lawler, E. E. III. (1971). *Pay and organizational effectiveness: A psychological view.* New York: McGraw-Hill.

Lawler, E. E. III, & Porter, L. W. (1963). Perceptions regarding management compensation. *Industrial Relations, 3,* 41–49.

Leung, K., & Bond, M. H. (1984). The impact of cultural collectivism in reward allocations. *Journal of Personality and Social Psychology, 47,* 793–804.

Lind, E. A., & Tyler, T. (1988). *The social psychology of procedural justice.* New York: Plenum.

Major, B. (1987). Gender, justice, and the psychology of entitlement. In P. Shaver & C. Hendrick (Eds.), *Review of personality and social psychology: Sex and gender* (Vol. 7, pp. 124–148). Newbury Park, CA: Sage.

Mark, M. M., & Folger, R. (1984). Responses to relative deprivation: A conceptual framework. In P. Shaver (Ed.), *Review of personality and social psychology* (Vol. 5, pp. 192–218). Beverly Hills, CA: Sage.

Martin, J. (1981). Relative deprivation: A theory of distributive justice for an era of shrinking resources. In L. L. Cummings & B. M. Staw (Eds.), *Research in organizational behavior* (Vol. 3, pp. 53–107). Greenwich, CT: JAI Press.

Martin, J. (1986). The tolerance of injustice. In J. M. Olsen, C. P. Herman, & M. P. Zanna (Eds.), *Relative deprivation and social comparison: The Ontario symposium* (Vol. 4, pp. 217–242). Hillsdale, NJ: Lawrence Erlbaum Associates.

Martin, J., Brickman, P., & Murray, A. (1984). Moral outrage and pragmatism: Explanations for collective action. *Journal of Experimental Social Psychology, 20,* 484–496.

Martin, J., Price, R., Bies, R., & Powers, M. (1979, August). *Relative deprivation among secretaries: The effects of the token female executive.* Paper presented at the Annual Meeting of the American Psychological Association, Toronto, Canada.

McCarthy, J. D., & Zald, M. N. (1977). Resource mobilization and social movement: A partial theory. *American Journal of Sociology, 82,* 1212–1241.

Miceli, M. P., & Lane, M. C. (1991). Antecedents of pay satisfaction: A review and extension. In K. Rowland & G. R. Ferris (Eds.), *Research in personnel and human resources management* (Vol. 9, pp. 235–309). Greenwich, CT: JAI Press.

Mowday, R. T. (1987). Equity theory and predictions of behavior in organizations. In R. Steers & L. Porter (Eds.), *Motivation and work behavior* (pp. 89–110). New York: McGraw-Hill.

Murphy-Berman, V., Berman, J. J., Singh, P., Pachauri, A., & Kumar, P. (1984). Factors affecting allocations to needy and meritorious recipients: A cross-cultural comparison. *Journal of Personality and Social Psychology, 46,* 1267–1272.

Painter, N. I. (1987). *Standing at armageddon: The United States, 1877–1919.* New York: Norton.

Patchen, M. (1961). *The choice of wage comparisons.* Englewood Cliffs, NJ: Prentice-Hall.

Pettigrew, T. (1964). *A profile of the Negro American.* Princeton, NJ: Van Nostrand.

Pettigrew, T. (1967). Social evaluation theory. In D. Levine (Ed.), *Nebraska Symposium on Motivation* (Vol. 15). Lincoln: University of Nebraska Press.

Pettigrew, T. (1971). *Racially separate or together?* New York: McGraw-Hill.

Prichard, R. A. (1969). Equity theory: A review and critique. *Organizational Behavior and Human Performance, 4,* 75–94.

Runciman, W. G. (1966). *Relative deprivation and social justice: A study of attitudes to social inequality in twentieth-century England.* Berkeley University of California Press.

Schwab, D. P. (1980). Construct validity in organizational behavior. In B. M. Staw & L. L. Cummings (Eds.), *Research in organizational behavior* (Vol. 2, pp. 3–43). Greenwich, CT: JAI Press.

Sears, D. O., & McConahay, J. S. (1970). Racial socialization, comparison levels, and the Watts riot. *Journal of Social Issues, 26,* 121–140.

Sinclair, R. C., & Mark, M. M. (1991). Mood and the endorsement of egalitarian macrojustice versus equity-based microjustice principals. *Personality and Social Psychology Bulletin, 17,* 369–375.

Smith, P. C., Kendall, L. M., & Hulin, C. L. (1969). *The measurement of satisfaction in work and retirement.* Chicago: Rand McNally.

Stouffer, S. A., Suchman, E. A., DeVinney, L. C., Star, S. A., & Williams, R. M., Jr. (1949). *The American soldier: Adjustment during Army Life* (Vol. 1). Princeton, NJ: Princeton University Press.

Sweeney, P. D., McFarlin, D. B., & Inderrieden, E. J. (1990). Using relative deprivation theory to explain satisfaction with income and pay level: A multistudy investigation. *Academy of Management Journal, 33,* 423–436.

Tyler, T. R. (1984). The role of perceived injustice in defendants' evaluations of their courtroom experience. *Law and Society Review, 18,* 51–74.

Tyler, T. R. (1987). Conditions leading to value-expressive effects in judgments of procedural justice: A test of four models. *Journal of Personality and Social Psychology, 52,* 333–344.

Tyler, T. R., Rasinski, K., & McGraw, K. M. (1985). The influence of perceived injustice on the endorsement of political leaders. *Journal of Applied Social Psychology, 15,* 700–725.

Walster, E., Berscheid, E., & Walster, G. W. (1976). New directions in equity research. In L. Berkowitz (Ed.), *Advances in experimental social psychology* (Vol. 9, pp. 1–43). New York: Academic Press.

Weiner, N. (1980). Determinants and behavioral consequences of pay satisfaction: A comparison of two models. *Personnel Psychology, 33,* 741–757.

2

The Social Context of Organizational Justice: Cultural, Intergroup, and Structural Effects on Justice Behaviors and Perceptions

Keith James
Colorado State University

org justice = percep. of org actions not perceptions of org. (handwritten annotation)

Although attention to organizational justice issues has increased substantially in recent years, there has as yet been relatively little integration across levels of analysis in justice theory and research (Brickman, Folger, Goode, & Schul, 1981; Greenberg, 1990). While some efforts to examine the role of more macro-level factors on organizational justice processes and outcomes have been under-taken (e.g., Kabanoff, 1991; Leung, 1988a), justice theory and research have been heavily balanced toward individualistic (intrapsychic and interpersonal) approaches (Brickman et al., 1981; Deutsch, 1975). Although individualistic approaches to justice have proven valuable, a more even balance of levels of analysis in work on organizational justice seems necessary to capture the complexity of justice processes in organizations. In line with this belief, this chapter is an effort to promote integration of social-context factors into organizational justice research and theory. Available research evidence and conceptual ideas on the effects of some macro- and meso-level factors on organizational justice are reviewed.

By organizational justice, we mean individuals' and groups' perceptions of the fairness of treatment (including, but not limited to, allocations) received from organizations and their behavioral reactions to such perceptions. This necessarily also involves examining influences on the behaviors of those who act for organizations in ways that impact on others' perceptions of organizational fairness. Culture (societal and organizational), intergroup relations (in the larger society and in organizations), and organizational structure are the major categories of factors examined for their implications for organizational justice. Some efforts to integrate the influences on organizational justice of these three categories of factors are woven throughout the chapter. The reader is warned, however, that a fully developed theoretical framework is not presented. The purpose of this chapter is to help begin a process of integration; the fruition of that process lies in the future.

CULTURE AND ORGANIZATIONAL JUSTICE

The number of cross-cultural studies of justice have increased in recent years, but the amount of available, especially quantitative, evidence is still limited. This is, in fact, true of all of the areas that are reviewed here, especially when one looks for studies conducted in organizational settings. There are, however, indications that culture exerts very important and wide-ranging effects on justice behavior, including even generally shaping the likelihood that individuals will experience feelings of injustice. The broad scope of established and potential effects of culture on justice perceptions and behaviors are reviewed in this section.

Culture and Concern with Justice.   Wallbott and Scherer (1986) and Babad and Wallbott (1986) review data (the two chapters cited discuss different elements of the same data set) from seven western-European countries (Belgium, France, Great Britain, West Germany, Italy, Spain, and Switzerland) plus Israel that indicate significant variations in the extent to which experienced injustice[1] is a source of anger for individuals of different nationalities. These authors found that experienced injustice was reported as the antecedent of feelings of anger in a range from 14% in France to 31% in Israel. Babad (1986) compared the anger experiences of Israeli Jews and Israeli Moslems using this same data set and also found a significant difference. Israel Jews reported that 24% of their anger was caused by experienced injustice, whereas the figure for Israeli Arabs was only 15%.

Gundykunst and Ting-Toomey (1988) took the data on anger and injustice from the seven European countries studied by Wallbott, Scherer, Babab, and their associates and tested whether Hofstede's (1980) scores for those countries on his four major dimensions of cultural variability would predict the tendency for injustice to trigger anger. The first of Hofstede's four dimensions is individualism/collectivism, which reflects the extent to which individual-level goals and personal experience versus group-level goals and group experiences are dominant. Masculinity/femininity is the second dimension and pits off achieve-

---

[1]Although the types of injustice included did not all involve organizations, many of the categories of injustice experiences described do seem to have involved business, school, work, or governmental organizations. The descriptions of the specific types of reported events that were subsumed under the label of "injustice" indicates that issues of both procedural and distributive justice were involved. Across all 8 countries, injustice was tied as the second most commonly reported source of anger, indicating the general importance of justice issues in people's lives.

ment orientation and abstract/object focus (masculine cultures) with quality-of-life and relationship focus (feminine cultures). Uncertainty avoidance is the third dimension and involves "the extent to which people feel threatened by ambiguous (social) situations and have created beliefs and institutions that try to avoid these" (Hofstede & Bond, 1984, p. 419). Finally, power-distance reflects beliefs that power differentials are natural, enduring, and based on the characteristics of the actors versus beliefs that power differentials are imposed for particular purposes in particular situations.

Gundykunst and Ting-Toomey found that power-distance scores strongly predicted (correlation of $-.86$)[2] the tendency to experience anger in response to injustice. The negative sign for this correlation indicates that the higher the power-distance score for a country, the lower was the percentage of total anger reported by individuals from that country that they attributed to injustice. Gundykunst and Ting-Toomey concluded that cultures that inculcate an acceptance of power differences lead individuals to expect, take for granted and, therefore, not get angry about, injustices. Conversely, in relatively low power distance cultures, there is less of a tendency to defer to power, which inclines individuals to react negatively when institutions or other individuals seem to be treating them unfairly.

Stern and Keller (1953) provided data from France (a country relatively high in power-distance); and Scase (1972) comparative data from Great Britain and Sweden (the former being higher in power-distance than the latter) that support the conclusion that cultures that are higher in power-distance lead to greater acceptance of individual and group-based inequality; whereas cultures that promote egalitarianism lead to less such acceptance. Rokeach's (1970) two-factor model of political ideologies (which seem best described as subcultural trends within cultures) may provide additional support for Gundykunst and Ting-Toomey's argument.

Rokeach proposed that patterns of difference in endorsement of two values, *equality* and *freedom* is what distinguishes what he viewed as the four major political ideologies (communism, socialism, capitalism, and fascism) found in societies. Power distance, as defined earlier, seems to incorporate both of these values. Rokeach looked for indications of beliefs about the value of freedom and equality in the writings of major communist, capitalist, fascism, and socialist theorists. In line with his predictions, he found that socialists endorsed both fairly strongly; communists had positive views of equality but negative views of freedom; capitalists endorsed freedom but were negative on equality; while fascists were negative about the value of both equality and freedom.

---

[2]Correlations with the other dimensions were not significant. At $-.41$, however, the one for uncertainty avoidance was of moderate size and would have been significant had the N of cases been at all reasonable. Because each *country,* not each individual, was a data point in Gundykunst and Ting-Toomey's (1988) analyses, the N was only 7.

Rokeach did not directly test for relations of these scores to justice-related behaviors but consideration of the patterns of actions by governments fitting into these ideological categories seems to support the connection. For instance, fascist disdain for both freedom and equality is congruent with the Nazi's brutal and biased treatment of both Germans and citizens of other countries during World War II. Similarly, the socialist governments of Northern Europe have been noted for their efforts to provide equal levels of material goods to all citizens and for the flourishing of sexual, social, and political freedoms under their aegis.

It seems that certain types of values or norms seem to lead to particular justice orientations. Even in individualistic cultures, organizationally or situationally induced orientations toward social harmony and social cohesiveness promote equality-based (or, sometimes, need-based) allocations; whereas orientations toward productivity and economic exchange promote equity-based allocations (Deutsch, 1975, 1985; Kerr & Slocum, 1987; Larwood, Kavanaugh, & Levine, 1978; Leventhal, 1976; Meindl, 1989). These outcomes seem partially linked to institutional type. Profit-making organizations, at least in the United States, seem to be generally oriented toward equity-based principles (Deutsch, 1975; Leventhal, 1976). It seems that because efficiency, economic concerns, and interest in maximizing individual performance in the short term tend to be the major goals in such organizations, equity (or exploitative) allocations and authoritarian/autocratic procedures are likely to be employed (Deutsch, 1975, 1985; Kabanoff, 1991; Kerr & Slocum, 1987; Nader, 1975). However, even in profit-making U.S. organizations, when egalitarianism, harmony, and relationship maintenance come to be the major goals, equality allocation principles and democratic, participative, negotiative procedures are likely to be used (Deutsch, 1975, 1985; Kerr & Slocum, 1987; Tyler & Lind, 1990).

Two other (other, that is, than power-distance) of Hofstede's major dimensions of culture, individualism/collectivism and masculinity/femininity, have also been proposed and demonstrated empirically to yield justice effects. Individualism/collectivism has received the most attention.

Individualism/Collectivism and Greed.   Recall that a major part of the conceptual focus of this dimension is on whether personal or group-related goals dominate. This sets the stage for one proposed relationship to justice: that excessive or distorted individualism in the United States may incline individuals to pursue their own goals at the expense of organizational or societal well-being; whereas collectivism in (especially) Japan gives organizations there an edge (e.g., Bellah, Madsen, Sullivan, Swidler, & Tipton, 1985; Mitchell & Scott, 1990; Ouchi, 1981).

Because of excessive individualism in the U.S. organization, members of U.S. companies are argued to be prone to greed and personal expediency at the expense of the rights, needs, and concerns of other organization members, the organization as a whole, or the larger society (Bellah et al., 1985; Mitchell &

Scott, 1990). Individualism is also proposed to lead organizations to ignore social responsibilities and to incline both organizations and individuals to unproductive disputes, including expensive legal battles (Hasegawa, 1986; Weisz, Rothbaum, & Blackburn, 1984). Collectivism in Japan, on the other hand, is proposed to lead to high cooperation, high motivation because of identification with the organization, and an intense sense of responsibility to ingroups on the part of individuals and organizations (Hasagawa, 1986; Ouchi, 1981; Weisz, Rothbaum, & Blackburn, 1984).

Others have argued that the depictions given here are caricatures that focus on only some characteristics and outcomes of individualism and collectivism (Spence, 1985; Waterman, 1981). They note some potentially positive consequences of individualism (e.g., creativity) and negative effects of collectivism (Hasegawa, 1986; Spence, 1985). It is clear that the implication that collectivism is "better" for organizations is a value judgment that needs to be qualified by the question of "better for what?"

In addition, both individualism and collectivism are complex constructs (Triandis, 1990; Triandis, Bontempo, Villareal, Asai, & Lucca, 1988). Situational (e.g., Katz & Hass, 1988) and organizational–cultural (Isabella, 1986) factors may help to determine which elements of societal culture will come into play in influencing justice-related actions. It may be that it is only when particular elements of individualism are dominant that extreme problems result in organizations and in society (Cushman, 1990; Spence, 1985). There also seem to be multiple specific types of collectivist cultures (Triandis et al., 1988). These seem to vary somewhat in how they influence behaviors within and toward organizations and organizational economic success (Hsu, 1971). One would like to see more, and more carefully controlled, studies exploring the circumstance in which and outcomes for which collectivism and individualism promote or inhibit individual and organizational success and yield benefits or damage to society. These should include examinations of the specifics of the processes behind such outcomes.

Individualism/Collectivism and Choice of Allocation Rule.   An argument that is somewhat related to the foregoing is that individualistic cultures promote equity approaches to allocations, whereas collectivistic cultures and value systems promote equality or need allocations (Deutsch, 1975; Hasegawa, 1986; Triandis, 1972, 1989). Leung and Bond (Bond, Leung, & Wan, 1982; Leung & Bond, 1982, 1984); Kashima, Siegal, Tanaka, and Isaka (1988); Mahler, Greenberg, and Hayashi (1981); Marin (1981); and Siegal and Shwalb (1985) produced data supporting the contention that individuals from some collectivistic cultures (those of China and Japan have received the most attention) do, indeed tend to allocate rewards more in line with the equality principle and individuals from individualistic cultures (e.g., the culture of the majority in United States; White Australian culture) more in line with the equity norm.

As noted earlier, the reverse of the effects just outlined also hold: Use of equity allocation principles promotes efficiency and individualism just as it is promoted by them; and use of equality allocations promotes group harmony and relationship maintenance just as it is promoted by them (Deutsch, 1975; Kabonoff, 1991; Kerr & Slocum, 1987; Mills & Clark, 1982). A related effect is that positive emotions seem to promote use of equality allocation principles, whereas negative emotions promote use of equity allocations (Sinclair & Mark, 1991). Group cohesiveness leads to positive emotions (McGrath, 1984). Thus, group cohesiveness may moderate allocational tendencies in part by way of individual emotional states.

Important complications and qualifications to the relationships of individualism/collectivism to equity and equality allocational tendencies seem to exist, however. First, greater use of equality norms by those from collectivistic traditions may require that the allocations be to ingroup members; allocations to outgroup members by collectivists may tend to follow equity principles even more strongly than outgroup allocations by individualists (Leung & Bond, 1984; Mahler et al., 1981; Marin, 1981). Collectivists may also be more likely to strongly pursue conflicts with outgroup members (Gundykunst, 1988; Leung, 1988b; Triandis, 1989). These outcomes seem to reflect a greater tendency toward ethnocentrism with increasing cultural collectivism (Hsu, 1971; Leung & Bond, 1984; Triandis, 1989).

In addition, given salient inequality of performance in work settings, even subjects from collectivistic cultures seem to endorse and make allocations that are somewhat equity-based, even with ingroup members (Bond, Leung, & Wan, 1983; Kashima et al., 1988; Leung & Bond, 1984, study 2). They apparently simply endorse equity principles somewhat less strongly and equality-principles somewhat more strongly than do individualists. Moreover, subjective "definitions" of ingroups seem to vary from collectivistic culture to collectivistic culture, and can be shifted by situational factors (Hsu, 1971; Leung & Bond, 1984; Triandis et al., 1988).

There is also some evidence of difference in need-based allocations across cultures that may also at least partly reflect the individualism/collectivism dimension although again the relationship is complex. Murphy-Berman and colleagues (Berman, Murphy-Berman, & Singh, 1985; Murphy-Berman, Berman, Singh, Pachauri, & Kumar, 1984) found that Hindu individuals from India (a relatively collectivistic culture) generally endorsed need-based allocations more strongly than individuals from the United States (a relatively individualistic culture). On the contrary, however, Kashima et al. (1988) found that salient need by a poor performer increased Australian (a relatively individualistic culture), but not Japanese (a relatively collectivistic culture) subjects' endorsement of equality allocations. Tornblom and Foa (1983) also review three studies conducted in Germany in which German students generally endorsed either the need or the

equality allocation principle. All of these studies also revealed culture by situation interactions on allocation rules.

Murphy-Berman and colleagues found in both of their studies that people from
the United States were much more inclined toward an equity principle and less
toward a need principle than people from India *when allocating positive outcomes.* When the outcomes to be distributed were negative (e.g., cuts in pay),
however, subjects from both the United States and India gave preference to those
with the greatest need (i.e., gave them less of the negative outcomes). Although
there was still some cultural difference in the degree of endorsement of need-
based allocations even with negative outcomes, it was substantially reduced.
German subjects in the studies discussed by Tornblom and Foa (1983) also
showed some variation in the type of principle endorsed (generally between need
and equality) depending on the type of outcome being allocated. In this case,
however, all of the types were positive: love, status, information, money, goods,
and services. In addition to greater impact of target need on Australian subjects'
allocations, Kashima et al. (1988) also found that target age influenced endorsement of equality allocation to a poor performer by Japanese, but not by Australian, subjects.

There also seem to be individual and group differences in indi-
vidualism/collectivism within cultures that may influence allocation tendencies
(Scott, 1965; Triandis, 1989; Triandis, Leung, Villareal & Clack 1985; Triandis
et al., 1988). Sex is a group category that seems to interact with cultural indi-
vidualism/collectivism to affect allocation norms. Murphy-Berman et al. (1984)
found a sex by culture interaction such that Americans of both sexes and Indian
males showed shifts toward greater endorsement of the need principle for negative, as compared to positive, outcomes. Indian females, however, favored need
in a consistent way regardless of outcome type. Evidence from several studies
indicates that American males are more likely than American females to adhere
to the equity principle. American females seem to be more inclined toward
equality or even self-sacrificing patterns of reward distribution (see partial reviews by Kahn, O'Leary, Krulewitz, & Lamm, 1980; and Major & Deaux,
1982). It has been argued (e.g., Kahn et al., 1980) that this reflects a greater
value placed on social relationships among American women because of cultural
socialization (see, however, Major, 1987 for an alternative explanation and a
review of supporting evidence).

Leung and Bond (1984) replicated the sex effect on allocations with American
subjects, but also found the opposite pattern (i.e., males more inclined toward
equality allocations and less toward equity allocations than females) among
(Hong Kong) Chinese subjects dealing with outgroup members. They argued that
women from collectivistic cultures should be even more collectivistic than males
from those cultures because gender roles generally put more group-maintenance
responsibilities on women. As such, they should also be most ethnocentric and,

thus, least likely to apply equality norms to outgroup members (see also Mahler et al., 1981; Strube, 1981; Triandis, 1989). If Leung and Bond's interpretation is correct[3], this reversal of the patterns for males and females between Americans (whose culture is relatively individualistic) and individuals from Hong Kong (whose culture is relatively collectivistic) would converge with other evidence to support the value explanation of male/female differences in allocations observed in American society.

Platow, McClintock, and Liebrand (1990) found a related outcome. They used subjects from a single culture but assessed (among other characteristics) their degree of individualism. They found that female individualists were more inclined toward fair allocations regardless of ingroup/outgroup distinctions; whereas male individualists were more inclined toward ingroup bias in allocations. These outcomes seem congruent with claims that individualistic cultures and values promote *both* interpersonal competitiveness *and* willingness to interact positively with strangers (e.g., Hsu, 1971; Triandis, 1989); and that these divergent effects of individualism are to some extent linked to sex roles. The results of Leung and Bond's (1984) study and that by Platow et al., (1990) would seem to indicate that the masculinity/femininity dimension of culture may be important to some aspects of organizational justice and may interact with individualism/collectivism in exerting its influence.

Masculinity/Femininity Effects on Justice.   Cultural masculinity/femininity is the third of Hofstede's dimensions that has been studied for it justice implications. The possibility of a main effect of cultural masculinity/femininity on justice-related behaviors has been examined in three studies; the possibility of a masculinity/femininity by individualism/collectivism interaction has been partially investigated in one.

In an outcome consistent with both Rokeach's work on ideologies and the idea that cultural femininity may mitigate against equity choices, Tornblom and Foa (1983) reported that subjects from socialistic and relatively feminine Sweden consistently endorsed equality allocation rules most strongly and equity rules least strongly across six categories (love, status, information, money, goods, and services) of outcomes. Nauta (1983) compared allocation patterns by individuals from the Netherlands with the patterns reported by Bond et al. (1983) for individuals from the United States and Hong Kong. In Hofstede's (1980) comparative study, the United States and the Netherlands were similar in indi-

---

[3]See, however, Leung and Iwawaki (1988) in which the interaction of culture (high- versus low-collectivism) and ingroup/outgroup membership showed only a non-significant trend. Also Leung, 1987, and Gabrenya, Wang, and Latane, 1985 in which degrees of collectivism were directly measured for groups of Chinese subjects from Hong Kong and Taiwan, respectively, and no sex differences were found; and Triandis et al., 1985, who report no sex difference in allocentrism among U.S. males and females.

vidualism but differed in masculinity/femininity. United States culture was relatively masculine and that of the Netherlands was one of the most feminine. Hofstede's results indicated that the cultures of Hong Kong and the Netherlands differ both on the individualism/collectivism and the masculinity/femininity dimensions. Nauta found that subjects from the Netherlands and Hong Kong did not differ in allocation tendencies used with others; but that subjects from both of those countries made more egalitarian allocations than did those from the United States.

Examination of the process behind these distributional tendencies did, however, yield a significant difference between the subject groups from the Netherlands and from Hong Kong. Although both groups seemed equally influenced by perceptions of the target's task competence, only those from the Netherlands were also significantly influenced by perceptions of the target's social-behavioral inputs (i.e., group-maintenance contributions). Based on these patterns, Nauta (1983) argued that when both individualism and femininity are relatively high in a culture, as in the case in the Netherlands, task inputs are considered important and equity allocation tendencies are present. But, these tendencies are tempered by substantial consideration given to socioemotional maintenance of the group. When collectivism is relatively high, as in Hong Kong, general egalitarian allocation norms for ingroups tend to be in effect. Thus, Nauta concluded that both cultural femininity and cultural collectivism can incline individuals toward more egalitarian allocations, but via somewhat different processes. If true, this would lead one to expect the strongest inclination toward egalitarianism, at least toward those perceived as being ingroup members, in cultural settings (or, after Triandis, 1989, in individuals with self-systems) high in both collectivism and femininity. This has not been empirically tested.

Leung, Bond, Carment, Krishnan, and Liebrand (1990) produced evidence that supported Nauta's allocational outcome results, but partially contradicted his process results. Leung et al. compared the reactions of Canadian and Dutch individuals to scenarios involving different potential procedures for dealing with an interpersonal conflict. Hofstede (1980) found the cultures of these two nations to be similar on three of four of his dimensions, but different on masculinity/femininity. The Dutch are substantially closer to the femininity pole than are (Anglophone) Canadians.

Recall that the masculinity/femininity dimension in part pits off interpersonal aggressiveness and competitiveness with cooperation and relationship orientation. Because of this, Leung et al. (1990) argued that Dutch subjects should be relatively more inclined toward harmony-enhancing procedures for handling conflicts; and Canadians relatively more toward confrontational procedures. Results of the study essentially supported these ideas[4].

---

[4]Both groups, however, actually rated the harmony-enhancing procedures more highly than the

Leung et al. (1990) also examined whether procedural preferences seemed to be mediated by instrumental beliefs about various procedure (i.e., beliefs about their utility for achieving process control and conflict resolution) or simply the degree to which interpersonal harmony was valued (the valance explanation). Their results provided support mainly for effects of instrumental beliefs, with valance mediation "only minimally supported." Thus, there is some dispute about the process(es) underlying the intercultural differences in organizational-justice tendencies reviewed earlier. This issue merits more detailed consideration.

Processes of Cultural Differences: Values or Instrumentality Beliefs? Results from tests of the two mediational possibilities (instrumental beliefs and values) in a previous study by Leung (1987) involving Americans and Hong Kong Chinese were similar to those of Leung et al. (1990). On the other hand, Leung and Lind (1986) found that their Chinese subjects' perceptions of the instrumental utility provided by non-adversarial procedures were unrelated to their perceptions of the desirability of such procedures.

Lind and Tyler (1988), based on a review of studies of preferences for justice procedures also concluded that the values behind procedural justice choices and preferences are the same cross-culturally. That is, that although some cross-cultural differences in procedural outcomes are seen, these are not due to differences in the valuation given to various (i.e., process control vs. harmony) possible outcomes of procedural choices but, rather, to cross-cultural differences in perceptions of which procedures best serve the same set of universally desired, that is to say, process-control, ends.

The direct quantitative evidence for this conclusion is, however, limited, contradictory (i.e., Leung and Lind's, 1986, results vs. the outcome of Leung's, 1987, study; Nauta, 1983 vs. Leung et al., 1990; Benjamin, 1975 vs. Lind, Erickson, Friedland, & Dickenberger, 1978), and mostly scenario-based. Moreover, even when instrumentality perceptions have been directly assessed and shown to be the better predictor of procedural choices, they still account for only a limited amount of the variance in those choices (e.g., at best, in Leung et al., 1990, 35% of the variance). Further, some nonquantitative (e.g., Hasegawa, 1986; Woo, 1989) and indirect evidence (Gabrenya, Wang, & Latane, 1985; Rokeach, 1970; Weisz et al., 1984) indicates possibly substantial culture-value influences on which outcomes are viewed as most important. It may be too early to have any substantial confidence in either the instrumental-utility of the valuation position and it may well be that both partially underlie observed cross-cultural differences in justice perceptions and allocations. Whether outcome-

---

confrontational ones. But Dutch subjects gave higher ratings to the harmony-enhancing procedures than did Canadians; and Canadians gave higher ratings to the confrontational procedures than the Dutch.

value or instrumental-utility beliefs exert more influence at any time may depend on the situation.

None of the studies to date in which instrumental and value-based mediational effects have been assessed and compared have included culture by situation interactions. This is especially important because at least some cultural orientations, such as collectivism, may represent more general tendencies to do what is seen as desirable (i.e., normatively appropriate for a particular situation according to one's ingroup—Hofstede, 1980) rather than what is desired (i.e., internalized as a preference) (Gabrenya et al., 1985; Hofstede, 1980; see also Hui & Triandis, 1986). Thus, striping procedural or distributive judgments of their context may increase the likelihood of supporting a common set of instrumental processes across cultures.

Lind and Tyler (1988) argued that the evidence indicates that situational factors seem to have only limited effects on procedural judgments. Several studies, however, have shown relatively substantial situation by culture effects. Some were discussed in the individualism/collectivism section earlier. Another, Leung and Lind (1986), indicated a significant sex of subject by status of the professional investigator(s) by procedure-type (adversarial versus nonadversarial) effect on procedural preferences for American, but not Chinese, subjects. In Sullivan, Peterson, Kameda, and Shimada (1981), the cultural background of the subjects was found to interact with the ingroup/outgroup status of the other party involved to influence procedural (Sullivan et al., 1981) choices. Other situation by culture interactions are discussed in the "Intergroup Relations" and "Organizational Structure" sections later. Subsequent to their 1988 book, even Lind and Tyler (Tyler & Lind, 1990) have acknowledged that situations, especially ingroup/outgroup distinctions, may exert important influences on justice perceptions and behaviors.

Further exploration of possible justice-related effects of ingroup/outgroup categories on justice perceptions and behaviors is, in fact, where we turn next.

INTERGROUP RELATIONS
AND ORGANIZATIONAL JUSTICE

Ingroup/Outgroup Processes. Individuals in complex modern societies bring many group memberships into any organization they join and joining any new organization tends to bring individuals memberships in several additional formal and informal groups (Kramer, 1991; McGrath, 1984). The salience[5] of

---

[5]After Oakes, 1987, salience here refers to the psychological prominence and influence of a social category, not to its perceptual prominence. As is indicated later in this section, perceptual prominence is one factor that can help trigger group salience, but there are other factors important to salience, as well, so that the salience and perceptual prominence constructs are not equivalent.

particular group memberships helps determine the extent and nature of intergroup competition. Kramer (1991) argued that when organization members' attend to a particular ingroup/outgroup distinction within the organization, intergroup competition and conflict becomes inevitable. Kramer (1991) tied this to literature on the commons dilemma (i.e., the observed tendency for individuals or groups to make excessive demands on finite resources that they share with others) by arguing that organizations are essentially a pool of shared resources for which those individuals and groups compete.

However, the "resources" for which groups compete include not only tangibles like money but also intangibles like status, power, and prestige (Tajfel & Turner, 1979; Turner, 1985). Because of this, competition and conflict can occur within organizations even between and among groups that are not at odds over objective goods or services that are in limited supply. According to Social Identity Theory (Tajfel, 1981; Tajfel & Turner, 1979), intergroup competition for esteem (status) is a major factor motivating group-related behaviors by individuals. The argument here is that individuals derive much of their personal identity and sense of self-worth from group memberships. Group memberships are argued, however, to have value only comparatively (see also Allen, Wilder, & Atkinson, 1983; Brewer, 1978). Group status (and, thus, to a substantial degree, individual self-esteem) necessitates intergroup comparison favorable to the ingroup.

Culture may induce general tendencies regarding breadth of individuals' social identifications, which can be with broad groups (e.g., humanity as a whole, a nation, an entire organization) or with narrower ones (a racial group, a community, a work team) (Hsu, 1971; Triandis, 1988). Culture may also partly determine nature of groups distinctions that tend to be the chronic focus of attention or tend to be more prone to situational activation (Tajfel & Turner, 1979). For instance, in the United States, racial/ethnic and sex distinctions tend to be chronically salient across a variety of situations (Allen et al., 1983; Tajfel & Turner, 1979). In Arabic countries, on the other hand, religion is generally relatively more and race relatively less important than in the United States. In Sweden and Iceland, sex tends to be generally less of a salient category than in the United States or the Arabic countries.

Relatively enduring circumstances within a particular organization can also influence which type of categories will be salient. For instance, in an organization in which sex ratios are highly skewed, sex categories will tend to become more salient unless some acute event or chronic feature of the organization makes another type of social identity strong enough to override it (Kanter, 1977).

Individual differences in chronic identification with an ingroup and empathy for an outgroup due to such things as history and personality (Markus, 1977) can also influence group salience and associated effects on justice perceptions and behaviors. For instance, Tougas, Dube, and Veilleux (1987) found that men whose identification with their own gender was relatively weak felt more "relative deprivation on behalf of other" (Runciman, 1966) (the "other" being women as a group, in this case) which, in turn, inclined them to be more supportive of affirmative action policies for women (see also, however, Tougas & Veilleux, 1990). These same authors also found that higher scores on perceptions of performance similarity between men and women were also positively associated with felt deprivation on behalf of women. If these outcomes can be generalized, then effects of the enduring importance of social categories to self, and of chronic conceptions of particular outgroups on justice perceptions and behaviors are indicated.

Dube and Guimond (1986) go further by proposing that individuals often have multiple conceptions for any single group, especially ones they are a part of or otherwise know well. They indicate that situations influences not only general group salience but also the salience of different specific conceptions of that group. Situationally induced shifts in the salience of specific conceptions of ingroup or outgroup might have important implications for justice behavior (Dube & Guimond, 1986; see also the discussion of work by Katz, Wackenhutt, & Hass, 1986, later).

Although intergroup competition and conflict seem to be influenced in important ways by ingroup/outgroup salience effects, competition and conflict also help to shape group salience; the influence is bidirectional (Kramer, 1991; Turner, 1985). Oakes (1987) argued and reviewed evidence indicating that intergroup effects are determined by a combination of accessibility of social categories and the fit or appropriateness of such categories to other existing circumstances. Thus, category accessibility plus situations that promote intergroup comparison or competition may combine to make it most likely that ingroup/outgroup distinctions will operate to influence organization members' perceptions and actions (James & Greenberg, 1989). A spiraling cycle ingroup/outgroup effects on organizational justice outcomes becomes possible.

Reactions to affirmative action programs may be one of the clearest examples of how organizational justice can be affected by the convergence of many of the processes just reviewed. Such programs combine both social categories (race and/or gender) that tend to be chronically powerful both because of cultural influences and because of what Allen et al. (1983) referred to as an "omnipresence of cues." They also involve situational enhancement of the salience of those categories because they are the focus of the program, because group ratios are usually skewed and because of competition for an important resource (jobs). Added to this are strong chronic group identifications by both advocates within the underrepresented group and racists/sexists within the majority. This pattern of influences may be why affirmative action policies often tend to trigger very high levels of emotion and intergroup conflict.

Influences on Organizational Justice Outcomes.   The implications of intergroup processes for organizational justice can be immense. One important impact is that awareness of ingroup/outgroup distinctions and intergroup competition can lessen concerns with applying justice rules equally to all individuals (Deutsch, 1985; Kramer, 1991; Tajfel & Turner, 1979; Tyler & Lind, 1990). One manifestation of this is simply the development and use of two sets of rules for allocations or procedures—one for "them" and one for "us." For instance, as noted previously, even among individualists distributions to members of strongly valued ingroups tend toward communal (equality) or need principles; but outgroup members tend to be dealt with on (at best) an equity basis (Deutsch, 1985; Mills & Clark, 1982).

An interesting study by Pfeffer and Langton (1988) of salary distributions in academic departments yielded results consistent with the idea that salient ingroup/outgroup distinctions affect allocations. Pfeffer and Langton found that salary differentials among department members tended to be greater the greater the heterogeneity of the department. That heterogeneity of education level and experience predicted pay differentials is unremarkable. However, sex heterogeneity was also a significant predictor of salary distributions even with education and experience controlled for, supporting the impact of salient ingroup/outgroup distinctions on allocations.

Similar effects can occur with procedures—there can be different sets that tend to be used with ingroup and with outgroup members (Nadler, 1975; Sullivan et al., 1981; Tyler & Lind, 1990). On occasion this may be beneficial, as in Adler (1987) who found that western women were able to effectively make deals with Japanese corporations even though Japanese gender-norms prevented Japanese women from obtaining anything other than low-level positions in those same corporations. Western women's status as *gaijins* (foreigners, but also translatable as "outsiders") was apparently more salient than their sex so that the standards that were applied to Japanese women were not seen as applicable to them.

Most sets of dual procedures for ingroup and outgroup members, however, are likely to favor the ingroup and thus be comparatively unfair for the outgroup (Deutsch, 1985; Nader, 1975; Tajfel & Turner, 1979; Turner and Associates, 1987; Tyler & Lind, 1990). For instance, Kanter (1977), Mullen and Baumeister (1987), and others (see James & Khoo, 1991; Pettigrew & Martin, 1987 for reviews) have argued and produced some evidence indicating that salience of sex or racial categories in organizations lead to biased appraisals and allocations.

Another possible organizational-justice effect of intergroup distinctions in organizations is that evaluations of the costs and benefits of actions and policies may be positively influenced more by benefits accruing to the ingroup, and negatively influenced less by costs born by outgroups (Dooley, 1984; Schein, 1985). This possibility does not, however, seem to have been subjected to much direct quantitative examination.

These differences in justice applications with ingroup and outgroup members involve what Deutsch (1985) and Opotow (1988), among others, refer to as *inclusionary* and *exclusionary* justice. To the extent that individuals apply justice principles only to members of the ingroup, justice becomes exclusionary. To the extent that justice principles and procedures are seen as universally applicable, they are inclusionary. At extremes of exclusion, the rules of justice are seen as not applying at all to some outgroup. In such cases, members of the ingroup are treated according to the moral code/values the individual has internalized while outgroups are used and abused as circumstances allow. Cultural forces may help to determine general tendencies toward inclusion or exclusion, as well as which types of group categories are most likely to be the focus of exclusionary practices when they do occur (Triandis, 1988).

There are a number of other moderating factors of ingroup bias. Some of these are targeted in the Social Identification Theory literature; others come from work on *fraternal deprivation* (i.e., feelings of injustice based upon an ingroup's disadvantage relative to an outgroup) within the larger area of relative deprivation and social comparison (e.g., Crosby, 1976; Martin, 1981, 1986; Runciman, 1966, 1968; Walker & Pettigrew, 1984).

It is relatively high-status and high-power groups that seem most likely to exhibit outgroup bias (Fernandez, 1981; Greenberg, Pyszcynski, & Solomon, 1986; Kanter, 1977; Sachdev & Bourhis, 1991; Tajfel & Turner, 1979). Members of such groups are most able to derive esteem (status) from them; thus outgroups are most likely to be perceived as threatening group-based esteem for members of relatively high-status groups. These individuals are, therefore, most likely to exhibit negative attitudes and actions toward outgroups (Greenberg et al., 1986; Tajfel & Turner, 1979). High status and power groups in organizations are, of course also most able to translate their beliefs, expectations, and fears into action (Er, 1989; Tajfel & Turner, 1979). This can lead to justice-related organizational problems such as efforts to exclude or harass women and minorities (Fernandez, 1981; Kanter, 1977).

Efforts by advantaged groups to preserve status and resource superiority can lead to efforts to institutionalize differences by supporting them with organizational norms, values and rules which are often unrelated to task performance (Fernandez, 1981; Kanter, 1977). Where these are generally internalized by all parties, systems tend to be stable regardless of inequities and inequalities of treatment and outcomes among groups.

Challenges to an institutionalized system, when they do occur, are a trigger for hostility toward outgroups; and threats due to other factors that trigger anxiety or fear can exacerbate conflicts based on threats to internalized status or value/belief systems (Greenberg, et al., 1986; Rosenblatt, Greenberg, Solomon, Pszszynski, & Lyons, 1989; Schein, 1985; Tyler & Lind, 1990). Institutionalization can thus set the stage for a cycle of challenge/threat/resistance between upstart groups and the establishment.

Ingroup Salience and Individual Responses to Organizational Justice. Identity salience and expectations associated with identities can influence reactions of those who receive allocations and experience procedures as well as those of persons who make allocations and create and implement procedures. This ties into an argument made by Wegner (1982), who proposed that the world can be seen either through the "lens" of group norms, values, goals, and outcomes; or through the "lens" of personal expectations, values, goals, and outcomes. Perceiving the world through the lens of the group is, according to Wegner, most likely when the group is seen as a unitary entity, which can occur because of perceptions of member proximity, similarity or attraction; due to knowledge of common agency or common fate; or due to "Figure/Ground" effects due to situational variations in ingroup and outgroup proportions or other cues for group-salience (see, e.g., James & Greenberg, 1989).

Perceptions of the fairness of observed events should vary depending on whether they are viewed according to salient group identities, or according to personal identity. Wegner argued that group-as-lens effects influence how individuals judge the justness of ingroup treatment. Evaluations of outcomes are posited to vary depending on whether conceptions linked to an ingroup or conceptions linked to self are the "lens" through which the evaluation is made.

Work by Major and her colleagues (see Major's, 1987, review) supports this view. They have produced evidence in several studies that sex differences in expected rewards exist due to real differences in rewards received for work by males and females within American society. Such sex-linked differences are internalized and made salient by situational circumstances (by, e.g., some degree of sex-segregation of job categories within an organization). The result is that women sometimes believe themselves to be fairly compensated even when they are receiving fewer rewards than male colleagues because they are using other women as their standard of comparison. Zanna, Crosby, and Loewenstein (1987) provide evidence that women who tend use the outcomes of males in similar positions as a reference (i.e., for whom comparably placed males are the salient comparison group) feel more discontented than women who use other women as points of comparison. Similar effects have been found to occur for groups other than women (see Martin, 1981; Taylor, Wood, & Lichtman, 1983; Walker & Pettigrew, 1984).

James and Cropanzano (1990) elaborated on and tested the idea that "lens" effects would influence use of information about an organization's justice practices and procedures. They activated either self-conceptions or conceptions of an ingroup so that one or the other would be the "lens" through which subsequent information would be viewed. They then gave subjects one of three descriptions of a combined procedural/distributive interaction between an ingroup member and an outgroup allocator.

James and Cropanzano hypothesized that when the self was the lens, equity concerns would be paramount and subjects would use information about an ingroup member primarily to determine whether equity principles were adhered to by the organization. Given group-as-lens, however, subjects were expected to use the information to determine typical organizational standards for their ingroup. The results indicated that internal, but not external, locus of control subjects did use the information in the predicted ways in the self and group conditions.

Organizational Justice and Group-Level Actions.   As noted earlier, group-status differences and associated allocational and procedural differences may be accepted by disadvantaged groups if they are linked to an internalized ideology and made to seem inevitable, or if they simply seem beyond any hope of change (Tajfel & Turner, 1979; Taylor, Moghaddam, Gamble, & Zellerer, 1986; Walker & Pettigrew, 1984). Disadvantaged groups may even exhibit outgroup favoritism if the existing status system is accepted (Sachdev & Bourhis, 1991; Tajfel & Turner, 1979).

Disadvantaged, lower status, or unjustly treated groups may only attempt to modify intergroup standing and outcomes under certain conditions. Some identified in the literature include: when the status system seems unstable—that is, when alternative systems can be envisioned and seem possible (Tajfel & Turner, 1979); when the distance between the groups is relatively small (Taylor et al., 1986; Walker & Pettigrew, 1984); when individualistic options seem blocked (Martin, 1981, 1986); when both procedural and distributive injustices based on group membership are salient (Taylor et al., 1986); when there is both distributive injustice *and* violation of internalized and valued moral standards (Deutsch, 1985); when both ingroup status and the particular foci of injustice are highly valued (Walker & Pettigrew, 1984); when circumstances promote *inter*group (as opposed to *intra*group) comparisons by the disadvantaged group (Martin, 1981; Turner, 1985; Walker & Pettigrew, 1984; Zanna et al., 1984); or when the disadvantaged group has or develops a strong ideology that promotes collective action against the higher status group (Guimond & Dube-Simard, 1983; Taylor & McKirnan, 1984).

It is not clear whether this list captures all of the major factors; nor which of the factors listed are most powerful; nor how they might interact to produce group efforts to change unfavorable/unjust intergroup patterns. The literature on fraternal deprivation does indicate, however, that although felt injustice based on feeling that one's group has been treated unfairly seems the exception rather than the rule even in situations of "objective" discriminatory treatment across groups, it leads to powerful effects when it does occur (Crosby, 1976; Dube & Guimond, 1986; Walker & Pettigrew, 1984). Thus, further research on the sources and processes of perceptions of group deprivation and how such perceptions influence subsequent actions is important. Research within organizational settings is especially needed.

Culture by Ingroup/Outgroup Interactions.   Effects due to ingroup/outgroup distinctions apparently interact with cultural values in several ways. Some of these were previously discussed. Some others follow.

Lind and Tyler (1990) imply that cultural power–distance should interact with ingroup/outgroup distinctions. They argued that "groups that value hierarchical or subgroup distinctions, and that vary their procedures depending on status or other intragroup distinctions, will be especially exclusionary in their denial of justice to outsiders" (p. 93). They argue, similarly, that where one's ingroup stresses a value of egalitarianism and equal justice for all, exclusionary justice practices should be less likely (see also Deutsch, 1975, 1985). Platow et al. (1990) provide some supporting evidence for this position. They found that the level of individuals' prosocial (cooperative) values influenced allocation biases such that those relatively high on such values generally made fairer allocations to outgroup members.

Rokeach's (1970) ideas and evidence, discussed in the *Culture* section, also seem congruent with Tyler and Lind's views about the relationship of ingroup egalitarianism/power–distance to inclination to take an exclusionary approach to justice. Another set of supportive evidence comes from research by Furnham (1985a, 1985b, 1987) indicating that native English speaking Whites in South Africa—a society characterized by high social stratification and status-based inequality—exhibit more outgroup bias than comparable British subjects, and believe more strongly that the world is a just place where individuals and groups get what they deserve.

Furnham (1985b, 1987—see also Bluen & Barling, 1983) has linked South African exclusionary practices and defense of the existing procedural and out-come inequalities to strong Calvinistic/Protestant-ethic elements in White South-African culture. Greenberg (1979) and Stake (1983) have shown that endorsement of the Protestant-ethic by Euro-American subjects is related to adherence to equity rather than equality or need allocation principles. Katz and his colleagues (Katz & Hass, 1988; Katz et al, 1986) recently also tied in-group/outgroup bias in the United States to the Protestant-ethic as a cultural component. They have also shown, however, that value systems are complex and exert complicated influences on outgroup bias.

Katz and his colleagues proposed that mainstream American culture has mul-tiple and sometimes contradictory value-trends which many people internalize. Specifically, they argue that both a long-standing and potent current of human-itarianism/egalitarianism (which they also call *communalism*) and an opposing, similarly long-standing and powerful Protestant-ethic value (which they some-times also label *individualism*) exist within mainstream American society. They provide evidence that situational factors can help activate either set of values and that attitudes toward outgroup members are then moderated by the active value-set. Activated humanitarianism/egalitarianism seems to promote more positive outgroup attitudes; activated Protestant-ethic ideas seem to promote more nega-tive outgroup attitudes. As it happens, most of the attitude items used by Katz and his colleagues are ones that deal with fairness of outcomes and procedures for an outgroup, bringing their research very much in line with the focus of this chapter.

ORGANIZATIONAL STRUCTURE, STATUS,
AND POWER

Justice principles, perceptions, and actions may be closely bound to the status, positional, and power systems of organizations. These factors have not often been included in research or theory, however.

The relationship between justice principles in organizations and the structuring of status and power seems to be reciprocal. Reward systems in organizations (with "reward" broadly defined to include power and status) are partly a function of ideology, but also seem to sometimes be used to create and enforce particular ideologies (Kerr & Slocum, 1987; Schein, 1985).

Power and status systems, once in existence, lead to allocational and procedural expectations and outcomes that can profoundly affect organizational operations. As noted in the intergroup relations section, above, efforts to perpetuate status and power differentials can become a focus of some organization members' behavior. Sampson (1986) even argued that virtually the sole purpose of unequal distributions in organizations is to help maintain the status and power system. A more moderate view is that power and status and existing reward levels affect perceptions, justifications, and endorsements of the existing organizational systems.

At a more fundamental level, those who benefit more from a particular system seem to possess more extensive rationales for it and be more committed to it (Fernandez, 1981; Furnham, 1985a; Lerner, 1980). In addition, at least in western societies, organizational positions that include evaluative responsibilities, as most positions of relative power and status do, seem to include a norm of assigning causality for behaviors and outcomes to individuals (see Beauvois & Dubois, 1988, for a research review and discussion). This norm should clearly influence allocations of positive (rewards) and negative (punishments) organizational outcomes by those with power by making them more likely to see both "good" and "bad" elements of performance as due to the individual. It should also increase the likelihood that the "just-world" (just-organization) phenomena (Lerner, 1980)—the tendency to see outcome differences as deserved—will occur among those in positions of power.

Subordinates, being less subject to the internality norm, should have different perceptions on both issues. Thus, it seems likely that those at lower levels in organizations might have less of a fundamental acceptance of existing organizational systems than will be found among those who are relatively privileged.

A study by Lansberg (1984) produced evidence of a more specific impact of position within organizational hierarchies on perceptions of fairness of allocational procedures. He found that (U.S.) upper and middle managers viewed equity-based allocation of a hypothetical windfall (i.e., unexpected and one-time) pool of bonus money as more fair than either equality or need based allocation. Lower-level employees from the same organizations, however, endorsed equity allocations significantly less, and equality allocations significantly more, than did the managers. In addition, although upper-level managers tended to support a scheme based on organization-wide equity (i.e., contributions to the entire organization), middle-level managers saw equity distributions within divisions of the organization as most desirable.

The greater tendency among those in less powerful positions to make external attributions combined with hierarchic differences in preferred allocation principles may make it more likely that those in positions of relatively low power will see the entire organizational system as unjust and attempt to change it. On the other hand, the fact that individuals in positions of relative power seem to have stronger internalized justifications for existing power/status levels and seem to be more likely to make internal attributions may make them more likely to feel personally (as opposed to as a group) unjustly treated by other individuals or groups in the organization. Kemper (1978) presented a theory that seems congruent with this view. He argued that individual affective reactions and the behaviors these trigger are largely determined by the implications of interactions between/among actors for the existing power and status structure.

In essence Kemper argued that situations are evaluated for their implications for individuals' or groups' expected power and status and in terms of whether those implications have been caused by self or by an other (person or group). Perceived situational diminutions or enhancements of power or status interact with the perceived causal agent for these effects to trigger different types of affect. Kemper proposed, for example, that when one's power in a situation falls below what one has come to expect and an other is seen as the source of this power deficiency, the result is *anarchy-rebelliousness*. This is described as a pattern of behavior aimed at destroying the power of the other.

Because those in positions of high power have (a) higher general power expectations, which may make it more likely that situations will occur in which their expectations are not met; and (b) a greater tendency to attribute causality to others rather than situations, they may be more likely to experience violations of power expectations and to see these as due to the actions of other persons or groups.

One interesting additional element of Kemper's theory is that he dealt with the precursors and outcomes not only of perceived deprivation but also of perceived excess. Thus, he proposed that excess power attributed to self leads to guilt and efforts at expiation; that excess power attributed to other leads to megalomania and exploitative behavior; and that excess status attributed to other leads to shame *cum* anger and withdrawal. Kemper's conceptions would seem to contain a wealth of possibilities for justice researchers.

It seems possible that power/status difference may interact with cultural power-distance values to affect justice perceptions/behaviors. Because power-distance reflects an acceptance and expectation of social stratification and a tendency to view power and status differences as internally based, it seems reasonable that those holding powerful and high status positions within cultural settings in which power-distance is high will tend to have the highest and most widely generalized expectations for power and status. They, should, therefore be even more likely to react negatively to situations in which their power/status deviates from their expectations. Within their own cultures (given relatively uniform adherence to the power-distance value and associated norms) such deviations may be unlikely. But they might become highly likely in interactions with persons from other cultures, such as occur in multinational organizations and international trade. These ideas are speculative but seem worthy of empirical tests.

Er (1989) proposed other effects of positions high and low in power in organizations and links power to other structural factors, as well. He argued that those with low power are generally poorly positioned to be assertive in pursuit of what they see as fair treatment, but argued that this will be especially the case in authoritarian organizations. He claimed that pursuit of perceived fairness by such individuals may lead to more stress than would sacrificing some of their rights. For supervisors, he proposed that a more dominant and assertive style is possible and typically seen, but that this approach must be tempered by support and empathy if the subordinate is not to experience substantial distress which can yield negative consequences in the future.

Among coworkers, Er viewed relative equality of power as leading to potential problems unless interdependence and norms of cooperation are high. He proposed that matrix and organic organizations are particularly prone to the frustrations and stresses due to individuals and groups requiring or seeing themselves as entitled to outcomes from others but lacking the power to obtain them. Finally, he argued that positions in organizations that give their incumbents relatively high levels of autonomy from others but also make others dependent on them for cooperation or assistance promote domineering and demanding behavior in interactions with fellow organization members.

Congruent with the latter point is evidence that even upper-level managers, who Landsberg (1984) found to be relatively strongly oriented toward the equity principle, show an increased tendency to endorse equality as the basis of allocations given high task interdependence (the opposite of autonomy) among organization members (Meindl, 1989). This is apparently due to a recognition that systems high in interdependence necessitate high levels of cooperation and harmony and that the unequal rewards in an equity-based allocation system can help disrupt both (Kerr & Slocum, 1987; Meindl, 1989).

Similarly, Landsberg's finding of a difference between upper and middle managers in the unit (organization-wide vs. within divisions) that they saw as the best basis for an equity system may be somewhat congruent with an argument made by Hegtvedt (1987) that the size of the group an allocator is responsible for influences how the allocation will be performed. Hegtvedt argued and produced some (albeit statistically weak) evidence that responsibility for allocating rewards within a larger unit (larger than, in his study, the dyads typically used in social psychological research) focuses attention on the group as an entity rather than on individuals. Upper-level managers, having responsibility for a larger number of people, would be expected to focus on larger units than middle managers. Thus, Landsberg's results may somewhat fit with Hegtvedt's argument.

Pfeffer and Langton (1988) produced some additional evidence that degree of autonomy, as well as some other structural factors, influence justice-related outcomes. Using data from 1,805 departments at 303 colleges and universities, they found support for a number of predictions about circumstances they expected to help shape salary distributions. Structural factors associated with degree of wage dispersion were: degree of task autonomy among members, with greater autonomy associated with greater salary dispersion; degree of use of consensus decision making on nonpersonnel issues (the more, the less salary inequality there tended to be); the size of the department (the more members, the greater salary dispersion tended to be); the availability of salary information (the more likely that it would become known, the less salary variation among members there tended to be); and the tenure of the department head/chair (the longer, the lower salary dispersion tended to be). Although acknowledging the likelihood of mutual causality in some of these relationships, Pfeffer and Langton argued that they do provide evidence of important connections between the structure of organizations and patterns of distributions of resources.

Hardy (1990) made a similar case, again based on examination of academic institutions. This time, however, the outcome studied was the types of procedures adopted to deal with circumstances that forced budget cuts. Her results led her to conclude that the structuring of power within different universities substantially shaped procedural choices. Those universities that had more centralization of power were more likely to cut departmental budgets unequally (or even to eliminate whole departments) than those in which power was more decentralized.

A related structural issue is that justice norms and procedures may sometimes, for some issues, tend to develop at the level of work units or other operating units, which differ from those at the organization-wide level. This could cause conflicts of policies and practices and may also trigger perceptions of organizational unfairness if comparisons across unit boundaries are made. I know of no research that has directly examined this issue. But it is congruent with the results of examinations of justice in societies, which show that local justice norms and procedures are often present that differ from, and sometimes conflict with, national principles and practices (Nader, 1975). It also fits with discussions of subcultures within organizations in the organizational literature (e.g., Martin & Siehl, 1983; Schein, 1985).

Kabonoff (1991) offered a different take on power, structure, and justice than the authors discussed earlier. He indicated that power involves both structural and process factors; in his scheme, organizational reinforcements and how they are patterned are the process elements of power. He argued that the power structure and the power process are somewhat independent. They may or may not be congruent, and the different types of matches and mismatches between them define different types of organizations.

For instance, where power is relatively equally distributed across the structure and the process is egalitarian, Kabonoff argued that there is congruence of structure and process that yields loyalty and high involvement. However, because such organizations do not tie rewards to performance, skill, or other variations (e.g., externally based prestige) in member inputs, performance motivation may suffer and conflicts over perceived inequities and inefficiencies are likely. These conflicts may tend to occur and recur frequently because power is not concentrated in a way that allow imposing views or compelling compliance; but they tend to be relatively unacrimonious.

Kabonoff's presentation is rich and seems a promising source of hypotheses for justice researchers. Kabonoff's scheme could also be integrated with some of the ideas about cultural/value and ingroup/outgroup effects discussed earlier.

Differences in societal cultural patterns should probably influence the type of power-structure/power-process combinations that will arise; and these combinations should influence other organizational norms and values. For instance, the equal-power structure/egalitarian-process type would seem most likely to occur in cultures low in high power distance, high in collectivism and high in femininity. Regardless of societal culture, however, if factors such as the resource-dependence aspects of the environment in which the organization existed did lead to development of an equal-power structure/egalitarian-process arrangement, low power-distance, collectivistic, and feminine orientations should be likely to evolve within the organization's culture.

Similarly, ingroup/outgroup relations should partially help shape organization type within Kabanoff's scheme, and be partially shaped by type. Thus, where ingroup/outgroup distinctions are salient (say, for instance, in an organization highly polarized on racial or sexual lines over an affirmative action program) and resource competition exists, we would expect pressure toward an unequal-power system regardless of other factors. As noted in the intergroup relations section, however, there might not be only one reinforcement pattern in such a setting, as Kabonoff indicated. Instead, one might see a dual-process pattern in which the group in power would tend more toward egalitarian reinforcement amongst themselves (because ingroup solidarity and cohesion is promoted by perceived intergroup conflict or competition); but tend toward the use of equity or exploitation in reinforcements for individuals from the outgroup. After Leung and Bond (1984) and Triandis (1989), collectivists would be expected to be respond most strongly to ingroup/outgroup distinctions in organizations in the way just described.

CONCLUSIONS

I stated in the introduction that this work is a beginning, not an end. It represents a review of where we currently stand in our understanding of the role of more macro factors in organization justice practices and outcomes; a call to colleagues to broaden the scope and increase the depth of existing conceptions about organizational justice; and an effort to stimulate some new lines of research.

The patient reader who has persisted with this chapter to this point will no doubt agree that the impacts of culture, structure, and intergroup relations on organizational justice seem complex. A personnel psychologist of my acquaintance is of the opinion that macro-level factors generally have such complex patterns of influence and interrelationship that it is, in fact, best to simply ignore them. I hope, however, that I have made the case in this chapter that their roles in organizational justice are both interesting and crucial. We can ignore those roles if our personal comfort or the exigencies of academia compel us to, but to do so makes it unlikely that a genuine understanding of justice principles and practices (or other aspects of organizations) will ever arise. Thus, there is nothing to be done except to take a deep breath and plunge ahead.

ACKNOWLEDGMENTS

I thank the teachers, students and friends from many worlds whose ideas, assistance, and examples have brought me to where this chapter finds me. Of the many, special thanks to these few: Mad Bear Anderson, Julie Chen, Dz-Lyang Chen, Russell Cropanzano, Mort Deutsch, Maru Fernandez-Esquer, Jeff Greenberg, Gillian Khoo, and Asiba Tupahache. They have tried to help me understand. If I do not, the failure lies with my faculties, not with their efforts. Kawankamish to you all.

REFERENCES

Adler, N. J. (1987). Pacific basin managers: A *Gaijin*, not a woman. *Human Resources Management, 26*, 169–191.

Allen, V. L., Wilder, D. A., & Atkinson, M. L. (1983). Multiple group membership and social identity. In T. R. Sarbin & K. E. Scheibe (Eds.), *Studies in social identity* (pp. 83–110). New York: Praeger.

Babad, E. Y. (1986). Appendix 8: The Israeli case: Minority status and politics. In K. S. Scherer, H. G. Wallbott, & A. B. Summerfield (Eds.), *Experiencing emotion: A cross-cultural study* (pp. 246–255). Cambridge, England: Cambridge University Press.

Babad, E. Y., & Wallbott, H. G. (1986). The effects of social factors on emotional reactions. In K. S. Scherer, H. G. Wallbott, & A. B. Summerfield (Eds.), *Experiencing emotion: A cross-cultural study* (pp. 154–172). Cambridge, England: Cambridge University Press.

Bellah, R. N., Madsen, R., Sullivan, W. M., Swidler, A., & Tipton, S. M. (1985). *Habits of the heart: Individualism and commitment in American life.* Berkeley, CA: University of California Press.

Benjamin, R. W. (1975). Images of conflict resolution and social control: American and Japanese attitudes toward the adversarial system. *Journal of Conflict Resolution, 19,* 123–137.

Beauvois, J., & Dubois, N. (1988). The norm of internality in the explanation of psychological events. *European Journal of Social Psychology, 18,* 299–316.

Berman, J. J., Murphy-Berman, V., & Singh, P. (1985). Cross-cultural similarities and differences in perceptions of fairness. *Journal of Cross-Cultural Psychology, 16,* 55–67.

Bluen, S. D., & Barling, J. (1983). Work values in white South African males. *Journal of Cross-Cultural Psychology, 14,* 329–335.

Bond, M. H., Leung, K., & Wan, K. C. (1982). How does cultural collectivism operate? The impact of task maintenance contributions on reward distribution. *Journal of Cross-Cultural Psychology, 13,* 186–200.

Brewer, M. B. (1978). In-group bias in the minimal intergroup situation: A cognitive-motivational analysis. *Psychological Bulletin, 86,* 307–324.

Brickman, P., Folger, R., Goode, E., & Schul, A. (1981). Macrojustice and microjustice. In M. J. Lerner & S. C. Lerner (Eds.), *The justice motive in social behavior* (pp. 173–202). New York: Plenum.

Crosby, F. (1976). A model of egotistical relative deprivation. *Psychological Review, 83,* 85–113.

Cushman, P. (1990). Why the self is empty: Toward a historically situated psychology. *American Psychologist, 45,* 599–611.

Deutsch, M. (1975). Equity, equality, and need: What determines which value will be used as the basis of distributive justice? *Journal of Social Issues, 31,* 137–149.

Deutsch, M. (1985). *Distributive justice: A social psychological perspective.* New Haven, CT: Yale University Press.

Dooley, D. (1984). Program evaluation. In D. Dooley (Ed.), *Social research methods* (pp. 302–326). Englewood Cliffs, NJ: Prentice-Hall.

Dube, L., & Guimond, S. (1986). Relative deprivation and social protest: The personal-group issue. In J. M. Olson, C. P. Herman, & M. P. Zanna (Eds.), *Relative deprivation and social comparison: The Ontario Symposium* (Vol. 4, pp. 201–216). Hillsdale, NJ: Lawrence Erlbaum Associates.

Er, M. C. (1989). Assertive behavior and stress. *Advanced Management Journal, 54,* 4–8.

Fernandez, J. P. (1981). *Racism and sexism in corporate life.* Lexington, MA: Lexington Books.

Furnham, A. (1985a). Just world beliefs in an unjust society: A cross-cultural comparison. *European Journal of Social Psychology, 15,* 363–366.

Furnham, A. (1985b). Adolescents' sociopolitical attitudes: A study of sex and national differences. *Political Psychology, 6,* 621–636.

Furnham, A. (1987). School children's perception of economic justice: A cross-cultural comparison. *Journal of Economic Psychology, 8,* 457–467.

Gabrenya, W. K., Wang, Y., & Latane, B. (1985). Social loafing on an optimizing task: Cross-cultural differences among Chinese and Americans. *Journal of Cross-Cultural Psychology, 16,* 223–242.

Greenberg, J. (1979). Protestant ethic endorsement and the fairness of equity inputs. *Journal of Research in Personality, 13,* 81–90.

Greenberg, J. (1990). Organizational justice: Yesterday, today, and tomorrow. *Journal of Management, 16,* 399–432.

Greenberg, J., Pyszcynski, T., & Solomon, S. (1986). The causes and consequences of need for self-esteem: A terror management theory. In R. F. Baumeister (Ed.), *Public self and private self* (pp. 189–212). New York: Springer-Verlag.

Guimond, S., & Dube-Simard, L. (1983). Relative deprivation theory and the Quebec nationalist movement: The cognitive-emotion distinction and personal-group deprivation issue. *Journal of Personality and Social Psychology, 44,* 526–535.

Gundykunst, W. B. (1988). Culture and intergroup processes. In M. H. Bond (Ed.), *The cross-cultural challenge to social psychology* (Cross-cultural research and methodology series, Vol. 11, pp. 165–181). Newbury Park, CA: Sage.

Gundykunst, W. B. and Ting-Toomey, S. (1988). Culture and affective communication. *American Behavioral Scientist, 31,* 384–400.

Hardy, C. (1990). Strategy and context: Retrenchment in Canadian universities. *Organizational Studies, 11,* 207–237.

Hasegawa, K. (1986). *Japanese-style management.* New York: Kondansha International.

Hegtvedt, K. A. (1987). When rewards are scarce: Equal or equitable distributions? *Social Forces, 66,* 183–207.

Hofstede, G. (1980). *Culture's consequences.* Beverly Hills, CA: Sage.

Hofstede, G., & Bond, M. (1984). Hofstede's culture dimensions: An independent validation using Rokeach's Value Survey. *Journal of Cross-Cultural Psychology, 15,* 417–433.

Hui, C. H., & Triandis, H. C. (1986). Individualism-collectivism: A study of cross-cultural researchers. *Journal of Cross-Cultural Psychology, 17,* 225–248.

Hsu, F.L.K. (1971). Psychosocial homeostasis and Jen: Conceptual tools for advancing psychological anthropology. *American Anthropologist, 73,* 23–44.

Isabella, L. A. (1986). Culture, key events, and corporate social responsibility. In J. E. Post & L. E. Preston (Eds.), *Research in corporate social performance and policy* (Vol. 8, pp. 175–192). Greenwich, CT: JAI Press.

James, K., & Cropanzano, R. (1990). Focus of attention and locus of control as moderators of fraternal justice effects. *Social Justice Research, 4,* 169–185.

James, K., & Greenberg, J. (1989). In-group salience, intergroup comparison, and individual performance and self-esteem. *Personality and Social Psychology Bulletin, 15,* 604–616.

James, K., & Khoo, G. (1991). Identity-related influences on the success of minority workers in primarily nonminority organizations. *Hispanic Journal of the Behavioral Sciences, 13,* 169–192.

Kabanoff, B. (1991). Equity, equality, power, and conflict. *Academy of Management Review, 16,* 416–441.

Kahn, A., O'Leary, V. E., Krulewitz, J. E., & Lamm, H. (1980). Equity and equality: Male and female means to a just end. *Basic and Applied Social Psychology, 1,* 173–197.

Kanter, R. M. (1977). *Men and women of the corporation.* New York: Basic Books.

Kashima, Y., Siegal, M., Tanaka, K., & Isaka, H. (1988). Universalism in lay conceptions of distributive justice: A cross-cultural examination. *International Journal of Psychology, 23,* 51–64.

Katz, I., & Hass, R. G. (1988). Racial ambivalence and American value conflict: Correlational and priming studies of dual cognitive structures. *Journal of Personality and Social Psychology, 55,* 893–905.

Katz, I., Wackenhut, J., & Hass, R. G. (1986). Racial ambivalence, value duality, and behavior. In J. F. Dovidio & S. L. Gaertner (Eds.), *Prejudice, discrimination, and racism* (pp. 35–60). New York: Academic Press.

Kemper, T. D. (1978). *A social interaction theory of emotions.* New York: Wiley.

Kerr, J., & Slocum, J. W. (1987). Managing corporate culture through reward systems. *Academy of Management Executive, 1,* 99–108.

Kramer, R. M. (1991). Intergroup relations and organizational dilemmas: The role of categorization processes. In L. L. Cummings & B. M. Staw (Eds.), *Research in organizational behavior* (Vol. 13, pp. 191–228). Greenwich, CT: JAI Press.

Lansberg, I. (1984). Hierarchy as a mediator of fairness: A contingency approach to distributive justice in organizations. *Journal of Applied Social Psychology, 14,* 124–135.

Larwood, L., Kavanagh, M., & Levine, R. (1978). Perception of fairness with three alternative economic exchanges. *Academy of Management Journal, 21,* 69–83.

Lerner, M. J. (1980). *The belief in a just world: A fundamental delusion.* New York: Plenum.

Leung, K. (1987). Some determinants of reactions to procedural models for conflict resolution: A cross-national study. *Journal of Personality and Social Psychology, 53,* 898–908.

Leung, K. (1988a). Theoretical advances in justice behavior: Some cross-cultural inputs. In M. H. Bond (Ed.), *The cross-cultural challenge to social psychology* (Cross-cultural research and methodology series, Vol. 11, pp. 218–229). Newbury Park, CA: Sage.

Leung, K. (1988b). Some determinants of conflict avoidance. *Journal of Cross-Cultural Psychology, 19,* 125–136.

Leung, K., & Bond, M. H. (1982). How Chinese and Americans reward task-related contributions: A preliminary study. *Psychologia, 25,* 32–39.

Leung, K., & Bond, M. H. (1984). The impact of cultural collectivism on reward allocation. *Journal of Personality and Social Psychology, 47,* 793–804.

Leung, K., Bond, M. H., Carment, D. W., Krishnan, L., & Liebrand, W.B.G. (1990). Effects of cultural femininity on preference for methods of conflict processing: A cross-cultural study. *Journal of Experimental Social Psychology, 26,* 373–388.

Leung, K., & Iwawaki, S. (1988). Cultural collectivism and distributive behavior. *Journal of Cross-Cultural Psychology, 19,* 35–49.

Leung, K., & Lind, E. A. (1986). Procedural justice and culture: Effects of culture, gender, and investigator status on procedural preferences. *Journal of Personality and Social Psychology, 50,* 1134–1140.

Leventhal, G. S. (1976). The distribution of rewards and resources in groups and organizations. In L. Berkowitz & E. Walster (Eds.), *Advances in experimental social psychology* (Vol. 9, pp. 91–131). New York: Academic Press.

Lind, E. A., & Tyler, T. R. (1988). *The social psychology of procedural justice.* New York: Plenum.

Lind, E. A., Erickson, B. E., Friedland, N., and Dickenberger, M. (1978). Reactions to procedural models for adjudictive conflict resolution: A cross-national study. *Journal of Conflict Resolution, 22,* 318–341.

McGrath, J. E. (1984). *Groups: Interaction and performance.* Englewood Cliffs, NJ: Prentice-Hall.

Mahler, I., Greenberg, L., & Hayashi, H. (1981). A comparative study of rules of justice: Japanese versus Americans. *Psychologia, 24,* 1–8.

Major, B. (1987). Gender, justice, and the psychology of entitlement. In P. Shaver & C. Hendrick (Eds.), *Sex and gender* (Review of *Personality and Social Psychology,* Vol. 7, pp. 124–148).

Major, B., & Deaux, K. (1982). Individual differences in justice behavior. In J. Greenberg & R. L. Cohen (Eds.), *Equity and justice in social behavior* (pp. 43–76). New York: Academic Press.

Marin, G. (1981). Perceiving justice across cultures: Equity vs. equality in Columbia and in the United States. *International Journal of Psychology, 16,* 153–159.

Markus, H. (1977). Self-schemata and processing information about the self. *Journal of Personality and Social Psychology, 35,* 63–78.

Martin, J. (1981). Relative deprivation: A theory of distributive injustice in an era of shrinking resources. In L. L. Cummings & B. M. Staw (Eds.), *Research in organizational behavior* (Vol. 3, pp. 53–107). Greenwich, CT: JAI Press.

Martin, J. (1986). When expectations and justice do not collide: Blue-collar visions of a just world. In H. W. Bierhoff, R. L. Cohen, and J. Greenberg (Eds.), *Justice in social relations* (pp. 317–335). New York: Plenum.

Martin, J., & Siehl, C. (1983). Organizational culture and counter culture: An uneasy symbiosis. *Organizational Dynamics, 12,* 52–64.

Meindl, J. R. (1989). Managing to be fair: An exploration of values, motives, and leadership. *Administrative Science Quarterly, 34,* 252–276.

Mills, J., & Clark, M. S. (1982). Exchange and communal relationships. In L. Wheeler (Ed.), *Review of personality and social psychology* (Vol. 3, pp. 121–144). Beverley Hills, CA: Sage.

Mitchell, T. R., & Scott, W. G. (1990). America's problems and needed reforms: Confronting the ethic of personal advantage. *Academy of Management Executive, 4,* 23–35.

Mullen, B., & Baumeister, R. F. (1987). Social loafing, social facilitation, and social impairment. In C. Hendrick (Ed.), *Group processes and intergroup relations* (Review of personality and social psychology, Vol. 9, pp. 189–206). Newbury Park, CA: Sage.

Murphy-Berman, V., Berman, J. J., Singh, P., Pachauri, A., & Kumar, P. (1984). Factors affecting allocation to needy and meritorious recipients: A cross-cultural comparison. *Journal of Personality and Social Psychology, 46,* 1267–1272.

Nader, L. (1975). Forums for justice: A cross-cultural perspective. *Journal of Social Issues, 31,* 151–170.

Nauta, R. (1983). Distributive behavior in a feminine culture. In J. B. Deregowski, S. Dziurawiec, & R. C. Annis (Eds.), *Expiscations in cross-cultural psychology: Selected papers from the sixth international conference of the International Association for Cross-Cultural Psychology* (pp. 371–380). Lisse, The Netherlands: Swets and Zeitlinger.

Oakes, P. (1987). The salience of social categories. In J. C. Turner and Associates, *Rediscovering the social group: A self-categorization theory* (pp. 117–141). Oxford, England: Basil Blackwell.

Ouchi, W. G. (1981). *Theory Z: How American business can meet the Japanese challenge.* Reading, MA: Addison-Wesley.

Opotow, S. (1988). *Outside the realm of fairness: Aspects of moral exclusion.* Paper presented at the Annual Meeting of the American Psychological Association, Atlanta.

Pettigrew, T. F., & Martin, J. (1987). Shaping the organizational context for black American inclusion. *Journal of Social Issues, 43,* 41–78.

Pfeffer, J., & Langton, N. (1988). Wage inequality and the organization of work: The case of academic departments. *Administrative Science Quarterly, 33,* 588–606.

Platow, M. J., McClintock, C. G., & Liebrand, W.B.G. (1990). Predicting intergroup fairness and intergroup bias in the minimal group paradigm. *European Journal of Social Psychology, 20,* 221–239.

Rokeach, M. (1970). *The nature of human values.* New York: Free Press.

Rosenblatt, A., Greenberg, J., Solomon, S., Pyszczynski, T., & Lyon, D. (1989). Evidence for terror management theory: I. The effects of mortality salience on reactions to those who violate or uphold cultural values. *Journal of Personality and Social Psychology, 57,* 681–690.

Runciman, W. (1966). *Relative deprivation and social justice.* London: Routledge and Kegan Paul.

Runciman, W. (1968). Problems of research on relative deprivation. In H. H. Hyman & E. Singer (Eds.), *Readings in reference group theory and research* (pp. 69–76). New York: The Free Press.

Sachdev, I., & Bourhis, R. Y. (1991). Power and status differentials in minority and majority group relations. *European Journal of Social Psychology, 21,* 1–24.

Sampson, E. E. (1986). Justice ideology and social legitimation. In H. W. Bierhoff, R. L. Cohen, & J. Greenberg (Eds.), *Justice in social relations* (pp. 87–102). New York: Plenum.

Scase, R. (1972). Relative deprivation: A comparison of English and Swedish manual workers. In D. Wedderburn (Ed.), *Poverty, inequality, and class structure.* Cambridge, England: Cambridge University Press.

Schein, E. (1985). *Organizational culture and leadership.* San Francisco, CA: Jossey-Bass.

Scott, W. (1965). *Values and organizations: A study of fraternities and sororities.* Chicago: Rand-McNally.

Siegal, M., & Schwalb, D. (1985). Economic justice in adolescence: An Australian-Japanese comparison. *Journal of Economic Psychology, 6,* 313–326.

Sinclair, R. C., & Mark, M. M. (1991). Mood and endorsement of egalitarian macrojustice versus equity-based microjustice principles. *Personality and Social Psychology Bulletin, 17,* 369–375.

Spence, J. T. (1985). Achievement American style: The rewards and costs of individualism. *American Psychologist, 40,* 1285–1295.

Stake, J. E. (1983). Factors in reward distribution: Allocator motive, gender, and Protestant ethic endorsement. *Journal of Personality and Social Psychology, 44*, 410–418.

Stern, E., & Keller, S. (1953). Spontaneous group references in France. *Public Opinion Quarterly, 17*, 208–217.

Strube, M. J. (1981). Meta-analysis and cross-cultural comparison: Sex differences in child competitiveness. *Journal of Cross-Cultural Psychology, 12*, 3–20.

Sullivan, J., Peterson, R. B., Kameda, N., & Shimada, J. (1981). The relationship between conflict resolution approaches and trust—A cross-cultural study. *Academy of Management Journal, 24*, 803–815.

Tajfel, H. (1981). *Human groups and social categories: Studies in social psychology.* Cambridge, Eng.: Cambridge University Press.

Tajfel, H., & Turner, J. C. (1979). An integrative theory of intergroup conflict. In W. G. Austin & S. Worchel (Eds.), *The social psychology of intergroup relations* (pp. 33–47). Monterey, CA: Brooks/Cole.

Taylor, D. M., & McKirnan, D. J. (1984). A five-stage model of intergroup relations. *British Journal of Social Psychology, 23*, 291–300.

Taylor, D. M., Moghaddam, F. M., Gamble, I., & Zellerer, E. (1986). Disadvantaged group responses to perceived inequality: From passive acceptance to collective action. *Journal of Social Psychology, 127*, 259–272.

Taylor, S. E., Wood, J. V., & Lichtman, R. R. (1983). It could be worse: Selective evaluation as a response to victimization. *Journal of Social Issues, 39*, 19–40.

Tornblom, K. Y., & Foa, U. G. (1983). Choice of distributive principle: Crosscultural evidence on the effects of resources. *Acta Sociologia, 26*, 161–173.

Tougas, F., Dube, L., & Veilleux, F. (1987). Privation relative et programmes d'action positive. *Revue canadienne des Sciences du Comportement, 19*, 167–176.

Tougas, F., & Veilleux, F. (1990). The response of men to affirmative action strategies for women: The study of a predictive model. *Canadian Journal of Behavioral Science, 22*, 424–432.

Triandis, H. C. (1972). *The analysis of subjective culture.* New York: Wiley.

Triandis, H. C. (1988). Collectivism v. individualism: A reconceptualisation of a basic concept in cross-cultural social psychology. In G. K. Verma & C. Bagley (Eds.), *Cross-cultural studies of personality, attitudes, and cognition* (pp. 60–95). New York: St. Martin's Press.

Triandis, H. C. (1989). The self and social behavior in differing cultural contexts. *Psychological Review, 96*, 506–520.

Triandis, H. C. (1990). Cross-cultural studies of individualism and collectivism. In J. J. Berman (Ed.), *Cross-cultural perspectives*: Nebraska Symposium on Motivation (Vol. 37, pp. 41–133). Lincoln, NE: University of Nebraska Press.

Triandis, H. C., Bontempo, R., Villareal, M. J., Asai, M., & Lucca, N. (1988). Individualism and collectivism: Cross-cultural perspectives on self-ingroup relationships. *Journal of Personality and Social Psychology, 54*, 323–338.

Triandis, H. C., Leung, K., Villareal, M. J., & Clack, F. L. (1985). Allocentric versus idiocentric tendencies: Convergent and discriminant validation. *Journal of Research in Personality, 19*, 395–415.

Turner, J. C. (1985). Social categorization and the self-concept: A social-cognitive theory of group behavior. In E. J. Lawler (Ed.), *Advances in group processes* (Vol. 2, pp. 77–122). Greenwich, CT: JAI Press.

Turner, J. C. and Associates (1987). *Rediscovering the social group: A self-categorization theory.* Oxford, England: Basil Blackwell.

Tyler, T. R., & Lind, E. A. (1990). Intrinsic versus community-based justice models: When does group membership matter? *Journal of Social Issues, 46*, 83–94.

Walker, I., & Pettigrew, T. F. (1984). Relative deprivation theory: An overview and conceptual critique. *British Journal of Social Psychology, 23*, 301–310.

Wallbott, H. G., & Scherer, K. R. (1986). The antecedents of emotional experiences. In K. S. Scherer, H. G. Wallbott, & A. B. Summerfield (Eds.), *Experiencing emotion: A cross-cultural study* (pp. 69–83). Cambridge, England: Cambridge University Press.

Waterman, A. S. (1981). Individualism and interdependence. *American Psychologist, 36,* 762–773.

Wegner, D. M. (1982). Justice and the awareness of social entities. In J. Greenberg & R. Cohen, (Eds.), *Equity and justice in social behavior* (pp. 77–117). New York: Academic Press.

Weisz, J. R., Rothbaum, F. M., & Blackburn, T. C. (1984). Standing in and standing out: The psychology of control in America and Japan. *American Psychologist, 39,* 955–969.

Woo, K. (1989). The people versus Fumiko Kimura: But which people? *International Journal of the Sociology of Law, 17,* 403–428.

Zanna, M. P., Crosby, F., & Loewenstein, G. (1987). Male reference groups and discontent among female professionals. In B. A. Gutek & L. Larwood (Eds.), *Women's career development* (pp. 28–41). Newbury Park, CA: Sage.

Reconciling Theoretical Differences Among Procedural Justice Researchers by Re-Evaluating What it Means to Have One's Views "Considered": Implications for Third-Party Managers

3

Debra L. Shapiro
University of North Carolina at Chapel Hill

Managers spend much of their time attempting to resolve employees' grievances or interpersonal disputes (Mintzberg, 1973), and consequently, managers often act as third-party interventionists (Karambaya & Brett, 1989; Kolb, 1989; Sheppard, 1983, 1984; Sheppard, Blumenfeld-Jones, & Roth, 1989). Ironically, researchers of conflict management are currently disputing over what the most effective third-party intervention is. All agree that the most effective dispute resolution procedure is one that causes grievants to perceive *procedural justice* (i.e., that the procedure is fair), but there is disagreement on what causes procedural justice. Specifically, controversy has centered on the relative merits of giving disputants *process control* or *outcome control* (Brett, 1986; Folger, 1986). Process control refers to control over what information gets heard, or expressed ("voiced") to a third party, and outcome control refers to control over the decisional outcome of a dispute. An understanding of the relative importance of process and outcome control in causing judgments of procedural justice has important implications for the design of dispute resolution (cf. Ury, Brett, & Goldberg, 1989) and other decision-making systems in organizations (cf. Folger & Greenberg, 1985), and consequently, for determining how managers should intervene in disputes.

In this chapter, I review evidence that has led most procedural justice researchers to conclude that process control (voice) is the key factor that enhances judgments of procedural justice. In addition, I review evidence supporting two competing theories for why this voice effect consistently occurs. A *value-expressive perspective* proposed by Tyler and his associates (Tyler, 1987; Tyler, Rasinski, & Spodick, 1985), says that disputants want to have voice because they value "having the chance to state their case irrespective of whether their state-

51

ment influences the decisions of the authorities" (Tyler, 1987, p. 333). In contrast, an *instrumental perspective,* proposed initially by Thibaut and Walker (1975, 1978) and more recently by Brett (1983, 1986), says that disputants want to have voice because the opportunity to express themselves allows them to (potentially) influence the third party's decision. Put differently, the instrumental perspective argues that disputants want to be *more than listened to;* additionally, they want to influence the listener. Thus, the instrumental perspective says that disputants value voice because it gives them indirect control (influence) over their outcomes.

If voice is valued, primarily, because it gives disputants indirect outcome control, then giving disputants direct outcome control (i.e., giving them the authority to resolve their own dispute) may be a more effective, and expedient, way to intervene. Or, if the third party wants to have the ultimate say in how a dispute gets resolved, then he or she should do something, beyond listening to the disputants, to give them feelings of indirect outcome control.

Recently, the "consideration" that a third party apparently gives to disputants' expressed views has emerged as a critical moderator, and mediator, of the voice effect (Lind, Kanfer, & Earley, 1990; Shapiro & Brett, 1991; Tyler, 1987). Interestingly, the importance of the third party's perceived consideration has led Tyler (1987) to conclude that this strengthens the validity of the value-expressive perspective, Shapiro and Brett (1991) to conclude that this strengthens the validity of the instrumental perspective, and Lind et al. (1990) to conclude that this provides support for, both, the value-expressive and instrumental perspectives. The reasons leading to these differential conclusions are reviewed in this chapter as well.

Perhaps most importantly, this chapter focuses on what it *means* to say that one's views were "considered." The available literature does not address this. Such an understanding should help researchers interpret the findings that have recently shown this construct to moderate and mediate the relationship between voice and procedural justice. In this chapter, theoretical arguments and preliminary data are presented that suggest that a third party's perceived degree of consideration is related to his or her perceived willingness to do something with the views expressed, minimally by using this information to guide his or her own, or other authorities', initial thinking. In other words, I argue that perceived consideration is related to the perception that it is possible to influence the listener's thinking. The chapter concludes with a revised theoretical model of procedural justice that by including perceptual intervening constructs that include *potential* (rather than actual) decision influence, unites the value-expressive and instrumental perspectives. Implications of this revised model for helping managers choose the most effective way to intervene in employees' disputes are discussed.

Before reviewing the procedural justice literature and the competing perspectives held within, I begin this chapter by highlighting why managers interested in effectively resolving employees' disputes can benefit from understanding what factors enhance perceptions of procedural justice.

PROCEDURAL JUSTICE: ITS IMPORTANCE
FOR DISPUTE MANAGEMENT

Before the seminal research of Thibaut and Walker (1975), researchers generally believed that perceptions of fair outcomes (distributive justice, or "equity") were key in reducing organizational conflict (Adams, 1963, 1965). However, resource constraints do not allow managers to always allocate all the entitlements employees deserve, and disputes among employees (especially regarding scarce resources) cannot always be solved with integrative ("win–win") solutions. Perceptions of distributive justice generally result when the basis of allocation decisions seems fair. Put differently, perceptions of distributive justice and procedural justice are typically positively correlated (see Folger & Greenberg, 1985; Lind & Tyler, 1988; Tyler 1990, for reviews). Thus, enhanced understanding regarding what factors influence perceptions of procedural justice can provide managers additional ways—beyond giving or promising their employees more resources—to reduce the propensity of employees to dispute with managers, or each other.

Factors Enhancing Procedural Justice

Researchers have examined the extent to which three factors influence judgments of procedural justice: process control, outcome control or actual influence, and more recently, the perceived sensitivity and fairness of a third party's interpersonal manner (Bies, Shapiro, & Cummings, 1988; Greenberg, 1990a; Greenberg, in press; Lind & Tyler, 1988). Because the controversy in the procedural justice literature has regarded the relative importance of process- versus outcome-control, this chapter focuses on studies pertaining to the importance of these factors.

The Relative Importance of Process- Versus Outcome-Control

Unfortunately, despite the controversy, the *empirical* literature of procedural justice tells us little about the relative importance of process- versus outcome-control. For, the bulk of laboratory and correlational (field) studies examining factors that influence perceptions of procedural justice have occurred in contexts where authorities (e.g., teachers, policemen, judges, experimenters)—instead of the disputing parties—have made decisions (see Lind & Tyler, 1988, for an extensive review). Relatively few studies have varied disputants' degree of outcome control. This may have contributed to Thibaut and Walker's (1975) seminal, and often supported, conclusion that it is variations in process control, not outcome control, that shape procedural evaluations.

Researchers who did experimentally vary outcome control typically did so by giving, or not giving, subjects the opportunity to reject a settlement offered by a third party (Houlden, LaTour, Walker, & Thibaut, 1978; Lind, Lissak, & Conlon, 1983). None of these studies examined participants' reaction to a procedure that would allow disputants to *develop* possible solutions, with the help of a third party, and to then choose which, if any, of these solutions was preferable. Such a procedure is characteristic of mediation, as it is practiced in the field (Kolb, 1983, 1989; Shapiro, Drieghe, & Brett, 1985). Instead, "mediation" was operationalized in the laboratory by giving subjects the opportunity to reject a third party's suggested settlement. In a laboratory study, Brett and Shapiro (1985) operationalized mediation two ways: first, as procedural justice researchers had operationalized it in the laboratory, and second, as they had observed mediation to be practiced in the field. Relative to subjects who were given the opportunity to, merely, reject the third party's suggested settlement (the typical laboratory operationalization of mediation), perceptions of procedural justice were significantly greater among subjects who had been given the opportunity to participate in developing the solutions that they chose among to resolve their dispute (the field operationalization of mediation). Moreover, the latter procedure was preferred over another procedure in which disputants had been given process control, but no outcome control. Thus, Brett and Shapiro concluded that procedures are perceived to be most fair when disputants have outcome control, *and* the opportunity to participate in developing the options that will be considered for the dispute's outcome.

Increasingly more researchers have found that giving grievants the opportunity to voice their discontent is not, in and of itself, sufficient to influence perceptions of procedural justice. Tyler (1987) found that this voice effect occurs only when those voicing their discontent perceive that the listener (e.g., a policeman or court judge) "considered" their point of view. Similarly, Shapiro and Brett (1991) found that providing disputants (coalminers) the opportunity to voice their grievances, via mediation or arbitration, significantly enhanced perceptions of procedural justice only when the disputants perceived that the mediator or arbitrator had "considered" what they had said. Lind et al. (in press) found that the opportunity to express opinions (about a task-related goal) resulted in greater levels of procedural justice when participants in their study were told that their expressed opinions would, rather than would not, be "taken into account" by the experimenter who had the authority to set the goal. Similar to the laboratory findings of Brett and Shapiro (1985), these latest findings seem to suggest that people want procedures that allow them to feel that they participated in developing (but not necessarily making) a decision that will affect them. Do these most recent findings support the instrumental or value-expressive perspectives, or both? These competing perspectives, as well as contrary opinions regarding the extent to which recent findings support them, are discussed next.

Instrumental Versus Value-Expressive Explanations for the Voice Effect

Proponents of the instrumental perspective say that people value the opportunity to voice their opinion because it provides them the opportunity to influence others' decisions (Brett, 1986; Leventhal, 1980; Thibaut & Walker, 1975). Under circumstances where voice does *not* provide this opportunity (e.g., because an authority's decision has already been made, and it is said to be final), proponents of the instrumental perspective would expect opportunities to express opinions to be received with disinterest. This would explain why, when the experimenter in Lind et al.'s (in press) study encouraged subjects to express opinions about a task-related goal, subjects voiced less information to the experimenter when told their opinions could not, rather than could, influence the goal; or conversely, why subjects who were told their views *would* be "taken into account" voiced more information.

Under circumstances where one perceives that expressed views cannot possibly influence another's decision, instrumental theorists would expect perceptions of procedural justice to, similarly, be unaffected by opportunities for voice. This is precisely the finding that Tyler (1987) and Shapiro and Brett (1991) observed: Voice did *not* significantly influence perceptions of procedural justice when those expressing themselves perceived that their views were not taken into consideration; but a positive impact of voice on procedural justice was observed when expressed views were apparently considered. If the perception of one's views receiving no consideration is synonymous with the perception that one's views were not taken into account, then one who perceives that a third party did not consider his or her expressed views probably perceives that the third party's decision was already made, and thus, that there was never any possibility of influencing his or her decision (cf. Lind et al., 1990). The importance of perceived consideration in the voice–procedural justice relationship would, then, be due to the importance of the perceived *possibility* of influence. For this reason, Shapiro and Brett concluded that the moderating and mediating impact of the third party's perceived consideration on the voice–procedural justice relationship supports the instrumental perspective.

Tyler (1987) concluded that his findings supported a value-expressive perspective because he observed a positive relationship between voice and procedural justice when controlling for civilians' *actual* influence on authorities' (policemens', judges') decisions. Others have similarly concluded that there are value-expressive aspects of voice because a positive relationship between voice and judgments of procedural justice existed, when controlling for judgments regarding one's *actual* influence on authorities' decisions (Tyler et al., 1985; see reviews by Lind & Earley, in press, and Lind & Tyler, 1988). Note this is not equivalent to finding that voice enhanced procedural justice under circumstances where people believed there was no possibility of influencing authorities' decisions. The latter relationship has yet to be found; it is necessary to support a noninstrumental, value-expressive perspective.

Lind et al. (1990) recently attempted to examine voice effects when people were told that their expressed opinions (about a task-related goal) would, versus would not, be "taken into account" by the experimenter who had the authority to set the goal. Despite this instruction, subjects in both of these groups perceived they had greater control over the assigned goal relative to subjects in a No Voice Condition, who were not given an opportunity to express opinions about the goal. Thus, the opportunity to express one's opinions apparently increased one's feeling of decision influence. Tyler (1987) similarly found that when citizens recalled interactions they had had with the police, courts, or both, those who felt that they had experienced higher levels of process control (i.e., greater opportunity to present their case) were also more likely to report feeling higher levels of decision control. Put differently, process control apparently enhanced feelings of "indirect outcome control," a consequence predicted by the instrumental perspective (Brett, 1986).

To repeat, support for the value-expressive perspective would need to show that voice enhances procedural justice under circumstances where people do *not* perceive that voice enhances their decision control. A test is still needed regarding the extent to which voice is valued under circumstances where those permitted to express opinions believe that nothing they say can possibly influence the listener's thinking.

The empirical data that are available has led to inconsistent conclusions. Contrary to the conclusions of, either, Shapiro and Brett (1991) or Tyler (1987), Lind et al. (1990) interpreted their findings to be supportive of, both, the instrumental and noninstrumental perspectives. Why? Recall that Lind et al. found that subjects in the Pre-Decision Voice Condition, who were told that their opinions could influence the experimenter's goal-related decision, perceived significantly more procedural justice than did subjects in the Post-Decision Voice Condition, who were told that nothing they said could change the decision. Although this contrast would suggest that the voice effect was due to its perceived instrumentality, Lind et al. also found that perceptions of procedural justice were greater among subjects who had post-decision voice rather than no voice opportunity at all.

Intuitively, the value-expressive aspects of voice should be expected to account for why people who were permitted to express post-decision opinions perceived greater levels of procedural justice than people who were permitted to express no opinion at all; however, recall that Lind et al. found the provision of voice opportunities to enhance subjects' feeling of outcome control (i.e., influence over the goal-related decision). Objectively, subjects in the Post-Decision and No Voice Conditions should have perceived no outcome control, and only perceptions of process control should have varied across these groups. Subjectively, however, subjects in the former group perceived greater outcome control, as well as greater process control, than did subjects in the latter group. Thus, Lind et al. stated: "If the enhanced feelings of control in the post-decision voice condition are the result of an illusion of control, . . . one could argue that the fairness findings could be accounted for entirely within an instrumental theory of procedural justice judgments, providing that they were based on subjective, rather than objective, control" (p. 14).

Lind et al. conducted mediation analyses (Baron & Kenny, 1986, p. 1177) to determine whether perceptions of outcome control mediated all of the voice effect. Before removing the variance accounted for by perceived control, 19% of the variance in procedural justice was attributable to the voice effect. After removing the variance accounted for by perceived control, only 3% of the variance in procedural justice was accounted for by the contrast between the Voice versus No Voice Conditions. Thus, nearly all of the voice effect was attributable to subjects' perceptions of control—even under circumstances where subjects, objectively, lacked outcome control. This led Shapiro and Brett (1991) to conclude that this finding supports an instrumental explanation for the voice effect. In contrast, Lind et al. concluded that their findings support, both, noninstrumental as well as instrumental explanations since subjects' perceived control accounted for "some, but not all, of the voice effect on procedural fairness ratings" (p. 15).

While Lind et al.'s conclusion is controversial, their findings have important implications. First, their findings suggest that predictions regarding the relationship between decision influence and procedural justice should be based on the degree of decision influence people perceive themselves to have in any given procedure—despite the objective characteristics, or instructions, of the procedure. Second, their findings suggest that there are, indeed, *two types of instrumentality: actual and potential.* Apparently, while Lind et al.'s (1990) subjects were told, in the Post-Decision Voice Condition, that they lacked actual decision influence (because the experimenter had already decided on the task-related goal), they nevertheless perceived that they had potential decision influence, because they believed their expressed opinions *might* influence the, apparently reversible, decision.

Different responses will be elicited by questions regarding actual (objective) rather than potential decision influence. Consequently, researchers interested in determining the extent to which voice is valued for value-expressive versus instrumental reasons should ask—not "How much did you influence the decision?"—but: "How strongly do you believe having the opportunity to express your views enhanced your chance of influencing the decision?", "How interested would you have been in voicing your opinion if you knew, in advance, that nothing you said could influence the decision?". If voice opportunities enhance perceptions of procedural justice, after controlling for people's perceptions of actual and potential instrumentality, then clearly there are significant value-expressive aspects of voice. Such a test has yet to be made. Or, has it?

GETTING ONE'S VIEWS "CONSIDERED":
A CLOSER LOOK

"How interested would you have been in voicing your opinion if you knew, in advance, that nothing you said could influence the decision?"; "How interested would you have been in voicing your opinion if you knew, in advance, that nothing you said would be taken into consideration?". Are these two questions significantly different? Note that by asking questions regarding possible influence, or instrumentality, we have naturally returned to a question regarding "consideration." Are perceptions regarding the potential instrumentality of expressed views related to the degree to which views are taken into consideration?

Lind et al.'s (1990) operationalization of what they called the instrumental versus noninstrumental voice conditions would suggest that they are. Recall that Lind et al. operationalized the Pre- versus Post-Decision Voice Conditions by varying the extent to which subjects' opinions could influence the experimenter's decision making. This was achieved by telling subjects in the Pre-Decision Voice Condition that the experimenter would take their opinions "into account," and telling subjects in the Post-Decision Voice Condition instead that their opinions would not be. Although these conditions were identified as instrumental versus noninstrumental voice conditions, respectively, they seem to represent, equivalently, Consideration versus Nonconsideration Voice Conditions, respectively.

Thus, Lind et al.'s operationalization of instrumentality was achieved by varying instructions regarding the listener's willingness to take expressed opinions into consideration. Moreover, Lind et al.'s finding that voice produced stronger procedural justice ratings in the Pre-Decision rather than the Post-Decision Voice Condition suggests that voice was valued more for its instrumental aspects than its value-expressive aspects; or put differently, valued more when the speaker believed that the listener would take what was said into consideration. This is precisely what Tyler (1987) and Shapiro and Brett (1991) found: The voice effect occurred in the presence—and not the absence—of the third party's perceived consideration. Thus, the recent findings regarding the importance of expressed views being apparently "considered" seem to support the instrumental perspective of process control.

This conclusion has been negated by Tyler (1987) because voice has been found to enhance perceptions of procedural justice even under circumstances where it failed to influence the authorities to decide in one's favor. But does one regret "voicing" opinions regarding a preferred political candidate, or voting, when the preferred candidate fails to get elected? Does one regret sending a resume to a potential employer when this results in a job rejection? Does an academic regret sending a manuscript to a potential journal outlet after the manuscript is rejected? Chances are that, in all of these cases, those who attempted to get the outcomes they sought would feel sorry they did not achieve them, but not regretful that they had tried.

Indeed, sometimes knowing that the outcomes one receives (good or bad) are a result of one's *own* efforts is more important than achieving a success. For example, a friend of mine recently expressed an interest in teaching part time in a university setting. Knowing that my own University is seeking part-time instructors to teach business communication (her expertise), I said I would be pleased to recommend her, and asked for a resume. She declined, saying that, if offered or not offered the teaching position, she wanted to be able to credit herself for the outcome. Put differently, my friend wanted the privilege of communicating her own laurels rather than see them expressed via someone else (me). If this anecdote stopped here, one could conclude that this illustrates support for the value-expressive perspective since it suggests that people value expressing their own views.

However, when one considers why my friend chose to express herself in the first place, one cannot escape the fact that it was her hope to gain a favorable decision. In addition, she wanted to feel that the outcome—good or bad—would be due to her influence. Thus, one could argue that the motive behind her expression was instrumental: to get a teaching position, and to feel that she influenced this outcome. It is important to note that my friend hoped for this outcome before mailing her resume and letter; she remains hopeful while awaiting the hiring decision. In the event that her request to teach results in a job rejection, the instrumental wish (hope) currently felt will not, then, become nonexistent. Most of the research testing for value-expressive aspects of voice have asked people, *after* receiving a (favorable or unfavorable) decision from an authority, the extent to which they valued having the chance to express their views (Tyler, 1987; Tyler et al., 1985). Research is needed to test why people have chosen to express themselves (e.g., go to court, send a resume) in the first place, ideally before they have learned of the results of their efforts. I predict that most will say that their choice to voice their opinion (e.g., in court or a resume) was based on their hope of possibly influencing the listener's/receiver's decision.

If rejected, this job candidate will probably want an explanation for the rejection decision. And if given an adequate explanation, my friend will probably see the decision, and the reasons or criteria guiding it, as fair (Shapiro, in press; Shapiro, Buttner, & Barry, in press). However, if given an explanation that indicates her materials were not carefully read (e.g., if told that full-time teaching positions, which she is not seeking, are unavailable), it seems likely that this job candidate will feel that inadequate consideration, or attention, was given to her materials; and hence, regretful that she took the time to send them.

This example suggests that the perceived consideration one gives to others' expressed views is likely to be enhanced when the listener offers an adequate explanation. It has also been suggested that if the criteria guiding the decision (which is presumably the substance of the explanation) is seemingly fair, then perceptions of procedural and distributive justice should result. Indeed, explanations for unfavorable decisions, such as job rejections (Shapiro et al., in press), resource-refusals (Bies et al., 1988), layoffs (Brockner, DeWitt, Grover, & Reed, 1990), and paycuts (Greenberg, 1990a), have been found to enhance perceptions of justice. This may be due to the possibility that providing explanations causes recipients to feel that their views, concerns, or feelings have been taken into consideration.

What, more generally, may cause people to perceive that a listener has taken their expressed views into consideration? Presumably, if a third party (e.g., policeman, court judge, mediator, or arbitrator) takes what has been voiced into consideration, then the third party's response should be, in some way, responsive to the views expressed. Note that I have suggested that the third party's response should be *in some way* "responsive".

This does *not* mean that the third party's response must support, either entirely or partially, the views expressed. For example, third parties can help disputing parties find *new* ways to satisfy both sides' interests, solutions that neither party alone may have thought to express. Or, it is possible that third parties will make decisions that are "representative" of what most others, but not every individual, in the organization have voiced as concerns or areas of grievance (Leventhal, 1980). Or, it is possible that, after listening to one's expressed concerns (e.g., regarding implications of an organizational change), the third party may correct misperceptions that may eliminate concerns, and thus make a decision that alters nothing objectively (e.g., if a new policy remains unchanged), but alters the grievant's acceptance of the change. Moreover, if the act of correcting another's misunderstanding enhances the third party's perceived expertise, or the perceived accuracy of the reasons/data guiding the decision, then the unchanged decision may be perceived to be more fair as well (Leventhal, 1980).

Judges, and people in general, typically offer explanations for actions or decisions, especially when they anticipate that the actions will be disliked (Bies, 1987). Such explanations generally serve a conflict-mitigating function (Greenberg, 1990b), and in the case of a court judge may be required by law (Bies, 1987). Thus, even when a third party does not support the views some have expressed, he or she is likely to show responsiveness to these views merely by offering an explanation. The proclivity of judges to do this could account for why Tyler (1987; Tyler et al., 1985) found that people who voiced grievances in court, and lost, nevertheless believed the procedure was fair.

Because voice has long been held as a critical factor influencing procedural justice, and because the voice effect was mediated by the third party's perceived consideration in both the Tyler (1987) and Shapiro and Brett (1991) studies, it is important that attention be given to what, in fact, this construct means to people who are asked to judge this interpersonal characteristic. What do people mean when they say another showed "consideration" or seemed to have "considered" their views? Although I have suggested that this means a listener has been, in some way, responsive, next I present results of a study designed to answer this question.

Having One's Views "Considered": What Does This Mean?

Because one can take others' expressed views "into consideration" only before—and not after—a decision has been made (cf. Lind et al., in press), and because the desire to voice opinions is typically stronger when an impending decision will have significant rather than insignificant effects (Vroom & Yetton, 1973), I examined people's (55 undergraduate business students) propensity to voice their opinion about an impending decision that would significantly affect them, and asked what it meant to have the listener take their views "into consideration." Via scenarios, I referred to a decision that the respondents knew had actually been rumored to be a possibility: the elimination of the undergraduate business program. Although university authorities had publicly denied even thinking about this option, rumors that this decision may be made persisted. This was probably due, not only to the incessant nature of rumors (Rosnow, 1980) but, to the fact that within the last 18 months, the university's school of business had been changed to the "Graduate School of Business", and the site chosen for the business school's new location was closer to the professional graduate schools than it was to the undergraduate campus. When I administered the scenarios to the undergraduate business students participating in this study, it was still being rumored that the final decision regarding the permanence of the undergraduate business program had not yet been made. After answering questions regarding whether and why the opportunity to voice one's opinion (to a Faculty Advisor) would be valued, all were asked two open-ended questions: (1) "What does it mean to say that someone has 'considered' your views?", and (2) "What would your Advisor have to SAY or DO to make you believe he or she was 'considering' your views?"

In the interest of examining whether perceived consideration is related more to perceptions of potential influence, or instrumentality, versus noninstrumentality, the open-ended responses were sorted, by two students unfamiliar with the instrumental or value-expressive perspectives, into one of two categories. The first category was characteristic of responses that said having one's views considered meant "being listened to" or "understood" or anything that did not specify that an action be taken beyond listening. Thus, the first category represented non-instrumental definitions of the consideration construct. The second category was characteristic of responses that said having one's views considered meant that the listener would take action to potentially help support the expressed

TABLE 3.1
Students' Responses to "What Does it Mean to Say One's Views are 'Considered'?"

Noninstrumental Definitions	Instrumental Definitions
32	21

Examples:

Someone has thought about what you said.	Someone accepts your point of view as a realistic option or course of action.
He or she listens to your views on the matter and forms an opinion, either for or against what you have said.	It means that the person has listened as objectively as possible, discarding their own stance/opinion, and weighed the thoughtfulness and applicability of the views to the situation. Also, the person will have to decide on a course of action given the new views presented.
It means they have thought about the situation and tried to place themselves in your shoes.	
He or she has compared your views with the problem and the pros versus the cons.	If someone says he or she is "considering" what you have said, and you haven't witnessed any action on his part after saying this, then it would mean very little. I would infer that he is just throwing my situation into the back of his mind and not really considering acting on it.
The person has listened attentively and thought about what I have said.	
The person has listened to your point of v iew and analyzed/examined it fairly.	
They truly listen to your views and consider the views themselves. They make a real effort to understand your viewpoint.	He or she may bring up opposite views but after weighing them against your views, he or she believes in your views and agrees with you.
When someone sets aside their views for a moment to listen to your views. They must try to imagine themselves as the other side.	They listen and understand your views, try to help your situation.
The person listens to my views openmindedly and carefully.	They have *openmindedly* listened to your points, tried to put themselves in your place, have given real thought to your position, are willing to reconsider their own opinion in light of what was said.
They have examined my views from *my* - perspective and have given unbiased and open-mined thought to them.	
It means that although the person may disagree with your views, he still listens to what you have said and is willing to discuss it.	The person has listened to your views, weighed them against his or her own, and come up with a final decision using my opinion as well as his or her own.
Someone actually listens and thinks about what you are saying and how you feel.	I think "considered" means they have listened to my ideas, thought about hem as having meaning, and then taken action or planned to go further with them.
They have listened to everything I have said and understand my situation.	
They have thought about the views thoroughly--weighed the pros and cons.	They have become open-minded to the fact that their solution or idea may not be the best way to handle an issue.
It means they have thought about how they would react and feel under the same circumstances.	This means that someone is weighing my opinion into his or her decision.

views. Thus, the second category represented instrumental definitions of the consideration construct.

Table 3.1 shows the number of responses that defined having one's views considered in a noninstrumental versus instrumental way. Table 3.2 shows the number of responses that described noninstrumental versus instrumental ways to show that one's views were being "considered." Several examples of responses in each of the categories are presented in the tables as well.

Interestingly, 22 (nearly half) of the respondents answered the two questions inconsistently, by defining "considered" in a noninstrumental way (e.g., listening openmindedly), but then describing evidence that one's views are being considered in an instrumental way (e.g., the listener must say that he or she will weigh expressed views into his or her decision making). Although the content analysis is unable to determine the relative importance of noninstrumental versus instrumental aspects of consideration, in many cases it appears that instrumental definitions and descriptions are *extensions* of apparently noninstrumental perspectives. For example, a response in Table 3.1 categorized as noninstrumental defines "considered" this way: "They truly listen to your views and consider the views themselves. They make a real effort to understand your viewpoint."

A response in Table 3.1 categorized as instrumental shares part of the latter definition—"They listen and understand your views . . ."—but then concludes this thought with "and try to help your situation." Similarly, another response in Table 3.1 categorized as noninstrumental says that "considered" means: "The person listens to my views openmindedly and carefully"; whereas another response, which repeats this, concludes with an instrumental focus, and hence is categorized as instrumental: "They have openmindedly listened to your points, tried to put themselves in your place, have given real thought to your position, are willing to reconsider their own opinion in light of what was said."

The same patterns are notable in Table 3.2. For example, the first response characterized as a noninstrumental action states: "I would be more likely to believe my advisor's "consideration" if he or she asked questions and took notes." Two responses characterized as instrumental in Table 3.2 share the idea that notetaking is important for demonstrating that one's views are being considered, but for instrumental reasons. One of these responses stated: "If he or she were taking notes on my points—as if he or she wanted to repeat them to someone else . . .", and the other stated, more specifically: "He or she would take notes on the points I was making and say that he or she would discuss those points with a Board member [someone at the university with power to influence the decision]."

As a preliminary test of the generalizability of these findings, I distributed a survey to 25 managers that asked them to imagine the following: They felt strongly opposed to an organizational change that the top management of their company was considering, and they had the opportunity to voice their opinion regarding this potential change. Among the questions they responded to on this

TABLE 3.2
Students' Responses to "What Must Your Advisor Say or Do to Show Your Views Were Being 'Considered'?"

Noninstrumental Actions	Instrumental Actions
22	29

Examples

I would be more likely to believe my advisor's "consideration" if she or she asked questions and took notes.	My advisor would not only say that she (or he) understood my views, but she would possibly write a letter or even speak to a member of the University's Board of Directors or the entire Board (probably after making sure that other students shared my own opinion).
He or she would have to simply show interest in what I was saying. Especially by putting in her comments on my opinion, whether she agreed or disagreed with me.	He would have to say he is concerned for my welfare and others like me and tht he agrees with my opinion and will express that opinion to the Board of Directors.
She (or he) would have to nod her head. Say things like "Yes, I understand your situation and the inconvenience." Give eye contact. Look concerned. Listen to what I said.	He or she would have to say that they understand my situation and that they believe it is unfair. Then they should say that they will try to do everything possible to keep the University from eliminating my major.
She (or he) would have to show she was listening by asking questions to better understand where I was coming from.	He would call up a member of the Board while I was sitting in the office, and set up an appointment to discuss this issue about my major. He (or she) would take notes on the points I was making and say that he would discuss those points with a Board member.
She or he would have to listen, act interested, ask me questions about how I feel, talk with me.	
She (or he) could be saying that some of my reasons were valid and/or she agrees with some of them.	He would have to agree to present my views to the Board for consideration and he would expand on my views.
She or he would have to listen well, but also jot down some ideas brought up in the conversation.	She would have to appear in front of the Board and tell the members of my views and support my views.
She (or he) would look interested, ask questions, possibly take notes on important points of my argument. Nods of agreement and patient listening without objections would show she was interested also.	He would have to tell me the process of how the elimination of my major could be stopped. He then would need to act on that process.
She (or he) would explain the reasons she was considering my views and also explain why she may not agree with all of them.	My advisor would look me in the eye, promise to inform the higher echelons of command in the University, and set up a future meeting to give their reaction.
She (or he) would have to listen openly to my points of view and be willing to discuss the pros and cons of eliminating the major.	If she (or he) said that she was considering my views to perhaps use at a trustees meeting, then I would believe her.
She would have to listen to my side and keep an open mind and really act like she cared.	If he were taking notes on my points—as if he wanted to repeat them to someone else; he could tell me how to appeal to the Board directly; he could help organize the other students in the major for protest; even small things like eye contact and giving me his full attention can make the difference between feeling important and feeling ignored.
My advisor would have to be attentive while I am talking; look interested about what I have to say. He (or she) would also have to discuss with me the statements I make and maybe even challenge my views so I would know she is listening to me.	

TABLE 3.3

Managers' Responses to "What Must an Authority Say or Do to Show Your Views Would, in Fact, be 'Considered'?"

Noninstrumental Actions	Instrumental Actions
10	15

Examples:

They would have to listen to my concerns and respond by allowing that they have understood them—perhaps be restating them in their own words. They would need to demonstrate patience, interest, and openness in their manner.

This person would have to ask me *why* I feel as I do, and really make an effort to understand my viewpoints.

She or he would have to echo my views back, so I know they heard them correctly, discuss each aspect of my views, and comment whether or not this part of the view would be considered, give me a follow-up date for a decision/response.

He would say he would consider; listen to my arguments; document important points and issues.

This authority must demonstrate an 'open' mind to the issue, show an interest in hearing me out and convey 'respect' for my opinion even if she or he is not in full agreement. Asking probing questions, seeking clarification or justification or even putting counteraguments shall help. Of course, this authority's track record and my perceptions shall also be a factor.

The authority would listen. If the person corroborated the intended change, I would then explain concisely my reasons for objection. I would be more encouraged if the person asked questions. I would ask for reasons for change. The quality and completeness of the answers would indicate sincerity and consideration.

This authority would need to 'actively listen'; that is, demonstrate that he or she understood my position by repeating it, or asking questions for clarification, or listing the key points, or using an example. Once he or she had time to think about my proposal, he or she would have to talk with me again and plainly state his or her reactions.

She or he would have to look me in the eyes while I am talking; not interrupt; not immediately counter with reasons; send a memo or letter later acknowledging my concerns.

She would have to take the time to meet with me to ask for my objections/opinions as they relate to the reorganization. I would expect notes to be taken and no "rebuttal" of my opinions—just clarification and a commitment to have them considered and related to senior management.

The authority would have to indicate in some way that he understood my arguments against the potential change. Then I would like him to better explain the reason for the change so I might better understand the change. Finally, I would like him or her to promise to present my arguments to top management.

He would have to be specific about what he was going to say to whom, and when; tell me by when he would get back with me; get back with me when promised and describe the encounter.

She or he would say "That's a good point" and then take action to correct the organizational change immediately (if my views are going to be considered, action is immediately taken).

He or she would have to demonstrate that they have heard and understood me. They would have to explain their positions in light of mine and exhibit willingness to reconcile them. He or she would have to say: Now that I understand your views, I will take them into consideration when I make my proposal.

They would need to listen to my thoughts and reasoning on the subject, in addition to my proposed solutions; we would map a strategy based on our discussion.

The authority would SAY: (1) I understand your point; I see your view; (2) you make some valid arguments; (3) I'll think more about your view and express this opinion to top management. The authority would DO: (1) Listen attentively and actively; (2) talk to others who represent a similar viewpoint; (3) express my opinion to top management.

The first thing he would have to say is that the decision (regarding the change) has in fact not already been made.

TABLE 3.3
(continued)

Noninstrumental Actions	Instrumental Actions
10	15

Examples:

She or he would say "I'll take your views into
consideration; please tell me more about that;
I'd like to think about your views."

The authority would make good eye contact
and listen effectively by responding to
statements I make so that I know he at least is
trying to understand my opinion. Restate it at
the end of the discussion. Give me a
reasonable amount of his time so I could
present my case.

survey was: "What would an authority have to 'say' or 'do' to make you feel that
your views would, in fact, be considered?" Similar to my previous findings, and
shown in Table 3.3, approximately half of the sample said noninstrumental
actions, and the others said instrumental actions, were necessary to demonstrate
that their views would be considered. Nearly all of the responses characterized as
instrumental action descriptions said that the listener would need to say that he or
she would repeat the expressed views to organizational authorities (senior or top
management) who had the power to prevent the organizational change. Interestingly, the last response in the instrumental category of Table 3.3 states that
the first action necessary to demonstrate that one's views will be considered is an
explicit statement by the authority/listener that his or her decision has not yet
been made. This was precisely the action that Lind et al. (1990) used to opera-
tionalize the instrumental (Pre-Decision) Voice Condition in their study; and
as I argued earlier, it appears here as an operationalization of consideration,
too.

IMPLICATIONS FOR THE THEORY
OF PROCEDURAL JUSTICE

The findings previously reported have several important implications. Perhaps
most importantly, these findings illustrate that people (business students and
managers) define having their views "considered," and describe evidence of
this, in ways that are noninstrumental and instrumental. A result of recognizing
that perceptions of consideration consist of noninstrumental and instrumental
aspects is that its importance in determining voice effects does not, necessarily,

provide support for the value-expressive perspective (Tyler, 1987). Indeed, using canonical analysis, Shapiro and Brett (1991) found the factor of perceived consideration to correlate more highly with a dimension that was strongly related to outcome control rather than process control; and for this reason concluded that its mediating impact on the relationship between voice and procedural justice supported the instrumental perspective. More research is needed to determine the relative importance of noninstrumental versus instrumental aspects of perceived consideration to ease our interpretation of this construct's moderating and mediating effects.

In many cases, people described the noninstrumental aspects of consideration (e.g., taking notes, listening openmindedly) as *means* to instrumental ends (e.g., sharing one's notes with influential others, being openminded to the possibility of changing one's initial thinking). Thus, even apparently noninstrumental aspects of consideration have instrumental implications. Consequently, whether an aspect of perceived consideration is interpreted to be noninstrumental or instrumental depends on why this aspect is important to the respondent. If, for example, openmindedness is valued because this suggests someone will listen unbiasedly, then it has noninstrumental appeal. If openmindedness (or the lack of bias) is valued because this suggests the listener is open to changing his or her initial thinking, then it has instrumental appeal.

Similarly, whether process control is valued for noninstrumental or instrumental purposes depends on why this procedural factor is important to the respondent. Research regarding the importance of process control in influencing perceptions of procedural justice has not asked respondents why they value process control, but only whether (and the extent) they do. Questions regarding why process control is valued will probably lead researchers to observe that it is valued for noninstrumental and instrumental reasons. But more importantly, similar to the findings reported earlier, the noninstrumental aspects of process control (e.g., a desire to be "heard") will probably be perceived, also, as means to instrumental ends (e.g., being heard will enhance the chance of possibly changing the listener's/decision maker's thinking).

The latter point is particularly important, for the studies comprising the procedural justice literature (cf. Lind & Tyler, 1988) have typically measured/manipulated objective levels of process control, decision control, and actual decision influence. Consequently, they are unable to speak to the importance of potential instrumentality, hence the possible positive relationship between apparent noninstrumentality and instrumentality. For example, the present author has been to court, and has valued the opportunity to appeal a traffic fine—despite my failure to "win" a favorable decision. The current literature would classify my persistent affinity for process control as evidence that I valued my voice opportunity for value-expressive reasons. However, I chose to visit court because I had hoped that presenting my case would result in a reduced, or cancelled, fine; that is, I saw potential instrumentality in doing so. Having failed,

I still valued the privilege to appeal an unfavorable decision (i.e., fine) because it gave me the chance of possibly modifying it.

It seems to me now, and it seemed to me then, that it is better to have voiced and lost than never to have voiced at all. The persistent appeal of slot machines—despite their inability to give everyone favorable outcomes—seems similarly due to the chance they offer everyone to hit the jackpot. Future research on procedural justice, and process control in particular, needs to measure the extent to which others, like me, value voice for the potential instrumentality ("jackpots") it offers.

Indirect support for this already exists. Recall that the voice effect has recently been found to occur moreso (Lind et al., 1990) or exclusively (Shapiro & Brett, 1991; Tyler, 1987) when expressed views seem to be "considered." Findings reported here, as well as Lind et al.'s (1990) operationalization of the Pre-Decision Voice Condition, suggests that a necessary condition for perceived consideration is the perception that the listener's decision has not yet been made; and therefore, the perception that the listener may possibly change his or her thinking. Many responses (by students and managers) defined having views "considered," and described evidence of this, by stating things that indicated they perceived possible decision influence. For example, the following quotes taken from Table 3.1 illustrate the perception that potential influence is possible: "[the listener] . . . accepts your point of view as a realistic option or course of action," "[is] willing to reconsider their own opinion in light of what was said," "[will] come up with a final decision using my opinion as well as his or her own," "[is] openminded to the fact that [his or her] solution or idea may not be the best way to handle an issue," "is weighing my opinion into his or her decision," "will have to decide on a course of action given the new views presented." Consequently, the occurrence of the voice effect in the presence, but not absence, of perceived consideration (Lind et al., 1990; Shapiro & Brett, 1991; Tyler, 1987) may be due to people's desire to have the chance to possibly influence the listener's (e.g., arbitrator's, mediator's, judge's) decision. Note that this suggests voice is valued for its potential instrumentality. Actual influence, or the third party's actual decision—which has been identified in the procedural justice literature as the sole measure of instrumentality (Tyler, 1987; Tyler et al., 1985)—has no relevance here.

Reconciling Theoretical Differences: A Revised Model of Procedural Justice

By giving closer examination to the construct of perceived consideration, and by highlighting the importance of potential—rather than actual—decision influence, I believe that previous controversies in the procedural justice literature can be resolved. First, perceived consideration has noninstrumental and instrumental meaning. Given the importance of perceived consideration in determining pro-

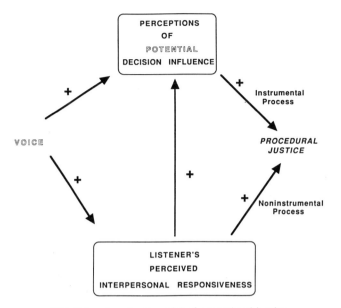

FIG. 3.1. A revised model of procedural justice.

cess control effects, these two dimensions of consideration need to be represented in a theoretical model of factors that influence perceptions of procedural
justice. The noninstrumental aspects of consideration referenced by the students
and managers in my studies were, more specifically, related to perceptions of
positive interpersonal responsiveness, such as the listener's perceived atten-
tiveness, patience, lack of bias, openmindedness, and empathy of understanding.
As argued earlier, the instrumental aspects of consideration referenced most in
my studies were related to perceptions of potential decision influence. Thus,
these two perceptions appear as critical predictors in the revised model of procedural justice shown in Fig. 3.1. They are labeled as *perceptions* because Lind
et al.'s (1990) findings demonstrate that procedural justice is influenced more by
perceived, rather than actual, characteristics.

An important implication of having perceptions as predictors of procedural
justice is that it removes the need to debate the importance of various, objective
structural characteristics (i.e., the degree of process control or outcome control
given to disputants). For this reason, structural factors have been deliberately
omitted from my model. An important implication of including noninstrumental
factors (i.e., perceptions of interpersonal sensitivity) and instrumental factors
(i.e., perceptions of potential influence) in the model is that value-expressive *and*
instrumental aspects of voice are recognized as significant determinants of procedural justice.

Recall that many students and managers who referenced noninstrumental aspects of consideration also said that such aspects had potential instrumental utility. Thus, it seems likely that the noninstrumental and instrumental aspects of consideration are not independent. This would account for why voice has been found to enhance feelings of decision control (Lind et al., 1990; Tyler, 1987). Clearly, this relationship should be strengthened when people perceive that the listener/decision maker is taking expressed opinions into consideration (cf. Lind et al., in press). For this reason, my model shows a positive relationship between the listener's perceived responsiveness and perceptions of one's own potential decision influence. An important implication of this proposed link is that it requires researchers to control for perceptions of potential (rather than actual) decision influence in future attempts to isolate value-expressive aspects of voice. Such a test should clearly demonstrate, more than past research has, the extent to which value-expressive versus instrumental reasons account for the voice effect.

Finally, there is an important implication of placing perceptions of potential instrumentality and the listener's responsiveness as intervening variables in the model. Doing so suggests that providing opportunities for voice is *not* necessary for producing perceptions of procedural justice. Next, in the discussion of implications for third party managers, I argue that as long as disputing parties perceive that they have had the opportunity to potentially influence a third party's (resolution) decision, *or* that the third party has been responsive to their concerns, perceptions of procedural justice will result.

IMPLICATIONS FOR THIRD PARTY MANAGERS

Numerous theories, from a variety of disciplines, have stated the importance of creating feelings of "participation" on the part of those who must accept or support a decision. For example, in the management literature, Vroom and Yetton (1973) theorized that when employees will be significantly affected by Management's decisions, and the decision's implementation will require employee support, greater levels of participative decision making will enhance the chance that employees will perceive the decision as fair, and support it. This same thinking also characterizes theories of enhancing employees' acceptance of change-related decisions (Kotter & Schlesinger, 1979) and decisions regarding dispute resolution (Ury et al., 1989). In the negotiation literature, integrative bargaining theorists (see reviews by Neale & Bazerman, 1991; Neale & Northcraft, 1991) have similarly argued that when agreements result from collaborative rather than dominating tactics, negotiators will perceive them to be more fair, and be more committed to them. In the psychology literature, compliance with others' requests has been said to be more likely when those asked to comply perceive that they have personal choice (or control) over doing so (Brehm, 1972; Cialdini, 1984).

Recognizing that maximal levels of participation in decision making, such as basing a decision on consensus, is not always practical, nor desirable, Vroom and Yetton (1973) proposed that a less participative style, called the *consultative* style of decision making, would still allow people to feel a sense of participation. Although the decision maker ultimately makes the decision in this approach, it is based on the opinions others express when consulted. Vroom and Yetton cautioned that for the consultative style of decision making to be effective, however, people whose opinions were consulted must believe that the decision maker would consider incorporating the expressed opinions.

It is believing in this possibility that creates the feeling of participation. Indeed, for this reason, Folger (1977) defined voice as a form of participative decision making. He stated, "Having voice in the system means having some form of participation in decision making by expressing one's own opinion . . ." (p. 109). Since having voice provides less control over another's decision than actual choice (or decision control) does, Greenberg and Folger (1983) later defined voice as an indirect form of participation, and Brett (1986) referred to voice as a form of "indirect outcome control."

Drawing from the array of theories mentioned here, and from Vroom and Yetton's notion of consultative decision making and its associated consequences, my model suggests that perceptions of procedural justice will result when people perceive that they have indirect outcome control; or, that a decision that is reached is one they had the opportunity to potentially influence. In addition to this, my model suggests that procedural justice will be perceived when the third party appears to have been responsive to others' (expressed or known) concerns. It should thus behoove managers to know what actions they can take to enhance these critical perceptions. Actions enhancing these perceptions are discussed next, each in turn.

Ways to Enhance Perceptions of Potential Decision Influence

The instrumental responses that appeared in each of the tables suggest several ways that managers can create the perception that others have potential influence over the decisions made in the workplace.

Consult Others' Opinions. One of the more obvious ways to create this perception—asking for others' opinions—does not appear in any of the tables. For all the participants in my studies responded to questions regarding what it meant to have their expressed views "considered," and therefore all assumed that their opinion had been consulted. Of course, this is not always the case. Indeed, it is rarely the case that managers intervene in employees' disputes with a consultative-like manner. Instead, managers generally intervene in employees' disputes in more authoritative ways, akin to the style of "umpires" (Kolb & Glidden, 1986), "inquisitors" (Sheppard, 1983), and "parents" (Sheppard et al., 1989).

People generally do not ask for others' opinions unless they feel a need for them. Consequently, the act of consulting another's opinion is likely to create the perception that it will be considered (Folger, 1977). Indeed, the strength of this tendency was observed in the Lind et al. (1990) study, when subjects felt enhanced levels of decision influence after voicing their opinion, even when told that their opinion could not influence the experimenter's (goal-related) decision. Thus, one action third-party managers can take to enhance disputing employees' perception that they can potentially influence the resolution decision is to, simply, consult the disputants for ideas and suggestions. The model illustrates this expectation by showing a positive relationship between voice and perceptions of potential decision influence, a prediction that supports the instrumental perspective.

Say the Decision is "Not Yet Made," or is "Correctable."   Another action likely to enhance disputing parties' feeling of potential influence is to explicitly state that a solution to the dispute has not yet been decided, or that a resolution decision, if made, is reversible or "correctable" (Leventhal, 1980). Such statements then allow the managers to say, with credibility, that the disputants' opinions regarding how to resolve the dispute will be "taken into consideration," and hence, part of the decision-making process. More specifically, managers can state that their decision will be "representative" of the views they hear; that is, it will ". . . reflect the basic concerns, values, and outlook of important subgroups [such as the disputing parties] in the population of individuals affected by the [decision]" (p. 44).

Be Interpersonally Attentive.   Other actions that managers can take to enhance the perception of potential decision influence regard how managers respond to the opinions that others express to them (which may, or may not, be solicited). As suggested by the instrumental responses in each table, when people respond to those who are voicing opinions by showing they are listening with full attention (e.g., by giving eye contact, taking notes), listening without preconceived notions (c.g., by not interrupting with objections), attempting to understand what is said (e.g., by restating what they heard, or asking for clarification), interested in helping (e.g., by saying they will share the expressed views with powerful others), and consequently, showing politeness and respect (cf. Tyler, 1987), such responses are likely to enhance the perception that one's views are being taken into consideration. And because a necessary condition for perceived consideration is that thought will be given to the views *before* making the decision, such responses are likely to enhance the perception that one has the possibility of influencing the decision.

Ways to Enhance Perceptions of Positive Interpersonal Responsiveness

Recall that I previously defined positive interpersonal responsiveness to be the noninstrumental aspects of perceived consideration, as suggested by the business students and managers in my studies. The noninstrumental aspects of consideration mentioned in my studies included all of the actions that were listed at the conclusion of the previous section.

Be Interpersonally Attentive.   Thus, for example, taking notes on what is being expressed can create the perception of potential decision influence (discussed earlier) and/or, simply, that the listener is being responsive. Elsewhere, such characteristics have been identified as the "interpersonal context of procedural justice" (Tyler & Bies, 1990), and as aspects of the noninstrumental perspective (Lind & Tyler, 1988). It is important to note that these interpersonal characteristics were identified by business students and managers as aspects that had noninstrumental *and* instrumental value. The extent to which these characteristics are intertwined with noninstrumental and instrumental aspects is illustrated, perhaps best, by the following response (shown in Table 3.2):

> If he or she were taking notes on my points—as if he or she wanted to repeat them to someone else; he or she could tell me how to appeal to the Board directly; he or she could help organize the other students in the major for protest; even small things like eye contact and giving me his or her full attention can make the difference between feeling important and feeling ignored.

Although this student began describing evidence of consideration in an instrumental way, he or she concluded this thought by making reference to apparently noninstrumental interpersonal actions (e.g., giving full attention) that would cause this student to feel personally valued (i.e., "important"). The group-value model of procedural justice (Lind & Tyler, 1988) says feelings of personal value result from having the opportunity to express one's views. This student's response suggests that these feelings result, more specifically, from expressing one's views to someone who is being positively interpersonally responsive. Surely, when a listener is unresponsive or destructively responsive (i.e., rude, for example, by rolling one's eyes with impatience or disgust), it is less likely that voicing will result in feelings of being valued. For this reason, my model shows perceptions of the listener's responsiveness, instead of feelings of personal or group value, as a critical intervening factor between voice and procedural justice.

Consult Others' Opinions and/or Listen Attentively.   It seems likely that the act of expressing one's views, particularly if the views were solicited, are likely to create the perception that someone is being interpersonally responsive. For, people do not generally ask for others' viewpoints unless they care to hear them; and even when unsolicited, social mores generally cause listeners to acknowledge those who speak to them. Thus, the model shows a positive relationship between voice and perceptions of the listener's interpersonal responsiveness.

Provide Explanations.   Finally, as I suggested earlier, another action managers can take to increase their perceived responsiveness is to take the time to explain the basis of the decision eventually reached. The importance of this is illustrated by the statement of one of the managers (shown in Table 3.3), who said: "I would ask for reasons for the change. The quality and completeness of the answers would indicate sincerity and consideration." Researchers (Bies et al., 1988; Brockner et al., 1990; Greenberg, 1990a; Shapiro et al., in press) have increasingly pointed to explanations as a means of mitigating employees' tendency to react to unfavorable decisions (e.g., resource-refusals, paycuts, layoffs) with negative affect and destructive work behaviors; yet, all have cautioned that the explanations must be judged to be "adequate" for their conflict-mitigating utility to be realized. Recent investigations have suggested that the interpersonal sensitivity of the explainer and the specificity and thoroughness of the explanation's substance are important determinants of explanations' perceived adequacy (Greenberg, 1990a, in press; Shapiro et al., in press). Such characteristics probably enhance the perception that the explainer cares about the recipients' feelings, and perhaps, wants to be responsive to the recipient's (expressed, known, or anticipated) concerns.

Choosing How to Intervene

How should managers intervene in employees' disputes? They should intervene with actions that will cause the disputants to perceive that they have the potential to influence the resolution decision, and that the third party manager is being responsive to their needs and concerns. When these two perceptions are produced (which I believe will be facilitated by the actions described earlier), then perceptions of procedural justice should result—*regardless of the objective characteristics of the intervention approach used.* More important than whether disputants have outcome control is whether disputants feel they have participated in developing the decision regarding the dispute's resolution (Brett & Shapiro, 1985), which may be achieved with maximally participative (consensus) or less participative (consultative) approaches (Vroom & Yetton, 1973). Similarly, more important than whether disputants have process control is whether disputants feel that their voice will be, or has been, considered (Lind et al., in press; Shapiro & Brett, 1991; Tyler, 1987). In summary, more important than whether disputants have process or outcome control is whether disputants feel they have a third party who will be responsive to their (expressed, known, or anticipated) needs, and the possibility of influencing (including appealing) their dispute's resolution.

The relative effectiveness of arbitration versus mediation procedures has been disputed in the procedural justice literature (Brett, 1986; Folger, 1986; Shapiro & Brett, 1991). In both procedures, disputants have process control; in only mediation do they also have decision control. If the third party (arbitrator or mediator) is perceived to be interpersonally responsive (e.g., by taking what is said into consideration), perceptions of potential decision influence should result, and both procedures should be viewed as equally fair. My model predicts this. Shapiro and Brett's (1991) findings support this. Managers should thus no longer agonize over which procedure to use when intervening in employees' disputes; instead, managers should turn their attention to which actions they can take to enhance the critical perceptions of being interpersonally responsive and offering disputants the potential to influence their dispute's resolution.

Having said this, it is important to note that mediators consult disputants' opinions regarding ways to potentially resolve their dispute; give disputing parties influence (final say) over the resolution decision, and therefore, identify this decision as not yet made; and interactively listen, by often restating what has been said and asking for clarification. Arbitrators do not do this, at least to the same degree. Findings that grievants generally prefer mediation over arbitration (Brett & Goldberg, 1983; Karambaya & Brett, 1989; Shapiro & Brett, 1991) may therefore be due to these differences. One implication is that managers ought to be trained to intervene with actions more akin to mediation than arbitration (Karambaya & Brett, 1989). Or, managers who wish to retain ultimate say over how employees' disputes are resolved should be trained to, nevertheless, say and do (the other) things that mediators do: consult disputants' opinions and interactively respond to them in a sensitive manner. Doing so enhances the chance of creating perceptions identified in my model as critical causes of procedural justice.

CONCLUSION

The revised model of procedural justice that I offer incorporates aspects that have been identified with noninstrumental (Lind & Tyler, 1988; Tyler, 1987; Tyler & Bies, 1990) and instrumental (Brett, 1986; Leventhal, 1980; Shapiro & Brett, 1991; Thibaut & Walker, 1975) theories of procedural justice. More importantly, it suggests that apparently noninstrumental aspects (e.g., speaking to one who is openminded and unbiased) can enhance perceptions of instrumentality: potential decision influence. Such a relationship can explain why there has been controversy about whether voice is valued, primarily, for noninstrumental or instrumental reasons. To say that voice is valued for both of these reasons does not reconcile the controversy (Lind & Tyler, 1988). For my findings suggest that the two categories of noninstrumental versus instrumental aspects are intertwined, and hence perhaps, not meaningfully distinguished. For this reason, my model has distinguished between perceptions of potential decision influence and the listener's perceived responsiveness. Perceived responsiveness is shown in the model to be both a noninstrumental consequence of voice and an antecedent to perceived (potential) instrumentality. Unlike previous models of procedural justice, my model excludes any reference to objective characteristics, such as process control and outcome control. By excluding these and including the notion of potential instrumentality, the model provides theoretical reconciliation.

I hope that the simplicity of my model, and its emphasis on perceptual antecedents to procedural justice, will encourage subsequent controversy that will be focused on how to deal with subjective determinants. It is my opinion that people looking for procedural justice, or any justice, do things (e.g., voice their opinion, choose to talk to someone with influential power, choose to talk to someone that will take their views into consideration), that will give them the possibility of influencing their outcomes. Having voiced this opinion, I hope procedural justice researchers and managers will take it, and my proposed model, into consideration. More specifically, I hope my expressed opinion might alter the way researchers subsequently study and measure antecedents of procedural justice, and the way managers intervene in employees' disputes. If I believed my expressed opinion had no possibility of influencing subsequent thinking or action regarding procedural justice and dispute resolution, I would not have voiced it.

REFERENCES

Adams, J. S. (1963). Toward an understanding of inequity. *Journal of Abnormal and Social Psychology, 67,* 422–436.

Adams, J. S. (1965). Inequity in social exchange. In L. Berkowitz (Ed.), *Advances in experimental social psychology* (Vol. 2, pp. 267–299). New York: Academic Press.

Baron, R. M., & Kenny, D. A. (1986). The mediator-moderator variable distinction in social psychological research: Conceptual, strategic, and statistical considerations. *Journal of Personality and Social Psychology, 51,* 1173–1182.

Bies, R. J. (1987). The predicament of injustice: The management of moral outrage. In L. L. Cummings & B. M. Staw (Eds.), *Research in organizational behavior* (Vol. 9, pp. 289–319). Greenwich, CT: JAI Press.

Bies, R. J., Shapiro, D. L., & Cummings, L. L. (1988). Causal accounts and managing organizational conflict: Is it enough to say it is not my fault? *Communication Research, 15*(4), 381–399.

Brehm, J. W. (1972). *Responses to loss of freedom: A theory of psychological reactance.* Morristown, NJ: General Learning Press.

Brett, J. M. (1983). *Procedural justice.* Paper presented at the national meeting of the Academy of Management, Dallas, TX.

Brett, J. M. (1986). Commentary on procedural justice papers. In R. Lewicki, M. Bazerman & B. Sheppard (Eds.), *Research on negotiation in organizations* (Vol. 1, pp. 81–90). Greenwich, CT: JAI Press.

Brett, J. M., & Goldberg, S. B. (1983). Grievance mediation in the coal industry: A field experiment. *Industrial and Labor Relations Review, 37,* 49–69.

Brett, J. M., & Shapiro, D. L. (1985). *Procedural justice: A test of competing theories.* Paper presented at the national meeting of the Law and Society Association, San Diego, CA.

Brockner, J., DeWitt, R., Grover, S., & Reed, T. (1990). When it is especially important to explain why: Factors affecting the relationship between managers' explanations of a layoff and survivors' reactions to the layoff. *Journal of Experimental Social Psychology, 26*(5), 389–407.

Cialdini, R. B. (1984). *Influence: How and why people agree to things.* New York: William Morrow.

Folger, R. (1986). Mediation, arbitration, and the psychology of procedural justice. In R. Lewicki, M. Bazerman, & B. Sheppard (Eds.), *Research on negotiation in organizations* (Vol. 1, pp. 57–79). Greenwich, CT: JAI Press.

Folger, R. (1977). Distributive and procedural justice: Combined impact of "voice" and improvement on experienced inequity. *Journal of Personality and Social Psychology, 35,* 108–119.

Folger, R., & Greenberg, J. (1985). Procedural justice: An interpretative analysis of personnel systems. In K. Rowland & G. Ferris (Eds.), *Research in personnel and human resources management* (Vol. 3, pp. 141–183). Greenwich, CT: JAI Press.

Greenberg, J. (1990a). Employee theft as a reaction to underpayment inequity: The hidden cost of paycuts. *Journal of Applied Psychology, 75*(5), 561–568.

Greenberg, J. (1990b). Looking fair vs. being fair: Managing impressions of organizational justice. In B. M. Staw & L. L. Cummings (Eds.), *Research in organizational behavior,* (Vol. 12, pp. 111–157). Greenwich, CT: JAI Press.

Greenberg, J. (in press). Stealing in the name of justice: Informational and interpersonal moderators of theft reactions to underpayment inequity. *Organizational Behavior and Human Decision Processes.*

Greenberg, J., & Folger, R. (1983). Procedural justice, participation, and the fair process effect in groups and organizations. In P. Paulus (Ed.), *Basic group process* (pp. 235–256). New York: Springer-Verlag.

Houlden, P., LaTour, S., Walker, L., & Thibaut, J. (1978). Preference for modes of dispute resolution as a function of process and decision control. *Journal of Experimental Social Psychology, 14,* 13–30.

Karambaya, R., & Brett, J. M. (1989). Managers handling disputes: Third-party roles and perceptions of fairness. *Academy of Management Journal, 32*(4), 687–704.

Kolb, D. M. (1983). *The mediators.* Cambridge, MA: MIT Press.

Kolb, D. M. (1989). Labor mediators, managers, and ombudsmen: Roles mediators play in different contexts. In K. Kressel & D. G. Pruitt and Associates (Eds.), *Mediation research: The process and effectiveness of third-party intervention* (pp. 91–114). San Francisco, CA: Jossey-Bass Publishers.

Kolb, D. M., & Glidden, P. (1986). Getting to know your conflict options. *Personnel Administrator, 31*(6), 77–90.

Kotter, J. P., & Schlesinger, L. A. (1979, March–April). Choosing strategies for change. *Harvard Business Review,* 106–114.

Leventhal, G. S. (1980). What should be done with equity theory? In K. J. Gergen, M. S. Greenberg, & R. H. Willis (Eds.), *Social exchange: Advances in theory and research* (pp. 27–55). New York: Plenum Press.

Lind, E. A., & Earley, P. C. (in press). Procedural justice and culture. *International Journal of Psychology.*

Lind, E. A., Kanfer, R., & Earley, C. (1990). Voice, control, and procedural justice: Instrumental and noninstrumental concerns in fairness judgments. *Journal of Personality and Social Psychology, 59*(5), 952–959.

Lind, E. A., Lissak, R. I., & Conlon, D. E. (1983). Decision control and process control effects on procedural fairness judgments. *Journal of Applied Psychology, 13,* 338–350.

Lind, E. A., & Tyler, T. R. (1988). *The social psychology of procedural justice.* New York: Plenum Press.

Mintzberg, H. (1973). *The nature of managerial work.* New York: Harper & Row.

Neale, M. A., & Bazerman, M. H. (1991). *Negotiator cognition and rationality*. New York: Free Press.

Neale, M. A., & Northcraft, G. B. (1991). Behavioral negotiation theory: A framework for conceptualizing dyadic bargaining. In L. L. Cummings & B. M. Staw (Eds.), *Research in organizational behavior* (Vol. 13, pp. 147–190). Greenwich, CT: JAI Press.

Rosnow, R. L. (1980). Psychology of rumor reconsidered. *Psychological Bulletin, 87*(3), 578–591.

Shapiro, D. L. (1991). Has the conflict-mitigating effect of explanations been overestimated?: An examination of explanation-effects under circumstances of exposed deceit. *Administrative Science Quarterly, 36,* 614–630.

Shapiro, D. L., & Brett, J. M. (1991). *Comparing the instrumental and value-expressive models of procedural justice under conditions of high and low decision control.* Paper presented at the national Academy of Management meeting, Miami, FL.

Shapiro, D. L., Buttner, E. H., & Barry, B. (in press). Explanations: What factors enhance their perceived adequacy? *Organizational Behavior and Human Decision Processes*, forthcoming.

Shapiro, D. L., Buttner, E. H., & Barry, B. (in press). Explanations: When are they judged adequate? *Best Papers Proceedings of the National Academy of Management,* Miami, FL.

Shapiro, D. L., Drieghe, R., & Brett, J. M. (1985). Mediator behavior and the outcome of mediation. *Journal of Social Issues, 41*(2), 101–114.

Sheppard, B. H. (1983). Managers as inquisitors: Some lessons from the law. In M. H. Bazerman & R. J. Lewicki (Eds.), *Negotiating in organizations* (pp. 192–213). Beverly Hills, CA: Sage.

Sheppard, B. H. (1984). Third-party conflict intervention: A procedural framework. In B. M. Staw & L. L. Cummings (Eds.), *Research in organizational behavior* (Vol. 6, pp. 141–190). Greenwich, CT: JAI Press.

Sheppard, B. H., Blumenfeld-Jones, K., & Roth, J. (1989). In K. Kressel, D. G. Pruitt and Associates (Eds.), *Mediation Research: The process and effectiveness of third-party intervention* (pp. 166–189). San Francisco, CA: Jossey-Bass.

Thibaut, J., & Walker, L. (1975). *Procedural justice: A psychological analysis.* Hillsdale, NJ: Lawrence Erlbaum Associates.

Tyler, T. R. (1987). Conditions leading to value expressive effects in judgments of procedural justice: A test of four models. *Journal of Personality and Social Psychology, 52,* 333–344.

Tyler, T. R. (1990). *Why people obey the law.* New Haven, CT: Yale University Press.

Tyler, T. R., & Bies, R. J. (1990). Beyond formal procedures: The interpersonal context of procedural justice. In J. S. Carroll (Ed.), *Applied social psychology and organizational settings* (pp. 77–98). Hillsdale, NJ: Lawrence Erlbaum Associates.

Tyler, T. R., Rasinski, K. A., & Spodick, N. (1985). Influence of voice on satisfaction with leaders: Exploring the meaning of process control. *Journal of Personality and Social Psychology, 48*(1), 72–81.

Ury, W. L., Brett, J. M., & Goldberg, S. G (1989). *Getting disputes resolved: Designing systems to cut the costs of conflict.* San Francisco, CA: Jossey-Bass.

Vroom, V., & Yetton, P. (1973). *Leadership and decision making.* Pittsburgh: University of Pittsburgh Press.

The Social Side of Fairness: Interpersonal and Informational Classes of Organizational Justice

4

Jerald Greenberg
The Ohio State University

What constitutes the fair treatment of people in organizations? Over the past three decades several different approaches have characterized the focus of scientists examining this important question. For many years, the study of fairness in organization was dominated by a *distributive justice* orientation, an approach that focused on outcomes—both how allocators distributed them, and how recipients reacted to those allocations (Greenberg, 1987a). Conceptualizations such as Adams' (1965) equity theory and Leventhal, Karuza, and Fry's (1980) allocation preference theory typify this orientation (for reviews, see Greenberg, 1982, 1987a, 1990a).

As this perspective gained dominance, an independent approach to the study of justice began to develop in Thibaut and Walker's (1975) pioneering studies of reactions to the procedures used to reach decisions in dispute-resolution contexts. Following this lead, researchers became interested in expanding the distributive justice orientation so as to include consideration of the processes by which outcomes are determined—that is, by adopting a procedural justice orientation (e.g., see Greenberg & Folger, 1983; Greenberg & Tyler, 1987). Since the 1980s, studies of procedural justice have rejuvenated both research and conceptual interest in matters of organizational justice, in large part due to the widespread applicability that such approaches have had in explaining a variety of organizational phenomena (Folger & Greenberg, 1985; Greenberg, 1990a). For example, research on procedural justice has shed considerable conceptual light on such important organizational concerns as performance appraisals (e.g., Greenberg, 1986, 1987b), employee compensation (e.g., Miceli & Lane, 1991), survivors' reactions to layoffs (e.g., Brockner & Greenberg, 1990), and managerial dispute resolution (e.g., Karambayya & Brett, 1989).

One byproduct of this considerable level of activity has been growing recognition that the original focus of both distributive and procedural justice is overly narrow in its emphasis on "structural" matters (Greenberg & McCarty, 1990; Tyler & Bies, 1990). That is, existing theories and research have tended to focus on the mechanisms by which distributive and procedural justice are accomplished. For example: (a) distributive justice researchers have focused a considerable amount of attention on questions such as "when are various distributive norms situationally appropriate?" (e.g., see Greenberg & Cohen, 1982; Törnblom, in press), and (b) procedural justice researchers popularly considered "what procedural elements (e.g., voice in decision-making, consistency of treatment, and the like) enhance the fairness of reward allocations?" (e.g., Greenberg, 1986, 1987a). This popular focus on matters of how fairness may be structured, although very important, has come at the expense of recognizing another important source of fairness perceptions—namely, the social determinants of fairness.

Beginning in the late 1980s several researchers have noted that when people are asked to report what constitutes unfair treatment, their responses focused on interpersonal rather than structural factors. For example, reports of inconsiderate, impolite treatment, and lack of consideration for others' feelings have been obtained in several open-ended questionnaire studies tapping perceived determinants of fairness (e.g., Messick, Bloom, Boldizar, & Samuelson, 1985; Mikula, Petrik, & Tanzer, 1990), and the importance of these factors has been established in examinations of retrospective accounts of fair treatment in a variety of organizational contexts (Bies & Moag, 1986; Tyler, 1986). Taken together, these studies provide strong agreement that the quality of interpersonal treatment one receives constitutes another source of perceived fairness, one that is not immediately recognized by the prevailing emphasis on the structural aspects of outcome distributions and procedures.

The purpose of the present chapter is to elucidate the status of these social determinants of justice. Given their prevalence in several contemporary investigations of organizational justice (e.g., Greenberg, 1990b, 1991b, 1991c, in press), such a task should prove beneficial by providing a useful platform from which to clarify and understand these factors. Toward this end, I begin the chapter by summarizing the current conceptual confusion regarding the interpersonal aspects of justice. I then seek to eliminate this confusion by proposing a rudimentary taxonomy that positions these social determinants relative to existing categories of justice. This sets the stage for reviewing some of the most recent empirical findings on the social determinants of justice. Because this research raises critical questions about the psychological mechanisms theorized to account for the impact of the social determinants of justice, the next section of the chapter focuses on these processes. The chapter then concludes by summarizing the current status of the social side of organizational justice.

CONCEPTUAL CONFUSION REGARDING THE STATUS OF SOCIAL ASPECTS OF JUSTICE

In one of the earliest conceptual statements regarding the social determinants of justice, Bies and Moag (1986) identified the term *interactional justice* to refer to people's sensitivity to "the quality of interpersonal treatment they [people] receive during the enactment of organizational procedures" (p. 44). It was Bies' (1986; Bies & Shapiro, 1987) contention that interactional justice should be understood as separated from procedural justice on the grounds that it represents the enactment of procedures rather than the development of procedures themselves.

Although others agreed that these so-called interactional factors were important—indeed, they were repeatedly identified in open-ended questionnaire studies of justice determinants (e.g., Messick et al., 1985; Sheppard & Lewicki, 1987)—they disagreed that the enactment of procedures was not truly a part of the procedural justice concept itself (Lind & Tyler, 1988). For example, Greenberg (1990a; Greenberg & McCarty, 1990) argued that so-called interactional justice may be best understood as an interpersonal aspect of procedural justice, and that the concept of procedural justice should be broadened to accommodate interpersonally based procedures. (This is in addition to the structural determinants of procedural justice imposed by Leventhal et al., 1980—consistency, lack of bias, accuracy, correctability, representativeness, and ethicality.) As a clue that the separate concept of interactional justice has given way to recognition that there is an interpersonal side of procedural justice, one need only consider the recent writings of Bies (e.g., Folger & Bies, 1989; Greenberg, Bies, & Eskew, 1991). Notably, Tyler and Bies (1990) eschewed the term *interactional justice* in favor of "the interpersonal context of procedural justice" (p. 81) and noted that procedural fairness judgments are influenced, in part, by the interpersonal treatment one receives.

Taking an intermediate position, Mikula et al. (1990) claimed that there is merit in recognizing that interactional justice is both a separate concept and that it may be subsumed under procedural justice. As they put it:

> It strikes us that both viewpoints are equally reasonable as long as one focuses exclusively on social situations of judgment and decision-making (e.g., allocation decisions . . .)—as the majority of justice research has done in the past. In those cases, interpersonal treatment relates mostly to the enactment of procedures. However . . . studies suggest a broader concept of interpersonal treatment which goes beyond situations of judgement and decision-making and includes all kinds of interactions and encounters. If one agrees to such a broad concept, it seems better to regard the manner of interpersonal treatment as an independent subject of justice evaluations rather than to subsume it under the concept of procedure. (p. 143)

Underlying Mijula et al.'s (1990) position is the notion that the justice of interpersonal treatment goes beyond the simple enactment of procedures; it also deals with the making of allocation decisions. Similarly, it was Bies and Moag's (1986) original contention that interpersonal treatment is an intermediary between procedures and outcome distributions. As such, it appears that the interpersonal aspects of justice—which thus far have been appreciated only from a procedural justice perspective—are also involved in the distributive side of justice. Indeed, it is this incompleteness of conceptualization that has led to the confusion and the controversy described here. It is my contention that what has been referred to as interactional justice may be legitimately recognized as a part of procedural justice because, under certain circumstances, it is. Likewise, it is also sometimes separated from procedural concerns, and an aspect of distributive justice. In my opinion, the confusion lies in the fact that the distinction between procedures and outcomes, while applied to the structural aspects of justice, has not yet been applied to the social aspects of justice. In other words, whereas theorists have concentrated on the procedural aspects of the social determinants of justice, they have not explicitly recognized the corresponding distributive aspects of the social determinants of justice. With this in mind, a taxonomy is proposed that seeks to clarify the role of social factors in conceptualizations of justice, one that integrates these factors into the existing distinction between procedures and distributions already popularized in the justice literature (Greenberg, 1987a, 1990a; Greenberg & Folger, 1983).

A TAXONOMY OF JUSTICE CLASSES

A taxonomy is proposed that is designed to highlight the distinction between the structural and social determinants of justice by noting their place in each of the two established types of justice—distributive and procedural. I begin by defining the dimensions from which the taxonomy is composed. Then, four justice classes are identified by cross-cutting the two dimensions. By highlighting the types of behaviors associated with each of the resulting justice classes, I intend to clarify the existing confusion concerning the interpersonal aspects of justice.

Defining Dimensions

The proposed taxonomy is formed by cross-cutting two independent dimensions: (a) category of justice—procedural and distributive, and (b) focal determinants—structural and social.

As established earlier and described in great detail elsewhere (e.g., Greenberg, 1987a; Walker, Lind, & Thibaut, 1979), distributive justice refers to the perceived fairness of outcome distributions (Homans, 1961), whereas procedural justice refers to the fairness of the procedures used to determine those outcomes

(Folger & Greenberg, 1985; Thibaut & Walker, 1975). In essence, the difference is based on the distinction between content and process that is basic to many of the social and philosophical approaches to the study of justice (for a review, see Cohen & Greenberg, 1982).

The distinction between structural and social determinants is based on the immediate focus of just action. In the case of structural determinants, justice is sought by focusing on the environmental context within which interaction occurs. By contrast, the social determinants of justice focus on the treatment of individuals. Thus, whereas the structural determinants ensure fairness by structuring a decision-making context, the social determinants ensure fairness by concentrating on the interpersonal treatment one receives. Accordingly, the act of following a prevailing rule of justice (e.g., distributing reward equitably; Leventhal, 1976) is structurally fair; the act of treating others in an open and honest fashion (e.g., providing adequate social accounts of decisions; Bies, 1987; Greenberg, 1990c) is socially fair. This distinction is analogous to one made in the conflict resolution literature (e.g., Neale & Bazerman, 1991) between solutions that focus on structure (e.g., the setting of a superordinate goal) and those that focus on interpersonal processes (e.g., teaching people to communicate more effectively).

Admittedly, at this point, these defining dimensions of the taxonomy may appear to be a bit abstract and in need of further elaboration. However, as the various justice classes are described in the following section, considerable substance promises to be added to the skeleton provided thus far.

Justice Classes

A taxonomy of justice is classes created by combining categories of justice with focal determinants of justice. The names given to the resulting classes are shown in Table 4.1.

Systemic Justice.   I use the term *systemic justice* to refer to the variety of procedural justice that is accomplished via structural means. This is the class of

TABLE 4.1
A Taxonomy of Justice Classes

Focal Determinant	Category of Justice	
	Procedural	Distributive
Structural	*Systemic justice*	*Configural justice*
Social	*Informational justice*	*Interpersonal justice*

justice that was originally studied by procedural justice scholars. For example, Thibaut and Walker (1975) noted that procedural justice requires structuring the dispute-resolution context such that disputants are given control over the process by which a resolution is sought.

The systemic justice class is also represented by Leventhal's (1980) proposed rules to evaluate the fairness of allocation procedures. Specifically, he claimed that fairness demands imposing procedures that allow for allocation decisions to be made such that they: (a) are consistent over people and time, (b) disallow expressions of bias, (c) are based on accurate information, (d) provide opportunities to modify and reverse decisions, (e) represent the concerns of all parties, and (f) are compatible with prevailing moral and ethical standards. These are all ways of structuring the context such that procedural justice is obtained. As such, they are examples of acts that promote systemic justice.

Configural Justice.   I use the term *configural justice* to refer to the variety of distributive justice that is accomplished via structural means. This is the class of justice that has been popularly studied by sociologists (e.g., Törnblom, in press) and social psychologists (Deutsch, 1975) interested in the pattern of resource allocations perceived as fair under various circumstances—hence, the term *configural*.

Distributions of reward may be structured either by forces to conform to existing social norms (e.g., equity, equality, and need have been popularly studied; Deutsch, 1975; Leventhal, 1976), or by the desire to attain some instrumental goal (e.g., promoting productivity or minimizing conflict; Greenberg & Cohen, 1982). These are all ways of structuring the context of reward allocations such that certain distributive patterns result. As such, they are examples of acts that promote configural justice.

Informational Justice.   I use the term *informational justice* to refer to the social determinants of procedural justice. Hence, informational justice may be sought by providing knowledge about procedures that demonstrate regard for people's concerns. Research has shown that an effective way of doing this is by providing people adequate social accounts of the procedures used to determine desired outcomes (Bies, 1987; Shapiro, this volume). Because it is typically the open sharing of information that promotes this class of justice, the term *informational* is used to identify it.

Information about procedures may take many forms. For example, research has shown that MBA job candidates believed that corporate recruiters treated them fairly to the extent that they presented honest and candid information and reasonable justifications for the decisions they made (Bies & Moag, 1986). Similarly, Bies and Shapiro (1987, 1988) found that people who received negative outcomes (such as being denied a job, or having a proposal rejected) were more likely to accept those results as fair when they received a reasonable explanation regarding the procedure used than when no such justification was provided. The role of informational justice also has been demonstrated in the domain of performance appraisal. Notably, Greenberg (1991a) had workers rate the fairness of the performance appraisals they received, and compared the ratings of those whose numerical evaluations were accompanied by written narratives explaining their ratings (the outcome, in this case) with those who received no such explanation. As expected, significantly higher perceptions of fairness were obtained when explanations were provided than when they were not. Thus, the use of explanations regarding the procedures used to determine performance ratings enhanced the perceived fairness of those ratings.

For explanations to be perceived as fair, however, they must also be recognized as genuine in intent (i.e., not merely ingratiatory) and based on sound reasoning. For example, fairness judgments tend to be enhanced when explanations are believed to be communicated without any ulterior motives (Bies, Shapiro, & Cummings, 1988), based on information that is logical to the outcome distribution at hand (Shapiro & Buttner, 1988), and based on legitimate factors (e.g., claims of mitigating circumstances as opposed to arbitrary judgments; Folger, Rosenfield, & Robinson, 1983). Taken together, such research suggests that the social aspects of procedural justice—that is, informational justice—constitutes an important element of reactions to procedural injustice.

Interpersonal Justice.   I use the term *interpersonal justice* to refer to the social aspects of distributive justice. Interpersonal justice may be sought by showing concern for individuals regarding the distributive outcomes they received. By contrast to informational justice, which focuses on knowledge of the procedures leading to outcomes, interpersonal justice focuses on the consequences of those outcomes directly. Empirical support for the distinction may be drawn from Greenberg's (1991a) study of the explanations given to account for employee performance ratings. In this investigation, evidence of distinct categorical differences was found between explanations that focused on providing information relevant to the rating (informational justice) and those that focused on expressions of remorse for the outcomes themselves (interpersonal justice).

Several examples of interpersonal justice variables may be noted. For example, Bies (1986) found that job candidates who were displeased with the outcomes they received (i.e., they were turned down) believed those outcomes to be fairer when the authority figure demonstrated concern for their plight than when no such concern was communicated. In another context, Tyler (1988) found that citizens' reactions to dealings with police and courts were highly influenced by the sensitivity shown to their problems by authorities. Namely, ostensible displays of politeness and respect for citizens' rights enhanced their perceptions of fair treatment by authorities. Finally, Mikula et al.'s (1990) open-ended questionnaire research tapping people's perceptions of fair and unfair treatment also identified several behaviors that fall into this category. For example, it may be said that complaints of "letting somebody down" and "selfish behavior" reflect a kind of failure to meet one's social obligations to a distribution of effort. As such, they represent violations of interpersonal justice.

It also makes sense to look at apologies as a tactic for enhancing interpersonal justice (see also Bies, 1987; Greenberg, 1990c). Because they involve expressions of remorse, apologies help harmdoers distance themselves from the negative effects of their actions (Tedeschi & Norman, 1985). Research by Greenberg (1991a) showed that apologies tend to be included in the written narratives that accompany performance appraisals, and are most frequently given to low performers. Interestingly, it also was found that the low-rated employees who received apologies for their low ratings accepted those evaluations as more fair than those who failed to receive apologies (Greenberg, 1991a). Such findings are consistent with additional evidence from other contexts showing that apologies are an effective means of reducing expressions of anger (Baron, 1990; Ohbuchi, Kameda, & Agarie, 1989).

Discussion

One of the major benefits of this taxonomy is that it expands our current understanding of the nature of the social determinants of justice beyond that provided by the current work on "interactional justice" (e.g., Bies & Moag, 1986; Bies & Shapiro, 1987). Indeed, the taxonomy proposes a solution to the current conceptual confusion regarding the status of interactional justice as a separate category of justice vs. an element of procedural justice. Because the definition of interactional justice refers to the "enactment of organizational procedures," it is clear that the social determinants of justice are involved in *both* procedural justice (i.e., the procedures used to determine outcomes) and distributive justice (i.e., the outcome resulting from enacting those procedures). Indeed, the present taxonomy distinguishes between those social determinants of justice that deal with procedures (termed *informational justice*) and those that deal with outcomes (termed *interpersonal justice*). In so doing, this taxonomy not only clarifies the role of the social determinants of justice, but does so in a manner that symmetrically expands the existing distributive-procedural dichotomy.

An important byproduct of recognizing both the distributive and procedural aspects of the social determinants of justice—that is, the interpersonal and informational justice classes—is that it promises to stimulate needed research. Traditionally, interpersonal justice has been less widely studied than its procedural counterpart, informational justice. Hopefully, by separating these justice classes from each other, the stage is set for conducting research that closely examines the separate effects of each one. Toward this end, given the advances made in recently completed research (presented in the following section), attention to the social determinants of justice promises to be the subject of increased empirical and conceptual activity.

RESEARCH ON THE ORGANIZATIONAL IMPACT
OF SOCIAL DETERMINANTS OF JUSTICE

Although several studies already cited help define the distinction between the informational and interpersonal justice classes, additional recent research has been conducted that closely examines the impact of these factors on various aspects of organizational behavior. In particular, three different domains have been studied to date—employee theft, acceptance of a corporate smoking ban, and employee reactions to corporate layoffs. Findings in each of these areas are summarized next.

Employee Theft

Based on the assumption that employees would engage in petty theft as a means of redressing an underpayment inequity, I undertook two experimental studies— a field quasi-experiment, and a follow-up laboratory study—that examined the extent to which the social determinants of justice mitigated theft reactions to underpayment inequity.

Participants in the first study (Greenberg, 1990b), were employees of three different manufacturing plants owned by the same parent company. The employees of all three plants, mostly clerical workers and low-level manufacturing operatives, had similar demographic characteristics, and had no opportunities to communicate with each other. In response to a cash-flow crisis caused by unexpectedly lost contracts, the company had decided that it was necessary to engage in the cost-cutting response of reducing the pay of all employees in two of the three plants by 15% for a period of 10 weeks. (These were the plants whose employees manufactured the products no longer needed due to the lost contracts.) The employees in these two plants received less pay than they had been receiving although they were expected to perform at a comparable level—hence, a naturalistic manipulation of underpayment inequity had occurred (Adams 1965).

With the cooperation of the parent company, the experimenter manipulated the manner in which the pay cut was explained to the workers in the two affected plants. Employees at one plant, selected at random, received an explanation that was high in both informational and interpersonal justice (in terms of the present taxonomy, a high social justice condition). Employees of the other plant received an explanation that was low on both these dimensions (low social justice condition). Specifically, in the high social justice condition, employees were provided with a great deal of information about the need for the layoffs (an elaborate and lengthy presentation involving the use of charts and graphs to detail the nature of the problem and the necessity of taking the action). They were also presented repeated expressions of remorse over the negative outcomes (e.g., "Will it hurt? Of course! But, it will hurt us all alike . . . it really hurts me to do this, and the decision didn't come easily"). By contrast, employees in the low social justice condition were given only minimal information about the need for the layoffs and its justification; the basis for the decision was not described. Moreover, only the most perfunctory expressions of apology or remorse were voiced. Thus, by manipulating the statements of company officials, either high levels or low levels of both informational and interpersonal justice were introduced. Finally, because no pay cuts were necessitated in the third plant, its employees constituted the control group.

The major dependent measure was the rate of employee theft. This was the company's standard measure of "shrinkage," the percentage of inventory unaccounted for by known uses (e.g., sales, waste, etc.). These measures were collected by persons blind to the study. Data were collected on a weekly basis over the 30-week study period—10 weeks before the pay cuts were instituted, 10 weeks during the pay cut period, and 10 weeks after normal pay was reinstated. As expected by equity theory, the workers whose pay was reduced (i.e., underpaid workers) responded to the resulting underpayment inequity by stealing—a way of attempting to raise their outcomes in an unauthorized manner. After the pay was reinstated, the theft rate returned to its lower, pre-pay cut levels. By contrast, those in the control group showed no changes in theft rate throughout the study period.

What is particularly interesting is how much the employees stole as a function of the nature of the information and interpersonal treatment they received. Employees who received low levels of information presented in an insensitive manner stole approximately 8% (compared to a base rate of approximately 3%), whereas those who received high levels of information presented in a highly sensitive manner stole slightly over 4%. This difference was not only statistically significant, but financially significant for the company that bore the cost of this undesirable behavior. Interestingly, those receiving the low social justice manipulations reported that they were treated more inequitably than those who received the negative outcomes, but were presented high social justice manipulations. However, those in the high social justice condition expressed no more inequitable treatment than those who were not underpaid (those in the control group). In addition, the data show that many of those in the high social justice condition responded to the inequity they experienced in another way as well—namely, by quitting their jobs. Specifically, whereas over 25% of the workers in the low social justice condition resigned in response to the pay cut, only about 2% did so in the high social justice condition (compared to 0% in the control group). In summary, these data clearly demonstrate that low levels of informational and interpersonal justice encourage expressions of inequity and several forms of behavioral redress—pilfering (to increase outcomes) or resigning (to leave the field).

Given that this initial field quasi-experiment used manipulations that combined both informational and interpersonal justice, a follow-up study was conducted in a laboratory setting in which the independent effects of the informational and interpersonal factors could be assessed independently (Greenberg, in press). The subjects were undergraduates who were promised an established fair pay rate, $5 per hour, to perform a clerical task. After performing the task a random half of the participants were told that they would be paid the $5 promised them, whereas the remaining participants were told they would be paid only $3. Informational justice was manipulated by varying the quality of the information used as the basis for establishing this rate of pay. Specifically, the high informational justice conditions were characterized by: (a) the use of directly acquired information, (b) from an expert source, (c) who is identified, and (d) that is double-checked with an independent source. By contrast, the low informational justice manipulations relied on: (a) the use of hearsay information, (b) from a person of undisclosed expertise, (c) who is not identified, and (d) that is not independently verified. Remarks meeting these criteria were tailored to the underpaid and equitably paid conditions separately. For example, in the underpayment/high informational justice condition, subjects were told:

> While you were working, I found out from my supervisor that our research sponsor is really only paying $3 instead of the $5 you were promised. As you can see from this document [experimenter shows participant fake budget figures], this is the amount that was planned in the original budget proposal. To make sure, I also called the project's budget officer and was reassured of this figure. Because of a typographical error, some participants did get $5, but this was a mistake. Starting now, you can get only $3.

By contrast, in the underpayment/low informational justice condition, subjects were told:

> While you were working, I heard from someone in the hall that our research sponsor is really only supposed to be paying $3, instead of the $5 you were promised. As a result, that's what I'll be paying you.

Following the administration of the informational justice manipulation, additional comments were made that created the interpersonal justice manipulation. These remarks varied in terms of the degree of caring and sensitivity shown the participant with respect to their pay rate. Specifically, the high interpersonal justice conditions were characterized by: (a) repeated expressions of remorse (or satisfaction) and (b) attempts to dissociate from (or associate with) the outcome. Low sensitivity conditions were characterized by: (a) expressions of disinterest with the participants' outcomes and (b) claims of greater concern with one's own personal outcomes. Remarks meeting these criteria were tailored to the underpaid and equitably paid conditions separately. For example, in the underpayment/high interpersonal justice condition, subjects were told:

You really got a bad deal and I feel very sorry for you. I know it's only a $2 difference, but I feel awful for misleading you. Please recognize that it's not my fault, and that I would pay you more if I could. You seem like such a nice person, I really hate to have to do this to you. I don't want to upset you. It's probably not much consolation, but I feel very badly about this myself.

By contrast, in the underpayment/low interpersonal justice condition, subjects were told:

That's the way it is; I don't make the rules around here. I really don't care how much you get paid. I don't care too much about how much others get; I'm more concerned about how much I get paid myself.

After the final interpersonal sensitivity remarks were made, the experimenter told the subjects that he had to rush down the hall to run another experimental session. With this, he reached into his hip pocket and removed a handful of $1 bills, quarters, nickles, dimes, and pennies, and placed this money on a nearby desk. The experimenter's seemingly disorganized state helped create the impression that he was unaware of the exact amount of money he put on the table. In keeping with this image, he said, "I have to go down the hall now to begin another session, so [reaching into his pocket] I'll just have to leave you some money to pay yourself with. I don't know how much is here, but it look's like there's more than enough for you. Just take the $5 ($3) you are supposed to be paid and leave the rest on the table." This procedure made it possible for participants to take as much money as they wanted without believing that the experimenter would be able to tell how much was actually taken. However, because in actuality, there was a total of $10.42 available (7 one-dollar bills, 6 quarters, 11 dimes, 12 nickles, and 22 pennies), it was possible to determine exactly how money was taken.

The results clearly showed that the amount of pay taken was dependent on payment equity in conjunction with the justice manipulations. For example, whereas no appreciable theft occurred among subjects who were equitably paid, the amount of theft was considerable among those who were underpaid. However, the amount of money underpaid workers took varied as a function of the informational justice and the interpersonal justice manipulations. Although the effect of these two factors did not interact with each other, each factor contributed to a reduction in the amount of money taken. That is, theft was reduced when levels of informational justice were high rather than low and when levels of interpersonal justice were high rather than low. In fact, when both factors were high, theft rate was lowest, and when both factors were low, theft rate was highest. In other words, each type of justice contributed additively to a reduction in theft behavior stimulated by the surprise instigation of inequitable treatment.

Acceptance of a Corporate Smoking Ban

Given how clear-cut the effects of interpersonal and informational justice have been shown to be on mitigating theft reactions to underpayment inequity, another study was undertaken to determine the extent to which the observed effects were generalizable to other types of negative behaviors. With this in mind, a study was undertaken to test the effectiveness of social justice manipulations on another important variable associated with effective organizational functioning—namely, acceptance of a corporate smoking ban (Greenberg, 1991b). Just as theft can cost companies a great deal, so too can the failure of workers to accept a smoking ban—especially if otherwise good workers who happen to smoke find the ban unacceptable and quit their jobs as a result. The research was undertaken with an interest in asking whether the introduction of social justice variables would enhance workers' acceptance of a corporate smoking ban.

Extrapolating from the above research on employee theft (Greenberg, 1990b, in press), I had reason to believe that the manipulations I had been using to mitigate theft reactions to underpayment could also be used to help facilitate acceptance of a corporate smoking ban. This notion was tested in the following manner. In meetings conducted by corporate officials, employees of a clerical services company were told that the company was about to introduce a company-wide smoking ban. Effective the following week, there would be a total ban on smoking on all company premises. Because the meetings were conducted in separate rooms, I had an opportunity to present separate groups of employees with different degree of information about the reasons for the smoking ban, and in ways that demonstrated different degrees of social sensitivity. The manipulations were similar to the ones used in the theft laboratory study (Greenberg, in press). Specifically, in the informational justice condition, employees were either presented with a great deal of information about the costs of smoking, the health and danger risks involved, and so on (the high informational justice condition) or were given very limited and superficial information about the negative effects of smoking on the company and its employees (the low informational justice condition). In addition, this information was presented in a manner in which either considerable social sensitivity was shown about the potential difficulty involved with giving up smoking on the job (the high interpersonal justice condition) or very little sensitivity was shown to the feelings of those affected (the low interpersonal justice condition).

In addition, because the smoking ban (unlike the pay cut that occurred in the earlier studies) did not affect all workers in the same way, an opportunity presented itself to study the manner in which the hypothesized effects may be qualified by the severity of the outcome. To do this, an independent variable (termed outcome severity) was composed by noting whether workers smoked on the job, and if so how much. Dichotomizing the distribution of the number of cigarettes smoked, levels of the variable were created by distinguishing between those who smoked less than the median amount (light smokers) and those who smoked more than the median amount (heavy smokers). One of the key dependent measures dealt with "acceptance of the smoking ban," an internally consistent group of three items tapping workers' willingness to go along with ban.

Several interesting results were found. Most notably, there was evidence for an egocentric bias. That is, the more severe the outcome (i.e., the more the worker smoked), the less the ban was accepted. This is consistent with several of my earlier studies in which it was found that what is fair is what benefits oneself (Greenberg, 1983, 1987c). However, this was qualified by the informational justice and interpersonal justice manipulations. Each of these factors interacted with the severity variable, but not with each other. As in the theft studies, each factor contributed some to the acceptance of the smoking ban; their combined effects were additive.

Interestingly, however, this effect was most pronounced among heavy smokers—that is, those who were most adversely affected by the ban. In other words, among heavy smokers, the introduction of high levels of informational justice and interpersonal justice effectively raised the acceptance rate of the smoking ban to levels approaching those of light smokers and nonsmokers. The effects of these variables were less pronounced among light smokers. Even more extreme, nonsmokers' acceptance of the ban was not at all influenced by the social justice manipulations; their level of acceptance was already asymptotically high. Hence, an interesting conclusion from this study is not only that the effects I noted for theft also occurred for acceptance of a corporate smoking ban, thereby showing generalizability, but also what was found with respect to when the effects occurred. Namely, the mitigating effects were greatest among those who were most adversely affected. From a practical perspective, this may be considered quite useful insofar as these were the workers who were most harmed—hence, the ones who were in greatest danger of quitting. Noting that these were, in fact, the participants who were most likely to benefit from the social justice manipulations, is encouraging with respect to the practical implications of the work.

These findings do not imply that the manipulations had no effects on nonsmokers; indeed they did. Although nonsmokers weren't affected by the information and the sensitivity in their acceptance of the ban, they were affected when it came to recognizing the fairness of the procedure the company used to introduce the smoking ban. In fact, with respect to ratings of fairness, all subjects agreed that the use of detailed information presented in a socially sensitive manner enhanced perceptions of the fairness of the way the smoking ban was instituted. That is, fairness perceptions were enhanced by increases in informational justice and increases in interpersonal justice. Each factor contributed to some of the variance in perceived fairness; the greatest levels of fairness were recognized when the levels of both variables were high.

At this point, an ethical aside is in order regarding the conduct of this study. The procedure called for subjects to receive one of four instructional sets (2 levels of informational justice x 2 levels of interpersonal justice) and then to complete the questionnaire. Although it would have been ideal, from an experimental perspective, to include a measure of actual compliance with the smoking ban, or perhaps acceptance of the ban at some time in the future, it was considered ethically necessary to use a procedure that would have otherwise invalidated the interpretation of such data. Specifically, because the earlier theft research (Greenberg, 1990b, in press) established that there was a substantial benefit associated with administering high levels of both the informational and interpersonal justice manipulations, it would have been considered ethically inappropriate to release any participants until they had actually been exposed to these treatments. As a result, the experimental sessions were not ended until all employees were thoroughly debriefed and then give the high levels of whatever variables were not earlier administered. Because such treatment was known to yielded beneficial outcomes, it was essential for them to be provided to all employees after they were temporarily withheld (i.e., before the questionnaire was completed). To release them in advance of such debriefing, although essential for the collection of compliance data, may have caused the employees undue stress and cost the company the consequences of such negative reactions. From a cost–benefit perspective, it was clearly essential to refrain from using any procedure that would have knowingly sustained employees' experienced distress.

Minimizing Negative Responses to Layoffs

Yet another domain in which the effects of social justice variables have been examined is reactions to layoffs among both victims and survivors (see Konovsky & Brockner, this volume). In this connection, a series of questionnaire studies by Brockner, Konovsky, Cooper, and Folger (1991) and an experimental investigation by Greenberg (1991c) paint a consistent picture of the beneficial effects of high levels of social justice variables.

In the first study by Brockner et al. (1991), victims of layoffs completed a questionnaire in which they indicated the extent to which they were given advance notice regarding their layoffs (an informational justice variable), the extent to which they were offered benefits that eased the financial costs of the layoffs, and their desire for governmental regulations designed to protect workers from layoffs. It was found that the less advance notice that was given (i.e., the less informational justice was recognized), the more the participants favored governmental regulation, especially when the financial effects of the layoffs were great. In other words, when minimal warning was given about the use of an undesirable procedure, people expressed a preference for actions that would minimize a recurrence of such situations.

In their follow-up study, Brockner et al. (1991) sent a questionnaire to employees who survived the layoffs of some of their fellow employees at the same organization. This time, the social justice measures included three intercorrelated questionnaire items tapping both interactional justice (e.g., clarity of the explanations given for the layoffs) and interpersonal justice (e.g., the extent to which layoff victims had news of the layoffs delivered in "a nice way"). The dependent measure consisted of judgments of organizational commitment. An interaction pattern similar to that of the previous study was found in these two studies as well. In other words, a significantly lower level of organizational commitment was expressed by survivors who believed that the layoff victims were treated in a socially unfair manner, especially when they believed that the effects of the layoffs were particularly severe (measured in terms of the percentage of persons laid off).

It is interesting to note the consistent pattern of findings in these studies despite the different measures. These findings are also similar to the pattern of interaction noted in Greenberg's (1991b) study of workers' reactions to a corporate smoking ban. In that study too, the most negative effects were found among those who experienced the most severe outcomes (i.e., the heaviest smokers) when the level of social justice was lowest. Clearly then, a consistent pattern of evidence shows that the reactions to social justice variables are qualified by the nature of the consequences involved. This makes sense when one considers that informational and interpersonal justice manipulations are, after all, designed to reduce the consequences of outcomes. As such, the interaction pattern may be taken as a summary of the combination of conditions under which negative reactions to negative treatment may be effectively mitigated. Viewed from this perspective, it makes a great deal of sense to find that the combination of poor treatment and poor outcomes sets the stage for the most negative reactions.

Although the Brockner et al. (1991) results are interesting, their questionnaire failed to separate the effects of interpersonal and informational factors. As such, the individual contributions of these variables to reactions to layoffs remains to be determined. Moreover, because Brockner et al. (1991) measured, but did not manipulate, social justice variables, their correlational study does not permit direct assessment of the causal effects of social justice variables.

An experimental study by Greenberg (1991b) eliminated these problems. The participants in this investigation were employees of an assembly plant who were asked to write brief narratives about what it was like to work for their company. Their responses were collected twice—once 6 weeks before any layoffs occurred, and again immediately after company layoff notices were distributed. The layoff notices were prepared in a fashion following from the independent manipulations of informational and interpersonal justice established in the researcher's earlier investigations in this area (Greenberg, 1990b, 1991b, in press). In other words, the informational justice variable was characterized by providing either lengthy explanations regarding the company's economic problems and the necessity for the layoff (high informational justice condition) or very limited statements of the problems involved (low informational justice condition). This information was combined with varying expressions of sympathy for the workers: either sincere expressions of sorrow for having to take this action (high interpersonal justice condition) or rather cool, detached statements regarding the business necessity of the action (low interpersonal justice condition). This information was presented to supplement notices indicating that either they were being laid off themselves (victim condition) or that some other company employees (survivor condition) were being laid off. (This information was, of course, true.)

The primary data consisted of raters' assessments of the affective tone of the workers' descriptive comments concerning their jobs. Data were available both before and immediately after the layoffs for both victims and survivors. The overall pattern of findings was remarkably similar to that obtained in Greenberg's (1991b) study of workers' reactions to a smoking ban. In fact, parallels can be drawn between those who were not directly adversely affected (nonsmokers and survivors) and those who were directly adversely affected (smokers and layoff victims). Specifically, it was found that descriptions of the company became more negative following the layoffs. However, consistent with a self-serving, egoistic perspective (Greenberg, 1983, 1987c), after the layoffs the victims expressed even greater negative reactions than the survivors. In addition, among the victims, the negative reactions were mitigated by the use of statements high in levels of informational and interpersonal justice. Indeed, the most negative reactions occurred among victims of layoffs receiving low levels of both informational and interpersonal justice. Although the survivors of layoffs were less strongly affected by the social justice manipulations, they were affected in the same relative pattern. (For ethical purposes, the participants were thoroughly debriefed as in the Greenberg, 1991b, study—that is, by being administered any beneficial treatments that were earlier denied.)

Summary

These findings not only conceptually corroborate those of Brockner et al. (1991), but they also extend the generalizability of several earlier studies showing a similar pattern of findings regarding the effects of informational and interpersonal justice. This research makes it clear that high levels of both informational and interpersonal justice, alone and/or together, are effective in mitigating the undesirable behavioral and attitudinal reactions to negative outcomes. Whether it was theft reactions to underpayment inequity, acceptance of a corporate smoking ban, or employees' affective reactions toward their companies following layoffs, providing employees with complete explanations regarding the procedures used in a way that showed sensitivity toward their unfortunate situations effectively reduced their negative reactions. That is to say, these manipulations reduced levels of theft, promoted acceptance of the smoking ban among those who were most adversely effected, and lowered negative affect toward the company following layoffs.

THEORETICAL QUESTIONS AND IMPLICATIONS

The taxonomy and research just reviewed highlight several critical conceptual issues in need of further development. In particular, several theoretical questions and implications raised by this work may be identified. The remainder of this chapter addresses two of these: (a) the processes underlying the mitigating influences of informational and interpersonal justice, and (b) the juxtaposition of the present approach with the group-value model of procedural justice (Lind & Tyler, 1988).

Processes Theorized to Underlie the Mitigating Influences of Informational and Interpersonal Justice: Some Possibilities

Given the high degree of consistency with which the mitigating effects of social justice variables have been observed over a variety of phenomena, it is appropriate to ask why the effect occurs. In other words, what are the underlying processes involved? Given the statistically significant interactions found between the social justice manipulations and the reaction measures, it may be said that the social justice variables moderate the relationship between the negative outcomes and the negative reactions (Baron & Kenny, 1986). However, the exact nature of the processes responsible for yielding different reactions to unfavorable outcomes is unclear. Indeed, as Baron and Kenny (1986) noted, the use of moderators sometimes leads to positing the existence of various mediational processes. In the present case, four distinct possibilities with respect to the nature of the mediational processes may be identified.

First, it may be the case that the social justice manipulations work by reducing the negativity of the outcome (Bies, 1987). Therefore, to the extent that the negative outcomes are made to seem not so bad, it is not surprising that the reactions may be not so negative. Evidence for this possibility is provided by Greenberg's (1990a) employee theft field quasi-experiment. Participants in that study expressed the greatest degree of payment inequity under the conditions in which the most extreme inequity-reduction behaviors occurred (that is, when social justice was low). To the extent that the social justice manipulations influenced perceptions of outcome fairness, it follows that reactions to outcome fairness would be qualified. Thus, the most negative behaviors occurred when the most inequitable payment was given—that is, when the lowest levels of social justice variables were administered. Despite this, the nature of the data made it impossible to test this effect directly. Specifically, because the behavioral reactions measured (i.e., theft rates) were collected at the aggregate level, they could not be correlated with individual perceptions of payment equity. As a result, it is not yet possible to claim that social justice manipulations moderate reactions to negative outcomes by virtue of the fact that they qualify the perceived fairness or negativity of those outcomes.

Second, it may be the case that the social justice manipulations work by qualifying people's willingness to respond in a negative fashion. That is, although people might continue to suffer from the negative outcomes, the social justice manipulations may minimize people's willingness to express themselves negatively. Indeed, previous research has shown that people do not always show discernible responses to felt inequities (Greenberg, 1984) and that direct inequity-reducing actions are not always taken even when inequitable conditions are recognized (Greenberg, 1987c; Mark & Folger, 1984). In cases in which authorities have displayed high degrees of social justice, attempting to justify the harm and minimize its impact, it makes sense that victims would feel somewhat obligated to refrain from expressing themselves in a disruptive manner. Likewise, an authority's ostensible displays of disregard for one's plight might stimulate, if not instigate, a disgruntled subordinate's willingness to respond in a negative fashion. As such, it may be that the processes of modeling (Bandura, 1986) and/or reciprocating others' behaviors (Gouldner, 1960) may account for the observed tendency for social justice manipulations to mitigate negative reactions to negative outcomes. However, in the absence of any direct tests of this possibility, this notion must remain within the realm of speculation.

A third possibility is that the social justice manipulations may influence, to some extent, both the level of outcome negativity experienced and the willingness to express oneself negatively in a simultaneous fashion. In other words, it is recognized that the first two possibilities are not mutually exclusive. Indeed, to the extent that one process occurs, it is possible that the other might also be triggered. Thus, some degree of moderation of both the negativity of the outcome and the willingness to respond in a negative fashion might occur. However, evidence in support of this possibility is lacking at this time.

A fourth possibility is that one social justice manipulation may influence the outcome negativity expressed and that the other may influence the willingness to express oneself negatively. For example, it might be that the sharing of information reduces the level of negative outcomes experienced, whereas the ostensible shows of concern for the outcomes received reduces the willingness to react negatively. Similarly, the reverse might also be possible. Namely, the sharing of information may reduce the willingness to react negatively whereas the ostensible shows of concern for the outcomes received might reduce the negativity of the outcomes.

Although direct support for this possibility has yet to be demonstrated, some preliminary findings are available to suggest that people's perceptions of fairness do, in fact, differentiate between the informational and interpersonal justice classes. For example, when Greenberg's (in press) laboratory subjects were asked to rate the fairness of the procedures used to determine their pay, the only differentiating factor was the degree of informational justice shown (procedures were perceived as significantly fairer under high informational justice conditions than under low informational justice conditions). Similarly, when these same subjects were asked to rate the fairness of the experimenter's treatment of them, the only differentiating factor was the degree of interpersonal justice shown (the treatment was perceived as significantly fairer under high interpersonal justice conditions than under low interpersonal justice conditions). To the extent that people are capable of differentiating between the various determinants of fairness, it is possible that each social justice class might be individually responsible for acting on a separate determinant of the reactions. Once again, however, in the absence of any direct evidence bearing on this possibility, it must remain within the realm of conjecture.

Juxtaposition to the Group-Value Model of Procedural Justice

In recent years, some key insight into the processes responsible for reactions to procedural injustices have been provided by the group-value model (Lind & Tyler, 1988; Tyler & Lind, 1992). Because some of these processes may be involved in the effects I have described here, I am devoting some space to discussing this approach vis-à-vis the present work. As becomes apparent, despite considerable agreement, some key sources of disagreement are noted that help to underscore the major assumptions of the present conceptualization.

During the past decade, questions about the mechanisms underlying the operation of procedural justice effects have been answered in terms of both the social control and the value-expressive opportunities they provide (Shapiro, this volume; Tyler, 1987). That is, fair distribution procedures are recognized as such because they either enhance one's control over desired outcomes (the control explanation; Thibaut & Walker, 1975) or because they provide an opportunity to strengthen long-term relationships with authority figures (the group-value explanation; Lind & Tyler, 1988). Although both control and noncontrol factors are clearly involved (e.g., see Lind, Kanfer, & Earley, 1990), mounting evidence (e.g., Tyler, 1989) suggests that control is not the only reason why people prefer to have input into the decisions affecting them. Specifically, the model suggests that because people in organizations focus on their long-term associations with authorities, they expect organizations "to use neutral decision-making procedures enacted by trustworthy authorities" and to treat them "with respect, dignity, and politeness" so that, over time, all group members will benefit fairly from being members of the group (Tyler, 1989, p. 837). Beyond neutrality and trust, the group-value model also specifies that group standing is also critical to fairness judgments. Elaborating on this, Lind (1988) said:

> To the extent that procedures provide signs that the perceiver has full status in the group, the procedures will be seen as fair. Thus, procedural justice will be high when the procedure emphasizes the importance of the person and the importance the group accords to the person's concerns and rights. The model therefore predicts that procedural fairness will be high for procedures that promote respectful or polite treatment or that dignify the concerns of people involved, because such treatment

symbolizes full status in the group. Conversely, procedures that are perfunctory, undignified, or impolite in the way they treat people are status-threatening and likely to be seen as unfair. (p. 14.)

Consistent with the group-value model, studies have shown that perceptions of fairness are related to the extent to which decision outcomes reflected the views of those involved (Miller, Jackson, Mueller, & Schersching, 1987) and show signs of good faith by the authorities involved (Leung & Li, 1990; Tyler, 1989).

These descriptions and this evidence make it clear that fairness is enhanced by the types of behaviors described by the informational and interpersonal justice classes identified in the present work. Clearly, I agree with Lind and Tyler (1988) that the social factors represent important determinants of fair treatment. I also acknowledge their suggestion that the underlying mechanism for perceptions of fairness in this case may be identification with group values. In other words, treating people with dignity and respect may make them feel welcome as members of a group or organization to which they value belonging.

However, I believe it is important to qualify Lind and Tyler's (1988) position by adding that the social determinants reflect not only the fairness of the procedures, but also the fairness of distributions themselves. Typically, it is not formal procedures, but individual actions taken that reflect concern for one's rights and well-being. For example, an individual who knowingly allocates insufficient quantities of needed resources to others, and who does so in a calculated, calloused fashion (e.g., by saying, "take this pittance, it's all I'm going to give you") is following a distributive practice that is unfair in both its enactment and its outcomes. Strictly speaking, no procedural violations may have occurred—if, for example, prevailing norms dictated that it was acceptable for the allocator to make distributive decisions without seeking others' input (Greenberg, Eskew, & Miles, 1991). Thus, although I agree with Lind (1988) that perfunctory, undignified, and impolite actions may be procedurally unfair, so too many distributive acts that are showcased in similar fashion. Because often distributive behaviors are not the result of any formal procedural guidelines, but rather, the result of an individual's decision making (e.g., Leventhal, 1980), it would be misleading to infer that such negative treatment would not be judged to be unfair. Indeed, it is not only the fairness of procedures but the fairness of outcomes themselves that demand the use of socially fair treatment. With this, I simply restate one of my major themes of this chapter—namely, that undesirable social treatment should be recognized as an element not only of procedural justice, but of distributive justice as well.

Having stated this, I reiterate a point I made in an earlier paper (Greenberg, 1990a): With all the recent attention paid to procedural justice, we run the risk of forgetting about distributive justice. The need to integrate both the procedural and distributive aspects of justice (including the social and structural determinants of each), I believe, is essential. Any social scientist who claims to study one aspect of justice without paying attention to the other is surely guilty of premature specialization. Given that definitions of procedural justice encompass distributive justice, separating one from the other is a most delicate operation— one that should be taken no more lightly than a surgeon operating on one half of the brain while neglecting the other half!

CONCLUSION

By elucidating the social determinants of fairness in organizations in this chapter, I have attempted to make advances along several important fronts. Given that people frequently cite various elements of social interaction when describing episodes of fair and unfair treatment, the present work sought to provide a useful framework for more precisely understanding the nature of these perceptions. Beyond this, the same conceptual taxonomy promises to be a useful tool for (a) clarifying existing confusion regarding the status of social determinants of justice relative to the prevailing procedural–distributive distinction, and (b) highlighting newly identified justice classes in need of further research attention. Despite several conceptual ambiguities unearthed by the present analyses (which themselves promise to expand the boundaries of conceptual thought about organizational justice), it is clear that the traditional emphasis on the structural determinants of justice has painted a picture of organizational justice that is painfully incomplete. I hope that on the basis of the arguments made in this chapter, the social determinants of justice—that previously have been recognized in an unsystematic fashion—will now be legitimized as a coherent, systematic complement to the structural determinants of both procedural and distributive justice.

ACKNOWLEDGMENTS

I gratefully acknowledge the helpful comments of Robert Bies, Joel Brockner, Russell Cropanzano, and Don Eskew on an earlier draft of this chapter.

REFERENCES

Adams, J. S. (1965). Inequity in social exchange. In L. Berkowitz (Ed). *Advances in experimental social psychology* (Vol. 2, pp. 267–299). New York: Academic Press.

Bandura, A. (1986). *Social foundations of thought and action.* Englewood Cliffs, NJ: Prentice-Hall.

Baron, R. A. (1990). Countering the effects of destructive criticism: The relative efficacy of four interventions. *Journal of Applied Psychology, 75,* 235–245.

Baron, R. M., & Kenny, D. A. (1986). The moderator-mediator variable distinction in social psychological research: Conceptual, strategic, and statistical considerations. *Journal of Personality and Social Psychology, 51,* 1173–1182.

Bies, R. J. (1986, August). Identifying principles of interactional justice: The case of corporate recruiting. In R. J. Bies (Chair), *Moving beyond equity theory: New directions in research on justice in organizations.* Symposium conducted at the meeting of the Academy of Management, Chicago, IL.

Bies, R. J. (1987). The predicament of injustice: The management of moral outrage. In L. L. Cummings & B. M. Staw (Eds.), *Research in organizational behavior* (Vol. 9, pp. 289–319). Greenwich, CT: JAI Press.

Bies, R. J., & Moag, J. S. (1986). Interactional justice: Communication criteria of fairness. In R. J. Lewicki, B. H. Sheppard, & B. H. Bazerman (Eds.), *Research on negotiation in organizations* (Vol. 1, pp. 43–55). Greenwich, CT: JAI Press.

Bies, R. J., & Shapiro, D. L. (1987). Interactional fairness judgments: The influence of causal accounts. *Social Justice Research, 1,* 199–218.

Bies, R. J., & Shapiro, D. L. (1988). Voice and justification: Their influence on procedural fairness judgments. *Academy of Management Journal, 31,* 676–685.

Bies, R. J., Shapiro, D. L., & Cummings, L. L. (1988). Causal accounts and managing organizational conflict: Is it enough to say it's not my fault? *Communication Research, 15,* 381–399.

Brockner, J., & Greenberg, J. (1990). The impact of layoffs on survivors: An organizational justice perspective. In J. Carroll (Ed.), *Applied social psychology and organizational settings* (pp. 45–75). Hillsdale, NJ: Lawrence Erlbaum Associates.

Brockner, J., Konovsky, M., Cooper, R., & Folger, R. (1991). *The interactive effects of procedural justice and outcome negativity on victims and survivors of job loss.* Manuscript submitted for publication.

Cohen, R. L., & Greenberg, J. (1982). The justice concept in social psychology. In J. Greenberg & R. L. Cohen (Eds.), *Equity and justice in social behavior* (pp. 1–41). New York: Academic Press.

Deutsch, M. (1975). Equity, equality, and need: What determines which value will be used as the basis for distributive justice? *Journal of Social Issues, 31*(3), 137–149.

Folger, R., & Bies, R. J. (1989). Managerial responsibilities and procedural justice. *Employee Responsibilities and Rights Journal, 2,* 79–90.

Folger, R., & Greenberg, J. (1985). Procedural justice: An interpretive analysis of personnel systems. In K. Rowland & G. Ferris (Eds.), *Research in personnel and human resources management* (Vol. 3, pp. 141–183). Greenwich, CT: JAI Press.

Folger, R., Rosenfield, D., & Robinson, T. (1983). Relative deprivation and procedural justification. *Journal of Personality and Social Psychology, 45,* 268–273.

Gouldner, A. W. (1960). The norm of reciprocity: A preliminary statement. *American Sociological Review, 25,* 161–179.

Greenberg, J. (1982). Approaching equity and avoiding inequity in groups and organizations. In J. Greenberg & R. L. Cohen (Eds.), *Equity and justice in social behavior* (pp. 389–435). New York: Academic Press.

Greenberg, J. (1983). Overcoming egocentric bias in perceived fairness through self-awareness. *Social Psychology Quarterly, 46,* 152–156.

Greenberg, J. (1984). On the apocryphal nature of inequity distress. In R. Folger (Ed.), *The sense of injustice* (pp. 167–188). New York: Plenum.

Greenberg, J. (1986). Determinants of perceived fairness of performance evaluations. *Journal of Applied Psychology, 71,* 340–342.

Greenberg, J. (1987a). A taxonomy of organizational justice theories. *Academy of Management Review, 12,* 9–22.

Greenberg, J. (1987b). Reactions to procedural injustice in payment distributions: Do the means justify the ends? *Journal of Applied Psychology, 72,* 55–61.

Greenberg, J. (1987c). Using diaries to promote procedural justice in performance appraisals. *Social Justice Research, 1,* 219–234.

Greenberg, J. (1990a). Organizational justice: Yesterday, today, and tomorrow. *Journal of Management, 16,* 399–432.

Greenberg, J. (1990b). Employee theft as a reaction to underpayment inequity: The hidden cost of pay cuts. *Journal of Applied Psychology, 75,* 561–568.

Greenberg, J. (1990c). Looking fair vs. being fair: Managing impressions of organizational justice. In B. M. Staw & L. L. Cummings (Eds.), *Research in organizational behavior* (Vol. 12, pp. 111–157). Greenwich, CT: JAI Press.

Greenberg, J. (1991a). Using explanations to manage impressions of performance appraisal fairness. *Employee Responsibilities and Rights Journal, 4,* 51–60.

Greenberg, J. (1991b). *Using socially fair procedures to facilitate acceptance of a corporate smoking ban.* Manuscript submitted for publication.

Greenberg, J. (1991c). *Social fairness and employees' reactions to layoffs.* Manuscript submitted for publication.

Greenberg, J. (in press). Stealing in the name of justice: Informational and interpersonal moderators of theft reactions to underpayment inequity. *Organizational Behavior and Human Decision Processes.*

Greenberg, J., Bies, R. J., & Eskew, D. E. (1991). Establishing fairness in the eye of the beholder: Managing impressions of organizational justice. In R. Giacalone & P. Rosenfeld (Eds.), *Applied impression management: How image making affects managerial decisions* (pp. 111–132). Newbury Park, CA: Sage.

Greenberg, J., & Cohen, R. L. (1982). Why justice? Normative and instrumental interpretations. In J. Greenberg & R. L. Cohen (Eds.), *Equity and justice in social behavior* (pp. 437–469). New York: Academic Press.

Greenberg, J., Eskew, D. E., & Miles, J. A. (1991, August). *Adherence to participatory norms as a moderator of the fair process effect: When voice does not enhance procedural justice.* Paper presented at the meeting of the Academy of Management, Miami.

Greenberg, J., & Folger, R. (1983). Procedural justice, participation, and the fair process effect in groups and organizations. In P. B. Paulus (Ed.), *Basic group processes* (pp. 235–256). New York: Springer-Verlag.

Greenberg, J., & McCarty, C. (1990). The interpersonal aspects of procedural justice: A new perspective on pay fairness. *Labor Law Journal, 41,* 580–586.

Greenberg, J., & Tyler, T. R. (1987). Why procedural justice in organizations? *Social Justice Research, 1,* 127–142.

Homans, G. C. (1961). *Social behavior: Its elementary forms.* New York: Harcourt, Brace, & World.

Karambayya, R., & Brett, J. M. (1989). Managers handling disputes: Third-party roles and perceptions of fairness. *Academy of Management Journal, 32,* 687–704.

Leung, K., & Li, W. K. (1990). Psychological mechanisms of process control effects. *Journal of Applied Psychology, 75,* 613–620.

Leventhal, G. S. (1976). The distribution of rewards and resources in groups and organizations. In L. Berkowitz, & E. Walster (Eds.), *Advances in experimental social psychology* (Vol. 9, pp. 91–131). New York: Academic Press.

Leventhal, G. S. (1980). What should be done with equity theory? In K. J. Gergen, M. S. Greenberg, & R. H. Willis (Eds.), *Social exchange: Advances in theory and research* (pp. 27–55). New York: Plenum.

Leventhal, G. S., Karuza, J., & Fry, W. R. (1980). Beyond fairness: A theory of allocation preferences. In G. Mikula (Ed.), *Justice and social interaction* (pp. 167–218). New York: Springer-Verlag.

Lind, E. A. (1988, August). *Theoretical controversy in procedural justice: Self-interest and group-volume models of perceived fairness in legal, political, and organizational contexts.* Paper presented at the meeting of the American Psychological Association, Atlanta.

Lind, E. A., Kanfer, R., & Earley, P. C. (1990). Voice, control, and procedural justice: Instrumental and noninstrumental concerns in fairness judgments. *Journal of Personality and Social Psychology, 59,* 952–959.

Lind, E. A., & Tyler, T. (1988). *The social psychology of procedural justice.* New York: Plenum.

Mark, M. M., & Folger, R. (1984). Responses to relative deprivation: A conceptual framework. *Review of Personality and Social Psychology, 5,* 192–218.

Messick, D. M., Bloom, S., Boldizar, J. P., & Samuelson, C. D. (1985). Why we are fairer than others. *Journal of Experimental Social Psychology 21,* 480–500.

Miceli, M. P., & Lane, M. C. (1991). Antecedents of pay satisfaction: A review and extension. In K. Rowland & G. R. Ferris (Eds.), *Research in personnel and human resources management* (Vol. 9, pp. 235–309). Greenwich, CT: JAI Press.

Mikula, G., Petrik, B., & Tanzer, N. (1990). What people regard as unjust: Types and structures of everyday experiences of injustice. *European Journal of Social Psychology, 20,* 133–149.

Miller, C. E., Jackson, P., Mueller, J., & Scherching, C. (1987). Some social psychological effects of group decision rules. *Journal of Personality and Social Psychology, 52,* 325–332.

Neale, M. A., & Bazerman, M. H. (1991). *Cognition and rationality in negotiation.* New York: The Free Press.

Ohbuchi, K., Kameda, M., & Agarie, N. (1989). Apology as aggression control: Its role in mediating appraisal of and response to harm. *Journal of Personality and Social Psychology, 56,* 219–227.

Shapiro, D. L., & Buttner, H. B. (1988, August). *Adequate explanations: What are they, and do they enhance procedural justice under severe outcome circumstances?* Paper presented at the meeting of the Academy of Management, Anaheim, CA.

Sheppard, B. H. & Lewicki, R. J. (1987). Toward general principles of managerial fairness. *Social Justice Research, 1,* 161–176.

Tedeschi, J. T., & Norman, N. (1985). Social power, self-presentation, and the self. In B. R. Schlenker (Ed.), *The self and social life* (pp. 293–322). New York: McGraw-Hill.

Thibaut, J., & Walker, L. (1975). *Procedural justice: A psychological analysis.* Hillsdale, NJ: Lawrence Erlbaum Associates.

Törnblom, K. Y. (in press). The social psychology of distributive justice. In K. Scherer (Ed.), *The nature and administration of justice: Interdisciplinary approaches.* Cambridge, England: Cambridge University Press.

Tyler, T. R. (1986). When does procedural justice matter in organizational settings? In R. J. Lewicki, B. H. Sheppard, & M. H. Bazerman (Eds.), *Research on negotiation in organizations* (Vol. 1, pp. 7–23). Greenwich, CT: JAI Press.

Tyler, T. R. (1987). Conditions leading to value-expressive effects in judgments of procedural justice: A test of four models. *Journal of Personality and Social Psychology, 52,* 333–344.

Tyler, T. R. (1988). What is procedural justice? *Law and Society Review, 22,* 301–335.

Tyler, T. R. (1989). The psychology of procedural justice: A test of the group-value model. *Journal of Personality and Social Psychology, 57,* 830–838.

Tyler, T. R., & Bies, R. J. (1990). Beyond formal procedures: The interpersonal context of procedural justice. In J. Carroll (Ed.), *Advances in applied social psychology: Business settings* (pp. 77–98). Hillsdale, NJ: Lawrence Erlbaum Associates.

Tyler, T. R., & Lind, E. A. (1992). A relational model of authority in groups. In M. Zanna (Ed.), *Advances in experimental social psychology* (Vol. 25). San Diego: Academic Press.

Walker, L., Lind, E. A., & Thibaut, J. (1979). The relation between procedural justice and distributive justice. *Virginia Law Review, 65,* 1401–1420.

HIRING, FIRING, AND EVALUATIONS

5 Self-Appraisal and Fairness in Evaluations

Robert Folger
Tulane University

Debra Lewis
Personnel Decisions, Inc.

Performance appraisals typically engender the same degree of enthusiasm as paying taxes. Appraisal review sessions can cause stress for both the employee being appraised and the manager doing the appraising. Often this level of discomfort on both sides means that only a perfunctory discussion takes place (viz., one that goes through the motions of appraisal without ever addressing substantive issues such as areas of disagreement). Indeed, employees sometimes report that no actual session ever took place, despite a manager's record of having conducted one. Such reports occur with enough frequency that some performance appraisal specialists describe the phenomenon as "the invisible performance appraisal."

Although people giving and receiving performance feedback may find the prospects daunting and the sessions themselves uncomfortable, performance appraisals can yield information central to human resources management. This chapter focuses on performance appraisal ratings as input to administrative decisions that govern the allocation of important organizational rewards (e.g., pay and promotions). Certainly other purposes of appraisal can be important. By providing feedback, for example, ratings can contribute to motivational, developmental, and "coaching" purposes. We instead restrict our attention to the use of self-appraisal (SA) for administrative purposes. As a form of input to administrative decision making, SA offers some promise for increasing the acceptability and perceived fairness of decisions.

This focus may sound like a waste of time to those who hold what seems to be the conventional wisdom—namely that using SAs for administrative purposes could not be more wrongheaded. As just one recent example, Campbell and Lee (1988) argued strongly against the use of SAs for anything other than developmental purposes. Most such arguments against SA for administrative purposes stem from suggestions that employee ratings may be inflated and hence may lead to leniency in supervisory ratings. We review arguments and counterarguments on that issue in the first section of this chapter.

That review identifies a justification for investigating how SAs might be used to make administrative decisions about organizational rewards. Additional arguments have been discussed in more detail elsewhere (Folger, Konovsky, & Cropanzano, in press). Our underlying rationale examines the costs and benefits associated with using SA. Rather than denying that some inflation might occur, we consider it a potential cost that might, under at least some circumstances, be outweighed by potential benefits associated with SA. Key to this cost–benefit form of analysis, the work of Thibaut and Walker on procedural justice (1975) suggests that many potential advantages of SA would stem from the manner in which it enhances perceptions of fairness regarding the appraisal system. Most notably, SA ratings represent a form of employee "voice" (cf. Folger, 1977). Much research has shown that numerous benefits flow from the manner in which voice enhances the perceived fairness of procedures (Folger & Greenberg, 1985). We review this fairness-based perspective on SAs after having first addressed the leniency issue and finding some other potential benefits to SA in addition to enhanced fairness.

Another fundamental reason for pursuing research on this topic stems from gaps in existing research. The study of SA ratings that inform administrative decisions, a topic of at least some theoretical interest, suffers as much from sheer neglect as from derision (cf. Roberson, Torkel, Klein, Korsgaard, & Diddams, 1989); we believe that the present state of affairs may reflect premature abandonment of issues to which very little empirical work has actually been directed. For that reason, we describe results from a research study centered on the potential advantages of using SAs as part of the evidence gathered to make administrative decisions. We do not deny that some aspects of thereby using SAs may prove problematic. Research on the more problematic aspects could languish, however, unless other findings provide evidence for at least some positive effects in the first place. Our study extends previous documentation in that regard.

Consistent with the theme of calling for more research, an additional section of the chapter deals with what remains unknown in this area. In particular, our investigation examined only one of several possible ways that SAs can be conducted. Consideration of some other possibilities helps point out the extent of the need for further investigations.

THE DEBATE JOINED: WHY BOTHER
TO SELF-APPRAISE?

For administrative rather than developmental purposes, why bother to collect SA data (e.g., by having employees rate themselves on the same BARS—behaviorally anchored rating scales—scales that their managers use as a precursor to assigning rewards based on merit)? In variants of pay-for-performance or other putatively meritocratic systems, for example, a manager's responsibilities often include rating employee performance and basing administrative decisions about pay raises on those ratings. What basis could there be for allowing employee self-ratings to influence the manager's decisions, thereby in effect allowing an employee to take part in determining his or her own pay? Surely anyone can predict in advance that such a method would only yield inflated ratings; after all, the use of self-ratings as input to pay-determining procedures gives employees a means of seeking maximum earnings by trying to gain management acceptance for the best possible rating. Some empirical evidence is consistent with that assumption (e.g., Mabe & West, 1982; Meyer, 1980; Thornton, 1980).

Campbell and Lee (1988) for the Orthodox Position

Campbell and Lee (1988) drew exactly that type of pessimistic conclusion based on one of the most recent reviews of the SA literature: "research aimed at finding some types of individuals . . . for whom self-appraisals can be used evaluatively seems to have little chance of success. . . . the above analysis suggests that, as evaluation devices, SAs will have only limited usefulness" (p. 307). Campbell and Lee argued that because of inevitable bias in SAs, managers should not use employee SAs for evaluative purposes as data on which to base administrative decisions; instead, the recommended procedure would prohibit all forms of SA except in exclusively developmental sessions stripped of any evaluative connotations. Although Campbell and Lee are not the only authors to adopt this line of reasoning, we focus on their arguments as both recent enough to reflect current developments and representative enough to reflect the state of orthodoxy in I/O psychology.

We find their conclusion unrealistic and strange, especially because employees obviously will engage in self-evaluation when management evaluation of their performance determines pay (i.e., they quite naturally will compare their own evaluation with management's). Certainly no separation of evaluation from development, nor special type of developmental session focused only on future behavior, could prevent employees from forming an opinion regarding whether pay they received reflected a proper evaluation. Restated, however, the Campbell and Lee line of reasoning in effect implies that when evaluating employees for the purposes of determining merit-based pay, a manager should disregard employees' opinions about the fairness of the determination—because that opinion about fairness would inevitably derive from self-evaluation (SA), which has no place in management's evaluation of employees. If a female employee, for example, believes that her performance deserves a higher rating than the supervisor gave, she has in effect made a judgment of unfairness based on comparison of the supervisory rating with her own informal SA rating (a mental reference point that exists whether or not she has a chance to express it or record it as a public rating).

Carried to its logical extreme, the argument implies that no session for discussion of evaluations need be conducted, which matches the practice of companies where employees learn about pay raises only when a different amount shows up in their paychecks. The argument, in fact, suggests that sessions for discussing evaluations should not be conducted, lest employees use those occasions for expressing their opinions about their performance (SAs). After all, the danger exists that a manager who learned of an employee's opinion in such a session might accidentally be influenced—a danger to be avoided at all costs because it would amount to influence from an inevitably biased source.

That characterization of Campbell and Lee's position exaggerates for the sake of effect but also raises questions about the assumptions on which their arguments rest. At the start of their discussion of SA as an evaluation tool, for example, they noted two possible evaluative uses of SA—for assessing intersource reliability and for addressing potential criterion deficiency. They pointed out that "intersource reliability can be considered a precondition for evaluation validity," with the consequence that "serious disagreement among sources raises fundamental concerns about the evaluation process as a whole" (p. 302). This first potential use of SAs for evaluative purposes requires a reasonable correlation between management and employee ratings; too great a discrepancy calls for abandoning any reliance on SAs.

Notice, however, that such an argument somewhat arbitrarily jumps to conclusions while suffering from a lack of internal consistency (reliability!) itself. The conclusion stems from an assumption—implicit here, but subsequently made explicit—that when management and labor disagree about labor's effectiveness, management must be right. Normally, however, disagreement between two sources implies that either source might be incorrect. The argument's inconsistency, moreover, comes from ignoring its own advice: If serious disagreement raises fundamental concerns about the process as a whole, then why ignore those concerns by simply using management evaluations as the default source of truth?

Related questions can be raised about Campbell and Lee's discussion of the second possible use of SAs in an evaluation system, namely for reducing criterion deficiency otherwise undiminished because available information sources do not all tap all the relevant performance dimensions (i.e., inadequate domain sampling). SA might, they acknowledge, provide "performance information that is either not obtained or impossible to obtain through other channels" (p. 302). Nonetheless, they dismiss that option as moot because of "the possibility that systematically biased SAs might reduce evaluation effectiveness, if they introduced more contamination than they decreased deficiency" (p. 303). The former possibility seemed to them more probable based on the empirical evidence they reviewed, which indicated to them that "the likelihood of systematic bias appears high"—a conclusion in turn based on the following observation: "Relative to supervisory evaluations, SAs suffer from inflation . . . and restriction of range. It is reasonable to assume that SAs used as complementary devices would reflect these same limitations, if supervisory evaluations were available for comparison" (p. 303).

Again the argument hinges on presuming the validity of one standard (a supervisor's) rather than another (an employee's), however, and Campbell and Lee explicitly acknowledged having chosen sides in that fashion: "because most organizations using supervisory ratings assume that such evaluations adequately capture true performance, that convention is maintained here" (p. 303). An even more subtle sign of adopting a management perspective by default appears in their Figure 1, a diagram showing the relationship between self- and supervisor's appraisal process. Three parallel columns of boxes display sources influencing ratings: a middle column labeled *distorting influences,* and columns on either side for employee and supervisor. The top row reflects cognitions about job requirements, and the middle box refers to the distorting influence of informational constraints. Although the diagram remains neutral in all other respects, here the underlying assumption intrudes dramatically. Arrows from the center box stretch out identically in both directions—pointing both to supervisor and employee, thereby implying that both might suffer from constraints on the information available to them. The rest of the label inside that box (after "informational constraints"), however, refers to "incorrect job perceptions *relative to manager*" (p. 304, italics added). The very theoretical framework itself, therefore, subtly reinforces assumptions about the priority of the supervisor's views.

Even granting by fiat the absence of supervisor error, this type of orientation has problematic consequences in practice, as implied by evidence that Campbell and Lee themselves reviewed. Referring to the role ambiguity literature, they mentioned its "strong evidence that employees often do not have a clear idea of what their supervisors expect" and that "the typical performance appraisal may not reduce ambiguity" (p. 304). If the supervisor has the best possible ideas about what behaviors maximize effectiveness, and the employee does not have a clue without advice from the supervisor, then obviously—taking this extreme case as the most dramatically consistent with Campbell and Lee's viewpoint— the employee will have maintained incorrect job perceptions during the period prior to evaluation. The hidden assumption that would have to be valid to make the supervisor's low evaluation of the employee correct, however, is that the employee is 100% guilty for his or her ignorance and the supervisor is 100% blameless. All supervisors who communicate perfectly, only to be cursed by employees with deaf ears, will fit this description fine; others (the rest of the real world), not so well.

Campbell and Lee did admit that constraints on information "also can reflect shortcomings in the supervisor's understanding of the employee's job" (p. 305) and cite Mitchell (1983) in that regard. Interestingly enough, they mention only two examples, and one concerned supervisors who have come from another company and as a result—presumably for only a short time—might have some inaccurate or incomplete impressions. The other example pertains to interdependent jobs where separating out individual contributions might be difficult. By implication, lack of proper knowledge by supervisors seems to be rare and limited to the occurrence of unusual circumstances. Yet elsewhere they admitted that supervisor misunderstanding can occur because of inadequate observation (e.g., Kane & Lawler, 1979; Wexley & Klimoski, 1984) and because of extensive manager responsibilities (Borman, 1978; Mintzberg, 1973).

They also acknowledged such potential sources of distortion in supervisor judgment as confirmation biases and the overly person-centered or trait-oriented impressions due to actor/observer biases. They placed greater emphasis on the self-serving bias that can inflate SAs, however, citing past research (e.g., Meyer, 1980; Shrauger & Osberg, 1981; Thornton, 1980; Tsui & Barry, 1986) that SAs can thereby create leniency by the supervisor. Their primary rationale for adopting that stance was the following citation: "Significantly, Shrauger and Osberg (1981) found that deliberate dishonesty is more likely to occur when SAs are used for decisions involving the allocation of scarce resources—a typical implication for SAs used evaluatively" (p. 307). That quotation, however, seriously misrepresents Shrauger and Osberg's literature review, which concluded that "self-assessments are at least as predictive of . . . [various] criteria as are other assessment methods against which they have been pitted" (p. 322). The relevant passage by Shrauger and Osberg (1981) actually reads as follows:

> Aside from the implicit assumption that people are not competent to evaluate their own behavior, suspicion regarding self-predictions stems mainly from the concern that people are not motivated to be candid in their self-appraisals. Skepticism runs particularly high in situations involving the allocation of scarce resources, such as jobs or admission to professional training. It is assumed that when the motivation for such resources is great, the predictive accuracy of self-reports relative to other criteria would be low. (p. 347)

Clearly this passage refers only to "suspicion" and "skepticism," and motives that might be "assumed"—not empirical evidence.

In point of fact, Shrauger and Osberg stated that "relevant data regarding that assumption are limited" (p. 347). They went on to note that although deliberate faking instructions have yielded unpredictive SAs "those obtained in situations designed to make candid responses potentially costly have still been more accurate than other predictors" (Shrauger & Osberg, 1981, p. 347). Their most fundamental conclusion was as follows: "When assessment is at least in part for the benefit of the person assessed, as it should usually be in applied settings, the need for dissimulation may be minimized" (p. 347). By contrast, Campbell and Lee (1988) concluded that the findings from the literature "suggest that employee self-appraisals may be distorted unconsciously. . . . we might expect individuals to deal with instances of poor performance by denying the events, by attributing the causes of performance to other sources, or by labeling such events as atypical" (p. 306).

Staw (1983; Staw & Boettger, 1990)
for Unorthodoxy (Heresy?)

The motto of the orthodox position, of which Campbell and Lee's review is only one recent example, might be as follows: When in doubt, management wins out. Moreover, a certain air of management paternalism characterizes the orthodox orientation. An advocate of orthodoxy might well be aghast at examples such as the rating-by-pay-envelope illustration, for example, insisting that appraisal specialists already recognize as sound practice the desirability of informing employees about the manner in which supervisors determine ratings—and of allowing employees a chance to question the results. In fact, we got exactly that reaction from a reader not associated with this volume, who shall go nameless. Yet that same person went on to insist, rather paradoxically, that we should recognize each of the following: (a) the need for an organization's authority structure; (b) the value of maintaining the power and responsibility of higher levels to pass judgment on lower levels; and (c) the benefit to preventing disputes, and hence the obligation not to encourage employees to dispute management's judgments. The paradox, of course, comes from the juxtaposition of that last advice (discourage questioning management judgment) with the earlier remark that obviously employees should be granted an opportunity to question the results of the ratings they receive from a supervisor.

Thus once again certain inconsistencies seem to stem from a staunch defence of the status quo views that recommend against using SAs as input to evaluations. Alternative views, for which we use work by Staw (1983; Staw & Boettger, 1990) as a representative example, suggest instead that management authority can be questioned without endangering the organization. As a matter of fact, Staw's line of reasoning finds merit in constructive criticism that emerges from lower levels. Such critiques, Staw has argued, can even be vital to the health and well-being of the organization.

Part of the basis for this alternative perspective comes from Katz and Kahn's (1966) warning about the dangers of an organization's relying "solely upon its blueprint of prescribed behavior"; inflexible prescriptions do not allow sufficiently for operating contingencies and fail to anticipate perfectly the nature of changes in the organization's environment. Some behaviors not prescribed by a firm's current directives, therefore, might actually be more functional than some of the behaviors that the firm has prescribed. Currently prescribed behaviors get institutionalized (possibly rigidified) not only because of outdated job descriptions, but also because of outdated performance evaluation forms.

Staw and Boettger (1990) took that warning to heart and examined the consequences of meeting or exceeding the standards for role behavior in a job (the equivalent of rating categories on an evaluation form). In addition to extrarole behavior that goes beyond expectations, they identified the category of "counterrole" actions in terms of behavior that differs from expectations. These behaviors "are part of neither a formal job description nor management's likely conception of the ideal employee," including some "neither anticipated nor seen as desirable by existing management"; also included are "quiet changes that people may introduce to revise or redirect their work roles" (p. 535). Clearly, at least some behaviors that differ from expectations in these ways will cause the supervisor's ratings of an employee to differ from the employee's. The construct of counter-role behaviors thus identifies another possible reason—overlooked by the orthodox view—for a difference between SA and supervisory ratings.

More importantly, Staw and Boettger questioned the orthodox view's presumptive capitulation to management by default when ratings differ. They pointed out that "standard role behavior—what most practitioners and researchers consider to be good performance—may not be so functional when roles are incorrectly specified" and demonstrated such effects in an empirical study. As they put it, "a worker who goes beyond the call of duty to accomplish a misconceived job may actually be more dangerous to an organization than a more mundane performer" (p. 537). In addition, they argued that the potential usefulness of counter-role behaviors pertains not only to the short term, when roles are misspecified, but also "as an investment toward longer-run adaptiveness, when current specifications . . . may no longer be applicable" (p. 537; see also Nemeth & Staw, 1989).

Among possible counter-role behaviors relevant to discrepancies between SAs and supervisor ratings of employees, one stands out in particular—the category to which Staw and Boettger refer as *task revision*, or "taking action to correct a faulty procedure, inaccurate job description, or dysfunctional role expectation" (p. 537). Of course, the very notion that a job description could be inaccurate or a task in need of revision runs counter to the orthodox perspective. Staw and Boettger, however, prefer heresy: "what supervisors or higher management desire may be dysfunctional or incorrect from a broader organizational perspective" (p. 555). The full extent of their heretical views has been aptly expressed in the following terms:

> Except on very simple tasks, where the path for correct behavior is self-evident, it is often unclear where the optimal direction of behavior lies. Thus, the notion that goals need to be 'correctly' specified is based on the fundamental assumption of hierarchical and prescient knowledge—that those in command know best where efforts should be placed. The rub . . . is that such confidently prescribed behavior may . . . be in error, since workers can often know more than a supervisor about the proper course of action (Mechanic, 1962), and because behavior . . . thought to be optimal may in fact be dysfunctional for longer-run effectiveness (Katz & Kahn, 1978). (p. 548)

Our views are similarly those of the heretics, as can be seen in a related line of reasoning expressed elsewhere (Folger et al., 1992).

We have framed these issues as a debate between orthodoxy and heresy, and in fact we were virtually accused of heresy by the anonymous reader mentioned earlier. Surprisingly, however, some of Campbell and Lee's comments can be re-interpreted as consistent with a more heretical point of view. Their recognition of increased content validity as a second use for SAs (other than intersource reliability), for example, acknowledged that SAs might diminish criterion deficiency if the employees' own ratings incorporated performance dimensions other than those identified by alternative evaluation sources (sources that SA data complement rather than merely confirm).

Campbell and Lee (1988) appear to have had in mind alternative sources other than supervisory ratings (e.g., non-rating data such as sales, capturing some aspects of performance yet nonetheless possibly deficient with respect to more intangible aspects of the job). As noted earlier, they expressed the opinion that SAs as complementary devices would show inflation and range restriction relative to supervisory ratings if the latter were available as a yardstick for assessing such tendencies. Their assumption seems to have been that SAs would presumably have had little or no use as complements to other sources unless the latter excluded supervisory ratings. Using sales data alone might suffer from criterion contamination if differences in territories and other external influences intruded, or might suffer from deficiency if service quality and behaviors enhancing customer satisfaction (and promoting repeat sales in the long run) did not also get taken into account. The lack of supervisory ratings in such cases could reasonably call for SAs as a proxy.

Our less orthodox re-interpretation of Campbell and Lee's comments, however, argues that SAs can diminish criterion deficiency (i.e., aid content validity) even when supervisory ratings are also in use. This possibility emerges directly from the Staw and Boettger analysis of task revisions as a counter-role behavior. Employees who revise their tasks out of concern for the organization's well-being may improve its effectiveness more than if they had performed only according to the supervisor's role expectations for them. Because the supervisor's ratings stem from those official role prescriptions, they constitute the greater source of criterion deficiency (not sufficiently tapping effectiveness dimensions), whereas the employee's actions—and hence perhaps the employee's own self-ratings—have greater validity.

Staw (1983) provided even more general lines of argument supporting such alternatives to orthodoxy. As he put it, "Too often . . . it is simply assumed that a set of evaluation procedures are effective once they are in place" (p. 37). Assuming that accurate performance ratings yield greater organizational effectiveness, Staw has pointed out, actually involves two different types of implicit theories: theories of individual performance, and theories of organizational effectiveness. The latter refers to aggregate assessments of organizational well-being as criteria; procedures at the organizational level are designed to embody features that will make them successful predictors of those aggregate criteria, given the correctness of the adopted implicit theory about causal relations between predictors and criteria. Thus the theory-in-use at this level assumes that proper value can be placed on particular ends (despite possible conflicting interests among constituencies) and that the organization possesses sufficient knowledge about the means to those ends (despite uncertainties associated with changing environments and technology).

Similarly at the individual level, employee behavior guided by organizational procedures should predict individual work products:

> Organizations, for example, prefer to reward people who complete their work accurately, produce more than others, help their co-workers, and exhibit some enthusiasm for the organization. Implicitly we have assumed that these factors are positive contributors to subunit, departmental, and organizational performance.

Unfortunately, implicit theories of performance can be incorrect, and seemingly positive behaviors can have negative effects. Workers turning out high quantities of products, for example, may do so only by means of excessively costly methods, or by creating inordinate amounts of scrap in the process, or by producing inferior quality work, or by endangering safety. Staw made an even harsher observation: "In fact, when we look at major organizational disasters, we often find highly motivated, well-monitored, and direct behavior—all moving in concert toward a corporate collapse" (p. 36).

Despite predictive problems betraying a lack of adequate understanding at both levels of implicit theory, "we may be more willing to recognize the vagaries of our theories of organizational effectiveness . . . than we are of our theories of individual performance" (p. 32). That statement provides one possible explanation for the deference to authority shown by the orthodox position, along with the recommendation of avoiding SAs for administrative purposes; such a practice might cause employees to call into question aspects of accepted practices and the organization's conventional wisdom about the best way to perform jobs. The advocates of orthodoxy, as well as practicing managers, may not realize the extent to which implicit theories of individual performance guide assumptions about the adequacy of rating scales. In addition, they may tend not to recognize how potentially problematic those theories are, even if they do realize that implicit theories are operating. The more the underlying theories are taken for granted and assumed correct, the greater the tendency to discount the value of having them questionned by employees with SAs discrepant from supervisory ratings.

Staw contended that we as organizational scientists "are more often surprised to learn that these simple assumptions can be wrong" (p. 32), so we can hardly blame others for not seeing the value of their assumptions' being questioned. Nonetheless, Staw (1983, p. 32) provided several ready examples of empirical data contradicting the commonly held assumptions embodied in most theories of individual performance: "More work sometimes causes bottlenecks (Weick, 1974); effort in the wrong direction can be worse than no effort at all (Kerr,

1975); absenteeism and turnover can have some positive as well as negative consequences" (Staw & Oldham, 1978)." Thus, some behaviors might look bad to supervisors and lead to low ratings of an employee's performance, when the employee's contribution to the firm's well-being was actually positive and deserving of high ratings. That scenario would entail the largest possible discrepancies between SAs and supervisory ratings, yet the SAs would be more accurate from the perspective of performance efficacy. Systems that did not permit SAs would thereby miss valuable information.

Differences between SAs and supervisor ratings are to be expected; the need for recognizing and understanding why and how employees may interpret their contributions from a different perspective than management's is a reason for encouraging supervisors to collect SA data and to discuss discrepancies in viewpoints. This need is especially critical when it is realized that such discrepancies may reflect something other than the lack of inter-rater reliability based on multiple sources' observations regarding the same object of judgment. An emphasis on reliability assumes implicitly that the object of judgment is the employee's *behavior* (as evidenced by the amount of attention in the PA literature dedicated to various behaviorally based rating systems). For the purpose of compensation and other reward-allocation decisions based on merit, however, the ultimate criterion is the individual employee's relative *performance contribution* to the effective functioning of the organization.

Closer examination of this performance criterion goes to the heart of a validity issue that Campbell and Lee (1988) pass over lightly in deferring to managers' judgments. Differences between supervisors' and subordinates' assessment ratings may reflect not so much different opinions about the individual employee's behavior, but the application of differential evaluative *weights* to various performance components. In turn, these weights may reflect differing viewpoints about what constitutes valid effectiveness. This point, along with Staw's analysis of counter-role behavior, task revision, and implicit theories of individual performance, sheds new light on the way that SAs can provide information relevant to reducing criterion deficiency.

Research by Schmitt, Noe, and Gottschalk (1986) illustrates this point's relevance. They compared school administrators' SAs with ratings by teachers and by the administrators' immediate supervisors. The ratings involved 15 dimensions on a behaviorally anchored rating scale and each person also made an overall performance rating. Regressions of these overall ratings on BARS scores showed significant differences among regression coefficients from all three sets of raters. In particular, Schmitt et al. noted the following tendencies: "The ratees [administrators] themselves seemed to most heavily weight efforts directed at curriculum, student progress, fiscal matters, and district–school coordination problems. Supervisors' overall judgments were most related to judgments of ratees' efforts to direct support services and student behavior, and to structure communication" (p. 135). The conclusion was that the raters were differentially "weighting those dimensions that would seem most salient to them" (p. 135).

With each group finding different aspects of the job to be relevant, the likelihood of criterion deficiency under such circumstances would be relatively high if decisions were based on ratings from only a single source. We suspect that this example illustrates a common workplace phenomenon, the probable occurrence of which should increase the higher the level of the position within the organizational hierarchy. As such, it also illustrates yet another reason for obtaining SAs and encouraging a discussion about differences of opinion between supervisor and employee.

Fairness as an Added Perspective

Elsewhere (Folger et al., in press), the previous discussion has been expanded to include a number of other considerations. Here we add only the several strands of argument related to the common theme of fairness. That SAs may reduce criterion deficiency, for example, can be rephrased as indicating SAs' contribution to distributive justice—fairness issues concerning the outcome of a decision. Where the outcome of performance appraisal involves the distribution of organizational rewards, then a more comprehensive criterion provides a fairer assessment of a person's contribution to the organization (cf. Greenberg, 1986b). Thus the procedure used—SAs incorporated as input to decisions about final performance appraisal ratings—serves as a means to a just end, namely the fair distribution of rewards among employees. This fairness perspective complements the perspective derived from Staw's arguments about the inherent incompleteness of unchallenged implicit theories of performance. Staw's arguments suggested that SAs might serve as a means to improving the well-being of the firm, especially its long-term capacity for innovation and adaptive performance (see also Bernardin & Beatty, 1984; Carroll & Schneier, 1982; Latham & Wexley, 1981). Here we merely point out that the same arguments apply equally well regarding SAs as a means to fair outcomes for employees.

SAs also have been hypothesized to increase the extent to which employees participate in the appraisal discussion (e.g., Burke, Weitzel, & Weir, 1978; Farh, Werbel, & Bediean, 1988; Latham & Wexley, 1981), and participation as a form of voice enhances the perception of procedural justice as the fairness of decision-making processes (cf. Folger & Greenberg, 1985). Within organizational contexts, for example, the benefits of process fairness have been demonstrated in terms of reactions both to pay raises (Folger & Konovsky, 1989), and to pay cuts (Greenberg, 1990). Additional findings have shown organizational advantages with respect to not only the survivors of layoffs but also the victims (Folger, Konovsky, & Brockner, 1990).

Those results have shown effects on various attitudinal measures, including organizational commitment. Other results have extended the evidence to the realm of organizational citizenship behaviors (Konovsky & Folger, 1991). Furthermore, experimental investigations have demonstrated related procedural justice effects under conditions where cause-and-effect inferences can be made with greater confidence (e.g., Cropanzano & Folger, 1989; Greenberg, 1987a; for a review, see Lind & Tyler, 1988). In addition, studies in the performance appraisal context show additional information consistent with the premise that participation enhances perceived fairness (e.g., Greenberg, 1986a, 1987b; Landy, Barnes-Farrell, & Cleveland, 1980).

Given the number of supportive studies and amount of indirect evidence, it is surprising to find so little systematic investigation of different kinds of methods for implementing SAs when they are used to determine pay raises. Both Bernardin and Beatty (1984) and Teel (1978) described a system whereby both supervisors and subordinates make independent assessments of performance, for example, but empirical studies of that system's effects were not cited. In the following section we provide some preliminary, small-scale evidence about the effects of a modification on such a system.

AN ILLUSTRATIVE STUDY

We took advantage of a unique opportunity to study a self-appraisal system in action. A chain of thrift stores allowed us to implement such a system in half of their stores, located in a South-Central metropolitan area and also in a number of the surrounding communities and towns. Although officially operating on a not-for-profit basis, this branch in fact has maintained a thriving business. The president of this local branch had consistently pursued a meritocratic philosophy (e.g., bonuses for superior performance). Within that context, therefore, employees had been told that performance appraisal ratings would be used for determining pay raises.

Working with management, we designed one particular way of incorporating self-appraisal ratings into the decision-making process. The following excerpts from a letter describing the review process to employees in advance (where *x*s replace the name of the head manager to whom the employees' store managers reported) indicate the sequence of events that accompanied self-appraisal in those randomly selected stores that implemented the new system:

1. Complete the attached performance review as indicated.

2. After you complete this form, give it to your manager.

3. Your manager will then review your evaluation of your performance, rate your performance, and add comments where appropriate.

4. Your manager will then review her ratings with *xxx*.

5. Your manager will then meet with you before [a specified date] to discuss the performance review. This meeting will allow both you and your manager to discuss the reasons for the ratings given.

6. Your manager will then forward the performance review to *xxx* for her review, comment, and signature.

Note a prominent feature of this system consistent with Thibaut and Walker's (1975) emphasis on the distinction between "process control" and "decision control": (a) Just as a civil dispute hearing allows voice by disputants during the *process* of evidence presentation and argument, this system for incorporating employee self-appraisal allows employees to voice their opinions about the "evidence" regarding their performance—both in the form of the self-appraisal ratings that they submit to their own store manager, and in the form of opportunities available during the performance review discussion. (b) Despite such "process control" by employees, the ultimate "decision control" resides with management (in this case, the final ratings being jointly determined by the store manager and the store managers' boss, xxx).

Data were gathered from employees (all female except one) of the nine retail stores in the local region of this thrift chain. All employees participated, making a total of 9 managers (who provided supplemental data) and 59 subordinates; the latter number was reduced to 40 for the respondents from whom we obtained complete data over time. The average employee was 43.5 years old, educated 11.2 years, and employed by the company for 31.9 months.

Pre-Appraisal Measures and Appraisal Ratings

In a pre/post fashion, one set of measures was taken prior to the manipulation that randomly (subject to sales volume equivalence) divided the stores into a group using traditional appraisal (TA) and a group using SA. A pretest of attitudes, administered to employees, surveyed responses to items on trust, job satisfaction, and the extent of voice. The voice items were developed by Folger and Konovsky (1989) as part of a 26-item set designed to measure components of procedural justice. The commitment items represent the short form of the Organizational Commitment Questionnaire developed by Mowday, Steers, and Porter (1979). The trust items represent a scale developed by Roberts and O'Reilly (1974) to assess employees' trust in their supervisors.

Additionally, the store managers responded to Organizational Citizenship Behavior (OCB) materials developed by Konovsky (1986); 10 items from a "diligence" factor were deemed best suited and were modified to fit this particular population. Modifications regarding the wording of the statements are recommended contingent upon the type of work being performed (Organ, 1988).

After these pre-measures had been obtained, store managers were trained on either of two methods of performance appraisal—TA (a review of traditional practices) and SA (similar material slightly condensed, with additional instructions about the new procedure and its rationale). At the conclusion of the appraisal training session, the managers were instructed to rate each of their employees. The instructions urged the managers to give valid ratings, but they were told the ratings were "for research purposes only" and that they did not need to adhere to these ratings during the formal appraisal process. The managers were allowed to keep a copy of these ratings.

The primary purpose of annual performance appraisals in these stores was to determine the amount of a forthcoming annual pay raise. The performance appraisal process began within a week of the training session. Each manager left with a form letter to each employee, which stated that the performance appraisal process was beginning and that outlined the steps involved. In addition to the letter, those in the self-appraisal group received the appraisal form, a slight modification of the form currently in use by the organization.

The TA method generated one overall rating from the average of sub-items on a performance appraisal form, whereas the SA method generated two in each case (one from the manager and one from the employee). In the SA group, an appraisal agreement score was computed as the subordinate's overall averaged rating minus the manager's overall averaged rating. To measure the extent of discrepancy between subordinate and supervisor, the number of discrepant ratings, as well as the magnitude of these discrepancies, were recorded.

Post-Appraisal Measures

Within 1 to 3 weeks following all performance appraisals, a Performance Evaluation Questionnaire (PEQ) was administered to capture employees' perceptions of the appraisal process. These PEQ items were partially adopted from the questionnaire employed by Roberson et al. (1989). Roberson et al.'s questionnaire items were taken from existing scales or items were developed for their research. An exploratory factor analysis by Roberson et al. produced the following subscales: contribution, influence, feedback, goalsetting, understanding, acceptance, agreement/fairness, and job responsibilities. In addition to the items that loaded on these subscales, another scale, respect (Greller, 1978), was also included. Also, items referring to potential specific constraints on performance were modified from Bernardin (1989) by meeting with a subject matter expert (the head manager of all the stores).

Four items measured the manager's satisfaction with, and perceptions of usefulness of, the appraisal process (adapted from Roberson et al., 1989). Managers responded to this form at the same time their employees responded to the survey performance appraisal questionnaire.

Further post-appraisal measures involved re-administering the employee attitude survey and the supervisory ratings of employee OCBs, which occurred about 12–15 weeks after the first wave. An additional scale added to the attitude survey included four items assessing employees' response to the outcomes (pay raise) of the performance appraisal—the 'satisfaction with the pay system' (pay raise) scale on Heneman's (1989) Pay Satisfaction Questionnaire.

Results and Discussion

We can summarize quickly a conclusive amount of overwhelming support regarding the positive effects of self-appraisal on reported perceptions about the appraisal discussion (for further details, see Lewis, 1990): Despite the small sample size, every discussion-related measure differed significantly such that the self-appraisal group displayed more positive reactions than the traditional group. The reactions from the two groups differed dramatically.

The remarkably positive results from those measures do not entirely coincide with the findings from the second post-appraisal questionnaire. Here self-appraisal had much less impact. In particular, only one measure—Trust—clearly surpassed the conventional .05 level, although our Organizational Citizenship Behavior measure came close (i.e., within rounding to hundreths). Those results came from an analysis of the posttest scores only, however, whereas a pre/post X self/traditional ANOVA revealed no significant effects. We thus conclude that immediately favorable ratings of the appraisal discussion itself tended not to have much carry-over impact with respect to a change in the time span and scope of dependent measures. Whereas SAs yielded positive results (i.e., more favorable employee attitudes) when employees responded within a short time after the appraisal review (1–3 weeks) and rated aspects of the discussion itself, little if any enhanced favorability appeared when employees responded some time later (12–15 weeks) and expressed their feelings regarding more general issues (voice, trust, and commitment).

Such results should not come as a great surprise nor constitute a serious criticism of self-appraisal. Primarily these findings demonstrate once again that a single intervention in one organizational subsystem (evaluation and reward) does not necessarily induce a profound or wholesale change in employee attitudes across the board. Moreover, our small sample probably precluded detecting any broad-range and temporally stable effects.

We sought to explore the nature of the results further by administering yet another questionnaire within a month after the last survey. It contained items used for two purposes: (a) To assess whether variations in employees' ease or anxiety during the review discussion might be associated with the other responses they reported, we administered a five-item Comfort index (e.g., "In general, how comfortable were you with the appraisal discussion?"). (b) To assess whether other responses might be associated with the perceived fairness of the raise that an employee received, we administered a two-item Raise Fairness scale. The first item of this latter index asked "How fair was your raise?" (with a 5-point, "very unfair" to "very fair," response scale). The second item asked "How acceptable was your raise when you compare it to your work performance?" (with a 5-point scale indicating levels that ranged from "very unacceptable" to "very acceptable").

Initially we examined the scores from both appraisal groups on each of these two new indices. The Comfort index yielded results showing that self-appraisal employees ($M = 19.1$) felt more comfortable with their review discussions than did traditionally appraised employees ($M = 13.6$), $p < .0001$. On the other hand, the Raise Fairness index produced corresponding scores ($M = 4.5$ vs. $M = 3.9$ for self appraisal vs. traditional, respectively) that did not differ significantly from one another, $p > .38$.

We also examined data from those new measures along with data from the previous survey. These further analyses involved using multiple regression to determine whether either of the new indices (Comfort or Raise Fairness) contributed uniquely to the variance in the prior survey's measures. One set of regression equations revealed that within the SA group alone, the inclusion of Comfort and Fairness as predictors contributed no variance to results from any of the third-wave measures over and above the variance contributed by respondents' pretest scores on those measures. Results from the corresponding set of regression equations within the TA group, however, showed that the Raise Fairness index contributed significantly to voice, trust, and organizational commitment ($p < .01$ in each case).

Those results indicate that to the extent traditionally appraised employees considered their raises to be fair, they also endorsed responses expressing certain types of opinions, emotions, and perceptions: namely, that the company generally gave them a voice, that they could trust their supervisors, and that they felt committed to the organization. No causal directionality can be determined, of course, so we cannot say whether TA employees allowed their thoughts and feelings about voice, trust, and commitment (which conceivably might be relatively stable) to influence their perceptions about the fairness of their raises. Nor can we know whether the reverse causal influence predominated instead, such that perceived raise fairness influenced responses to voice, trust, and commitment. Regardless whether either of those directional paths of causal influence (or joint influence by an unknown third cause) operated within the TA group, however, the results show that no such tendencies operated within the SA group.

We speculate that the introduction of SA may in some sense weaken or even tend to sever possible links between the perceived fairness of organizational rewards and attitudes toward the organization. When appraised traditionally, those links may remain strong and in place, such that employees have every reason to maintain similar attitudes toward the organization and the rewards it dispenses (i.e., good reward, good organization; bad rewards, bad organization). When reviewed by methods that incorporate self-appraisal into the decision-making process, however, employee responses regarding voice, trust, and commitment tend to be expressed at levels that vary independently of differences in the perceived fairness of raises.

Thus an interesting psychological mechanism might be brought into play as a function of how performance appraisal discussions are conducted. The results suggest that perceptions of pay-raise fairness either influence or fail to influence other employee responses depending on whether a traditional or self-appraisal discussion was held. Such results imply that a fair process can blunt the impact of outcome-related effects, consistent with other findings in the procedural justice literature.

Finally, we have seen first hand that the advantages of self-appraisal may not be garnered without cost. Specifically, we can point to a 15% increase in ratings that occurred within the self-appraisal group as evidence *potentially* consistent with past caveats about inflationary tendencies (even though it could reflect yielding to the accurate parts of employee views). Rather than dwelling on that evidence as consistent with advice against using self-appraisals, however, we see the cost–benefit analysis as itself in need of closer examination and possible reappraisal.

Our alternative view of the cost–benefit relations cannot be developed fully here (but see Folger et al., 1992), but it essentially coincides with the viewpoint expressed by Staw (1983) that we reviewed earlier. The Staw account places somewhat greater emphasis on an openness regarding issues of authority. If performance ratings stem from *theories* that act as interpretive lenses through which objective reality must be viewed, or as screens through which aspects of that reality must pass (e.g., some being selectively filtered out), then the role of authority no longer looms so sacrosanct. Each employee will have a theory of performance, and a supervisor in charge of rating that employee may have a *different* theory of performance (e.g., they may disagree about what constitutes good performance, or about the means–ends relations between behaviors and productivity).

If nothing else, self-ratings used as an impetus for discussion in performance review sessions can help to expose discrepancies in implicit theories of performance. Among possible consequences of ultimate organizational benefit, for example, some might be prompted by the very existence of self-ratings that are more favorable to the employee than are the ratings of the same employee by the management representative who acts both as an independent rater and the final arbiter of the discrepancies (with possible assistance from a higher level of management). Note that no assumption need be made that the self-ratings are necessarily wrong (i.e., too high), but only that they differ in a direction that would be of benefit to the employee. When the "official" management rater weighs in with a lower rating, the discrepancy is bound to become the basis for discussion; indeed, our study showed as much. We argue that those discussions can become a very constructive basis for exposing the discrepant theories of performance.

In summary, our results showed that when SA ratings were used in an evaluation process associated with administrative decisions about pay raises, many positive changes in perceptions and attitudes occured. Our data revealed such changes most clearly with respect to perceptions and attitudes about the performance review discussions themselves. If nothing else, those findings should encourage some interest because performance review discussions are normally dreaded so much. Our data represent a single case in which some positive effects occured. Once such effects occur, we have a firmer basis for declaring that they can occur and hence that they will occur under at least some circumstances—the next issue being when they are most likely to occur.

Phrasing the matter in those contingency terms emphasizes that SAs used administratively need much more research. More than our small sample or other methodological problems of these preliminary data, the generalizability question looms largest of all. Investigation of other methods might show whether effects are produced only by one particular manner of implementation.

VARIATIONS ON SA IMPLEMENTATION

In working with management to design and incorporate SA ratings as a basis for determining pay raises, we were struck by the many options for implementation—and by the lack of guidance in the literature regarding which options might be most efficacious. Because the orthodox position has advised against using SAs in that fashion, virtually no systematic research has been conducted to examine the possible impact from variations in implementation. Given this lack of empirical work and the evidence of some promise for SAs found in our data and other studies, we hope to encourage more comprehensive investigation of the relevant issues by presenting in the following discussion a description of some variations potentially worth investigating. In each case we begin by identifying one aspect of the procedure as implemented in our study, and then we discuss various options.

First note that for research purposes, we asked store managers at the end of the training session to complete an appraisal form rating their employees. Thus those managers had already made a preliminary set of ratings before seeing the employee SAs. Although we collected those ratings for analysis, we doubt that managers had much of a sense of strong commitment to specific scores. Moreover, we allowed managers to keep a copy for themselves but doubt that those prior ratings had much if any influence at the time when the store managers made official ratings to be seen by the head manager.

Alternative procedures obviously could include variations in which supervisors made no written ratings of any kind prior to seeing employee SAs. Psychologically, the absence of prior written ratings removes a source of added commitment to one's own opinions. We hypothesize that when such sources *do* exist, leniency should be reduced. Investigators who want to check on the maximum extent to which a supervisor's exposure to employee SAs fosters leniency in the subsequent supervisory ratings, therefore, would need to ensure that no prior supervisory ratings had been made in the current review period. The disadvantage of that approach, on the other hand, is that the absence of any check on supervisors' pre-existing assessments of their employees removes all opportunities to determine how much SAs can influence supervisors' opinions about employee competence.

Although any prior supervisory ratings could induce some degree of commitment to one's own opinion, the nature of different circumstances under which such ratings occur could produce different amounts of commitment. Investigations of such variations might simultaneously reveal differences in leniency. Our procedure probably induced only a very minimal degree of advanced commitment at best, for example, and hence gave fairly free rein for leniency tendencies to emerge. Perhaps the only way to induce any less commitment, other than the option of no previous written ratings discussed above, would involve instructions for the supervisors to record their own private ratings in advance (with a guarantee that the records would never be obtained, thereby also precluding their research use for assessing influence).

Moving in the direction of inducing more commitment and hence presumably less leniency, another variation would involve a public rating made to the supervisor's boss prior to the receipt of employee SAs. Presumably that type of advance commitment might hold down leniency to the greatest extent possible, although even stronger steps could conceivably be taken. A supervisor might be required not only to submit those ratings in advance to the boss, for example, but also to hold a joint discussion with that boss in which the two of them came to consensus before receiving the employee SAs. Such a procedure might also give the boss the opportunity to try to induce some comparability across units (raters), as well as the opportunity to influence the shape of the distribution of ratings (e.g., informally, rather than through use of a formal forced distribution system).

At the next stage of the process, we had store managers receive SA forms that had been completed by employees in advance of the appraisal discussion session. Those managers thereby had the opportunity to learn about the employees' opinions prior to meeting with employees for a review of the ratings. This procedure allowed the opportunity for managers to reflect about the meaning of the SA ratings before having to discuss any differences of opinion with employees; the opportunity for reflection also took place before the employees had a chance to discover those differences.

Alternatively, consider the consequences when each go into the discussion "cold" (i.e., having filled out a rating form but not knowing the ratings on the other person's form). On the one hand, the on-the-spot discovery of a discrepancy might generate a climate of flexibility, perhaps induced by the sheer necessity of having less time to think about the nature of the discrepancy before formulating a response (i.e., not working from as entrenched and well-defended a position as might be the case when time for thinking up those defenses and rehearsing their justification had been available by virtue of advance awareness of the other's ratings). On the other hand, surprise discrepancies might instead induce an even more intense degree of defensiveness, perhaps related to feeling caught off guard and having the reaction associated with the threat of being figuratively backed into a corner. Because of the difficulty of bringing theory and a priori hypotheses to bear on this situation, we think it is ripe for investigation.

Instead of the employee not knowing what initial impressions a supervisor has, which may have put employees at a disadvantage in the system we used and also characterizes the option just discussed, employees might be given the supervisor's initial ratings prior to the review session. Two options of this sort exist: one in which the tables are turned relative to our system, such that employees have advance information of a type that supervisors do not have; the other in which both parties have advance information about the initial ratings of the other. We suspect that in practice, the choice among all such options will be guided more by management considerations rather than theory. Nonetheless, interesting differences in the climate of the discussion could presumably emerge as the result of those variations. The structure of a system might convey symbolic messages, for example, in which case the equality connotations of the mutually pre-informed system might generate a greater climate of trust. This equalizing also removes the supervisor's advantaged position of prior knowledge, however, and might lead to a more combative discussion than when the combination of the supervisor's position of authority and access to greater prior information made the supervisor more influential and the employee more acquiescent. Any such effects might be even stronger as regards the comparison between the two systems that place one party versus the other in the advantaged position.

Note also that in the system used at the SA stores of our study, the store managers then rated employees, showed those ratings to their supervisor for discussion to consensus, and subsequently conducted the review session with employees. Just as one of the previously discussed options included a public rating made to the supervisor's boss prior to the receipt of employee SAs, our procedure thus also made the store manager's opinions public to someone else before the employee learned about them (the difference being that in our study, those opinions made public to the store managers' boss had been formed only after the store managers learned their employees SAs). Again, therefore, this publicly declared position should induce stronger commitment and hence ultimately yield less leniency than in the absence of public disclosure. As an alternative, the procedures we used could be implemented in the same manner up to this point, but dropping the step of consultation with someone higher in authority. This might allow more of a chance for leniency to emerge, and it would also not allow the higher-up authority an early chance to establish uniformity across raters or an informal chance to influence ratings in the direction of forced distribution.

In addition, countless variations might be considered as options for the discussion session itself; that is, little attention has been given to special steps that might used for conducting that session when discussion about discrepancies between supervisory ratings and SAs takes place. Training sessions for supervisors are common, for example, but perhaps these discussions might go better if employees also undertook training in regard to the use of rating scales for evaluating performance. In addition, both supervisors and employees might be given training in conflict management, so that disagreements get handled constructively.

At the final step, our system included one more opportunity for the head manager to review the ratings upon which store managers and employees had mutually agreed. This procedure has at least one potential advantage, from the store managers' point of view, in that some diffusion of responsibility can occur. The prior involvement by the head manager at an earlier step allows the store manager to claim some lack of responsibility for ratings considered overly harsh (because they had been jointly agreed upon with the advice and consent of the more senior authority); adding this additional review could provide another such opportunity. If nothing else, the store manager might be in a position to say that any drastic changes could be challenged in the final review, and too much change overall might not be approved because the head manager, after all, had already found the earlier (pre-discussion) ratings to be reasonable. These aspects of the procedure allow supervisors some sense of security against an onslaught of challenges, and so they might be expected to counteract tendencies toward leniency.

Overall, a delicate balance needs to be preserved: Our review of optional methods of implementation has indicated that chances to curtail leniency exist at various stages of the process, and that an attack on leniency can be mounted in a number of alternative ways. At the same time, our arguments about the need to learn from employees (for the sake of company effectiveness and long-run innovation)—and about the need for fairness—suggest (a) that SA scores higher than supervisory ratings might reflect truth rather than error, and (b) that an over-zealous attempt to stamp out inflated ratings, especially when employees are sincere in their opinions, can create the impression that management does not take SAs seriously and goes through the motions in bad faith (as a somewhat Machiavellian co-optation effort aimed only at creating the *appearance* of fairness).

CONCLUSION

We found promising effects from SA in a small-scale demonstration study. In contrast with orthodox advice, those SAs were used for the administrative purpose of making pay-raise decisions. We have argued in the abstract that the orthodox advice fails to take into account the extent of possible inaccuracies, irrelevancies, and contamination in supervisors' "implicit theories" about performance. We also believe that SA review discussions about discrepant ratings can provide supervisors with valuable information (e.g., about performance constraints and competing priorities) that fosters their ability to modify those theories of performance, bringing assumptions more in line with the day-to-day realities that employees experience on the job.

Of course, self-interest may cause employees to package such information in a favorable light. Employees who view SAs as a bargaining opportunity may inflate ratings as a self-interested ploy aimed at getting higher salaries. The temptation to assume the worst about employee motives makes it essential that arguments for SA not rest entirely on the need for task revision and the updating of implicit theories. Rather, fairness considerations also strengthen the case; judgments that affect another person's livelihood should not be made with no regard for the other person's point of view.

Folger can report first-hand experience in having used a system similar to the one implemented in the thrift stores. During the last year of an administrative term when numerous staff people reported to him, he discovered that the use of SAs has an additional property generally neglected by accounts in the literature: Discussions about rating discrepancies help to convince the manager about the importance of careful observation and recordkeeping throughout the year. We speculate that no amount of training nor exhortation to observe such practices can be as compelling as the experience of having to defend views based on shaky evidence. If for no other reason, that salubrious effect alone warrants renewed attention to SAs.

Having tried to make a case that SAs warrant further investigation, we end on the note sounded by the preceding section. The paucity of research on SA used administratively can only be rectified by a change in the thinking of the industrial and organizational science community. Rather than being persuaded to abandon that use of SAs when few variations have been systematically investigated, researchers should study the effects of those variations and hold the more open-minded view characteristic of science until further data have been collected. Moreover, those who would deny employee self-expression about pay prospects via SAs should bear the responsibility of designing some other system for garnering employee acceptance, enhancing perceived fairness, and granting employees those rights that they would surely demand as citizens in situations outside the workplace.

REFERENCES

Bernardin, H. J. (1989). Situational constraints and performance appraisal. Unpublished manuscript.

Bernardin, H. J., & Beatty, R. W. (1984). *Performance appraisal: Assessing human behavior at work*. Boston: Kent.

Borman, W. C. (1978). Exploring upper limits of reliability and validity in job performance ratings. *Journal of Applied Psychology, 63*, 135–144.

Burke, R. J., Weitzel, W., & Weir, T. (1978). Characteristics of effective employee performance review and development interviews: Replication and extension. *Personnel Psychology, 31,* 903–919.

Campbell, D. J., & Lee, C. (1988). Self-appraisal in performance evaluation: Development versus evaluation. *Academy of Management Review, 13,* 302–314.

Carroll, S. J., & Schneier, C. E. (1982). *Performance appraisal and review systems.* Glenview, IL: Scott, Foresman.

Cropanzano, R., & Folger, R. (1989). Referent cognitions and task decision autonomy: Beyond equity theory. *Journal of Applied Psychology, 74,* 293–299.

Farh, J., Werbel, J. D., & Bedeian, A. G. (1988). An empirical investigation of self-appraisal-based performance evaluation. *Personnel Psychology, 41,* 141–156.

Folger, R. (1977). Distributive and procedural justice: Combined impact of "voice" and improvement on experienced inequity. *Journal of Personality and Social Psychology, 35,* 108–119.

Folger, R., & Greenberg, J. (1985). Procedural justice: An interpretive analysis of personnel systems. In K. Rowland & G. Ferris (Eds.), *Research in personnel and human resources management* (Vol. 3, pp. 141–183). Greenwich, CT: JAI Press.

Folger, R., & Konovsky, M. A. (1989). Effects on procedural justice, distributive justice, and reactions to pay raise decisions. *Academy of Management Journal, 32,* 115–130.

Folger, R., Konovsky, M. A., & Brockner, J. (1990). *A dual-component view of responses to injustice.* Paper, presented at the National Academy of Management meeting, San Francisco, CA.

Folger, R., Konovsky, M. A., & Cropanzano, R. (1992). A due process metaphor of performance appraisal. In B. M. Staw & L. L. Cummings (Eds.), *Research in organizational behavior* (Vol. 14, pp. 129–177). Greenwich, CT: JAI Press.

Greenberg, J. (1986a). Determinants of perceived fairness of performance evaluations. *Journal of Applied Psychology, 71,* 340–342.

Greenberg, J. (1986b). The distributive justice of organizational performance evaluations. In H. W. Bierhoff, R. L. Cohen, & J. Greenberg (Eds.), *Justice in social relations* (pp. 337–351). New York: Academic Press.

Greenberg, J. (1987a). Reactions to procedural injustice in payment distributions: Do the means justify the ends? *Journal of Applied Psychology, 72*(1), 55–61.

Greenberg, J. (1987b). Using diaries to promote procedural justice in performance appraisals. *Social Justice Research, 1,* 219–234.

Greenberg, J. (1990). Employee theft as a reaction to underpayment inequity: The hidden cost of pay cuts. *Journal of Applied Psychology, 75,* 561–568.

Greller, M. M. (1978). The nature of subordinate participation in the appraisal interview. *Academy of Management Journal, 21,* 646–658.

Heneman, H. G. (1989). Pay satisfaction. In K. M. Rowland & G. R. Ferris (Eds.), *Research in personnel and human resources management* (Vol. 3, pp. 115–139). Greenwich, CT: JAI Press.

Kane, J. S., & Lawler, E. E. (1979). Performance appraisal effectiveness: Its assessment and determinants. In B. M. Staw (Ed.), *Research in organizational behavior* (Vol. 1, pp. 425–478). Greenwich, CT: JAI Press.

Katz, D., & Kahn, R. L. (1966). *The social psychology of organizations.* New York: Wiley.

Katz, D., & Kahn, R. L. (1978). *The social psychology of organizations* (2nd ed.). New York: Wiley.

Kerr, S. (1975). On the folly of rewarding A, while hoping for B. *Academy of Management Journal, 18,* 769–783.

Konovsky, M. A. (1986). *Antecedents and consequences of informal leader helping behavior: A structural equation modeling approach.* Unpublished doctoral dissertation, Indiana University, Bloomington.

Konovsky, M. A., & Folger, R. (1991). The effects of procedures, social accounts, and benefits level on victims' layoff reactions. *Journal of Applied Social Psychology, 21,* 630–650.

Landy, F. J., Barnes-Farrell, J., & Cleveland, J. N. (1980). Perceived fairness and accuracy of performance evaluation: A follow-up. *Journal of Applied Psychology, 65,* 355–356.

Latham, G., & Wexley, K. (1981). *Increasing productivity through performance appraisal.* Reading, MA: Addison-Wesley.

Lewis, D. M. (1990). *Self-appraisal versus traditional performance appraisal: Perceptions of procedural justice.* Unpublished doctoral dissertation, Tulane University, New Orleans.

Lind, E. A., & Tyler, T. R. (1988). *The social psychology of procedural justice.* New York: Plenum Press.

Mabe, P. A., III, & West, S. G. (1982). Validity of self-evaluation of ability: A review and meta-analysis. *Journal of Applied Psychology, 67,* 280–296.

Mechanic, D. (1962). Sources of power of lower participants in complex organizations. *Administrative Science Quarterly, 7,* 249–364.

Meyer, H. H. (1980). Self-appraisal of job performance. *Personnel Psychology, 33,* 291–295.

Mintzberg, H. (1973). *The nature of managerial work.* New York: Harper & Row.

Mitchell, T. R. (1983). The effects of social, task, and situational factors on motivation, performance, and appraisal. In F. Landy, S. Zedeck, & J. Cleveland (Eds.), *Performance measurement and theory* (pp. 39–47). Hillsdale, NJ: Lawrence Erlbaum Associates.

Mowday, R. T., Steers, R. M., & Porter, L. W. (1979). The measurement of organizational commitment. *Journal of Vocational Behavior, 14,* 224–247.

Nemeth, C. J., & Staw, B. M. (1989). The tradeoffs of social control and innovation in groups and organizations. In L. Berkowitz (Ed.), *Advances in experimental social psychology* (Vol. 22, pp. 175–210). New York: Academic Press.

Organ, D. W. (1988). *Organizational citizenship behavior: The good soldier syndrome.* Lexington, MA: Lexington Books.

Roberson, L., Torkel, S. J., Klein, D., Korsgaard, M. A., & Diddams, M. D. (1989). *Self appraisal and perceptions of the appraisal discussion: A quasi-experimental field study.* Unpublished manuscript.

Roberts, K. H., & O'Reilly, C. A. (1974). Measuring organizational communication. *Journal of Applied Psychology, 59,* 321–326.

Schmitt, M., Noe, R. A., & Gottschalk, R. (1986). Using the lens model to magnify raters' consistency, matching, and shared bias. *Academy of Management Journal, 29,* 130–139.

Shrauger, J. S., & Osberg, T. M. (1981). The relative accuracy of self-predictions and judgements by others in psychological assessment. *Psychological Bulletin, 90,* 322–351.

Staw, B. M. (1983). Proximal and distal measures of individual impact: Some comments on Hall's performance evaluation paper. In F. Landy, S. Zedeck, & J. Cleveland (Eds.), *Performance measurement and theory* (pp. 31–38). Hillsdale, NJ: Lawrence Erlbaum Associates.

Staw, B. M., & Boettger, R. D. (1990). Task revision: A neglected form of work performance. *Academy of Management Journal, 33,* 534–559.

Staw, B. M., & Oldham, G. R. (1978). Reconsidering our dependent variables: A critique and empirical study. *Academy of Management Journal, 21,* 539–559.

Teel, K. (1978). Self-appraisal revisited. *Personnel Journal, 57,* 364–367.

Thibaut, J., & Walker, L. (1975). *Procedural justice: A psychological analysis.* Hillsdale, NJ: Lawrence Erlbaum Associates.

Thornton, G. (1980). Psychometric properties of self-appraisal and job performance. *Personnel Psychology, 33,* 263–271.

Tsui, A., & Barry, B. (1986). Interpersonal affect and rating errors. *Academy of Management Journal, 29,* 586–598.

Weick, K. (1974). *Reward concepts: Dice or marbles.* Unpublished paper, Cornell University, Ithaca, NY.

Wexley, K. N., & Klimoski, R. (1984). Performance appraisal: An update. In K. M. Rowland & G. D. Ferris (Eds.), *Research in personnel & human resources management* (Vol. 2, pp. 35–79). Greenwich, CT: JAI Press.

6 Managing Victim and Survivor Layoff Reactions: A Procedural Justice Perspective

Mary A. Konovsky
Tulane University

Joel Brockner
Columbia University

Since the early 1980s and in the foreseeable future, job layoffs have been and will be frequent within organizations. More than half of the Fortune 1,000 companies have undergone some significant restructuring causing the elimination of both white- and blue-collar jobs since 1980 (Leana & Feldman, 1988). Between 1987 and 1991 more than 85% of the Fortune 1,000 firms downsized their white-collar work force, affecting more than 5 million jobs. More than 50% downsized in 1990 alone (Cameron, Freeman, & Mishra, 1991). The current economic recession is another factor contributing to job loss through layoffs. *Business Week* estimates that as many as 51,000 jobs were lost during July 1991, due to the recession (Cooper & Madigan, 1991).

Because of the ever-present threat of layoffs among both blue- and white-collar workers and the associated loss of quality of life, layoffs constitute a significant social problem. Furthermore, and as we discuss in detail later, layoffs have direct consequences for organizational effectiveness. It is imperative, therefore, that organizational researchers study the layoff process so that we may begin to understand the effects of layoffs on individual functioning and on organizational effectiveness. This chapter provides such an effort. We begin by summarizing the literature examining individuals' reactions to layoffs. We then focus on one important determinant of those reactions: fairness in layoff decision making. Using the empirical and theoretical literature on fairness in layoff decision making, we then propose guidelines for managers who must plan and implement layoffs.

REACTIONS TO LAYOFFS

Layoffs generally have adverse effects on the individuals who are laid off (hereafter referred to as layoff victims), the individuals who remain with the organization following a layoff (hereafter referred to as layoff survivors), and on the organization itself. Each of these foci of layoff effects has important implications for organizational effectiveness. Among survivors, for example, layoffs may lead to high levels of job insecurity. Not only does high job insecurity put layoff survivors at emotional risk, but job insecurity may ultimately influence organizational functioning through its negative effects on survivor productivity and morale (Brockner, in press). Somewhat more obviously, victims also experience negative consequences from layoffs. Traditionally, research on victims' layoff reactions has been concerned with outcomes not directly related to organizational performance (e.g., psychological distress of layoff victims). Presumably, because the psychological and economic distress suffered by layoff victims occurs during the post-layoff period when those individuals are no longer associated with the organization, victims' reactions to layoffs have been cause for little management concern (Konovsky & Folger, 1991). The problem of unemployment can no longer be considered the exclusive worry of the individual who is laid off, however, because layoff victims increasingly issue accusations and direct aggressive emotions toward managers of organizations who are now partially blamed for the occurrence of layoffs. Furthermore, questions about managements' responsibility for massive layoffs have been raised by governmental agencies as well (Leana & Ivancevich, 1987).

We discuss the research investigating victims' and survivors' reactions to layoffs, including the psychological and physiological effects of layoffs and the effects of unemployment on the families of layoff victims. We follow this with a review of the literature investigating victim and survivor expressions of resentment directed toward the organization.

Layoff Victims' and Survivors' Individual Functioning

Leana and Ivancevich (1987) suggest three aspects of individual functioning: psychological, physiological, and family relations, that are affected when individuals lose their jobs. Most of the research on these topics examines layoff victims and ignores layoff survivors.

Job loss has been associated with numerous aspects of psychological dysfunction among layoff victims. Job loss, for example, is associated with reductions in self-esteem, positive affect, and life satisfaction (Leana & Ivancevich, 1987). Job loss also is related to increased apathy, passivity, depression, anxiety, and hostility (e.g., Feather & Barber, 1983; Stokes & Cochrane, 1984). One recent longitudinal study comparing the employed and unemployed found, for example, that unemployed individuals are more depressed and report more negative moods

(Winefield, Winefield, Tiggemann, & Goldney, 1991). Psychiatric illnesses are also more frequently reported among the unemployed (Stafford, Jackson, & Banks, 1980). Finally, Rhine (1984) and Corbett (1985) found exceedingly high suicide rates among those displaced by plant closings.

In addition to psychological symptomatology, job loss also is also associated with increased physiological symptomatology. In general, the unemployed report more health deterioration following a job termination (Payne, Warr, & Hartley, 1980). Headaches, stomach upset, sleep problems and lack of energy are frequently reported among the unemployed (Cochrane & Stopes-Roe, 1980; Pearlin & Lieberman, 1979). O'Brian and Kabanoff (1979) and Cook, Cummings, Bartley, and Shaper (1982) found more evidence of cardiovascular dysfunction among terminated workers. In one study conducted by Cobb and Kasl (1977), deaths among unemployed men due to cardiovascular dysfunctioning were over three times the expected level. Kahn (1981) concluded that job loss had an adverse impact on physical health with the threat of unemployment triggering some physiological changes long before actual job loss occurred.

Family relations also suffer as a result of job loss. Increased marital friction and stress are reported among couples in which the husband had lost his job (Fagin, 1981; Moen, 1976). Furthermore, relationships with children are affected by the father's job loss. Children of the unemployed are found to experience strained relationships with peers, to be more moody at home, to have increased school problems, and to feel distrustful, immobilized, helpless, and victimized (Buss & Redburn, 1983; Liem & Rayman, 1982). Children also report a decline in their perceptions of their fathers' status and parental authority following job loss (Elder, 1973). Unemployed fathers direct more aggression and hostility toward their children (Leventman, 1974) and unemployment is thought to be one of the most common precipitators of child abuse (Justice & Justice, 1976).

Finally, layoffs affect the economic well-being of those who are laid off and their families. In a survey of 460 laid-off workers from Pittsburgh and Florida, Leana and Feldman (1988) report that two fifths of the sample took new jobs in which their pay was reduced by at least 30%; one fifth of the sample had taken a pay cut of at least 50% of their former salary at their new jobs. Only one sixth of those laid off were employed in jobs that paid more than their previous job. Cameron et al. (1991) reported that more than one half of the one million American managers laid off in 1990 took pay cuts of 30% to 40% of their former salaries to obtain new jobs.

Perhaps because of the startling economic and psychological ramifications of layoffs for those who lose their jobs, the effects of layoffs on survivors are often overlooked. Sufficient evidence does exist, however, to conclude that the functioning of layoff survivors is also at risk during and after the layoff process. Co-worker dismissal may, for example, engender job insecurity (i.e., anxiety) in layoff survivors (Brockner, Grover, Reed, & DeWitt, 1992). Survivor guilt is also a common reaction among layoff survivors (Brockner, Davy, & Carter,

1985). The mere fact that survivors fare better than those laid off can produce feelings of guilt because survivors may believe that they, rather than those individuals actually laid off, could have been the layoff victims (Adams, 1965).

Layoff Victims' and Survivors' Resentment Toward Their Employers

Organizational researchers have not investigated layoff reactions directed toward organizations and their management as extensively as the effects of layoffs on individual functioning (Konovsky & Folger, 1991). The little research that does exist, however, suggests that layoffs, indeed, are associated with victim and survivor expressions of resentment directed toward the organization and its managers. We first discuss victim expressions of organizational resentment and then we turn to survivor expressions of resentment.

Baik, Hosseini, and Ragan (1987) were among the first to investigate layoff victims' reactions directed toward organizations and their managers. They noted that laid-off workers may seek direct redress for job loss by instituting lawsuits for unjust discharge and discrimination. More than two thirds of all cases brought under the Age Discrimination in Employment Act of 1967 were precipitated by discharge and involuntary retirement actions by employers (Schuster & Miller, 1984). Layoffs also result in increased pressure for legal regulation of layoffs, such as that embodied in the recently enacted Worker Adjustment and Retraining Notification Act—which requires employers to provide at least 60 days advance notice in the event of plant closings or large-scale layoffs. Baik et al. (1987) found that when employees attribute job loss to the employer rather than to environmental factors, they desire greater legal protection from layoffs. Konovsky and Folger (1991) found that layoffs perceived to be unfair also result in an increased desire for regulation of layoffs among layoff victims. Finally, layoffs may result in anti-company campaigns such as the one directed toward Chrysler's 1987 Christmas closing of its Kenosha, Wisconsin plant that received extensive adverse publicity on prime-time network news (Feldman & Leana, 1989). Anti-company campaigns may decrease the ability of organizations to recruit qualified employees in the future (Gannon, 1971). Baik et al. (1987) found that when employees attribute their job loss to their last employer, they are unwilling to informally help their former company recruit new workers. Konovsky and Folger (1991) found that the perceived fairness of a layoff influenced employees' willingness to recruit for a former employer.

Layoff reactions that adversely impact organizational effectiveness also occur among layoff survivors. The adverse effects of layoffs on survivor attitudes including job involvement, organizational commitment, and job satisfaction, and survivor behaviors including absenteeism, turnover, and productivity have been demonstrated in a number of studies by Brockner and his colleagues.

Brockner, Grover, and Blonder (1988) and Brockner, DeWitt, Grover, and

Reed (1990), for example, demonstrated that layoffs adversely impact survivors' job involvement. Survivor organizational commitment, job satisfaction, and absenteeism and turnover intentions are also frequent casualties of the layoff process (e.g., Brockner, Grover, Reed, DeWitt, & O'Malley, 1987; Brockner et al., 1990; Davy, Kinicki, Scheck, & Sutton, in press). Turnover is an especially critical problem following layoffs, and frequently layoffs result in increased turnover among a firm's most valuable employees (Greenhalgh & Jick, 1979). Finally, survivors report sometimes exerting less work effort as layoffs occur in their organizations (Brockner et al., 1990). Greenhalgh (1982) suggested that job insecurity is one cause of this reduced productivity. Brockner et al. (1992) found that productivity decreased most among those layoff survivors who are either extremely high or extremely low in job insecurity.

The empirical evidence previously discussed established that layoffs can have negative effects on both layoff victims and survivors and that those effects are frequently detrimental to organizational performance. The potentially adverse effects of layoffs on organizations and individuals have motivated researchers to explore the factors that determine the nature of layoff reactions. The next section reviews the literature regarding the influence of one such factor, procedural justice, on victims' and survivors' layoff reactions.

PROCEDURAL JUSTICE AND LAYOFF REACTIONS

Although more than one theoretical framework may be applied to analyzing the effects of layoffs, we believe that procedural justice theories provide a potent framework for explicating layoff reactions. This is because the layoff process consists of a series of events in which victims and survivors evaluate the fairness of layoff procedures (Brockner & Greenberg, 1990). Managers determine, for example, how to downsize their organizations, layoffs being only one such mechanism to accomplish that goal. Once a decision to layoff has been made, managers also determine how to decide who to lay off, how to implement the layoff, and finally, how to inform individuals that they will be laid off. At each of these choice points, managers must determine the best course of action for the organization and its employees. Because procedural justice influences victim and survivor layoff reactions directly (and thus indirectly influences organizational effectiveness), understanding the influence of procedural justice on layoff reactions is imperative for the successful management of layoffs.

Historically, justice theories focused on distributive justice or the perceived fairness of decision outcomes. Beginning with the ground-breaking work of Thibaut and Walker (1975), organizational justice researchers realized that how a decision is made also influences individuals' reactions to the allotment of resources. *Procedural justice* is the term most commonly used to refer to how decisions are made or the perceived fairness of decision-making procedures.

Thibaut and Walker (1975) focused on the distribution of control in decision making and propose that individuals view procedures as means to an end of improving their own decision outcomes. They focused on two aspects of control: process control and decision control. Process control refers to the extent of control over decision-making procedures and decision control refers to the extent of control over the actual decision outcomes. In his model of procedural justice, Leventhal (1980) also focused on control and proposed six factors influencing individuals' perceptions of fairness, including the ethicality, consistency, lack of bias, accuracy, representativeness and correctability of the decision-making procedures.

Greenberg (1990) differentiated among two salient procedural justice elements in the organizational setting: the structural characteristics of decision making and the interpersonal characteristics of decision making. The structural characteristics of a decision include the formal policies and procedures used by the organization to make decisions. One important structural characteristic of layoff decision making, for example, is the amount of advance notice given to those who are laid off. Prior to the time that managers were required to give employees 60 days notice of an impending layoff, management did not generally provide employees much notification that layoffs would occur. Kaufman (1982) reported that 80% of employers provided less than 4 weeks' notice of impending terminations. One additional structural aspect of procedural justice in layoff decision making includes the criteria that are used to determine who to layoff. Sometimes performance criteria or seniority are used. Alternatively, the layoff victims may be randomly selected.

The interpersonal aspects of procedural justice refer to the type of interpersonal treatment people receive throughout the layoff process, including the adequacy with which the layoff decisions are explained (Bies & Moag, 1986). Management may, for example, provide varying levels of information when explaining to both layoff victims and survivors why a layoff is necessary. Management may also exhibit varying levels of respect and dignity when informing the individuals who are to be laid off. We next review the empirical research that has examined the structural and interpersonal elements of procedural justice as they influence victim and survivor layoff reactions.

Procedural Justice and Victims' Layoff Reactions

The reactions of layoff victims include those related to their attitudes toward their former employer. Two layoff victim reactions have been empirically examined: the willingness of layoff victims to recruit for a former employer and layoff victims' desire for legal regulation of layoffs. Earlier we discussed the potential importance of these layoff victim reactions for organizational effectiveness; now we discuss the link between procedural fairness in layoff decision making and the occurrence of these responses.

One of the few studies to investigate layoff victim reactions assesses both victims' desire for legal regulation of layoffs and their willingness to recruit for their former employers. Konovsky and Folger (1991) surveyed 353 individuals who had been laid off from organizations across a variety of industries for an average of 4.5 months. They investigated the effects of the structural characteristics of the layoff decision (i.e., decision-making accuracy, absence of bias, and ethicality) and the interpersonal justice of the layoff decision making (i.e., how the layoff decision is communicated). In addition to these two indicators of procedural justice, Konovsky and Folger also assessed the effects of social accounts, or the explanations management provides concerning why the layoffs were necessary. Finally, Konovsky and Folger investigated the effects of the outcomes individuals receive when they are laid off (i.e., the extent of the severance benefits). The results of this study indicate that procedural fairness decreases layoff victims' desire for regulation of layoffs and strengthens layoff victims' willingness to recruit for their former employer. The structural elements of layoff decision making (e.g., advance notice) and the manner in which those decisions are communicated influenced victims' layoff reactions in a positive manner. The amount of severance benefits received and the actual justifications management provided for the occurrence of the layoffs, on the other hand, explain no unique variance in victims' layoff reactions.

Rousseau and Anton (1988) and Baik et al. (1987) provide further evidence that interpersonal justice is important for determining layoff victims' reactions. Rousseau and Anton presented experimental subjects with hypothetical scenarios in which an individual had been laid off. Subjects in this study read plausible accounts for the layoff that were provided by management (e.g., "a combination of economic factors and technological changes"). Those subjects receiving plausible explanations rated the layoff as less unfair than did subjects who learned of no such reasons. This research indicates that the credibility of managements' explanations for layoffs can influence victims' reactions to layoffs. The research described also indicates that the structural and interpersonal aspects of procedural justice are important determinants of victims' reactions to layoffs.

Further research on victims' responses to layoffs (Brockner, Konovsky, Cooper-Schneider, Folger, Martin, & Bies, 1992) investigates the conditions under which the two aspects of procedural justice previously discussed are especially important for determining layoff victim responses. This survey of 218 layoff victims examined the joint effects of procedural justice (both structural and interpersonal) and outcome negativity on layoff victim responses. Outcome negativity is assessed by asking layoff victims to report the level of severance benefits they received following their layoff; the lower the benefits, the greater the outcome negativity. Brockner et al. (1992) found that when outcome negativity is low, there is little relationship between procedural justice and victims' desire for regulation of layoffs. When outcome negativity is high, however, there is a strong (inverse) relationship between procedural justice and victims' desire for regulation of layoffs.

Procedural Justice and Survivors' Layoff Reactions

Organizational justice researchers have also examined the influence of procedural justice on survivor reactions to layoffs. Brockner et al. (1990), for example, established the effects of the interpersonal aspects of procedural justice on survivors' organizational commitment, work effort, and turnover intentions. These researchers surveyed 597 individuals employed in a chain of retail stores that experienced layoffs in the previous 6–9 months. Survey respondents rated how clearly top management and supervisors had explained the reasons for the layoffs. In general, survivors reacted more favorably when they felt that they had received clear explanations of the reasons for the layoff. However, the relationship between clarity of explanation and survivors' reactions interacted with factors believed to affect survivors' need for information. For example, when the layoff was an unusual event for the organization, or when the bases used to decide who would be laid off versus retained was unclear, there was an especially strong relationship between the clarity of the explanation for the layoff and survivors' reactions. That same study also revealed that survivors' prior attachment to the layoff victims moderated the relationship between clarity of explanation and survivors' reactions. Respondents reported the greatest decline in organizational commitment when they identified with or felt attached to the layoff victims and when the organization failed to provide clear explanations for the layoffs.

One interesting pattern of results emerging from studies on both layoff victims and survivors is the form of the interaction between procedural justice and the negativity of the outcomes associated with the layoff. Specifically, procedural justice is frequently a stronger determinant of survivor and victim layoff reactions when outcome negativity is high rather than low. Brockner et al. (1992) conducted a study specifically designed to assess the nature of the interaction between procedural justice and outcome fairness on both survivor and victim reactions to layoffs. The results pertinent to layoff victims were discussed in the preceding section and only those results for layoff survivors will be discussed at this point. We should emphasize, however, that the pattern of results is the same for both layoff victims and survivors.

Brockner et al. (1992) conducted two field studies to examine the interactive effects of procedural justice and outcome negativity on survivor reactions to layoffs. Study 1 investigated the effects of the interpersonal aspects of procedural justice and outcome negativity on survivors' organizational commitment. Outcome negativity was comprised of survivors' perceptions of the adequacy of organizational caretaking (e.g., severance benefits) extended to layoff victims, and in particular, how well such caretaking would provide for their needs were they to be laid off. The results indicated that when interpersonal justice was absent, layoff survivors reported a considerably larger decrease in organizational commitment when outcome negativity was high rather than low. The perception of high interpersonal justice, however, considerably reduced the effects of out-come negativity on organizational commitment. Survivors, in other words, react most negatively when outcome negativity is high and interpersonal justice is low. The second study conducted by Brockner et al. (1992) revealed a similar pattern of results. In this study, 150 full-time employees of a financial services organiza-tion that had undergone layoffs 5 to 7 months prior to the study were surveyed. Outcome negativity was operationalized by measuring the severity of the layoff (the percentage of workers laid off). Once again, under conditions of low inter-personal justice, organizational commitment decreased more when outcome negativity was high rather than low; when interpersonal justice was high, the relationship between outcome negativity and organizational commitment was greatly reduced.

One shortcoming of the studies by Brockner et al. is that the victim and survivor samples were not drawn from the same organization. As a result, it is impossible to compare the magnitude of procedural justice's effects on layoff survivors and victims. Greenberg (1991) provided data from a quasi-experimen-tal study indicating that the effects of procedural justice are more pronounced on layoff victims compared to layoff survivors. Greenberg manipulated interperson-al justice by presenting either more or less information regarding the company's economic problems and the necessity for the layoff. Both victims and survivors were asked to make judgments about what it was like to work in the company. Raters judged pre-manipulation and post-manipulation summaries written by victims and survivors and found that the descriptions of working for the company became more negative following the layoff. Among the layoff victims, the nega-tive reactions were most severe under conditions of low levels of procedural justice. Layoff survivors displayed a similar pattern of layoff reactions, although the magnitude of the survivors' responses was less than that for victims. These results are analogous to Brockner et al.'s (1992) if we make the (reasonable) assumption that the outcome of the layoff is more negative for victims than survivors.

Davy, Kinicki, Scheck, and Sutton (in press) provided further evidence of the importance of procedural justice in influencing survivor layoff reactions. Unlike the survivor studies just described, these researchers examined the structural aspects, rather than the interpersonal aspects, of layoff decision making. Data were obtained from 120 employees working for a high-tech firm that was down-sizing its work force at the time of the first survey. The procedural justice measure assessed employees' voice in setting procedures involving pay, company policy and procedures, and organizational change. The results of this study indicate that voice has a positive and direct impact on survivors' perceptions of the fairness of the layoff decision-making process. Further, the fairness of the layoff process is positively associated with organizational commitment and job satisfaction. These attitudes are, in turn, negatively associated with absenteeism and turnover intentions.

Collectively, this research indicates some similarities in the ways that victims and survivors respond to layoffs. Specifically, both the interpersonal and structural aspects of layoff decision-making procedures are associated with a variety of layoff reactions including victims' desire for regulation of layoffs and survivors' organizational commitment and work effort following a layoff. Additionally, a consistent pattern of interaction effects exists in both victim and survivor samples. Layoff victims and survivors have the most negative reactions to layoffs when outcome negativity is high and procedural fairness is low. This pattern of findings indicates that procedural justice can mitigate the influence of the negative outcomes associated with layoffs on victims and survivors.

We now turn to a discussion of the theoretical implications of the empirical findings discussed earlier concerning the victims and survivors of layoffs. We then discuss the practical implications of those findings for managing the layoff process.

UNDERSTANDING THE EFFECTS OF PROCEDURAL JUSTICE ON LAYOFF REACTIONS

The research reviewed previously suggests that both layoff victims and survivors are influenced by the fairness of the procedures used to implement layoffs. These findings raise the question of why decision-making procedures are so important in the layoff context. We discuss three theoretical approaches that have made their way into the procedural justice literature: the self-interest or instrumental model, referent cognitions theory, and the group-value model. We discuss these differing theoretical perspectives in the context of explaining the afore-mentioned interaction between procedural justice and outcome negativity.

The nature of the interaction—an example of which is provided in Table 6.1—can be described in three ways:

1. As long as the outcomes associated with the decision are more positive (or not so negative), then the impact of procedural fairness on individuals' reactions is relatively small (i.e., the ends justify the means).

2. As long as the procedures used to make or implement the decision are more fair, then the impact of outcome negativity on individuals' reactions is relatively small (i.e., the means justify the ends).

3. One group will react much more negatively than all others: those who believe that their outcomes are relatively negative and the procedural fairness is relatively low.

It is worth noting that this interaction effect has been found on numerous occasions, not only among layoff victims and survivors, but across a wide array of laboratory and organizational settings (Folger & Martin, 1986; McFarlin & Sweeney, 1990).

TABLE 6.1
Victims' and Survivers' Reactions as a Function of Outcome Negativity and Procedural Fairness

Victims' Reactions[a]

| | | Outcome Negativity | |
		High	*Low*
Interactional	Low	4.08	3.63
Justice	High	3.41	3.56

Survivors' Reactions[b]

| | | Outcome Negativity | |
		High	*Low*
Interactional	Low	4.18	5.27
Justice	High	6.14	5.76

[a]The victim's dependent measure was desire for legal regulation of layoffs that ranged from 1 to 5; higher scores reflect a greater desire for governmental regulation of layoffs (i.e., more negative reactions to job loss).

[b]The survivor's dependent measure was change in organizational commitment that ranged from 1 to 11; lower scores reflect a greater decrease in organizational commitment, relative to the pre-layoff period. Neutral point (no change) = 6.

The Self-Interest or Instrumental Model

The self-interest or instrumental model was originally developed by Thibaut and Walker (1978); it assumes an egoistic view of human nature, in which people are primarily concerned with receiving tangible and material outcomes from their exchanges with groups and organizations (e.g., money, promotions, and interesting work). The self-interest or instrumental model may explain the interaction effect described in Table 6.1 in at least two ways. First, because peoples' primary motive is to receive desired outcomes, procedural considerations should have little impact provided that the outcomes are relatively favorable (i.e., the ends justify the means).

This reasoning not only implies that outcome negativity and procedural fairness will interact, but also that outcome negativity should have a main effect (in the statistical sense) on victim and survivors' reactions. In fact, the main effect of outcome negativity was not statistically significant in both the victim and survivor sample studied by Brockner et al. (1992). Nevertheless, it still may be possible to explain the outcome by procedure interaction by adopting a longer-term perspective on individuals' relationships with organizations. Specifically, procedural fairness may influence individuals' beliefs about the amount of desired outcomes they can expect from the organization over time. As long as the procedures for making and implementing resource allocation decisions are fair, people may believe that they will receive their (dare we say fair) share of desired outcomes. As a result, their reactions to the organization may be less influenced by the outcomes of the current exchange than if fair procedures were absent (along with the lack of assurance that things would "even out" over time). This reasoning may explain why survivors' organizational commitment is less influenced by outcome negativity when the procedural fairness is perceived to be relatively high rather than low.

At first blush, this logic seems hard-pressed to explain the interactive effect of outcome and procedural variables on victims' reactions. After all, victims no longer have a relationship with their former organization; therefore, how can they possibly be concerned with whether outcomes will even out over time? One possibility is that victims will take a longer term perspective not with their former organization, but with past and future employers in general. Recall that victims' reactions in the Brockner et al. (1992) study are operationalized in the form of their desire for legal and governmental regulation of layoffs. If negative outcomes are coupled with unfair procedures, then layoff victims may be most desirous of having a third party (like the government) step in to assure that layoffs are handled better in the future. From an instrumental or self-interest perspective, third-party intervention in how layoffs are managed may lead layoff victims to believe that they will receive more positive (or less negative) concrete outcomes from organizations over time.

Future research needs to evaluate these speculations. For now, it is important to note that the reasoning previously discussed provides a possible conceptual extension to Thibaut and Walker's (1975) initial theorizing about the self-interest model. Thibaut and Walker argued that procedural fairness is important because it influences peoples' judgments of the outcomes they expect to receive over time from a *specific* other party to the relationship. Our speculation is that if the self-interest model is correct, it may be because people adopt a longer-term perspective with the general category of entities represented by the specific party.

Referent Cognitions Theory

Originally proposed by Folger (1986), referent cognitions theory (RCT) also places heavy emphasis on the tangible, concrete outcomes that people receive from their exchanges with organizations. The particular focus of RCT is how people come to define outcomes as relatively favorable or not. According to Folger, people compare their current outcomes to those "that might have been," or easily imagined alternative outcomes. The alternative outcomes against which people compare their current outcomes may be influenced by a range of factors, including others' outcomes, one's past outcomes, one's aspired to outcomes, or some objective standard. Attitudes depend on the difference between present outcomes and those that might have been. For example, layoff victims and survivors will experience resentment towards the organization when their outcomes fall short of those that might have been.

Procedural fairness becomes relevant to the referent cognitions analysis in that it may shape victims' and survivors' perceptions of alternative outcomes that could have emerged (but did not). If procedures are unfair, then both groups have a basis for believing that other outcomes could have emerged, if only fair procedures had been followed. For example, if people receive negative outcomes as a result of a procedure that allowed them little or no input into the process, they are more likely to feel resentful than if the same outcomes were preceded by procedures that did allow them to participate. RCT may explain why victims and survivors react much more negatively in the High Outcome Negativity/Low Procedural Fairness condition relative to all other conditions. High outcome negativity sets the stage for expressions of resentment toward the organization. When negative outcomes are coupled with the perception of low procedural fairness, then victims and survivors have an even stronger basis for thinking that more positive outcomes could have occurred.

Similar outcome by procedure interactions consistent with RCT have been obtained under controlled laboratory conditions. In one study (Folger, Rosenfield, & Robinson, 1983), for example, subjects failed to obtain a desirable reward as a result of procedures that varied in fairness. In the low procedural fairness condition, scoring procedures were changed arbitrarily, whereas in the high procedural fairness condition, people were given cogent explanations of the reasons for the change. Subjects also were told what their outcomes would have been if the scoring procedure had not been changed. In the high referent outcomes condition they were told that their outcomes would have been much better than those they actually received, whereas in the low referent outcomes condition they were told that their outcomes would not have been any better than those that they actually obtained. The results showed that people are much more resentful in the low procedural fairness/high referent outcomes condition than in all other conditions. The fact that the form of the interaction in the laboratory is similar to that exhibited in correlational field surveys of layoff victims and survivors lends internal validity to the latter findings.

Group-Value Theory

The group-value model was developed by Lind and Tyler (1988), partially in response to the finding that instrumental models did not provide a complete explanation of how procedural justice variables influence people. The assumptions underlying what it is that people want from their group (including organizational group) memberships are quite different than in the case of instrumental models. Rather than being concerned with concrete, tangible, and material rewards, people wish to develop their senses of self-identity and self-worth. Interpersonal relationships in general and group membership in particular give people the opportunity to validate the correctness of their beliefs and behavior, thereby promoting a clearer self-identity. Groups also provide frequent evaluations to people, including the extent to which they are accepted, respected, and held in high regard.

Given the premium that people place on the more symbolic and psychological rewards meted out by group members, it stands to reason that people should hold in high regard groups and organizations that follow fair decision-making procedures. Fair procedures communicate to people that they are being treated in a dignified and respected way, thereby enhancing their feelings of self-worth. In fact, we found a main effect for procedural justice in our studies of layoff victims and survivors (Brockner et al., 1992). In general, people reacted more favorably when procedural fairness was relatively high.

The group-value model also explains the outcome negativity by procedural fairness interaction displayed in Table 6.1. Given that people value fair treatment for its symbolic value, their feelings toward the organization are less influenced by the negativity of the tangible outcomes associated with the layoff. That is, the felt presence of procedural justice reduces the relationship between outcome negativity and victims' and survivors' attitudes toward the organization. Thus, like the instrumental explanation, the presence of procedural fairness has important symbolic value and therefore reduces the relationship between outcome negativity and victims' and survivors' reactions. The key difference between the instrumental and group-value explanations rests in that which is symbolized by high fairness. According to the instrumental explanation, fair treatment symbolizes that victims and survivors can expect to receive their share of tangible, concrete outcomes over time. According to the group-value model, fair treatment symbolizes respectful and dignified treatment, thereby enhancing victims' and survivors' feelings of self-worth.

Future Research Directions

In calling attention to the self-interest, referent cognitions, and group-value models, we are not saying that these are the only explanations of the outcome negativity by procedural fairness interaction, nor of the effects of procedural justice more generally. For example, the interaction may reflect a "social legitimacy" effect. When outcomes are negative, individuals may feel resentful toward the organization; after all, no one likes to lose. However, we have been socialized not to always express our anger and resentment when our outcomes fall short of aspirations. Instead, it is more socially acceptable to be a "good loser." When unfair procedures are associated with the decision yielding negative outcomes, then our inhibitions about expressing the resentment (due in part to the negative outcomes) may be lowered. Most of us can accept that we will not always get the outcomes that we want. It would be far more unpalatable to acknowledge that the procedures underlying the decisions were unfair. Put differently, it seems more socially legitimate to complain about unfair procedures than negative outcomes. Thus, it may be the combination of negative outcomes (which arouse resentment) and unfair procedures (which entitles people to express the resentment) that leads people to react most negatively. Of course, this is precisely the nature of the interaction reported in Table 6.1. We are not aware of any research bearing on this explanation, but it seems worth evaluating.

We also are not advocating that future research consist of critical tests pitting one theoretical explanation against another explanation, as if to determine which one is "right" or "wrong." It would seem far more useful to keep in mind the distinctions between theories, and devote future research to determining the conditions under which (and/or the people for whom) one theory is more appropriate than the other. Thibaut and Walker (1975) already have established that instrumental concerns explain some of the variation in peoples' reactions to procedural fairness. Lind and Tyler (1988) have just as assuredly convinced us that instrumental motivations do not present the entire picture, and that issues of self-identity and self-worth also are important to people. Thus, both viewpoints (as well as RCT) have empirical backing.

Future research may profitably proceed by specifying when instrumental concerns are especially important versus when group-value considerations predominate. For example, those high in their economic need to work may be especially sensitive to procedural justice variables as they inform them of their financial status in the group or organization. Individuals who are highly committed to the organization, and thereby derive a strong sense of self-identity and self-worth from their organizational affiliation, may become especially bothered by unfair procedures shown by the organization. Their decline in commitment may reflect a concern that the relationship is threatened, along with their self-identity and self-worth (Brockner, Tyler, & Cooper-Schneider, 1992). In summary, future research needs to move beyond the current position that both instrumental and group-value factors matter. We need to know more about the circumstances under which one or the other is especially salient in employees' minds.

PROCEDURAL JUSTICE AND MANAGING LAYOFFS

The research on the effects of procedural justice on victim and survivor responses to layoffs is important not only because it contributes to the development of organizational justice theories but also because it addresses an area of human resources management where proactive management practices may be especially valuable. Successful management of layoffs can benefit not only the organization, but also the individual people affected by layoffs, including victims, survivors, and their families. We first discuss the implications of the empirical research on procedural justice for layoff victims, followed by a discussion of the implications of procedural justice research for layoff survivors.

Managing Layoffs to Respect the Rights of Victims

Earlier we reviewed research indicating that layoffs can have unfavorable effects both on victims' individual functioning and on victims' reactions to organizations and their managers. Victims of layoffs not only experience depression and anxiety, but they also, under some conditions, resent management and retaliate by filing discrimination suits, supporting the legal regulation of layoff, and refusing to assist the organization in future recruiting.

Given the psychological and economic importance of victims' layoff responses, the general guideline provided by the research on procedural justice and victim layoff reactions would be for managers to be as procedurally sensitive as possible throughout the layoff decision-making process. The empirical literature suggests that two aspects of procedural justice, the structural and interpersonal elements, both need to be managed throughout the layoff process.

One framework for understanding the structural elements of procedural justice is provided by Leventhal (1980). He proposed that fair procedures (a) are consistent, (b) suppress bias, (c) use accurate information, (d) provide opportunities to correct errors, (e) represent appropriate parties, and (f) follow ethical standards. Konovsky and Folger (1991) demonstrated that a measure of layoff procedures based on Leventhal's conceptualization is, indeed, associated with victims' layoff reactions. Theory and research suggest, therefore, that layoff decision-making should follow, as closely as possible, the recommendations of Leventhal as translated into the layoff context. Using accurate information to make layoff decisions is one prominent example of how managers can employ fair layoff decision-making procedures. If layoff victims are to be selected according to performance criteria, for example, then accurate performance criteria are absolutely necessary to ensure that the layoff procedures are perceived as fair. Not only is accurate information necessary, but once a decision rule is determined, it must be consistently applied. Race, gender, age, or nationality, for example, should have no bearing on determining who should be laid off.

Providing adequate advance notice to layoff victims is an additional structural element of procedural justice. Kaufman (1982) suggested several ways in which pre-notification may be helpful to both organizations and employees. Pre-notification permits more time for planning both the phase-out programs and individual employee retraining, relocation, or reemployment efforts. Employees may also respond positively rather than negatively if they feel their employer is attempting to buffer the adverse consequences of job loss. Finally, pre-notification also encourages organizational, union, and community initiatives in the form of job placement, counseling, and training programs.

The study of Konovsky and Folger (1991) also indicated that the nature of the interpersonal treatment accorded layoff victims is critical in determining their reactions to being laid off. Communication with layoff victims, therefore, should exemplify consideration and a concern for victims' needs. A sensitivity to the plight of the layoff victim is also important. In addition to treating victims with dignity and respect, the reasons for the layoffs should be clearly communicated to the layoff victims.

Although outcome negativity and procedural justice variables seem functionally equivalent—as measured by their effects on the victims and survivors of job loss—there is at least one key difference between outcome and procedural considerations. The direct economic costs to the organization of acting in a procedurally fair manner probably are much lower than the costs associated with packages including severance pay and outplacement counseling, which are designed to reduce the negativity of the outcomes associated with the layoff. We are not advocating that organizations, in managing the layoff, ignore the factors that influence outcome negativity. If management offered virtually nothing tangible to the layoff victims, it is doubtful that procedural justice would compensate for such negative outcomes. However, from a cost effectiveness perspective, reasonably adequate caretaking provisions (to reduce outcome negativity), coupled with high levels of procedural justice in implementing the layoff, may be the most prudent way to manage the reactions of victims of job loss.

Managing Layoffs to Respect the Rights of Survivors

The research on layoff survivors, as with layoff victims, indicates that both the structural and interpersonal elements of procedural justice influence survivor reactions to layoffs. Furthermore, the research indicates that survivor layoff reactions are likely to be more negative under some conditions than others. Next we discuss both the importance of fair procedures and the importance of circumstance in influencing survivor layoff reactions.

As with layoff victims, the presence of fair procedures, especially those procedural aspects pertaining to interpersonal treatment (e.g., management communicating not only with the layoff victims but also with the layoff survivors in a kind and respectful manner), are important in mitigating the effects of layoffs on survivors. Structural aspects of procedural justice, such as having a voice in decision-making, are also important determinants of survivor layoff reactions. The use of fair procedures alone in layoff decision-making, however, may not be enough to convince those who remain with the organization that fairness is important in the organization. In addition to observing fair procedures such as providing clear explanations for a layoff, therefore, managers should also build an organizational culture that, in general, emphasizes procedural justice.

In addition to emphasizing fair procedures in general, the research on layoff survivors suggests several factors that moderate the effects of procedural fairness on survivors' reactions. One such factor is the degree of prior identification the survivor had with the layoff victims. When survivors are attached to or identify closely with the victims of layoffs, fair procedures are especially important in influencing survivor reactions to layoffs (Brockner, et al.; 1987). Furthermore, when survivors are highly committed to the organization prior to the layoffs, they are also likely to be especially sensitive to the use of fair procedures during layoffs (Brockner, Tyler, & Cooper-Schneider, 1992). These factors moderating the relationships between fair procedures and layoff survivors' reactions could be potentially used to identify survivors that are at high risk for especially negative layoff reactions. Managers could take extra effort to ensure that these high risk survivors receive the reassurance (i.e., fair treatment) that they need to continue to function effectively in their jobs.

Other circumstances also influence the importance of fair procedures and their effects on layoff survivors. Survivors' need for information, uncertainty levels, and the importance of the layoff outcomes moderate the effects of procedural justice on survivor layoff reactions (Brockner et al., 1990). So, for example, when the layoff decision was an unusual event or when survivors anticipated a lack of organizational caretaking during the layoff process, the absence of a clear explanation for the layoffs was especially detrimental to survivors' organizational commitment. Once again, these moderating factors indicate circumstances under which management should be especially careful to observe fair procedures during a layoff.

CONCLUSIONS

Layoffs will continue to present a dilemma to organizations and their managers because job loss not only has detrimental effects on the functioning of layoff survivors and victims, but also because layoffs can have negative effects on the organization's bottom line. Observing procedural justice throughout the layoff decision-making process, however, can substantially reduce the negative impact of layoffs on victims, survivors, and the organization. The sincere observance of fair procedures, and not the mere appearance of fairness, promises to be a major factor in obtaining any advantages that layoffs can provide organizations.

REFERENCES

Adams, J. S. (1965). Inequity in social exchange. In L. Berkowitz (Ed.), *Advances in experimental social psychology* (Vol. 2, pp. 267–299). New York: Academic Press.

Baik, K., Hosseini, M., & Ragan, J. (1987). *Attributing job loss from company layoff practices and circumstantial cues: Would job losers rather recruit for former employers or sue them?* Paper presented at the annual meeting of the Academy of Management, New Orleans, LA.

Bies R. J., & Moag, J. S. (1986). Interactional justice: Communicating criteria of fairness. In R. J. Lewicki, B. H. Sheppard, & B. H. Bazerman (Eds.), *Research on negotiation in organizations* (Vol. 1, pp. 43–55). Greenwich, CT: JAI Press.

Brockner, J. (in press). Managing the effects of layoffs on survivors. *California Management Review.*

Brockner, J., Davy, J., & Carter, C. (1985). Layoffs, self-esteem, and survivor guilt: Motivational, attitudinal, and affective consequences. *Organizational Behavior and Human Decision Processes, 36,* 229–244.

Brockner, J., DeWitt, R. L., Grover, S., & Reed, T. (1990). When it is especially important to explain why: Factors affecting the relationship between managers' explanations of a layoff and survivors' reactions to the layoff. *Journal of Experimental and Social Psychology, 26,* 389–407.

Brockner, J., & Greenberg, J. (1990). The impact of layoffs on survivors: An organizational justice perspective. In J. S. Carroll (Ed.), *Applied social psychology and organizational settings* (pp. 45–75). Hillsdale, NJ: Lawrence Erlbaum Associates.

Brockner, J., Grover, S., & Blonder, M. D. (1988). Factors predicting survivors' reactions to work layoffs: A field study. *Journal of Applied Psychology, 74,* 436–442.

Brockner, J., Grover, S., Reed, T., & DeWitt, R. (1992). Layoffs, job insecurity, and survivors' work effort: Evidence of an inverted-U relationship. *Academy of Management Journal, 35,* 413–425.

Brockner, J., Grover, S., Reed, T., DeWitt, R., & O'Malley, M. (1987). Survivors' reactions to layoffs: We get by with a little help for our friends. *Administrative Science Quarterly, 32,* 526–541.

Brockner, J., Konovsky, M. A., Cooper-Schneider, R., Folger, R., Martin, C., & Bies, R. J. (1992). *The interactive effects of procedural justice and outcome negativity on victims and survivors of job loss.* Manuscript submitted for publication.

Brockner, J., Tyler, T., & Cooper-Schneider, R. (1992). *The influence of prior commitment to an institution on reactions to perceived unfairness: The higher they are, the harder they fall.* Manuscript submitted for publication.

Buss, T. F., & Redburn, F. S. (1983). *Mass unemployment: Plant closings and community mental health.* Beverly Hills: Sage.

Cameron, K. S., Freeman, S. J., & Mishra, A. K. (1991). Best practices in white-collar downsizing: Managing contradictions. *Academy of Management Executive, 5,* 57–73.

Cobb, S., & Kasl, S. V. (1977). *Termination: The consequences of job loss* (Report No. 76-1261). Cincinnati, OH: National Institute for Occupational Safety and Health Research.

Cochrane, R., & Stopes-Roe, M. (1980). Factors affecting the distribution of psychological symptoms in urban areas of England. *Acta Psychiatrica Scandinavica, 61,* 445–460.

Cook, D. G., Cummings, R. O., Bartley, M. J., & Shaper, A. G. (1982). Health of unemployed middle-aged men in Great Britain. *Lancet, 5,* 1290–1294.

Cooper, J. C., & Madigan, K. (1991, September 9). Employment. *Business Week,* p. 24.

Corbett, J. (1985). *A study on unemployment in the Nom-Yough valley and its impact on social and psychological functioning.* McKeesport, PA: Nom-Yough Community Mental Health and Mental Retardation Center.

Davy, J. A., Kinicki, A. J., Scheck, C. L., & Sutton, C. L. (in press). Developing and testing an expanded model of survivor responses to layoffs: A longitudinal field study. *Journal of Vocational Behavior.*

Elder, R. J. (1973). *Children of the great depression: Social change in life experience.* Chicago: University of Chicago Press.

Fagin, L. (1981). *Unemployment and health in families* (DHSS Publication No. ISBN 0/902650/23/8). Washington, DC: U. S. Government Printing Office.

Feather, M. T., & Barber, J. G. (1983). Depressive reactions and unemployment. *Journal of Abnormal Psychology, 92,* 185–195.

Feldman, D. C., & Leana, C. R. (1989, summer). Managing layoffs: Experiences at the Challenger disaster site and the Pittsburgh steel mills. *Organizational Dynamics,* 52–64.

Folger, R. (1986). Rethinking equity theory: A referent cognitions model. In H. W. Bierhoff, R. L. Cohen, & J. Greenberg (Eds.). *Justice in social relations* (pp. 145–162). New York: Plenum.

Folger, R., & Martin, C. (1986). Relative deprivation and referent cognitions: Distributive and procedural justice effects. *Journal of Experimental Social Psychology, 22,* 531–546.

Folger, R., Rosenfield, D., & Robinson, T. (1983). Relative deprivation and procedural justifications. *Journal of Personality and Social Psychology, 45,* 268–273.

Gannon, M. J. (1971). Sources of referral and employee turnover. *Journal of Applied Psychology, 55,* 226–228.

Greenberg, J. (1990). Organizational justice: Yesterday, today, and tomorrow. *Journal of Management, 16,* 399–432.

Greenberg, J. (1991). *Social fairness and employees' reactions to layoffs.* Manuscript submitted for publication.

Greenberg, J., & Folger R. (1983). Procedural justice, participation, and the fair process effect in groups and organizations. In P. Paulus (Ed.), *Basic group process* (pp. 235–256). New York: Springer-Verlag.

Greenhalgh, L. (1982). Maintaining organizational effectiveness during organizational retrenchment. *Journal of Applied Behavioral Science, 18,* 155–170.

Greenhalgh, L., & Jick, T. D. (1979). *The relationship between job insecurity and turnover, and its differential effects on employee quality level.* Paper presented at the annual meeting of the Academy of Management, Atlanta.

Justice, B., & Justice, R. (1976). *The abusing family.* New York: Human Services Press.

Kahn, R. L. (1981). *Work and health.* New York: Wiley.

Kaufman, H. G. (1982). *Professional in search of work: Coping with the stress of job loss and unemployment.* New York: Wiley.

Konovsky, M. A., & Folger, R. (1991). The effects of procedures, social accounts, and benefits level on victims' layoff reactions. *Journal of Applied Social Psychology, 21,* 630–650.

Leana, C. R., & Feldman, D. C. (1988). Individual responses to job loss: Perceptions, reactions, and coping behaviors. *Journal of Management, 14,* 375–389.

Leana, C. R., & Ivancevich, J. M. (1987). Involuntary job loss: Institutional interventions and a research agenda. *Academy of Management Review, 12,* 301–312.

Leventhal, G. S. (1980). What should be done with equity theory? In K. J. Gergen, M. S. Greenberg, & R. H. Willis (Eds.), *Social exchange: Advances in theory and research* (pp. 27–55). New York: Plenum.

Leventman, P. G. (1974). *The technical professional: A study in career disillusionment.* Unpublished doctoral dissertation, Bryn Mawr College, Bryn Mawr, PA.

Liem, R., & Rayman, P. (1982). Health and social costs of unemployment: Research and policy considerations. *American Psychologist, 37,* 1116–1123.

Lind, E. A., & Tyler, T. R. (1988). *The social psychology of procedural justice.* New York: Plenum Press.

McFarlin, D. B., & Sweeney, P. D. (1990). *Distributive and procedural justice as predictors of outcome satisfaction.* Paper presented at the Society for Industrial and Organizational Psychology, Miami Beach, FL.

Moen, P. (1976). Family impact of the 1975 depression: Duration of unemployment. *Journal of Marriage and the Family, 41,* 561–572.

O'Brian, G. E., & Kabanoff, B. (1979). Comparisons of unemployed and employed workers on work values, locus of control, and health variables. *Australian Psychologist, 14,* 143–154.

Payne, R. L., Warr, P., & Hartley, S. (1980). *Social class and the experience of unemployment.* MCR/SSRCSAPU memo 549.

Pearlin, L. I., & Lieberman, M. A. (1979). Social sources of emotional distress. *Research in Community and Mental Health, 1,* 217–248.

Rhine, B. (1984). Business closings and their effects on employees: The need for new remedies. *Labor Law Journal, 35,* 268–280.

Rousseau, D. M., & Anton, R. J. (1988). Fairness and implied contract obligations in terminations: A policy capturing study. *Human Performance, 1,* 273–289.

Schuster, M., & Miller, C. S. (1984). An empirical assessment of the Age Discrimination in Employment Act. *Industrial and Labor Relations Review, 38,* 64–74.

Stafford, E. M., Jackson, P. R., & Banks, M. H. (1980). Employment, work involvement and mental health in less qualified young people. *Journal of Occupational Psychology, 53,* 291–304.

Stokes, G., & Cochrane, R. (1984). A study of the psychological effects of redundancy and unemployment. *Journal of Occupational Psychology, 57,* 309–322.

Thibaut, J., & Walker, L. (1975). *Procedural justice: A psychological analysis.* Hillsdale, NJ: Lawrence Erlbaum Associates.

Thibaut, J., & Walker, L. (1978). A theory of procedure. *California Law Review, 66,* 541–566.

Tyler, T. R. (1989). The psychology of procedural justice; A test of the group value model. *Journal of Personality and Social Psychology, 57,* 830–838.

Winefield, A. H., Winefield, H. R., Tiggemann, M., & Goldney, R. D. (1991). A longitudinal study of the psychological effects of unemployment and unsatisfactory employment on young adults. *Journal of Applied Psychology, 76,* 424–431.

7

Criticism (Informal Negative Feedback) as a Source of Perceived Unfairness in Organizations: Effects, Mechanisms, and Countermeasures

Robert A. Baron
Rensselaer Polytechnic Institute

A key task performed by managers is that of providing feedback to their subordinates—letting these persons know how well they are doing with respect to meeting the established standards of their organization or work group. When such feedback can be favorable in nature, most managers experience little difficulty in performing this task; communicating good news, after all, is a fairly pleasant task. Transmitting negative feedback, however, is a very different story. Many managers report considerable anxiety and dismay when confronted with the job of telling another person that her or his performance is below acceptable standards. True—there are exceptions to this general rule; a few persons do seem to relish the opportunity to crush another's ego and observe the signs of despair and frustration that often accompany being informed of one's failure (Baron, 1979; Baron & Richardson, 1992). Fortunately, however, such persons are indeed the exception; most managers strongly dislike the task of delivering negative feedback (Larson, 1989).

Why do managers find this to be such a troubling and unpleasant chore? Several factors seem to play a role. First, they anticipate negative reactions on the part of the recipients of such feedback—reactions that can lead to distinctly unpleasant interpersonal exchanges. In recent surveys conducted by myself and my students, managers have reported that they expect subordinates to react to negative feedback with such strategies as excuse-making, anger, and even with such tactics as pretending to accept a criticism as valid while actually rejecting it as unjustified (Baron, 1991). Clearly, such encounters are ones most persons wish to avoid.

Second, and closely related to this first point, managers are reluctant to deliver negative feedback to subordinates because they fear that doing so will adversely affect their working relationships with these persons. They anticipate that delivering negative feedback to subordinates will introduce elements of mistrust and annoyance into their relationships, and will actively interfere with the friendly relations they strive so hard to achieve. After all, they seem to reason, friends don't rain on each others' parades. The logic behind such assumptions may be questionable, but they do seem to play a role in managers' reluctance to deliver negative feedback to others.

Third, but by no means least, managers, like everyone else, have been on the receiving end of negative feedback. Thus, they fully realize how painful and upsetting such information can be. Being familiar with these facts, they are reluctant to deliver such information to subordinates—or to anyone else, for that matter.

In sum, the fact that most managers are disinclined to deliver negative feedback is far from surprising. The understandable nature of such reluctance, however, in no way mitigates its potentially harmful effects. Because managers shy away from the task of delivering negative feedback, they often refrain from commenting on inadequate performance by subordinates. In many cases, they would rather ignore such problems than deal with them head on. Unfortunately, of course, this communicates precisely the wrong message to subordinates: inaction by managers informs them, perhaps erroneously, that what they are doing *is* acceptable. The result? Problems that should have been the focus of negative feedback tend to intensify over time, until it becomes impossible for managers to overlook them any longer, or until they are unable to hold their annoyance—and their tempers!—in check. At this point, negative feedback is, finally, delivered. But because the problems that provoke it are now severe rather than moderate, and because managers may be in a highly emotional state (e.g., strongly annoyed, irritated, frustrated), such feedback is **not** delivered in the most desirable or helpful manner. In fact, as I have noted previously, the negative feedback delivered in such situations can often be described as *destructive* rather than *constructive* in nature (see Fig. 7.1; Baron, 1988b, 1990b). As this term suggests, such feedback can have a number of unfortunate effects. And among these, I believe, is the potential to serve as a source of **perceived injustice** in many organizational settings.

In the remainder of this chapter I focus on this proposal. More specifically, I attempt to accomplish five related tasks. First, I distinguish more clearly between constructive and destructive criticism and describe the negative effects often produced by the former type of feedback. Second, I examine when and how destructive criticism can lead to perceptions of injustice or unfair treatment on the part of the recipients of such feedback. Third, I comment on the relevance of the self-serving bias and related attributional processes to this process. Fourth, I summarize some of the negative effects that may follow from criticism-produced feelings of injustice. Finally, I consider steps that can be taken to alleviate such problems—techniques for delivering negative feedback in ways that do not anger

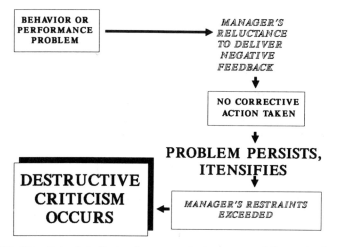

FIG. 7.1.   Potential effects of managers' reluctance to deliver negative feedback to subordinates.

or annoy recipients, and techniques for "repairing the damage" once such criticism has occurred.

DESTRUCTIVE CRITICISM: ITS NATURE AND EFFECTS

The term *criticism* (which I use as a synonym for informal negative feedback in the remainder of this chapter), has an interesting linguistic history. The root of the word is the Greek term *kritikos,* which means discernment. So, the term *criticism* meant, originally, the ability to be discerning, as in theater *critics* or restaurant critics. We do not, in fact, expect such persons to be harsh or pitiless in all cases; rather, we hope that they will indeed be discerning—able to notice, and call our attention to what is both good and bad in plays and restaurants. In recent decades, however, the word "criticism" has taken on a much harsher meaning. This can be readily demonstrated. Imagine that your own boss stated: "Come into my office for a few minutes; I want to criticize you." Clearly, in this context you would anticipate that what would soon follow would be anything but pleasant. In short, the term *criticism* has come, in common use, to be synonymous with such terms as *harsh, biting, stern, unpleasant,* and so on.

In fact, there is no reason why the delivery of negative feedback must involve any of these features. In careful analyses of the nature of such feedback, Weisinger (1981, 1989) has proposed that the content of negative feedback—the basic message that performance has fallen short of accepted standards—can be separated both distinctly and readily from the style in which this information is

TABLE 7.1
Constructive Versus Destructive Criticism

Constructive Criticism	Destructive Criticism
Specific in content	General in content
Does not contain threats	Contains threats
Does not make attributions concerning causes of poor performance	Attributes poor performance in internal causes
Considerate in tone, content	Inconsiderate in tone, content
Timely, prompt	Not timely, delayed
Delivered in appropriate setting	Delivered in inappropriate setting

Note. Based on suggestions by Weisinger (1989).

delivered. Thus, negative feedback that takes account of several basic rules should be described as effective or, as I prefer, *constructive,* while feedback that ignores or violates these rules can be described as ineffective or *destructive.* More specifically, destructive criticism can be defined as negative feedback that angers recipients or induces other reactions (emotional or cognitive) that cause them to reject the feedback offered out of hand, with little or no careful processing of the information provided. In contrast, constructive criticism is negative feedback that does not induce such reactions among recipients and which, as a result, stands a much better chance of being subjected to careful, controlled processing (Srull & Wyer, 1988). What factors or characteristics are most important in determining whether a specific instance of negative feedback belongs in one category or the other? Weisinger's analysis plus the findings of a large body of research on the effectiveness of feedback (e.g., Ilgen, Fisher, & Taylor, 1979; Larson, 1986) indicate that the ones listed in Table 7.1 are most crucial.

Destructive criticism, then, is negative feedback that is inconsiderate in style and content—it is indeed harsh, biting, and sarcastic, and takes no account of the feelings or emotional reactions of the recipients. Similarly, such criticism often contains threats—statements indicating that negative outcomes will follow if the recipient does not change her or his behavior in a specific manner (Shapiro & Bies, 1991). Third, destructive criticism often includes internal attributions; it affixes blame for poor performance squarely on the recipients, and on such factors as their lack of motivation, ability, or commitment. Fourth, destructive criticism is not timely; it is delivered long after the events in question have occurred—and when they may seem completely irrelevant to the current situation. Fifth, destructive criticism is general rather than specific. It indicates that something is wrong, but it does not specify precisely where and how performance has been inadequate, and therefore offers little if any clue as to how the situation (or performance) can be improved. Finally, such criticism is delivered at inappropriate times and in inappropriate settings—for example, in the presence of others rather than in private, and at times when the recipient can do little or nothing to respond to the criticism.

What are the effects of destructive criticism? I have conducted a series of studies focused on precisely this issue, so empirical data is available to address this point (Baron, 1988b, 1990b). In these studies (most of which were conducted in the laboratory), participants performed a relatively interesting task (devising a marketing plan for a new product), and then received feedback on their work from an accomplice. In both the constructive and destructive criticism conditions, this feedback was negative: Subjects received low numerical ratings on scales assessing their originality, creativity, effort, knowledge of potential markets, and so on. However, the written comments accompanying these ratings were distinctly different in the two conditions. In the constructive criticism condition, the comments were written to be specific in content, considerate in tone, to avoid attributions concerning the causes of subjects' poor performance, and contained no threats. For example, with respect to originality, the comments stated: "I think you were too conventional and unwilling to try anything very new." In contrast, in the destructive criticism condition, the comments were written to violate the guidelines described earlier; thus, they were inconsiderate in tone, general, attributed poor performance to internal factors, and included threats. For example, again with respect to originality, the written comment stated: "I don't think you could be original if you tried. Dull stuff."

The key question in this research was straightforward: Would subjects respond differently to these two styles of criticism despite the fact that in both cases, the underlying numerical ratings of their performance were identical? The findings of several related studies left little doubt. On virtually every dependent measure gathered, subjects exposed to destructive criticism demonstrated more negative reactions. As compared to those receiving constructive criticism, persons exposed to destructive criticism reported stronger feelings of anger and tension, stronger tendencies to resolve interpersonal conflicts through avoidance but weaker tendencies to resolve them through collaboration, lower self-set goals, and lower feelings of self-efficacy (Baron, 1988b, 1990b). In addition, studies conducted in organizational settings indicate that both managers and subordinates perceive destructive criticism as an important cause of conflict in their organizations, and as undermining effective working relationships (Baron, 1990b, 1991a). In short, it appears that where negative feedback is concerned, it is not simply the information that one has performed poorly that matters; the style in which this information is conveyed is important too. As I now point out, this theme has been one of growing importance in recent research on justice in organizational settings (cf. Tyler & Bies, 1990).

THE INTERPERSONAL CONTEXT OF
ORGANIZATIONAL JUSTICE: BEYOND OUTCOMES
AND PROCEDURES

As noted by Cropanzano (chapter 1, this volume), justice research can be construed as having focused, in turn, on two major aspects of perceived fairness: *distributive justice*—the allocation or division of various available resources among parties to an exchange (Adams, 1965; Crosby, 1976) and *procedural justice*—the processes by which such allocation decisions are reached (Folger & Greenberg, 1985; Thibaut & Walker, 1975). Both perspectives have proven valuable and have shed much light on the nature of justice in organizational settings (Cropanzano & Folger, 1989; Greenberg, 1988). Recently, however, a third perspective has received increasing attention. This perspective is, perhaps, most clearly described by Tyler and Bies, who noted that "people's judgments of procedural fairness are influenced by the quality of interpersonal treatment they receive from decision makers . . ." (1990, p. 88). In other words, there has been growing recognition, in recent years, that fair allocation of available resources in accordance with established procedures is not all there is to perceptions of organizational justice. In addition, the interpersonal treatment people receive within this context—the style adopted by resource allocators or decision makers—is important too. More specifically, what seems to matter is people's attributions concerning the motives of decision makers, explanations offered by these persons for their actions, adherence to ethical standards, apparent concern for their rights and welfare, and many other factors. So, in order for people to conclude that they have been treated in a fair manner and that exchanges have been just, something more than distributive and procedural justice seems to be required. And that is, succinctly, the perception that those involved in making decisions concerning reward allocations have behaved in a socially appropriate manner and demonstrated the kind of respect most individuals believe they deserve. As one old comment that appeared in countless Hollywood Westerns of the 1930s and 1940s put it, "Smile when you say that, pardner . . ."

A considerable body of empirical evidence lends support to the contention that this interpersonal context is an important one for understanding the nature of organizational justice. For example, consider a study conducted by Bies (1986). He asked MBA students to describe situations in which they felt fairly or unfairly treated during the job recruitment process. The students' replies demonstrated considerable concern with such factors as the recruiter's honesty, courtesy, and concern for their personal rights, as evidenced by a lack of questions about such matters as marital status. In addition, and perhaps more surprising, these job candidates indicated concern with such factors—their interpersonal treatment by the interviewers—regardless of whether they were ultimately offered a job. So style (how they were treated interpersonally) seemed to be as important to these students as the actual outcome of the process.

Several additional studies suggest that individuals often reach conclusions about the fairness of procedures on the basis of actions by the persons who enact them (i.e., decision makers; Bies & Moag, 1986; Tyler, 1988). In one series of studies on this issue, Bies and his colleagues (e.g., Bies, 1987; Bies, Shapiro, & Cummings, 1988) have examined the effects of accounts—decision makers' explanations for their actions—on perceptions of procedural and allocation fairness. For example, in one of these studies, Bies et al. (1988) asked MBA students to describe a recent situation in which they made a request to their boss that was rejected. After doing so, they rated the extent to which their boss offered an explanation for this rejection—a *causal account*. Subjects also rated the adequacy of the reasoning offered in support of the account, and the boss's apparent sincerity. Finally, they rated the extent to which they became angry after the boss's refusal, the extent to which they felt they were treated unfairly in the situation, their disapproval of their boss, and the extent to which they complained about the decision to persons at higher levels in the organization. Results indicated that both the perceived adequacy of the reasoning behind the causal account and its perceived sincerity influenced subjects' reactions. The more adequate the reasoning in the boss's refusal and the greater his or her sincerity, the lower subjects' reported feelings of anger, unfairness, and disapproval, and the lower their tendency to complain to higher-ups. These findings suggest that fairness in such situations is influenced by social factors and attributions, as well as by the actual decision reached.

I have obtained closely related results in a series of studies concerned with the role of attributions in organizational conflict (Baron, 1985, 1988a, 1990a). In these studies, subjects negotiated with an accomplice who adopted an extreme initial position and then made very few concessions during the exchange of offers and counteroffers that followed. At various points during the session, the accomplice offered various explanations for his or her confrontational actions. In various conditions, the accomplice attributed this behavior to (a) orders from superiors to be tough, (b) the sincere belief that his or her position was a fair one, or (c) his or her own personal competitiveness. Not surprisingly, subjects responded more negatively to the accomplice when this person attributed confrontational actions to personal characteristics than when he or she attributed the same actions to sincere beliefs in his or her own position or to external factors (orders from superiors). In addition, some findings suggested that perceptions of the accomplice's fairness, too, varied with these attributional conditions. Subjects rated the accomplice as being least fair when this person attributed his or her "tough stance" to personal competitiveness, but as most fair when the accomplice attributed the same behavior to the sincere belief that his or her position was a fair one. These findings lend support to the view that social factors—in this case causal attributions—play an important role in perceptions of organizational fairness.

Related research by Tyler (1988) extends this principle to a somewhat different context—that involving interactions between citizens and both the police and the courts. Tyler found that in assessing the fairness of these public organizations, individuals weigh their personal treatment by police officers and court officials as heavily as the actual outcomes they experience or the procedures involved. Once again, then, interpersonal factors appeared to be quite important to individuals in judgments of fairness, even in cases where the stakes are high indeed.

It is in this interpersonal context that the nature of negative feedback—whether it takes the form of constructive or destructive criticism—comes sharply into focus. Virtually everyone would agree that negative feedback has one primary—and rational!—purpose: helping recipients to improve. When criticism is delivered in a constructive manner (i.e., when it is considerate, timely, avoids threats, and so on), I contend, it is perceived as stemming primarily, if not entirely, from this basic motive. When, in contrast, it is delivered in a destructive manner (i.e., when it is inconsiderate, not timely, includes threats, assigns blame), I suggest, it is perceived as stemming from other motives, for example, desires on the part of the critic to assert her or his authority, to put the recipient in "his or her place," to get even for past wrongs by the recipient, and so on.).

I have recently obtained support for these predictions in several studies (Baron, 1991a). In these investigations, managers from several different companies were asked to describe instances in which they criticized, or were criticized by, another person. Then, they were asked to answer a series of questions pertaining to their reactions to the criticism and their perceptions of the motives behind it. Focusing for the moment on managers' reactions when they were the recipients of criticism, results indicated that the greater the extent to which managers perceived the criticism as constructive (i.e., specific, considerate, and so on), the more they perceived it as stemming from the critic's desire to help them do their job better ($R^2 = .44, p < .05$). Similarly, the more they perceived the criticism as constructive in nature, the greater the extent to which they rated it as fair ($R^2 = .78, p < .01$). These findings, and those in related research (e.g., Bies, 1990) indicated that negative feedback—and especially the manner in which it is delivered—can play a key role in judgments of organizational justice. As Tyler and Bies noted: ". . . the interpersonal treatment that people receive from decision makers is an important consideration in people's evaluation of procedural justice" (1990, p. 83).

COMPLICATIONS IN THE PROCESS: THE SELF-SERVING BIAS STRIKES AGAIN

Social perception is a ubiquitous process, but if recent research on this topic (and on social cognition generally) points to any conclusion it is this: Our constructions of the social world are subject to many forms of potential bias and error (Smith & Kida, 1991). One of the most important of these occurs with respect to attributions and is known as the *self-serving bias* (Miller & Ross, 1975). Briefly, it refers to our tendency to attribute desirable outcomes to internal causes, but undesirable ones to external factors. Put another way, the self-serving bias leads us to take credit for positive results, but to blame others (or additional external causes) for negative ones. The self-serving bias is powerful, and has been observed in many different contexts (e.g., Maass & Volpato, 1989). For example, in research closely related to the present line of reasoning, Baumeister and his colleagues (Baumeister, Stillwell, & Wotman, 1990) asked male and female subjects to provide autobiographical accounts of instances in which (a) they had been angered by another person, and (b) they had been the cause of another's anger. Content analyses of these reports indicated that perceptions of these two classes of incidents differed in many respects. Moreover, and more to the point, many of these differences seemed to reflect the operation of the self-serving bias. Thus, when reporting on incidents in which they had been victims of anger-provoking actions by others, subjects tended to describe the perpetrator's actions as stemming from arbitrary, incoherent, or even contradictory motives, as involving lasting harm, and as damaging to their relationship with this person. In contrast, when reporting on incidents in which they had been the anger-provoker, subjects described their behavior as stemming from uncontrollable impulses or external factors beyond their control, as being isolated incidents unlikely to produce lasting harm, and as unlikely to damage their relationship with the victim. In addition, while victims perceived their anger in the situation as justified and reasonable, perpetrators tended to perceive such anger as surprisingly—and inexplicably—strong.

On the basis of these findings, Baumeister proposed a model of interpersonal conflict in which perpetrators perform actions that, from their perspective, are reasonable and legitimate. Victims, however, perceive these actions as inexplicable provocations, stemming primarily from sheer malice. Yet, despite such perceptions, victims appear to suppress open expressions of anger in many cases: they don't want to give the anger-provoker the satisfaction of seeing how upset they are, or don't want to encourage further unpleasantness. As a result, perpetrators continue their actions until—at some point—victims can no longer hold their tempers in check. Now it is the turn of perpetrators to perceive another's actions of inexplicable and mysterious; after all, the victims have not given them any prior indication that they objected strongly to the anger-provoking actions, so why are they so angry now?

If this process sounds similar to the one outlined at the start of this chapter, in which managers refrain from delivering negative feedback to subordinates until they can no longer tolerate unacceptable actions by these persons, this is intentional. Many of the same elements seem to be involved. In the context of Baumeister et al.'s (1990) model, managers may be viewed as victims of anger-provoking actions by subordinates. Like the victims in this model, they stifle overt expressions of their anger or annoyance—until they are unable to do so any longer. The emotional outbursts that follow then take the form of destructive criticism, and can, as I have found in several studies (Baron, 1988b, 1990b) produce negative effects on motivation and working relationships.

Additional evidence in support of this model, and in support of the operation of the self-serving bias, is provided by the study described earlier (Baron, 1991). As may be recalled, participants in that investigation described incidents

TABLE 7.2
Perceptions of Own and Others' Criticism

Measure	Criticism to Others	Criticism Received
Anger felt by critic	3.77	5.42
Fairness of criticism	6.23	4.83
Criticism stemmed from desire to help	5.84	3.79
Criticism stemmed from desire to get even	2.07	4.20

Note. Ratings on 7-point scales; $p < .05$ in all cases.

in which they were the recipient of criticism and in which they were the critic. The survey they completed asked participants to rate the criticism they delivered or received on a number of different dimensions. On the basis of the self-serving bias, I predicted that they would rate their own criticism more favorably. For example, they would report more positive and appropriate relations while delivering criticism than when receiving it, and would perceive their own criticism as stemming from more desirable motives than criticism they received from others. As shown in Table 7.2, this is precisely what occurred. Subjects reported less anger while delivering criticism than when receiving it, $F (4, 20) = 11.23, p < .001$, and described criticism they delivered as stemming from more desirable motives than criticism they received from others, $F (7, 17) = 5.35, p < .002$. In other words, the self-serving bias did seem to operate, and operate strongly, in the context of informal negative feedback.

These findings, in turn, suggest the existence of powerful internal barriers to the acceptance of criticism. Recipients, it appears, are predisposed to view such feedback as unjustified, as poorly delivered, and as stemming from motives that are, at the least, suspect in nature. In order for criticism to gain acceptance, therefore, it seems imperative that it be delivered in accordance with the guidelines noted above—that it be considerate, timely, free of threats, and so on. Recipients appear to be too sensitive to such information to permit any other course of action.

PERCEPTIONS THAT CRITICISM HAS BEEN UNFAIR: ADDITIONAL NEGATIVE EFFECTS

So far in this discussion, I have described the nature of destructive criticism and outlined some of its potential negative effects. In this section, I broaden the context of this discussion somewhat by focusing on some effects that may follow when criticism is perceived as unfair by its recipients.

As noted earlier, the primary purpose of negative feedback is that of helping the recipient improve. In other words, criticism is a form of social influence—it is designed, after all, to produce some change in the behavior of the persons toward whom it is directed. Is it effective in this regard? That, in a sense, is the crux of the entire matter. In some instances, and to some extent, criticism does indeed succeed in producing such change. In a recent investigation conducted with managers from a large manufacturing company, participants were asked to rate the extent to which criticism produces a wide range of effects (Baron, 1991b). Results indicated that the managers perceived criticism as producing such effects as desired changes in recipients' behavior ($M = 4.65$), and increments in recipients' motivation ($M = 4.58$; all ratings were made on a 7-point scale ranging from "likely to occur" to "very unlikely to occur.") However, the same managers also reported that criticism yielded such counterproductive effects as causing recipients to change negatively ($M = 3.50$), to become angry and reject the criticism ($M = 3.43$), and to become less confident of their own abilities ($M = 3.27$). Clearly, then, the picture is mixed with respect to the efficacy of criticism in producing desired change.

Certainly the effectiveness of criticism in this respect depends strongly on the style in which it is delivered—the extent to which it is constructive or destructive in nature (Baron, 1990b; Weisinger, 1989). However, I contend that the success of criticism in producing its desired goal of change is strongly mediated by recipients' perceptions of the extent to which it is fair. Moreover, I suggest that the nature of such mediation can be understood in the context of recent cognitive models of persuasion (e.g., Petty & Cacioppo, 1986). When criticism is perceived as being fair, the information it contains is subjected to careful scrutiny and elaborate processing. Persuasion then occurs through what, in recent models of persuasion, is termed the *central route*. In contrast, when criticism is perceived as being unfair or unjustified, relatively little processing of the information it contains follows. In this case, persuasion (and subsequent change) occurs through what is known as the *peripheral route,* and will occur only if the criticism is accompanied by powerful persuasion cues—information relating to the expertise, attractiveness, or status of the would-be persuader. Given that criticism perceived as unfair tends to elicit reactions that may interfere with the operation of such persuasion cues (e.g., anger, annoyance, feelings of being victimized), as well as competing cognitive processes (e.g., vigorous efforts at excuse-generation), persuasion seems highly unlikely in this context (see Fig. 7.2).

In summary, it is suggested here that perceptions regarding the fairness of informal negative feedback play a crucial role in the extent to which such information attains its primary goal: inducing desired change on the part of recipients. To the extent these proposals are confirmed by subsequent research, it would appear that managers and others faced with the task of delivering such feedback should take every step at their disposal to assure that their comments are viewed as being fair and justified. What steps are helpful in this regard? It is to this question that I turn next.

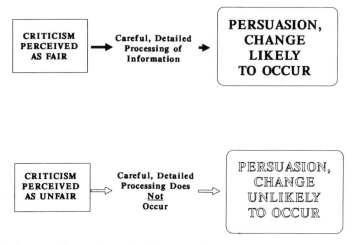

FIG. 7.2.   Effects of perceived fairness of criticism on information processing and persuasion.

ENHANCING THE EFFECTIVENESS OF CRITICISM:
SOME PRACTICAL STEPS

Although managers certainly play many different roles, they are, after all, often hired to *manage*—to oversee and supervise others. And as noted previously, this function involves providing such persons with the feedback they need to enhance their performance. Knowing how to deliver criticism in an effective manner, therefore, is a skill that most, if not all managers, will find useful. In this final section, I focus on steps that managers and others with authority can take to improve their own performance in this crucial respect.

Designing Criticism to be Effective: Following the Basic Guidelines

The first and most obvious step managers can take to enhance their success as providers of negative feedback is to follow the guidelines for effective or constructive criticism presented earlier. Because these have been presented elsewhere, there is no need to repeat them here. However, I would like to add two points. First, before criticizing another person, it is crucial that future critics examine their own motives. "Why am I going to deliver this negative feedback?" should be the first, and most fundamental question. If the answer is anything other than "To help this person improve," it is time to delay—and think again!

Second, criticism should have a strategic element. Before criticizing another person, a would-be critic should consider such questions as these: "What do I hope to accomplish through this criticism—what do I wish to change?" and "Can the recipient actually change in this manner?" Unless the precise goal(s) of criticism are clear, it may quickly turn into an empty exercise in verbal abuse. Similarly, if the recipient can't change—he or she lacks the needed skills or information; it is too late to alter a course of action—there is little or no justification for delivering criticism. These are basic points all persons about to engage in criticism should address.

Assure That the Procedures Surrounding the Criticism are Fair

In their insightful analysis of the interpersonal context of procedural justice, Tyler and Bies (1990) noted that even formal decision-making procedures afford decision makers some latitude and discretion. This is certainly true with respect to informal negative feedback. Managers have the option of deciding when, where, and how such feedback is delivered. In view of this fact, it seems important that they take steps to assure that recipients perceive their decisions in this respect to be fair and rational ones. In other words, they should do everything in their power to assure that criticism is not perceived as a random, arbitrary, haphazard event, stemming as much from managers' bad moods as from more formal procedures. This involves attention to the following issues:

1. *Leave room in the process for employees' viewpoints:* Managers should begin criticism sessions by noting that what follows is based on their perceptions; thus, it is not unshakable "fact," and is open to correction on the basis of input from employees. This suggests openness to employees' viewpoints, and may enhance perceptions that the procedures are fair (e.g., Tyler, 1987).

2. *Apply criteria for assessing performance consistently across employees:* When delivering negative feedback, critics should do everything in their power to assure recipients that what follows is based on consistently applied criteria. In other words, they should assure that all subordinates are assessed on the same criteria, and that criticism is tied closely to these consistent standards (Greenberg, 1986).

3. *Avoid any suggestion of personal bias:* As noted earlier, recipients of criticism are all too ready to perceive it as stemming from less than compelling causes, or even from the personal malice of critics. Related perceptions center around the belief that critics are acting out of personal bias—dislike for the recipients, racial or ethnic prejudice, and related factors. Clearly, managers should strive to overcome such perceptions on the part of subordinates. It is important that both appear to be unbiased (Greenberg, 1989), and that they actually be unbiased in these and other respects. Failure to accomplish these goals will undermine their efforts to induce desirable change on the part of the recipients of criticism.

COUNTERING THE EFFECTS OF DESTRUCTIVE CRITICISM: WHAT TO DO WHEN THE GUIDELINES HAVE BEEN VIOLATED

Perfection is a quality that lies beyond human grasp; it can be imagined, but it is, by definition, impossible to achieve. This is certainly true with respect to the delivery of informal negative feedback. Despite their best efforts, no manager will be able to criticize others in a completely flawless manner. And in fact, most will find that on occasion, they do lose their tempers and say things to subordinates that violate at least one of the guidelines for effective criticism. What can be done to repair the damage produced by such exchanges? I examined this issue in two studies, one conducted in the laboratory and the other carried out in an organizational setting. Results of both investigations agreed in suggesting that negative effects resulting from instances of destructive criticism can be countered in several ways. The most successful of these involve direct apologies for the inappropriate criticism, and efforts to attribute such criticism to external causes (e.g., felt role requirements, externally imposed high standards). Both of these procedures appear to mitigate the anger and annoyance generated by destructive criticism, and to restore working relationships to their former state. Interestingly, procedures involving the opportunity to voice complaints about harsh criticism were ineffective in this respect. Indeed, they actually seemed to increase feelings of anger on the part of recipients. These findings agree with evidence gathered in the study of *catharsis,* suggesting that such procedures are often ineffective in reducing anger and overt aggression and may, in fact, actually intensify such reactions (e.g., Baron & Richardson, 1992).

To summarize, it appears that the effects of destructive criticism can be reduced by various procedures. Managers and others who err in this manner, therefore, should not despair; if they act promptly and carefully, the negative effects that often result from such criticism *can* be lessened. One cautionary note: The repeated use of such corrective actions may tend to lessen their effectiveness; after all, how many times can a manager apologize for angry outbursts? Thus, the guiding principle where criticism is concerned should be prevention, not repair of damage already done. Where providing others with informal negative feedback is concerned, therefore, the old adage about the relative merits of prevention and cure is one worth keeping firmly in mind.

REFERENCES

Adams, J. S. (1965). Inequity in social exchange. In L. Berkowitz (Ed.), *Advances in experimental social psychology* (Vol. 2, pp. 267–299). New York: Academic Press.

Baron, R. A. (1979). Aggression, empathy, and race: Effects of victim's pain cues, victim's race, and level of instigation on physical aggression. *Journal of Applied Social Psychology, 9,* 103–114.

Baron, R. A. (1985). Reducing organizational conflict: The role of attributions. *Journal of Applied Psychology, 70,* 434–441.

Baron, R. A. (1988a). Attributions and organizational conflict: The mediating role of apparent sincerity. *Organizational Behavior and Human Decision Processes, 41,* 111–127.

Baron, R. A. (1988b). Negative effects of destructive criticism: Impact on conflict, self-efficacy, and task performance. *Journal of Applied Psychology, 73,* 199–207.

Baron, R. A. (1990a). Attributions and organizational conflict. In S. Graham & V. Folkes (Eds.), *Attribution theory: Applications to achievement, mental health, and interpersonal conflict* (pp. 185–204). Hillsdale, NJ: Lawrence Erlbaum Associates.

Baron, R. A. (1990b). Countering the effects of destructive criticism: The relative efficacy of four potential interventions. *Journal of Applied Psychology, 75,* 235–245.

Baron, R. A. (1991). *The use and impact of criticism (informal negative feedback) in organizations.* Unpublished manuscript, Rensselaer Polytechnic Institute, Troy, NY.

Baron, R. A., & Richardson, D. (1992). *Human aggression* (2nd ed.). New York: Plenum.

Baumeister, R. F., Stillwell, A., & Wotman, S. R. (1990). Victim and perpetrator accounts of interpersonal conflict: Autobiographical narratives about anger. *Journal of Personality and Social Psychology, 59,* 994–1005.

Bies, R. J. (1986). Identifying principles of interactional justice: The case of corporate recruiting. In R. J. Bies (Ed.), *Moving beyond equity theory: new directions in research on justice in organizations.* Symposium conducted at the meetings of the Academy of Management, Chicago, IL.

Bies, R. J. (1987). The predicament of injustice. In B. M. Staw & L. L. Cummings (Eds.), *Research in organizational behavior* (Vol. 9, pp. 290–318). Greenwich, CT: JAI Press.

Bies, R. J. (1990). Managing conflict before it happens: The role of accounts. In M. A. Rahim (Ed.), *Managing conflict: An interdisciplinary approach* (pp. 83–91). New York: Praeger.

Bies, R. J., & Moag, J. S. (1986). Interactional justice: Communication criteria of fairness. In R. J. Lack, B. H. Sheppard, & M. H. Bazerman (Eds.), *Research on negotiations in organizations* (Vol. 1, pp. 43–55). Greenwich, CT: JAI Press.

Bies, R. J., Shapiro, D. L., & Cummings, L. L. (1988). Causal accounts and managing organizational conflict: Is it enough to say it's not my fault? *Communication Research, 15,* 381–399.

Cropanzano, R., & Folger, R. (1989). Referent cognitions and task decision autonomy: Beyond equity theory. *Journal of Applied Psychology, 74,* 293–299.

Crosby, F. (1976). A model of egoistical relative deprivation. *Psychological Review, 83,* 85–113.

Folger, R., & Greenberg, J. (1985). Procedural justice: An interpretive analysis of personnel systems. In K. Rowland & G. Ferris (Eds.), *Research in personnel and human resource management* (Vol. 3, pp. 141–183). Greenwich, CT: JAI Press.

Greenberg, J. (1986). Determinants of perceived fairness of performance evaluations. *Journal of Applied Psychology, 71,* 340–342.

Greenberg, J. (1988). Cultivating an image of justice: Looking fair on the job. *Academy of Management Executive, 11,* 155–158.

Ilgen, D. R., Fisher, C. D., & Taylor, M. S. (1979). Consequences of individual feedback on behavior in organizations. *Journal of Applied Psychology, 64,* 349–371.

Larson, J. R., Jr. (1986). Supervisor's performance feedback to subordinates: The role of subordinate performance valence and outcome dependence. *Organizational Behavior and Human Decision Processes, 37,* 391–408.

Larson, J. R., Jr. (1989). The dynamic interplay between employees' feedback-seeking strategies and supervisors' delivery of performance feedback. *Academy of Management Review, 14,* 408–422.

Maass, A., & Volpato, C. (1989). Gender differences in self-serving attributions about sexual experiences. *Journal of Applied Psychology, 19,* 517–542.

Miller, D. T., & Ross, M. (1975). Self-serving biases in the attribution of causality: Fact or fiction? *Psychological Bulletin, 82,* 313–325.

Petty, R. E., & Cacioppo, J. T. (1986). The elaboration likelihood model of persuasion. In L. Berkowitz (Ed.), *Advances in experimental social psychology* (Vol. 19, pp. 123–205). New York: Academic Press.

Shapiro, D. L., & Bies, R. J. (1991). *Threats, bluffs, and disclaimers: Their effects on negotiator power, fairness, trustworthiness, and performance.* Manuscript submitted for publication.

Smith, J. F., & Kida, T. (1991). Heuristics and biases: Expertise and task realism in auditing. *Psychological Bulletin, 109,* 472–489.

Srull, T. K., & Wyer, R. S. (1988). *Advances in social cognition: A dual model of impression formation.* Hillsdale, NJ: Lawrence Erlbaum Associates.

Thibaut, J., & Walker, L. (1975). *Procedural justice: A psychological analysis.* Hillsdale, NJ: Lawrence Erlbaum Associates.

Tyler, R. R. (1987). Conditions leading to value expressive effects in judgments of procedural justice: A test of our models. *Journal of Personality and Social Psychology, 52,* 333–344.

Tyler, T. R. (1988). What is procedural justice? *Law and Society Review, 22,* 301–335.

Tyler, T. R., & Bies, R. J. (1990). Beyond formal procedures: The interpersonal context of procedural justice. In J. S. Carrol (Ed.), *Applied social psychology and organizational settings.* Hillsdale, NJ: Lawrence Erlbaum Associates.

Weisinger, H. L. (1981). *Nobody's perfect.* Los Angeles: Stratford Press.

Weisinger, H. L. (1989). *The critical edge: How to criticize up and down your organization and make it pay off.* Boston: Little Brown.

8 Justice Considerations in Employee Drug Testing

Mary A. Konovsky
Tulane University

Russell Cropanzano
Colorado State University

The percentage of organizations performing some type of drug testing varies widely with the type of industry, size of the company, nature of the work, and geographic location (Axel, 1989; Blum, 1989; Murphy & Thornton, 1991). Nevertheless, some general estimates of the prevalence of drug testing are available. Lahey (1986) reported, for example, that about 25% of all Fortune 500 companies conduct some form of drug screening. In a survey of 669 organizations, Axel found that a little under 50% of organizations tested for illicit substances. In a similar field study involving 125 companies, Blum placed the figure at a very similar 46%. Finally, in a recent study by Murphy and Thornton (1991), nearly 41% of the organizations examined were likely to engage in some form of screening. In each study it is likely that the survey was slanted toward larger organizations who are more likely to test. Nevertheless, these figures indicate that a large proportion of the American work force will be tested for drug use at least some time in their careers. Indeed, Murphy, Thornton, and Reynolds (1990) noted that the number of workers tested could be more than 4 million—and this figure only includes organizations regulated by the federal government.

THE EMERGENCE OF DRUG TESTING IN THE UNITED STATES

Drug testing emerges out of many people's fears of widespread substance abuse (Reinarman, Waldorf, & Murphy, 1988; Sloman, 1979). This concern began to grow during the 1960s. Against a backdrop of social change, there was a spread of new values concerning drug use and a notable increase in drug use among two

171

groups of young adults. The first of these was upper middle-class college students whose highly publicized use of drugs such as marijuana resulted in concern over the effects of marijuana on cognitive tasks and school performance. The second emerging group of drug users was American service personnel. The increased prevalence of drug use, especially among military personnel, ultimately led to an increase in drug testing. Here we trace the development of the events leading to widespread use of drug testing, beginning with the use of illicit drugs by middle-class students and military personnel, to concern over academic and military performance.

The "Hang" Loose Ethic

Goode (1972) and Johnson (1973) noted that a new set of cultural values arose during the 1960s. Trice and Roman (1972) termed these values the *hang loose* ethic. Among other things, this ethic rejected traditional values, including those opposing drug use. This new set of attitudes was not limited to the United States, but was also observed among many young Western Europeans (Battegay, Ladewig, Mühlemann, & Weidmann, 1976).

Research by Groves (1974) and Walters, Goethals, and Pope (1972) documented the rise of drug use among the young during this time period, and noted that this increase was associated with alternative or so-called "hippie" lifestyle. In the United States the increase in drug use (e.g., marijuana, in particular) has continued to the present time. Although it may currently be leveling off somewhat (Horgan, 1990), national surveys by both Cook (1989) and Voss (1989) show relatively high rates of marijuana use, the incidence of which is highest among the young. Given the age of many of those drug users, and the fact that they were often students, many people were concerned that marijuana use might exert detrimental effects on academic performance. This concern manifested itself in laboratory studies of cognitive performance (Murray, 1986) and field studies of academic performance (e.g., Gergen, Gergen, & Morse, 1972; Robbins, 1974). Although conducted in different settings and examining different outcomes, these two types of studies share a common theme of concern with mental impairment associated with marijuana use. We therefore briefly review those studies here.

Marijuana and Performance

There now appears to be some consensus that individuals' cognitive performance deteriorates under conditions of marijuana intoxication (see reviews by Murray, 1986, and Pugliese, 1973). Cropanzano and Konovsky (in press) noted that marijuana has adverse effects at all stages of information processing. When under the influence of marijuana, for example, there is evidence that subjects have trouble maintaining attention on complex tasks (Casswell & Marks, 1973;

MacAvoy & Marks, 1975), show decreased ability to retain information in short-term memory (Abel, 1970; Tinklenberg, Melges, Hollister, & Gillespie, 1970), have difficulty transferring material from short-term to long-term memory (Dornbush, Fink, & Freedman, 1971; Gianutsos & Litwack, 1976), and exhibit retrieval problems (Clark, Hughes, & Nakashima, 1970; Miller, Drew, & Kiplinger, 1972). In addition, marijuana intoxication causes poorer performance on traditional intelligence tests (Gilbert, 1970; Kiplinger, 1970) and interferes with judgments of time (Hollister & Gillespie, 1970) and distance (Roth et al., 1973).

Collectively, the evidence presented is convincing that marijuana contributes to decrements in cognitive performance. There are, however, important limitations in these studies. In particular, all of the studies examined cognitive performance while the individual was under the influence of marijuana. It is less certain that marijuana inhibits academic performance for the casual or recreational user who abstains while actually performing the requisite tasks. Several field studies have addressed this issue and the results are mixed. Johnson (1973) found that marijuana users made worse grades; Gergen, Gergen, and Morse (1972) found they made better grades; and Blum (1989) found no relationship between casual marijuana use and academic performance.

One additional limitation of the studies on the influence of marijuana on cognitive performance is the cross-sectional nature of the samples. Two longitudinal studies conducted by Mellinger, Somers, Bazell, and Manheimer (1978) and Shedler and Block (1990) overcome this design deficiency. The results of those two studies are intriguing. These authors found that most marijuana smokers were casual and moderate in their use. Marijuana users were also found to be better adjusted than were abstainers. In both studies, however, there was a subgroup of chronic and heavy users who made worse grades and were more poorly adjusted than casual users. In other words, marijuana may be associated with performance decrements only among a relatively few heavy users.

Drug Use During the Vietnam War and the Military Response

During the Vietnam War, drug use spread throughout the American military (Robbins, 1974). Although marijuana was commonly used, a variety of other substances were also available (Robbins, 1978). Rock and Silsby (1978), for example, report substantial abuse of Methaqualone among service personnel stationed in Europe. Drug use became so extensive by 1975 that approximately 47% of the recruits inducted into the Navy reported pre-service drug experience (Crawford, Thomas, & Thomas, 1976).

Concern over the high rates of drug use in the military was exacerbated by a series of studies showing that military personnel drug use was associated with undesirable behaviors. Roffman and Sapol (1970), for example, found that soldiers stationed in Vietnam who used marijuana had more disciplinary problems than those who abstained from drug use. Similarly, Kolb, Nail, and Gunderson (1975) found that military drug users were less likely to be promoted and more likely to incur disciplinary action than non-drug users. A later study by Blank and Fenton (1989) found that Naval recruits who tested positive for marijuana were more likely to leave the service than those who did not test positive for marijuana. Indeed, after only 2½ years, 43% of the marijuana positive group had left the Navy. Finally, in a more extensive study of Naval personnel, McDaniel (1988) examined the relationship of use of a variety of drugs to the likelihood of an unsuitability discharge. McDaniel found that pre-service drug users were more likely to be discharged, although the effect sizes were all quite small (all r's between .04 to .07).

One problem with the research on drug use and behavior problems in the military is that many of these studies' results suffer from criterion contamination. One of the principal reasons that participants in these studies were discharged and disciplined is drug use. As a result of this type of relationship between drug use and discharge, definitive conclusions concerning the causal relationship between drug use and disciplinary problems cannot be drawn on the basis of these studies (cf. Normand, Salyards, & Mahoney, 1990). Regardless of any methodological flaws in their data collection, the US military nevertheless turned to drug testing to correct behavioral problems of its personnel (Blank & Fenton, 1989). Drug testing may have been reasonably successful in lowering the rate of drug use because by 1985, the reported incidence of marijuana use among Naval personnel had dropped to approximately 10% (Bray et al., 1986).

Drug Testing Spreads to Other Domains

Concerned over the high prevalence of drug use in American society (Cook, 1989; Voss, 1989) and encouraged by the apparent success of military drug testing, the US government began to encourage screening (cf. Hoffman & Silvers, 1987; Quayle, 1983) and drug testing spread rapidly through both the public and private sectors. Lahey (1986) reported that 25% of all Fortune 500 companies tested employees and/or applicants, and Hoffman and Silvers (1987) noted that by 1986 drug testing had become a $2 billion a year industry.

Given the rapid increase in the use of drug testing as a personnel selection device, research on the validity of drug testing as a screening device began to emerge. Much of this research focused on the link between using illicit substances and undesirable work behaviors. In the public sector, for example, the validity of an extensive drug-testing program devised by the US Postal Service has been examined. Normand, Salyards, and Mahoney (1990) found that marijuana use was associated with a greater rate of absences but not turnover or accidents in the United States Postal Service. Cocaine use, on the other hand, was associated with both absence and turnover rates. The generally weak results for accidents may have been due to the low base-rate. In another study of postal workers, Zwerling, Ryan, and Orav (1990) reported that individuals testing positive for either marijuana or cocaine had a higher rate of turnover. In addition, these individuals were apt to have their first injuries, accidents, and disciplinary actions at an earlier date than workers who tested negative for cocaine and marijuana.

Results from the private sector are somewhat less consistent than those from public sector organizations. In a study conducted at a large utility company, for example, Sheridan and Winkler (1989) found that employees who tested positive for drugs (usually marijuana) had more absences, accidents, and injuries than those testing negative. However, Horgan (1990) noted that this company tested "for cause." That is, employees were much more likely to be tested following an accident. Consequently, the possibility of criterion contamination as an alternative explanation for these results cannot be ruled out. Another study of utility workers conducted by Sheridan and Winkler (1989) also yielded mixed and inconsistent results.

In a study of railroad workers, Taggart (1989) found that a positive drug test was associated with more accidents. Lewy (1983), on the other hand, examined a drug-screening program in a hospital. He found that the baserate for drug use was low (about 2.6%) and he concluded that drug testing was not useful. Normand et al. (1990), however, noted that Lewy did not test for marijuana. This is by far the most widely used illicit substance. Hence, Lewy's findings might actually underestimate the true incidence of drug use. In another hospital study, Parish (1989) found that drug tests were not significantly related to retention, performance, or work evaluations. However, Zwerling et al. (1990) argued that the Parish study suffered from a small sample size.

Kandel and Yamaguchi (1987) conducted a large-scale survey of individuals in a variety of occupations. These authors report that drug use is indeed associated with job separation. However, their results are at least partially explained by the lifestyle of drug users and not to the direct effects of the illicit substance. In another large-scale survey of mostly private sector employees, Newcomb (1988) also found that marijuana use was correlated with turnover. In addition, marijuana smoking was also associated with workplace vandalism. These associations were small, however. Newcomb also reported that cocaine use did not predict either job separation or vandalism.

In one unique experimental study, Kagel, Battalio, and Miles (1980) randomly assigned people to marijuana use and no marijuana conditions. Subjects lived in the wing of a hospital and participated in a token economy. Kagel et al. found no evidence that marijuana lowered job performance. The design of their study, however, did not allow them to examine other undesirable behaviors such as disciplinary actions, turnover, and absenteeism.

Although the evidence is not definitive, it is reasonable to expect that at least under some circumstances drug testing will enhance productivity and other desirable work behaviors. (See Cropanzano & Konovsky, in press, for a more extended discussion of the validity of drug testing.) In spite of its potential benefit to organizations, however, drug screening has its critics (Hoffman & Silvers, 1987; O'Keefe, 1987; Wish, 1990). One of these criticisms is that drug-testing procedures violate employee rights. This may or may not be the case, however, depending on how drug testing is conducted. We now turn our attention to this issue and examine the variety of drug-testing procedures available to organizations.

THE CHARACTERISTICS OF DRUG-TESTING PROGRAMS

Drug-screening programs vary along many dimensions, and organizations mix and match the various components into a variety of different policies. The methods selected for testing are likely to have implications for the program's acceptability and validity, and frequently these two objectives are at cross-purposes. For example, some organizations often provide advance notice of drug tests. Such a policy is typically seen as more fair and less a violation of employee rights (Stone & Kotch, 1989). The downside of advance notice, of course, is that it affords substance users the opportunity to evade detection. A similar opportunity is offered if testing is only conducted as part of pre-employment screening. A job applicant could abstain from drug use until after being hired and begin again anew when he or she started working. On the other side of the coin, there are also many circumstances when the fairest test is likely to be the most accurate. Some types of drug tests yield unacceptable levels of false positives (Irving et al., 1984). Lacking a second screening, such tests will inevitably misidentify many innocent people. For this reason, a follow-up test is widely recommended (Dwyer, 1989; Stevens, Surles, & Stevens, 1989), simultaneously increasing both the validity and the acceptability of drug testing.

Excepting, for the moment, the important issue of worker reactions, there has been a paucity of research examining the effectiveness of various testing programs. We do not know, for instance, which combination of policies yields the highest utility to the organization. The central problem seems to be the number of techniques currently available to employers. On the one hand, this is a positive development because it allows organizations to tailor screening programs to their own unique needs. To take a simple example, an airline may only require testing for individuals in areas related to public safety (e.g., pilots and mechanics). It might be less crucial to test booking agents. This flexibility of drug-testing policies, however, also has negative side-effects. The proliferation of different drug-testing programs has made it difficult for researchers to examine the effectiveness of any one. This task has been so arduous that most of the work to date has focused on enumerating the various options and assessing the frequency with which they are employed (Axel, 1989; Blum, 1989). Two issues limit this work.

First, drug-testing dimensions examined are not in any sense exhaustive. Each study focuses on relatively few attributes, such as the existence of an Employee Assistance Program (EAP) and the conditions of testing (e.g., random vs. advance notice). Second, these studies have sometimes not been guided by any comprehensive taxonomy. Hence, it is difficult to organize the findings into an integrated perspective that could offer guidance to managers when they are designing drug testing programs.

Lorber and Kirk (1987) have proposed one taxonomy of drug-testing program characteristics. They suggest that the attributes of drug-testing programs can be classified into four general dimensions, posed as four questions: Who is the subject of the testing? What are the circumstances that lead to testing? What are the administrative procedures used in testing? What are the consequences of failing the test?

Although useful, these four dimensions are still quite broad. As such they offer little specific guidance into the actual mechanics of designing a viable drug-screening program. As a result of this limitation, Murphy and Thornton (in press) designed a more thorough list of 56 program characteristics that could potentially be incorporated into a taxonomy for screening systems. Interestingly, Murphy and Thornton noted that their specific attributes can be roughly subsumed by the four broader dimensions proposed by Lorber and Kirk (1987).

Some examples can make this point clearer. Under the "Who is the subject of the testing?" dimension, Murphy and Thornton (in press) considered such elements as testing applicants vs. current employees and random testing versus reasonable suspicion. When considering the circumstances that lead to testing (what Murphy & Thornton, 1991, called "testing policy decisions"), specific elements included the presence or absence of a written policy and whether or not the program was implemented with employee participation. The broader dimension of "administrative procedures" subsumes the presence of periodic searches, supervisory training in detecting drug use, and follow-up testing. Finally, under Lorber and Kirk's "consequences" dimension, Murphy and Thornton (in press) discussed the possibilities of not offering an applicant a job, termination, or mandatory treatment.

Using this more complete list, Murphy and Thornton (in press) developed and validated an extensive survey instrument for describing organizational drug-testing policies. In a recent study, Murphy and Thornton (1991) analyzed the procedures used by 77 public and private organizations. These findings are reviewed next along with evidence from earlier studies. Taken together, this research provides a reasonably comprehensive picture of the types of testing procedures used in American organizations.

Who is the Subject of the Testing?

In general, a person is most likely to get tested if there is a reasonable suspicion that he or she is using drugs. A reasonable suspicion could be based on a variety of factors, such as behavioral characteristics, lower work performance, or the occurrence of an accident. Of those organizations that test for drugs, Blum (1989) reported that about 96% conduct tests under conditions of reasonable suspicion. Murphy and Thornton (1991) place this figure at a somewhat lower 65.7%. It is also common for organizations to screen after some mishap. Blum reported that a little over 20% of the companies he surveyed test after an accident. The Murphy and Thornton (1991) data show a higher rate of 38% for testing following an accident. Other groups of individuals are tested less frequently. Random screening of incumbents, for example, is only employed by about 7% of the companies that test for drug use (Blum, 1989). Murphy and Thornton (1991) reported a substantially higher figure for random screening of 31%. The reasons for the discrepancies between these two studies are not entirely clear. In addition to testing current employees, job applicants are also quite likely to be screened. Murphy and Thornton (1991) reported that of companies who tested for drug use, 78% screen prospective hires. Blum (1989) reported a similar 74%.

What are the Circumstances That Lead to Testing?

Although fairness perceptions are likely to be enhanced when employees are allowed to participate (Cropanzano & Konovsky, in press; Konovsky & Cropanzano, 1991), Murphy and Thornton (1991) found that many companies implement drug screening without consulting their workers. In fact, of the nonparticipative options presented in the Murphy and Thornton (1991) survey, about 30% of the organizations used at least one of them. Fortunately, most companies do provide their workers with written descriptions of their screening policy (Axel, 1989; Murphy & Thornton, 1991). Interestingly, some of these written policies have become fairly inclusive in attempting to control worker behavior. Axel noted that 70% of the policies include testing for at least some prescription drugs, and 25% attempt to regulate off-the-job behavior.

What are the Administrative Procedures Used in Testing?

Most companies that use employee drug testing train their supervisors to recognize symptoms of substance use (Axel, 1989; Murphy & Thornton, 1991). Most will re-test samples after the first positive test. This important practice, however, is far from universal. Murphy and Thornton (1991) reported that about 31% of employers do not conduct follow-up, confirmatory tests. Finally, most organizations do not use controversial security procedures such as drug sniffing dogs and searches. However, many do. Axel (1989) found that 36% of her sample engaged in at least some of these procedures. For searches only, Murphy and Thornton (1991) report a much lower figure of 17%.

What are the Consequences of Failing the Test?

In more than 94% of cases when an applicant fails a test, he or she is not offered a job (Murphy & Thornton, 1991). Guthrie and Olian (1989) report that 71% of the organizations that test, reject job applicants following a single confirmed positive drug test. Blum (1989) indicated, however, that when companies are faced with difficulties in staffing, they are sometimes forced to hire individuals after a positive test.

For job incumbents the consequences of drug testing generally include discipline or treatment. In terms of discipline, Murphy and Thornton (1991) found that approximately 30% of current workers who test positive for drugs are likely to be fired, although a large percentage may be suspended. Guthrie and Olian (1989) reported that 16% of companies will dismiss an employee who fails a single test. The treatment option generally involves sending employees to an EAP. This service can be either an internal or external program. Blum (1989) reported that of the companies she surveyed, only 20% had testing but no EAP. Another way to look at this data is to note that of the testing organizations, roughly 40% did not offer the treatment option. Axel (1989) reported more encouraging data. She noted that 75% of the testing organizations in her sample also offered an EAP. Hence, the treatment option is made widely available, but it is not universal.

CONSIDERING FAIRNESS IN THE DESIGN OF DRUG-TESTING PROGRAMS

As discussed earlier, drug-testing programs vary in their operational characteristics and consequences. Not surprisingly, employees' attitudes toward drug testing also vary as a result of the operational characteristics and consequences of drug testing. In the next section, we provide a general overview of employee attitudes toward drug testing and then turn to considerations of fairness in employee drug testing.

Employee Attitudes Toward Drug Testing

Although drug testing is an intrusive personnel selection and evaluation device (e.g., Garland, Giacobbe, & French, 1989) and is often considered a threat to employee rights (e.g., O'Keefe, 1987), much of the available data indicate that employees have surprisingly favorable attitudes toward drug testing. Hanson (1990), for example, provided one assessment of employee attitudes toward drug testing. In a sample of 333 railroad employees, 34% of the respondents thought drug testing, in general, was effective. Sixty-three percent thought pre-employment testing was justifiable. Roman and Blum (in press) also provided survey data indicating favorable drug-testing attitudes among a random sample of

Georgia adults ($N = 524$). This survey, which was conducted in 1986, indicated that nearly 13% of the participants strongly approved of drug screening and 37% approved. Nearly 50% of Georgia adults, therefore, reported positive attitudes toward drug testing. Drug testing may be associated with positive employee attitudes because the perceived need for drug testing may be great due to the magnitude of our society's drug problem. Alternatively, drug testing may be associated with positive employee attitudes because of the potentially deleterious effects of drugs on the ability of an organization to conduct its business. Drug testing, for example, may lead to more positive perceptions concerning workplace and public safety (Reid, Murphy, & Reynolds, 1990).

Although a surprising number of individuals report favorable attitudes toward drug testing, there is also evidence that unfavorable attitudes toward drug testing exist. At least one survey (Masi, 1987) found that many organizations were displeased with drug testing. Additionally, in the survey by Roman and Blum (in press) described earlier, 28% of the participants disapproved and 18% of the participants strongly disapproved of drug testing. In Hanson's (1990) study, 23% of the railroad workers thought drug testing, in general, was not effective. Hanson also found that only 16% of his survey respondents agreed that random testing of current employees was fair. Likewise, Murphy, Thornton, and Reynolds (1990) found that college students viewed random screening of current employees most negatively of all methods of sampling for drug testing.

Because of the potential for employees to have negative reactions to drug testing, the design of drug-testing programs is becoming an increasingly salient management issue. Negative employee responses to drug testing are of special concern because of their potential impact on current employees' attitudes and performance. Discontent with drug testing can undermine the productivity of current employees (Konovsky & Cropanzano, 1991). Poorly conducted drug testing, in other words, may reduce work place drug use at the expense of other more positive employee work attitudes and behaviors. Negative responses to drug testing may also impact an organization's prospective employees. Crant and Bateman (1989) demonstrated, for example, that the use of drug testing can have a negative impact on prospective employees' attitudes toward an organization and their intentions to apply for employment in that organization. In order to gain the most positive benefits from drug-testing programs, therefore, those programs must be designed in a manner that will not lead to negative employee perceptions.

One important determinant of employees' reactions to drug testing is the perceived fairness of the drug-testing program. Crant and Bateman (1989) were among the first organizational researchers to propose that fairness was an important factor influencing employee reactions to drug testing. Subsequent to Crant and Bateman, other organizational researchers also concluded that justice considerations are critical throughout the drug-testing process (e.g., Konovsky & Cropanzano, 1991; Stone & Kotch, 1989). Justice philosophers (e.g., Dworkin,

1977; Rawls, 1971) support this perspective. Considerations of fairness are paramount, according to Rawls (1971), when allocation of resources rationally regarded as advantageous or disadvantageous occurs. Certainly the outcomes commonly linked to drug testing (e.g., termination) can be regarded as advantageous or disadvantageous, and therefore ones where fairness considerations will prevail.

Next we review the empirical evidence investigating the relationship between drug testing and employees' fairness perceptions. Specifically, we focus on two factors that influence employees' fairness perceptions: the perceived procedural justice and distributive justice of drug testing. We then describe the implications of this literature for designing drug-testing programs.

Drug-Testing Fairness

Organizational justice researchers have demonstrated that employee fairness perceptions are a function of both distributive and procedural justice (e.g., Folger & Greenberg, 1985; Greenberg, 1990). Distributive justice refers to the fairness of the outcomes received as a result of drug testing. As a result of a positive drug test, for example, an organization's policy may indicate termination of a current employee or a no hire decision for a prospective employee as the appropriate action. Other organizations, however, may provide rehabilitation or treatment in response to a positive drug test. Procedural justice in the drug-testing context refers to the fairness of the methods associated with a drug-testing program. The amount of advance notice and the clarity of the explanations provided for drug testing are two examples of the procedures associated with drug testing. We first discuss the drug-testing literature describing the influence of distributive justice on employee fairness perceptions. We then turn to a discussion of procedural justice and its influence on fairness perceptions in the drug-testing context.

We have made choices in the following discussion to classify drug-testing program characteristics as procedures or outcomes. We classify, for example, the decision made as a result of a positive test as an outcome and the presence or absence of an appeal process as a procedure. In some cases, the classification decisions are ambiguous. The issue of confidentiality or who has access to the drug-test results has both procedural and outcome qualities. Confidentiality has procedural qualities in that it is related to due process considerations. Deciding to provide the results of a drug test to someone, however, also refers to a decision outcome. It is not surprising that real life events do not logically and perfectly fit into mutually exclusive and exhaustive categories. There is empirical evidence that research subjects also do not have a mutually exclusive and exhaustive classification scheme for distinguishing among justice elements. Konovsky and Cropanzano (1991) found, for example, a high correlation ($r = .76$) between procedural and distributive fairness perceptions, indicating the propensity of research subjects to use interrelated categories in judging fairness dimensions. In spite of the imperfect nature of applying the distributive/procedural justice taxonomy to drug-testing program components, we have classified elements of drug-testing programs as procedures or outcomes for the purposes of organizing our discussion. We are, nevertheless, aware of the imperfect nature of our classifications and the need for further empirical investigation to determine the essential characteristics that determine whether a drug-testing program element is perceived to be a procedure or an outcome.

Distributive Justice.   Early research on organizational justice (e.g., Adams, 1965) identified outcome fairness as a major contributor to individuals' reactions to management decisions. Outcome fairness is most often conceptualized as the ratio of one's inputs to outcomes (e.g., Adams & Freedman, 1976). Inputs, according to distributive justice theory, consist of work inputs (i.e., contributions) and outcomes consist of work outcomes (i.e., rewards or inducements) (Greenberg, 1990). Factors related to both inputs and outcomes are relevant to employee reactions to drug testing; furthermore, drug-testing researchers have examined both those justice elements.

With regard to the inputs to drug testing, several factors have been examined in the empirical literature. The characteristics of the jobs to be tested are one relevant factor. Job characteristics often define the risk associated with performing some jobs under the influence of drugs. Additionally, job characteristics indicate other information that people use to judge the danger of performing a job. Drug testing is more likely to be accepted in jobs that involve high levels of perceived risk to the public than in those where the hazards associated with drug impaired performance are minimal (Guthrie & Olian, 1989) or when testing procedures are unrelated to the job (Lumsden, 1967). Murphy, Thornton, and Prue (1991) and Stone and Vine (1989) examined the issue of perceived danger and found that employees' reactions to drug tests depended in part on whether employees' impaired performance led to a high degree of danger. When the characteristics of a job were judged to lead to danger when performed under the influence of drugs, drug testing was perceived to be more fair than when the risk of danger was low.

Another input into the distributive justice equation is the type of drug an individual is using. In a survey including three samples ($N = 371$) of college undergraduate students, Murphy, Thornton, and Reynolds (1990) found consistent evidence indicating that individuals react less favorably to alcohol testing than to testing for other drugs, even though alcohol abuse may do more damage to the national economy (Bureau of National Affairs, 1986). Testing for alcohol was more controversial and associated with less favorable attitudes toward drug testing than testing for any other illicit drugs. Participants made few distinctions among illicit drugs. In a study presenting vignettes to 128 undergraduate business majors, Stone, O'Brien, and Bommer (1989) examined only illicit drugs and also found no differences in influence of different illicit drugs on perceptions of drug testing fairness.

The reasons for conducting drug tests are additional relevant inputs whose influence on perceptions of drug testing fairness has been empirically examined. Stone, Stone, and Pollock (1990) found that the presence of a precipitating event (e.g., suspected use, decline in performance) influenced individuals' reactions to drug testing. A sample of 141 employed subjects read a scenario, presenting, among other details, the manipulation of the presence and type of precipitating event. Drug testing was perceived to be more fair when it followed both a performance decrease and an accident than when there was no performance decline and no accident.

Evidence also exists that the perceived need for drug testing influences fairness perceptions. Crant and Bateman (1990) had 163 undergraduate business students role play college graduates who were seeking employment. They found that job applicants were more likely to have favorable attitudes toward the organization and greater intentions to apply for employment when a drug-testing program not only was present, but there was a high perceived need for drug testing.

Crant and Bateman (1989) suggested several factors that may influence the perceived need for drug testing. Company size is one such factor. In a survey of 500 human resource executives, Gomez-Mejia and Balkin (1987) found that larger firms were more likely to have drug-testing programs. Furthermore, Madonia (1984) found that organizational size was positively associated with alcohol and drug use rates. Of employees in organizations with less than 3,000 workers, 42% reported that drug use was a moderately serious or very serious problem. In companies with more than 3,000 employees, 72% reported that drug use was moderately or very serious. Based on the greater prevalence of drug use in large compared to small organizations, Crant and Bateman (1989) concluded that the perceived need for drug testing may be greater in large organizations.

Employee characteristics also may influence the perceived need for drug testing. Surprisingly, being a drug user does not appear to be consistently and negatively related to the perceived need for drug testing. Bensinger (1987) demonstrated, for example, that many potential job applicants who are not drug users object to employee drug testing. Stone and her colleagues (e.g., Stone & Bowden, 1989) have also demonstrated that drug use does not consistently predict negative attitudes toward drug testing. In contrast to those findings, Garland et al. (1989) reported a survey of 692 undergraduate students enrolled in sophomore and junior levels management courses that indicated that students who used drugs, smoked cigarettes, and stole from their employers were more likely to oppose drug screening. In another study of college students, Murphy, Thornton, and Reynolds (1990) replicated the finding that individuals who use drugs are less approving of drug screening.

Additional employee characteristics other than drug use history may also influence the perceived need for drug testing. Garland et al. (1989), for example, demonstrated that business students who were religious fundamentalists or who had an authoritarian personality were more likely to approve of drug tests than students who were not religious fundamentalists or authoritarian. Murphy et al.

(1991) and Stone and Kotch (1989) found that the perceived need for drug testing was largely independent of employment suitability as indicated by grade point average, job offers received, or previous employment experience. One implication of this latter finding is that an additional cost of drug testing may be that organizations will lose highly qualified employees because of a drug-testing program.

The other half of the distributive fairness equation is the outcome of drug testing. The primary outcome of a drug-testing program is the decision to take some action against individuals submitting positive specimens. Some organizations choose to terminate individuals testing positive for drugs, whereas other organizations will provide treatment options. Stone and Kotch (1989) used a sample of 73 blue-collar workers and a vignette methodology to determine the effects of the consequences of a confirmed, positive drug test on employee attitudes. They found employees rated drug-testing programs as more fair when rehabilitation rather than termination was provided in response to a positive drug test. Other research also demonstrates that drug-testing programs are judged more positively when rehabilitation rather than termination is the outcome. Gomez-Mejia and Balkan's (1987) survey demonstrated that human resource executives judged drug testing programs more positively when organizations used rehabilitation than when they used termination. In their survey of college students, Murphy et al. (1990) also demonstrated that loss or denial of a job was seen as less desirable than rehabilitation. In this survey, whether an individual was a job applicant or current employee also influenced students' reactions' to the consequences of a drug test. Termination was seen as less justifiable for current employees than not hiring job applicants. Finally the appropriateness of termination versus rehabilitation may be moderated by additional factors. Using a sample of employed individuals who read appropriate vignettes, Stone et al. (1990) demonstrated that the use of termination as a consequence for non-compliance with drug testing was viewed as more fair when an accident had occurred than when no accident had occurred.

Procedural Justice.   Although the importance of distributive justice to fairness perceptions is substantial, subsequent research has identified additional factors associated with justice perceptions. Thibaut and Walker (1975), for example, demonstrated that the procedures associated with decision-making have an impact on fairness perceptions (see also Folger & Greenberg, 1985).

Due to the complex and multifaceted nature of the procedures associated with drug testing, it is helpful to further differentiate among those factors. Greenberg (1990) noted that procedural justice refers to at least two elements: (a) the structural characteristics of a decision, and (b) the quality of the interpersonal treatment associated with decision making (see Bies & Moag, 1986, for a review). The structural elements of procedural justice refer primarily to those decision-making procedures stipulated by the formal policies of the organization.

Policies regarding chain of custody would be one example of the structural elements of procedural justice in drug testing. Leventhal (1980) provided a comprehensive model of procedurally fair structural characteristics when he noted that fair procedures include input from all affected parties (representativeness rule), are consistently applied (consistency rule), suppress bias (bias-suppression rule), are as accurate as possible (accuracy rule), are correctable (e.g., provide for appeals) (correctability rule), and are ethical (ethicality rule).

Bies (1987) developed the concept of the interpersonal aspects of procedural justice that refers to the quality of the interpersonal treatment received during the implementation of a procedure such as drug testing. Crant and Bateman (1989) applied the concept of interpersonal justice to the drug-testing context when they noted that the explanations or social accounts offered by managers often influence employee perceptions of drug-testing fairness.

One study by Konovsky and Cropanzano (1991) demonstrated the importance of both procedural justice factors in the drug-testing context. Konovsky and Cropanzano surveyed 255 employees in a pathology testing laboratory concerning their perceptions of the structural aspects of procedural fairness, interpersonal fairness, and outcome fairness of the organization's drug-testing program. The results of this survey indicated that only procedural and interpersonal fairness influenced employees' reactions to drug testing. Specifically, fair procedural structure was positively associated with management trust and affective organizational commitment and interpersonal fairness was associated with affective commitment and job satisfaction. Furthermore, fair procedural structure was also positively associated with employee performance. This study was the first to demonstrate that procedural justice in drug testing can effect not only employee attitudes, but also employee performance.

Although the study by Konovsky and Cropanzano indicated that procedural fairness influenced employee reactions to drug testing, this study did not address the specific drug-testing program components that contributed to employee fairness perceptions. Additional research on employee reactions to drug testing, however, suggests several specific factors may contribute to employees' fairness judgments.

A survey of human resource managers from 43 companies conducted by Gomez-Mejia and Balkin (1987) provided one overview of the types of factors that may affect procedural fairness perceptions in the drug-testing context. These factors closely parallel those suggested by Leventhal. The human resource managers surveyed by Gomez-Mejia and Balkin reported, for example, that accuracy in drug testing was an important component for drug-testing effectiveness. The correctability of personnel decisions based on drug testing was an additional factor of importance identified in this study. They found that when drug testing was implemented with union support (e.g., provided worker voice), human resource managers considered the program to be more effective. Additional factors influencing human resource managers reactions to drug testing and associated with the correctability rule included a chance to appeal a negative decision.

Although no studies of drug testing have explicitly examined the importance of each of Leventhal's rules in determining fairness perceptions, the study by Gomez-Mejia and Balkin is strongly suggestive of the importance of those rules for determining fairness perceptions in the drug-testing context. An additional survey conducted by Reid, Murphy, and Reynolds (1990) also provides an indication of the procedural elements of drug testing that may contribute to employee fairness perceptions. Employees participating in this survey reported being concerned about test accuracy, management harassment, invasion of privacy, discrimination, and humiliation of sample collection procedures. Test accuracy was the strongest concern expressed by survey participants. The survey by Reid, Murphy, and Reynolds also indicated that employees' reported likelihood of accepting a job offer was affected by the nature of an organization's drug-testing policies.

Additional indications of a relationship between drug-testing procedures and employees' fairness perceptions are provided by a series of studies by Stone and her colleagues. Using vignettes with employed workers, Stone and Kotch (1989) demonstrated that employees perceived drug testing to be more fair when advance notice for a drug test was provided. Using a sample of 128 college students, Stone et al. (1989) replicated the advance notice results. They found that more advance notice had positive effects on fairness perceptions. Additionally, students indicated they were less likely to accept jobs in organizations that provided no advance notice of drug testing.

Stone and her colleagues also examined the methods used to select employees for drug testing. In a sample of 98 employees of a Southwestern chemical firm, Stone and Bowden (1989) found that participants' fairness perceptions and the likelihood they would accept a job offer were lower when random selection for drug testing was used than when all job applicants were tested for drugs or when testing was "for cause." In a comparison of testing all applicants versus testing only those suspected of drug use, fairness perceptions and intentions to accept a job offer were more negative when all applicants were tested. These results were similar to those found by Murphy et al. (1990) using three student samples. Stone and Bowden also found, however, that their results needed to be qualified by an additional consideration: the timing of the drug test. When drug tests were conducted prior to a job offer, random selection was perceived more negatively than either testing all applicants or testing only those applicants suspected of drug use. After an applicant had received a job offer, however, there were no differences in fairness perceptions or job acceptance intentions between random selection and testing all job applicants. Random testing, however, was viewed more positively than testing only those suspected of drug use.

One aspect of fair interpersonal treatment is to adequately explain decision procedures—particularly after a negative outcome (Bies, 1987; Bies & Shapiro,

1987). Stone and Bommer (1990) provided evidence that the justification organizations gave for drug testing affected individuals' responses. Vignettes describing two justifications for drug testing were provided to employed individuals who were taking an executive development course. Stone and Bommer found an interaction between drug-testing justification and the method used to select who to test. When the justification included testing for societal reasons and when individuals were selected for testing based on suspected drug use, employees viewed drug testing positively and they were likely to remain with the organization. In contrast to this, when a safety justification was provided, individuals responded more positively to random testing than testing based on suspected drug use.

Designing a Fair Drug-Testing Program

The results of the studies previously discussed indicate that managers concerned with reducing negative reactions to drug testing should consider the factors that influence employees' fairness perceptions when they design testing programs. These factors include those related to both procedural justice and distributive justice. With regard to enhancing perceptions of distributive justice, both inputs and outcomes of drug testing need to be considered in program design. The available data indicate the importance of several inputs into the drug-testing decision. Drug testing will be perceived to be more fair, for example, if testing is conducted only where job characteristics indicate risk or danger of drug use, when there is a reason for testing (e.g., an accident), and when the perceived need for drug testing is high. Perceived need may be high in large companies where drug use is generally more prevalent. The central outcome of a drug-testing program is whether to terminate or rehabilitate an individual who tests positive for drug use. The available evidence indicates that treatment is considered more fair than termination for current employees. Not hiring a prospective employee who tests positive for drug use, however, does not have a serious negative effect on fairness perceptions.

With regard to enhancing perceptions of procedural and interpersonal fairness in drug testing, several program design factors must be considered. The available evidence indicates that test accuracy is extremely important in the formation of employee perceptions of drug-testing fairness. The method of selecting employees for testing is also critical. In general, random selection has a negative effect on fairness perceptions, although this depends on whether job applicants or current employees are being tested and the reasons for testing (societal versus safety). The availability of an appeal process and advance notice are also important factors influencing employees' perceptions of the fairness of drug testing. Because of the evidence suggesting that procedural justice is linked not only to employee fairness perceptions but also to employee performance, the inclusion of fair procedures into drug-testing programs is especially critical.

One emergent pattern in the empirical research on justice in drug testing is that of interactions among the factors influencing employee reactions to drug testing. Stone et al. (1989), for example, examined three two-way interactions resulting from combining all pairs of the following drug-testing program characteristics: type of drug tested, amount of advance notice, and presence or absence of direct visual monitoring of sample collection. The type of drug tested for and amount of advance notice interacted to predict both individuals' fairness perceptions and job acceptance intentions. Advance notice and visual monitoring interacted to predict job acceptance intentions but not attitudes toward drug testing. No significant interactions were found between type of drug use detected and direct visual monitoring and the two dependent variables: attitudes toward drug testing and job acceptance intentions. This complex pattern of results demonstrates that managing single components of drug-testing programs in isolation from one another may not be sufficient to achieve the desired results and that managers will need to become increasingly sophisticated in anticipating the complex interactions that occur among the different justice components in the drug-testing context. We currently have, however, no theoretical basis for predicting the presence or absence of interactions among the different program elements affecting employee responses to drug testing, and therefore, this is one area where empirical evidence can not yet be used to supply simple rules for designing drug-testing programs.

Although the foregoing recommendations are based on the existing empirical evidence, some caution is warranted in the adoption of those recommendations. According to Reid et al. (1990), none of the factors influencing the effects of drug-testing on the attitudes and behaviors of those who are subject to testing has yet received sufficient attention. Furthermore, not all of the characteristics of drug-testing programs have been examined alone or in combination with other factors for their influence on employee fairness perceptions. Reid, Murphy, and Reynolds regard drug testing as an area where practice has preceded science and therefore conclude that it is not possible, at this time, to state which individual or organizational characteristics will affect the perceived fairness of drug testing. Only further drug-testing research investigating the factors influencing employee fairness perceptions and the interactions among those factors will clarify this issue.

REFERENCES

Abel, E. L. (1970). Marijuana and memory. *Nature, 227,* 1151–1152.

Adams, J. S. (1965). Inequity in social exchange. In L. Berkowitz (Ed.), *Advances in experimental social psychology* (Vol. 2, pp. 267–299). New York: Academic Press.

Adams, J. S., & Freedman, S. (1976). Equity theory revisited: Comments and annotated bibliography. In L. Berkowitz & E. Walster (Eds.), *Advances in experimental social psychology* (Vol. 9, pp. 43–90). New York: Academic Press.

Axel, H. (1989). Characteristics of firms with drug testing programs. In S. W. Gust & J. M. Walsh (Eds.), *NIDA Research Monograph 91: Drugs in the workplace: Research and evaluation data* (pp. 139–150). Washington, DC: National Institute on Drug Abuse.

Battegay, R., Ladewig, D., Mühlemann, R., & Weidmann, M. (1976). The culture of youth and drug abuse in some European countries. *The International Journal of the Addictions, 11,* 245–261.

Bensinger, C. C. (1987). *Attitudes toward drug screening: Implications for organizational recruitment.* Unpublished master's thesis, Rensselaer Polytechnic Institute, Troy, NY.

Bies, R. J. (1987). The predicament of injustice: The management of moral outrage. In L. L. Cummings & B. M. Staw (Eds.), *Research in organizational behavior* (Vol. 9, pp. 289–319). Greenwich, CT: JAI Press.

Bies, R. J., & Moag, J. S. (1986). Interactional justice: Communication criteria of fairness. In R. J. Lewicki, B. H. Sheppard, & B. H. Bazerman (Eds.), *Research on negotiation in organizations* (Vol. 1, pp. 43–55). Greenwich, CT: JAI Press.

Bies, R. J., & Shapiro, D. L. (1987). Interactional fairness judgments: The influence of causal accounts. *Social Justice Research, 1,* 199–218.

Blank, D. L., & Fenton, J. W. (1989). Early employment testing for marijuana: Demographic and employee retention patterns. In S. W. Gust & J. M. Walsh (Eds.), *NIDA Research Monograph 91: Drugs in the workplace: Research and evaluation data* (pp. 139–150). Washington, DC: National Institute on Drug Abuse.

Blum, R. H. (1969). *Students and drugs* (Vol. 2). San Francisco, CA: Jossey-Bass.

Blum, T. C. (1989). The presence and integration of drug abuse intervention in human resource management. In S. W. Gust & J. M. Walsh (Eds.), *NIDA Research Monograph 91: Drugs in the workplace: Research and evaluation data* (pp. 245–269). Washington, DC: National Institute on Drug Abuse.

Bray, R. M., Marsden, M. E., Guess, L. L., Wheeless, S. C., Pate, D. K., Dunteman, G. H., & Iannacchione, V. G. (1986). *Worldwide survey of alcohol and nonmedical drug use among military personnel.* Research Triangle Institute, RTI/3306/06-2FR.

Bureau of National Affairs (1986). *Alcohol and drugs in the workplace: Costs, control, and controversies: A BNA special report.* Washington, DC: Author.

Casswell, S., & Marks, D. F. (1973). Cannabis-induced impairment of performance on a divided attention task. *Nature, 241,* 60–61.

Clark, L. D., Hughes, R., & Nakashima, E. N. (1970). Behavioral effects of marijuana. *Archives of General Psychiatry, 23,* 193–198.

Cook, R. F. (1989). Drug use among working adults: Prevalence rates and estimation methods. In S. W. Gust & J. M. Walsh (Eds.), *NIDA Research Monograph 91: Drugs in the workplace: Research and evaluation data* (pp. 17–32). Washington, DC: National Institute on Drug Abuse.

Crant, J. M., & Bateman, T. S. (1989). A model of employee responses to drug-testing programs. *Employee Responsibilities and Rights Journal, 2,* 173–190.

Crant, J. M., & Bateman, T. S. (1990). An experimental test of the impact of drug-testing programs on potential job applicants' attitudes and intentions. *Journal of Applied Psychology, 75,* 127–131.

Crawford, K. S., Thomas, P. J., & Thomas, E. D. (1976). *Pre-service drug usage among Naval recruits: A 5-year trend analysis.* NPRDC TR 756TQ-45.

Cropanzano, R., & Konovsky, M. (in press). Drug use and its implications for employee drug testing. In G. R. Ferris & K. M. Rowland (Eds.), *Research in personnel and human resources management.* Greenwich, CT: JAI Press.

Dornbush, R. L., Fink, M., & Freedman, A. M. (1971). Marijuana, memory, and perception. *American Journal of Psychiatry, 128,* 194–197.

Dworkin, R. (1977). *Taking rights seriously.* Cambridge, MA: Harvard University Press.

Dwyer, D. J. (1989). Don't "just say no" to drug testing in the workplace: Some recommendations for developing and implementing policy. *Employee Responsibilities and Rights Journal, 2*(4), 275–287.

Folger, R., & Greenberg, J. (1985). Procedural justice: An interpretive analysis of personnel systems. In K. Rowland & G. Ferris (Eds.), *Research in personnel and human resources management* (Vol. 3, pp. 141–183). Greenwich, CT: JAI Press.

Garland, H., Giacobbe, J., & French, J. L. (1989). Attitudes toward employee and employer rights in the workplace. *Employee Responsibilities and Rights Journal, 2,* 49–60.

Gergen, M. K., Gergen, K. J., & Morse, S. J. (1972). Correlates of marijuana use among college students. *Journal of Applied Social Psychology, 2,* 1–16.

Gianutsos, R., & Litwack, A. R. (1976). Chronic marijuana smokers show reduced coding into long-term storage. *Bulletin of the Psychonomic Society, 7,* 277–279.

Gilbert, J. G. (1970). Drugs in memory improvement in normal aging. *Psychopharmacology Bulletin, 6,* p. 21.

Gomez-Mejia, L. R., & Balkin, D. B. (1987). Dimensions and characteristics of personnel manager perceptions of effective drug-testing programs. *Personnel Psychology, 40,* 745–763.

Goode, E. (1972). *Drugs in American society.* New York: Knopf.

Greenberg, J. (1990). Organizational justice: Yesterday, today, and tomorrow. *Journal of Management, 16,* 399–432.

Groves, W. E. (1974). Patterns of college student drug use and lifestyles. In E. Josephson & E. E. Carroll (Eds.), *Drug use: Epidemiological and sociological approaches.* Washington, DC: Hemisphere.

Guthrie, J. P., & Olian, J. D. (1989). *Drug and alcohol testing programs: The influence of organizational context and objectives.* Paper presented at the annual meeting of the Society for Industrial and Organizational Psychology, Boston, MA.

Hanson, A. (1990, July). What employees say about drug testing. *Personnel,* 32–36.

Hoffman, A., & Silvers, J. (1987). *Steal this urine test: Fighting drug hysteria in America.* New York: Penguin Books.

Hollister, L. E., & Gillespie, H. K. (1970). Marijuana, ethanol, and dextroamphetamine. *Archives of General Psychiatry, 23,* 199–207.

Horgan, J. (1990). Test negative: A look at the "evidence" justifying illicit-drug tests. *Scientific American, 262*(3), 18–22.

Irving, J., Leeb, B., Foltz, R. L., Cook, C. E., Bursey, J. T., & Willette, R. E. (1984). Evaluation of immunoassays for cannabinoids in urine. *Journal of Analytical Toxicology, 8,* 192–196.

Johnson, B. D. (1973). *Marijuana users and drug subcultures.* New York: Wiley.

Kagel, J. H., Battalio, R. C., Miles, C. G. (1980). Marijuana and work performance: Results from an experiment. *The Journal of Human Resources, 15,* 373–395.

Kandel, D. B., & Yamaguchi, K. (1987). Job mobility and drug use: An event history analysis. *American Journal of Sociology, 92,* 836–878.

Kiplinger, G. F. (1970). Humor motor and mental performance as influenced by cannabis. *Clinical Pharmacology and Therapy, 11,* 808–815.

Kolb, D., Nail, R. L., Gunderson, E. K. E. (1975). Pre-service drug abuse as a predictor of in-service drug abuse and military performance. *Military Medicine, 104,* 104–107.

Konovsky, M. A., & Cropanzano, R. (1991). The perceived fairness of employee drug testing as a predictor of employee attitudes and job performance. *Journal of Applied Psychology, 76,* 698–707.

Lahey, J. W. (1986). Whose rights are violated? *National Safety and Health News, 133*(6), 26–31.

Leventhal, G. S. (1980). What should be done with equity theory? In K. J. Gergen, M. S. Greenberg, & R. H. Willis (Eds.), *Social exchange: Advances in theory and research* (pp. 27–55). New York: Plenum.

Lewy, R. (1983). Preemployment qualitative urine toxicology screening. *Journal of Occupational Medicine, 25*(8), 579–580.

Lorber, L. Z., & Kirk, J. R. (1987). *Fear itself: A legal and personnel analysis of drug testing, AIDS, secondary smoke, VDT's*. Alexandria, VA: ASPA Foundation.

Lumsden, H. (1967). The plant visit: A critical area of recruiting. *Journal of College Placement, 27*, 74–84.

MacAvoy, M. G., & Marks, D. F. (1975). Divided attention performance of cannabis users and nonusers following cannabis and alcohol. *Psychopharmacologia, 44*, 147–152.

Madonia, J. F. (1984, June). Managerial responses to alcohol and drug abuse among employees. *Personnel Administrator*, 134–139.

Masi, T. (1987, March). Company responses to drug abuse from AMA's nationwide survey. *Personnel, 64*, 40–46.

McDaniel, M. A. (1988). Does pre-employment drug use predict on-the-job suitability? *Personnel Psychology, 41*, 717–729.

Mellinger, G. D., Somers, R. H., Bazell, S., & Manheimer, D. I. (1978). Drug use, academic performance, and career indecision: Longitudinal data in search of a model. In D. B. Kandel (Ed.), *Longitudinal research on drug use* (pp. 157–177). New York: Wiley.

Miller, L., Drew, W. G., & Kiplinger, G. F. (1972). Effects of marijuana on recall of narrative material and Stroop Colour-Word performance. *Nature, 237*, 172–173.

Murphy, K. R., & Thornton, G. C., III. (1991). *Characteristics of employee drug testing policies*. Manuscript submitted for publication.

Murphy, K. R., & Thornton, G. C., III. (in press). Development and validation of a measure of attitudes toward employee drug testing. *Educational and Psychological Measurement*.

Murphy, K. R., Thornton, G. C. III, & Prue, K. (1991). Influence of job characteristics on the acceptability of employee drug testing. *Journal of Applied Psychology, 76*, 447–453.

Murphy, K. R., Thornton, G. C. III, & Reynolds, D. H. (1990). College students' attitudes toward employee drug testing programs. *Personnel Psychology, 43*, 615–631.

Murray, J. B. (1986). Marijuana's effects on human cognitive functions, psychomotor functions, and personality. *The Journal of General Psychology, 113*, 23–55.

Newcomb, M. D. (1988). *Drug use in the workplace: Risk factors for disruptive substance abuse among young adults*. Dover, MA: Auburn House.

Normand, J., Salyards, S. D., & Mahoney, J. J. (1990). An evaluation of preemployment drug testing. *Journal of Applied Psychology, 75*, 629–639.

O'Keefe, A. M. (1987, June). The case against drug testing. *Psychology Today, 29*, 34–35, 38.

Parish, D. C. (1989). Relation of the pre-employment drug testing results to employment status: A one year follow-up. *Journal of General Internal Medicine, 4*, 44–47.

Pugliese, A. C. (1973). The effects of drugs on learning and memory: A review of the literature. *The International Journal of the Addictions, 8*, 643–656.

Quayle, D. (1983). American productivity: The devastating effect of alcoholism and drug abuse. *American Psychologist, 38*, 454–458.

Rawls, J. (1971). *A theory of justice*. Cambridge, MA: Harvard University Press.

Reid, L. D., Murphy, K. R., & Reynolds, D. H. (1990). Drug abuse and drug testing in the workplace. In K. R. Murphy & F. E. Saul (Eds.), *Psychology in organizations: Integrating science and practice* (pp. 241–263). Hillsdale, NJ: Lawrence Erlbaum Associates.

Reinarman, C., Waldorf, D., & Murphy, S. B. (1988). Scapegoating and social control in the construction of a public problem: Empirical and critical findings on cocaine and work. *Research in Law, Deviance, and Social Control, 9*, 37–62.

Robbins, L. N. (1974). *The Vietnam drug user returns* (Final Report, Special Action Monograph, Series A, No. 2). Washington, DC: U.S. Government Printing Office.

Robbins, L. N. (1978). The interaction of setting and predisposition in explaining novel behavior: Drug initiations before, in, and after Vietnam. In D. B. Kandel (Ed.), *Longitudinal research on drug use* (pp. 179–196). New York: Wiley.

Rock, N. L., & Silsby, H. D. (1978). Methaqualone abuse among U.S. army troops stationed in Europe. *The International Journal of the Addictions, 13*, 327–335.

Roffman, R., & Sapol, E. (1970). Marijuana in Viet Nam: A survey of use among Army enlisted men in two southern corps. *International Journal of Addictions, 5*, 1–42.

Roman, P. M., & Blum, T. C. (in press). Employee assistance and drug screening programs. In D. R. Gerstein & J. H. Henrick (Eds.), *Treating drug problems* (Vol. 2). Washington, DC: National Academy of Sciences Press.

Roth, W. T., Tinklenberg, J. R., Whitaker, C. A., Darley, C. F., Kopell, B. S., & Hollister, L. E. (1973). The effect of marijuana on tracking task performance. *Psychopharmacologia, 33*, 259–265.

Shedler, J., & Block, J. (1990). Adolescent drug use and psychological health: A longitudinal inquiry. *American Psychologist, 45*, 612–630.

Sheridan, J. R., & Winkler, H. (1989). An evaluation of drug testing in the work-place. In S. W. Gust & J. M. Walsh (Eds.), *Drugs in the work-place: Research and evaluation data* (pp. 195–216). Rockville, MD: National Institute on Drug Abuse.

Sloman, L. (1979). *Reefer madness*. New York: Grove Press.

Stevens, G. E., Surles, C. D., & Stevens, F. W. (1989). A better approach by management in drug testing. *Employee Responsibilities and Rights Journal, 2*(1), 61–71).

Stone, D. L., & Bommer, W. (1990, August). *Effects of drug testing selection method and justification provided for the test on reactions to drug testing.* Paper presented at the 1990 meeting of the National Academy of Management, San Francisco, CA.

Stone, D. L., & Bowden, C. (1989). Effects of job applicant drug testing practices on reactions to drug testing. In F. Hoy (Ed.), *Academy of Management Best Paper Proceedings* (pp. 190–195). Washington, DC: Academy of Management.

Stone, D. L., & Kotch, D. A. (1989). Individuals' attitudes toward organizational drug testing policies and practices. *Journal of Applied Psychology, 74*, 518–521.

Stone, D. L., O'Brien, T., & Bommer, W. (1989). *Individuals' reactions to job applicant drug testing practices.* Paper presented at the Annual Conference of the American Psychological Society, Washington, DC.

Stone, D. L., & Vine, P. (1989). *Some procedural determinants of attitudes toward drug testing.* Paper presented at the annual conference of the Society for Industrial and Organizational Psychology, Boston, MA.

Stone, E. F., Stone, D. L., & Pollock, M. (1990). *The effects of precipitating events and coerciveness of the procedures on individuals' reactions to drug testing.* Unpublished manuscript.

Taggart, R. W. (1989). Results of the drug testing program at Southern Pacific Railroad. In S. W. Gust & J. M. Walsh (Eds.), *NIDA Research Monograph 91: Drugs in the workplace: Research and evaluation data* (pp. 97–108). Washington, DC: National Institute on Drug Abuse.

Thibaut, J., & Walker, L. (1975). *Procedural justice: A psychological analysis.* Hillsdale, NJ: Lawrence Erlbaum Associates.

Tinklenberg, J. R., Melges, F. T., Hollister, L. E., & Gillespie, H. K. (1970). Marijuana and immediate memory. *Nature, 226*, 1171–1172.

Trice, H. M., & Roman, P. M. (1972). *Spirits and demons at work: Alcohol and other drugs on the job.* Ithaca, NY: Hoffman Printing Co.

Voss, H. L. (1989). Patterns of drug use: Data from the 1985 National Household survey. In S. W. Gust & J. M. Walsh (Eds.), *NIDA Research Monograph 91: Drugs in the workplace: Research and evaluation data* (pp. 33–46). Washington, DC: National Institute on Drug Abuse.

Walters, P. A., Goethals, G. W., & Pope, H. G. (1972). Drug use and life-style among 500 college students. *Archives of General Psychiatry, 26*, 92–96.

Wish, E. D. (1990). Preemployment drug screening. *Journal of the American Medical Association, 294*, 2676–2677.

Zwerling, C., Ryan, J., & Orav, E. J. (1990). The efficacy of preemployment drug screening for marijuana and cocaine in predicting employment outcome. *Journal of the American Medical Association, 264*, 2639–2643.

9

An Investigation Into the Relationship of Fairness and Customer Satisfaction With Services

Elizabeth C. Clemmer
Public Policy Institute, American Association of Retired Persons

The United States is moving from a manufacturing to a service economy, with as much as 66% of the gross national product and 80% of new jobs now attributed to the service sector. At the same time Americans are increasingly dissatisfied with many of the services they purchase. Services in fields as diverse as medicine, education, banking, transportation, and communication are routinely criticized in the national press, with academic research offering support for the widespread perception of dissatisfaction with service quality (e.g., Schutz & Casey, 1983).

The growing importance of services, coupled with this widespread dissatisfaction has led to research efforts directed at understanding the basis for customer evaluation of service experiences. This chapter reviews research on the evaluation of services, discusses the relationship between services and other organizational settings, and suggests ways in which findings from the extensive literature on justice and fairness in organizations may help clarify our understanding of customers' evaluation of services. Finally, a study is presented that tests the extent to which customers' conceptualizations of fairness and justice in service encounters are associated with their satisfaction with services.

Research on Services

Services Differ From Goods. It is useful to examine the differences between products and services for these differences help to explain why the evaluation of services is complex. Researchers generally agree that there are three factors that distinguish services from goods (Schneider & Bowen, 1984). The first is intangibility: Goods are tangible objects—refrigerators, computer chips, a stick of

193

chewing gum—but services are intangible. Thus, the attributes that would lead a customer to be pleased with a visit to the opera are less tangible than those that create satisfaction with a refrigerator. Shostack (1977) described a continuum of market entities, with products such as soft drinks or refrigerators at the tangible end, and services such as education or consulting at the opposite or intangible pole. In between are products such as cosmetics that have intangible aspects, or fast food outlets that include tangible and intangible components.

The second difference between goods and services is in production. Goods are first produced and inventoried, then sold and finally, consumed. In contrast, services are usually sold, then produced, and often consumed simultaneously with production. A person arranges for or purchases a cleaning service before someone arrives to "produce" the service, but the vacuum cleaner itself, would have been produced before purchase. Restaurant meals are consumed at the time of production itself.

The third distinguishing characteristic is that customers usually have a role in the production of services, but not in the production of goods. Customers describe their wishes to the cleaning service or explain their symptoms to the doctor. But customers do not participate in the production of goods—they do not typically describe their wishes to the vacuum cleaner manufacturer.

It is this characteristic, customer participation, that is particularly relevant to organizational issues. Customers often provide a significant portion of the raw material or input into the production process by providing essential information, for example, describing their needs or preferences in detail, or, with a doctor, describing their history and symptoms. When the service has a self-serve component then customers are also part of the transformation process. For example, at self-serve gasoline pumps, at bank automated teller machines (ATMs), or in fast food restaurants, customers carry their own food to the table and later clear off the table. This customer participation in the input and/or transformation process has led researchers to label customers "partial employees" (Bowen & Schneider, 1988). That the customer functions as a partial employee argues for including the customer as an important component in the functioning of organizations, certainly in the functioning of service organizations.

The distinctions between goods and services underscore the heterogeneity of service encounters. These encounters vary from customer to customer and from day to day, making the systematic evaluation of services more complex than that of goods. The foregoing discussion has also illustrated another source of complexity—the great variety of types of services within what is generally referred to as the service sector of the economy.

Service Types.   Telephone service, education, theater entertainment, medical care, and police, for example, all vary along many dimensions, but all are services. Lovelock (1980, 1984) has developed a classification scheme that looks at such dimensions as the focus of the service, the relationship with the customer, the customization, the judgment of the service provider, the role of fluctuating demand, and the location of the service.

For example, hairdressing focuses on the customer's body, and education on the mind, whereas banking and drycleaning focuses on "things"—assets or clothing. With insurance one has a formal and long-standing relationship, whereas with a restaurant the relationship is short term. Medical care and much police work are customized and require extensive judgment and expertise, education requires expertise but is often delivered in large classes with little customization for individual customers, and fast food offers some customization but requires little judgment from the providers. Services in which demand fluctuates, such as transportation or restaurants, differ from those where it is constant, such as insurance. Finally, services such as lawn care companies come to the customer, whereas others, such as hairdressers or airlines, require the customer to come to the service, and still others deal by mail or electronically, such as credit card companies. The range of services along Lovelock's dimensions further illustrates the difficulty in developing evaluation concepts that apply across all services.

Evaluation of Services.   The most extensive evaluation effort to date is that of Parasuraman, Zeithaml, and Berry (1985, 1986) who developed a scale to measure service quality. Their scale (SERVQUAL) comprises five rating factors: reliability of the service, responsiveness of personnel, assurance or competence, empathy, and tangibles such as equipment. The authors stress that their scale is designed to measure service quality and that such quality is the result of cognitive and global assessments, in contrast with satisfaction that captures a more emotional reaction to a specific experience. Quality measures ask for a factual response, whereas satisfaction questions tap into customers' feelings. Unfortunately, there has been no other comprehensive research effort creating a valid measure for evaluating customers' satisfaction with their service experiences.

Service Organizations and Justice

Systems Concepts and Service Organizations.   In the traditional systems model, the customer is part of the external environment that absorbs or purchases the organizational output, thereby providing the economic support that allows the organization to purchase more raw materials or inputs and to transform these into new outputs (Katz & Kahn, 1978). The customer is part of the feedback loop, but clearly external to the organization itself.

Recall, however, that in the production of services the customer often becomes a "partial employee" (Bowen & Schneider, 1988), providing essential inputs in the form of instructions or other information, and frequently doing part of the actual work of producing the service. Although the customer is not technically inside the organizational boundary, the customer is performing some of the same functions related to inputs and transformations that are performed exclusively by organizational employees in the production of manufactured goods. By extension then, those concepts that have proven useful in understanding employee reactions and behaviors in other organizational settings may also be fruitful in comprehending customer reactions and behaviors in service encounters.

The research on organizational justice described elsewhere in this volume dramatically illustrates the importance of justice in employees' reactions to organizational events. If customers are partial employees, these constructs may also illuminate our understanding of how customers evaluate their service experiences.

Justice Research and its Application in Service Settings.   Past research in justice theory has occasionally been done in service settings. Although these studies were done to test the validity or relationships of particular justice constructs, rather than to test the applicability of justice constructs in service encounters, these earlier studies do indicate that the justice concepts discussed elsewhere in this volume may apply in service settings. For example, several equity theory studies support the notion that satisfaction with services is related to fairness. Fisk and Coney (1982), in a scenario study, showed that "passengers" who learned they had paid more than a "friend" for the same flight expected lower quality service during the flight. In another scenario study, Folkes (1984) varied the reasons for poor service outcomes and found, as hypothesized, that customers chose different means to restore equity depending on whether the provider was at fault or had control over the outcome. Swan, Sawyer, Van Matre, and McGee (1985) surveyed hospital patients after their discharge and found a relationship between perceptions of equity and overall satisfaction and return intentions.

Other studies testing the importance of procedural fairness in determining satisfaction have also been done in service settings. For example, Tyler and Caine (1981) reported on two studies showing that perceptions of procedural justice influenced students' overall evaluation of teachers. Tyler and Folger (1980) found that perceptions of procedural justice influenced satisfaction with citizen encounters with the police. This relationship held both when police were acting in their role as authority figures (i.e., in stopping citizens for potential violations) or when they functioned more as service providers (i.e., in responding to a citizen call). Subsequent work by Tyler (1989, 1990) continues to show the weight that citizens place on both the fairness of procedures and the manner in which they are treated (e.g., respect, politeness, dignity) as they evaluate their encounters with courts and police. These studies by Tyler, as well as the equity studies, suggest that justice in service experiences may, like experiences in other types of organizational settings, have both procedural and distributive components.

Components of Justice in Service Experiences.   Researchers of services have begun to recognize that service encounters involve both a process and an outcome. Gronroos (1984) first investigated this distinction, referring to *technical quality* as the object of the service, for example, the hotel room and bed, and *functional quality* as the interactions with the customer. This technical quality describes the distributive or outcome component of service. The functional quality represents both the procedures followed in delivering the service and the manner in which the customer is treated. This functional quality is analogous to the principles usually considered as aspects of procedural justice (cf. Leventhal, 1980). The functional quality also captures aspects of what Bies and Moag (1986) called interactional justice and Sheppard and Lewicki (1987) referred to as process principles—the manner in which one party treats another during the carrying out of procedures and the decisions about outcomes. Tyler's research (1987a, 1987b, 1989) has also shown the importance of such interactional principles as respect and politeness in communications.

Gronroos' (1984) survey of Swedish service firm executives underscored the importance of this functional quality. A strong majority (91%) of the executives believed that if personnel behavior was "customer-oriented and service-minded" during the encounter, that this would compensate for temporary problems with technical (i.e., distributive or outcome) quality.

The significance of service distributions or outcomes, procedures, and interactional quality has been recognized intuitively by other service researchers and by service providers. The service quality measure developed by Parasuraman et al. (1988) includes items that capture these constructs. The typical "We want your opinion" reply card given to customers in restaurants and hotels includes questions on outcomes (tastiness of food), procedures (waiting time, reservation policies), and interactions (courtesy and friendliness of personnel).

In summary, there appears to be ample evidence that justice or fairness matters in service encounters, and that the specific constructs of justice used in other organizational settings provide useful hypotheses for exploring how customers evaluate these service encounters. The next sections describe such an exploration.

HYPOTHESES

First, it was hypothesized that service fairness can be categorized into fair outcomes, fair procedures, and fair interactions.[1] For example, restaurant patrons

---

[1]Recent research has moved away from regarding interactional justice as a separate construct and has instead integrated it with procedural justice, considering politeness, respect, and dignity as aspects or principles of procedural justice (Folger & Bies, 1989; Tyler & Bies, 1989). Interactional

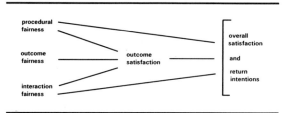

FIG. 9.1.   Hypothesized model of service fairness.

care about the food itself (the outcome), the restaurant policies (such procedures as waiting, or the handling of problems), and the courtesy or respect with which they are treated (interactions). It was also hypothesized that each category has principles (for example, courtesy or respect as principles of interactional fairness).

Second, it was hypothesized that perceptions of fairness in procedures and interactions are related to satisfaction with outcomes, and also to overall satisfaction and return intentions. This hypothesis is summarized in Fig. 9.1.

METHOD

Overview

The methodology presented here had two phases. The first or qualitative phase was designed to identify the principles or rules of justice or fairness relevant in the receipt of services. In the second, or quantitative phase, these justice principles served as the structure for a retrospective questionnaire that tested whether procedural and interactional principles were related to distributive satisfaction, overall satisfaction or return intentions. The research settings were fast food restaurants, "nice" (i.e., "tablecloth" restaurants), visits to doctors, and visits to banks.

Methodological Issues

Following the lead of earlier researchers (e.g., Greenberg, 1986; Sheppard & Lewicki, 1987) I used open-ended questionnaires, and then had the responses sorted, in order to discover the principles of service fairness. First, 94 customers described their fair or unfair experiences with various services. Next, 32 other

---

justice is treated separately in the study reported here because its intuitive importance in service encounters is supported by other justice studies showing it to be important in any assessment of fairness (see discussion by Greenberg, 1990 this volume). The merits of retaining the separate construct are discussed later in this chapter.

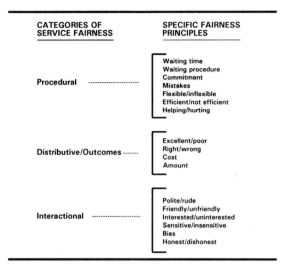

FIG. 9.2.   Fairness principles for services.

customers sorted the resulting 263 statements into the three categories of justice (distributive, procedural, and interactional). Then, in extensive pretesting, a list of principles or attributes was defined for each of the categories.[2] Finally, within each category, 12 other customers sorted the statements into principles for that category. A criterion of 67% agreement was used in each sorting. The sorting process resulted in 17 principles of service fairness (see Fig. 9.2).

These principles were used to develop questionnaire items. The final questionnaire consisted of 6 scales and 64 items. Three scales were based on the principles within each of the three fairness categories. The other three scales measured the constructs of distributive satisfaction, overall satisfaction with the service encounter, and intention to return to that service provider.

Other customers were then asked to respond to the questionnaire (n = 446). First, customers were randomly assigned to one of the four service settings, and one of three types of experiences: their most recent experience with that service, an unsatisfactory experience, or a satisfactory one. Next, to assist their recall, they wrote a description of the experience. Finally, they answered the scale items.

It was thought that using service settings in which customers believe procedures and interactions to be less important than outcomes would offer the most

[2]Because it was considered likely that principles identified in earlier research (e.g., Greenberg, 1986; Sheppard & Lewicki, 1987) might be applicable, it is not yet clear whether similar principles apply across all situations. One of the purposes of this study was to explore the principles that apply in service settings.

stringent test of the hypothesis, while services in which procedures and interactions were deemed very important would likely lend support for the hypothesis. The four services were selected from among several for which customers (n = 37) rated the importance of procedures, interactions, and outcomes. These ratings indicated that customers believed interactions and procedures to be relatively important to satisfaction with nice restaurants and doctors, and relatively unimportant to satisfaction with fast food restaurants and banks.

Undergraduate students served as customers for all phases of the research. The disadvantage in using students for research is that results may not generalize to the broader population. There are reasons to believe that this problem may not be severe in this instance. First, these students were describing or responding to their own individual service experiences, not to a scenario or to a laboratory manipulation of a service experience. Second, other studies done in non-university settings (e.g., in real-life court settings, or among voters) have found few differences in reactions or evaluations based on demographic characteristics such as age, income, or gender (e.g., Tyler, 1984, 1987b; Tyler & Folger, 1980).

RESULTS OF QUALITATIVE PHASE

The descriptions and subsequent sorting of fair and unfair experiences indicated that service fairness could be categorized into distributive, procedural, and interactional justice. No new categories emerged from the sorting process. Within the three categories, 17 themes or justice principles emerged. Thus, the sorting procedure offered support for the first hypothesis—that service fairness can be categorized by outcomes, procedures, and interactions, and that specific principles were associated with each category.

The sorting during the qualitative phase yielded similar proportions of statements across all fairness categories for fast food and nice restaurants and doctor visits. For banks, however, the results were different. A higher proportion of bank experiences were sorted into the procedural fairness category and a lower proportion were distributive in nature than was the case for the other three services.

RESULTS OF QUANTITATIVE PHASE

There were no significant differences based either on types of services or types of recall experiences. Therefore, all responses were analyzed together. The correlation between overall satisfaction and return intentions was high ($r = .86$) and these two constructs were averaged to form a single main dependent measure.

The relationships presented in the hypothesized model were examined in two steps. First, distributive satisfaction was regressed on the principles of dis-

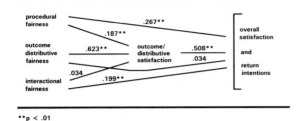

**p < .01

FIG. 9.3. Beta weights for regression of distributive satisfaction, overall satisfaction, and return intentions.

tributive, procedural, and outcome fairness. The analyses offered partial support for the second hypothesis: Procedural fairness principles did explain a significant amount of variance beyond that explained by distributive and interactional fairness principles, but interactional fairness principles did not contribute additional explained variance.

Next, the average of overall satisfaction and return intentions was regressed on the three sets of fairness principles and distributive satisfaction. Together these principles, along with distributive satisfaction, explained 79% of the variance in the dependent measure [F (4,441) = 412.16, p < .0001]. This high percentage is evidence that fairness is related to customer satisfaction with services, and indicates that survey items, based on people's actual fair and unfair experiences, quite adequately captured the constructs of overall satisfaction and return intentions. Figure 9.3 presents the beta weights for each relationship.

As already mentioned, in the quantitative analyses there were virtually no differences between the services. The ratings used to select services for the study had indicated that customers believed procedural and interactional fairness were more important in visits to nice restaurants and doctors and less important in visits to banks or fast food restaurants. The survey responses showed otherwise. Tests of the interactions between the four services and the three categories of service fairness showed no significant differences. Cross validation tests indicated high correlations (r > .80) between the various regression equations. These tests offered further evidence that type of service played virtually no role in determining the relative importance of the fairness categories. Thus, the survey results offered support for the single model of service fairness shown in Fig. 9.1.

DISCUSSION

Theoretical Implications for the Study of Justice

This study extends the justice research into a new arena. Most justice research has examined the reactions to the decisions of authority figures. Organizational justice looks at the reactions of employees to decisions by managers and supervisors, while other justice research has probed responses to teachers, police, or judges.

The present research on service settings is qualitatively different in two ways from these other studies. First, service encounters typically do not involve authority figures. Even when such encounters are with authority figures, for example, doctors, the client has the alternative of leaving and choosing another doctor. Although this alternative may sometimes be inconvenient, it is an alternative rarely available to employees, citizens, or students. Second, in service settings the customer is typically there by choice and it is the customer who usually makes the basic decisions on the nature of the encounter—on what to order or for what problem to request assistance. In sum, in service settings, the customer is more likely to be in a position of equality or even superiority than is the employee, citizen, or student in other justice research.

Thus, it is noteworthy that this research in service settings supports a basic finding from the organizational research, that procedural issues affect people's satisfaction with outcomes independent of the actual distribution (Greenberg, 1990; Lind & Tyler, 1988).

The present research stands in contrast, however, to recent work tending to integrate the construct of interactional justice with procedural justice (see Greenberg, 1990, for a summary of this trend). The quantitative analyses reported here show that procedural and interactional fairness each contributed uniquely to customers' satisfaction. The sorting process in the qualitative phase also supports separating the two constructs. For example, sorters placed bias experiences in the interactional category, not in procedural fairness as other research has suggested (e.g., Leventhal, 1980). Sorters argued that examples of bias more typically represented the behavior of individual service personnel, rather than an establishment's procedures. The point is not that procedural and interactional justice are orthogonal, which they are not, but rather that there may be utility in considering them separately.

There are other differences with previous research efforts. Although changes in labelling or definitions make comparisons of various justice principles across studies difficult, the similarities indicate that it may be possible eventually to develop a list of principles that apply in widely different settings.

Other organizational research has shown that different aspects of justice are differentially related to various measures of employee attitudes. For example, Folger and Konovsky (1989) reported that procedural justice was more strongly related to employees' organizational commitment than was distributive justice, a finding that appears to be at variance with the present study. Indeed, in this study return intentions—ostensibly a service setting analog to organizational commitment—were determined, on the basis of correlational and factor analyses, to capture the same construct as overall satisfaction with the service experience. The apparent discrepancy with Folger and Konovsky may be explained by differences between the types of organizational and service experiences in the two studies. Because it is relatively easy to decide not to return to a service provider, overall satisfaction may be the key factor determining return intentions after a service encounter. An employee's decision to leave an organization is more problematic, however, and organizational commitment may overlap much less with satisfaction with various aspects of the organization.

The foregoing suggests that at least some of the apparent differences in findings in other organizational justice research may be a result of particularities in encounters with the service sector, or, perhaps, with the particular services chosen for this study. This argues both for more research in service settings, and for a greater effort at resolving differences across justice studies (cf. Greenberg, 1990).

Implications for the Study of Services

The findings support the hypothesis that the fairness categories and principles are related to satisfaction with services. Such findings suggest that other measures of service satisfaction need to take fairness issues into account.

The findings also underscore the importance of outcomes or distributions in service satisfaction. Researchers investigating customer evaluation of services have paid relatively little attention to service outcomes. The SERVQUAL measure developed by Parasuraman et al. (1988), for example, contained no items on the quality of outcomes although some items dealt with outcomes by implication (e.g., items on provider competence or reliability). Services researchers may have overlooked outcomes in part because of the difficulty in developing measures. Compared with manufactured goods, the intangibility of services and the involvement of the customer in production make the measurement of service outcomes much more complex than the assessment of manufactured products.

Common sense tells us, however, that customers use services in order to obtain a particular outcome, a meal, for example, or a financial transaction, or medical treatment. The beta weights for distributive fairness reported in Fig. 9.3 indicate the need to address outcomes explicitly in any discussion of customer evaluations of service encounters.

Service managers and researchers are highly aware of the distinctions between types of services (e.g., Lovelock, 1980, 1984). This study found no significant differences between services. The finding is all the more noteworthy since the services had been chosen based on an empirical test showing that customers believed interactional and procedural justice were more important in certain services than in others.[3] The results reported here indicate that in customers'

---

[3]Customers had been asked to rate the importance of outcomes, procedures, and interactions for doctor visits, banks, education (college courses), fast food restaurants, nice restaurants, and supermarkets.

actual service experiences (in contrast with their abstract beliefs about comparative importance) procedural and interactional fairness are important, at least in these four quite different settings.

In this regard it is interesting to note that Parasuraman et al. (1988) also found virtually no differences across services for the various dimensions of service quality. They validated their scale across four services (banks, credit card companies, long-distance telephone service, and appliance repair shops) and separate factor analyses showed essentially identical factor structures for each service. The differences between service types that concern providers and researchers may be less important to customers.

This study has highlighted the role of fairness and justice in customer satisfaction, and has suggested principles that show how such fairness in service might be conceptualized (see Fig. 9.2). As such, the research has a very practical application. The principles that emerged in this research can function as guidelines to managers, or as a checklist. Because the principles represent the customers' point of view, they provide useful insight to service organizations by pointing out the areas where fair or unfair treatment of customers is likely to result in high or low satisfaction and a returning or withdrawing customer.

Limitations of the Study and Suggestions for Future Research

Two limitations were discussed earlier. First, undergraduate students served as customers for all phases of the study, generating descriptions of fair and unfair experiences, sorting these statements, pretesting the survey items, and responding to the survey. The use of undergraduates always raises issues of generalizability. Often this concern is heightened because the study is done in a laboratory or is based on scenarios. In this instance, the research is derived entirely from the students' personal experiences.

It is, of course, entirely possible that persons aged 18–23 pursuing a college education have qualitatively different service encounters than the general population. Indeed, students occasionally recounted instances of age discrimination ("Because I was younger I was treated poorly") and these statements were sorted into the bias principle within the interactional justice category. The bias these students experienced they attributed to their age. Other customers, however, may experience bias that they attribute to gender, race, status, or socioeconomic differences. The essential point, however, is that many people believe they experience bias for one reason or another. Naturally, to assure the generalizability of these findings, research using a more random sample of the population is needed.

The other limitation mentioned earlier is variation in types of services. Services differ along numerous dimensions, and a study such as this one must necessarily be limited to only a few different services. No claim can be made that this research is applicable to other services. The fact that there were no differences between the four services in this study, or in the work of Parasuraman et al. (1988) suggests the need for research that explicitly seeks to determine the limits of generalizability across service types. It may well be, for example, that justice matters less in services with rare or very brief encounters between customer and provider (e.g., with credit card companies). These issues deserve exploration.

A limitation not discussed heretofore is common method variance or response—response bias. Such bias undoubtedly influenced the magnitude of the explained variance, but it is not likely it accounted for all the effects. The differential strength of the relationships between the three categories of fairness and the dependent measure, the fact that each category contributed uniquely to the explained variance, and the fact that interactional fairness was not related to distributive satisfaction as had been expected, all indicate that the bias was a partial, not a determining, factor.

Because the study was correlational in design, it can not be assumed that fair or unfair experiences cause satisfaction or dissatisfaction. Perhaps, the reverse is the case and satisfaction with a service may lead customers to perceive fairness. Previous experimental work on justice has established that fairness leads to satisfaction, however, and other longitudinal studies also support this causal interpretation (e.g., Tyler, 1987a).

It is quite possible that the findings exaggerate the extent to which customers are actually concerned with fairness in service encounters. The survey items were based on experiences that customers described when asked to recount a fair (or unfair) service encounter. Although customers readily related their experiences and told why they were fair (or unfair), they may not, on their own, consider fairness a crucial issue. In this regard, it should be noted that research in marketing has indicated that confirmation of expectations is an important component of satisfaction (e.g., Churchill & Surprenant, 1982). The present study did not assess the comparative explanatory power of fairness and expectancy confirmation in customer satisfaction. The one study that did include measures of both constructs, Swan et al.'s (1985) study of patients' satisfaction with their hospital experiences, found that both equity considerations and expectations strongly affected both satisfaction and return intentions.

Research that compares the predictive power of a range of constructs is clearly needed. Qualitative approaches may also be fruitful. Customers might be asked simply to describe service experiences or describe noteworthy features of service experiences. Content analysis could determine the extent to which issues of fairness and justice, as well as other constructs, were raised independently by customers.

CONCLUSIONS

The study reported here adds to the literature on organizational justice by demonstrating that the construct of justice or fairness does apply in service settings and that there are principles of service fairness which are related to customers' satisfaction with their service encounters. Earlier research showing that procedural fairness contributes uniquely to satisfaction, above the contribution of distributive fairness, was supported. The research also offers support to the notion that interactional fairness, while not orthogonal with procedural fairness, may constitute a distinct construct. Finally, the results here suggest that customers have similar concerns in very different types of service encounters.

ACKNOWLEDGEMENTS

This chapter is based mainly on my dissertation at the University of Maryland. I am very grateful to my advisor, Benjamin Schneider, for his assistance on this and other projects.

REFERENCES

Bies, R. J., & Moag, J. S. (1986). Interactional justice: Communication criteria of fairness. In R. J. Lewicki, B. H. Sheppard, & M. H. Bazerman (Eds.), *Research in organizational behavior.* (Vol. 9, pp. 289–319). Greenwich, CT: JAI Press.

Bowen, D. E., & Schneider, B. (1988). Services marketing and management: Implications for organizational behavior. In B. M. Staw & L. L. Cummings (Eds.), *Research in organizational behavior* (Vol. 10, pp. 43–80). Greenwich, CT: JAI Press.

Churchill, G. A., & Surprenant, C. (1982). An investigation into the determinants of customer satisfaction. *Journal of Marketing Research, 19,* 491–504.

Fisk, R. P., & Coney, K. A. (1982). Postchoice evaluation: An equity theory analysis of consumer satisfaction/dissatisfaction with service choices. In H. K. Hunt & R. L. Day (Eds.), *Conceptual and empirical contributions to consumer satisfaction and complaining behavior* (pp. 9–16). Bloomington, IN: School of Business, Indiana University.

Folger, R. & Bies, R. J. (1989). Managerial responsibilities and procedural justice. *Employee Responsibilities and Rights Journal, 2,* 79–90.

Folger, R., & Konovsky, M. A. (1989). Procedural justice, distributive justice, and reactions to pay raise decisions. *Academy of Management Journal, 32,* 115–130.

Folkes, V. S. (1984). Consumer reactions to product failure: An attributional approach. *Journal of Consumer Research, 10,* 398–409.

Greenberg, J. (1986). Determinants of perceived fairness of performance evaluations. *Journal of Applied Psychology, 71,* 340–342.

Greenberg, J. (1990). Organizational justice: Yesterday, today, and tomorrow. *Journal of Management, 16,* 399–432.

Gronroos, C. (1984). A service quality model and its marketing implications. *European Journal of Marketing, 18,* 36–44.

Katz, D. & Kahn, R. L. (1978). *The social psychology of organizations, rev.* New York: Wiley.

Leventhal, G. S. (1980). What should be done with equity theory? In K. J. Gergen, M. S. Greenberg, & R. H. Willis (Eds.), *Social exchange: Advances in theory and research* (pp. 27–55). New York: Plenum Press.

Lind, E. A. & Tyler, T. R. (1988). *The social psychology of procedural justice.* New York: Plenum Press.

Lovelock, C. H. (1980). Towards a classification of services. In C. W. Lamb & F. M. Dunne (Eds.), *Theoretical developments in marketing* (pp. 72–78). Chicago: American Marketing Association.

Lovelock, C. H. (1984). *Services marketing*. Englewood Cliffs, NJ: Prentice-Hall.

Parasuraman, A., Zeithaml, V. A., & Berry, L. L. (1985). A conceptual model of service quality and its implications for future research. *Journal of Marketing, 49*, 41–50.

Parasuraman, A., Zeithaml, V. A., & Berry, L. L. (1988). SERVQUAL: A multiple-item scale for measuring consumer perceptions of service quality. *Journal of Retailing, 64*, 12–40.

Schneider, B. & Bowen, D. E. (1984). New services design, development, and implementation and the employee. In W. R. George & C. E. Marshall (Eds.), *Developing new services* (pp. 82–101). Chicago: American Marketing Association.

Schutz, H. & Casey, M. (1983). Consumer Satisfaction with occupational service: Quality, frequency, attitudes, information sources. In R. L. Day & H. K. Hunt (Eds.), *International fare in consumer satisfaction in complaining behavior* (pp. 81–86). Bloomington, IN: School of Business, Indiana University.

Sheppard, B. H., & Lewicki, R. J. (1987). Toward general principles of managerial fairness. *Social Justice Research, 1*, 161–176.

Shostack, G. L. (1977). Breaking free from product marketing. *Journal of Marketing, 41*, 73–80.

Swan, J. E., Sawyer, J. C., Van Matre, J. G., McGee, G. W. (1985). Deepening the understanding of hospital patient satisfaction; Fulfillment and equity effects. *Journal of Health Care Marketing, 5*(3), 7–18.

Tyler, T. R. (1984). The role of perceived injustice in defendant's evaluations of their courtroom experience. *Law and Society Review, 18*, 51–74.

Tyler, T. R. (1987a). Conditions leading to value-expressive effects in judgments of procedural justice: A test of four models. *Journal of Personal and Social Psychology Research, 52*, 333–344.

Tyler, T. R. (1987b, September). *Why people follow the law: Procedural justice, legitimacy, and compliance.* Paper presented at the meeting of the American Psychological Association, New York.

Tyler, T. R. (1989). The psychology of procedural justice: A test of the group-value model. *Journal of Personality and Social Psychology, 57*, 830–838.

Tyler, T. R. (1990). *Why people follow the law: Procedural justice, legitimacy, and compliance.* New Haven, CT: Yale University Press.

Tyler, T. R. & Bies, R. J. (1989). Beyond formal procedures: The interpersonal context of procedural justice. In J. S. Carroll (Ed.), *Applied social psychology and organization settings.* (pp 77–88). Hillsdale, NJ: Lawrence Erlbaum Associates.

Tyler, T. R. & Caine, A. (1981). The influence of outcomes and procedures on satisfaction with formal leaders. *Journal of Personality and Social Psychology, 41*, 642–655.

Tyler, T. R. & Folger, R. (1980). Distributional and procedural aspects of satisfaction with citizen-police encounters. *Basic and Applied Psychology, 1*, 281–292.

III

JUSTICE AT THE ORGANIZATIONAL AND INTERORGANIZATIONAL LEVEL

10

Is There Justice in Organizational Acquisitions? The Role of Distributive and Procedural Fairness in Corporate Acquisitions

Maryalice Citera
Joan R. Rentsch
Wright State University

Marks and Mirvis (1986) reported that 50% to 80% of organizational combinations are considered financial failures, and most are plagued by negative employee reactions. The most prevalent type of organizational combination is the acquisition. Acquisitions occur when one organization (acquiring) takes over another (acquired). Typically in an acquisition, the management from the acquiring organization has more decision-making power in the reallocation of resources than the acquired management (Levinson, 1970).

Research indicates that during acquisitions, employees from both organizations suffer from high levels of psychological and physical stress (Marks & Mirvis, 1985, 1986). Due to inherent power differentials in acquisitions, however, acquired employees tend to experience more uncertainty and stress than acquiring employees. Acquisition stress has been shown to result in such negative reactions as high turnover, decreased productivity, and low morale (e.g., Hayes, 1979; Kitching, 1967; Rockwell, 1968; Sinetar, 1981; Walsh, 1988, 1989).

Recently, researchers have recognized the long-term consequences of these negative reactions to acquisitions, but no dominant theoretical perspective explaining the psychological processes in acquisitions has emerged. The organizational justice literature offers one theoretical approach for understanding the many consequences of acquisitions. Organizational justice refers to the distribution of outcomes and the procedures used to make these distributions. Acquisitions, due to their very nature, involve many human resource allocations and redistribution decisions. The application of justice theory to acquisitions may help explain the problems frequently associated with acquisitions and suggest ways to avoid or resolve these problems. Next, we briefly review the acquisition process. Then we describe distributive and procedural justice and how these concepts may apply to acquisitions in general. Finally, we discuss several applications of justice concepts in managing acquisitions.

THE ACQUISITION PROCESS

An acquisition is an ongoing and complicated process that occurs over several years. Management must deal with this difficult process, while maintaining the organization's day-to-day business operations. The acquisition process consists of two primary stages: planning and implementation (Schweiger & Weber, 1989).

During the planning stage, the acquiring organization selects an acquisition candidate, contacts the candidate about the possibility of an acquisition, gathers information concerning the value of the acquisition candidate, and attempts to negotiate a deal with the candidate (Schweiger & Weber, 1989). At this time, the acquisition candidate may actively seek a suitable alternative acquirer, defend itself against a takeover, or try to negotiate a deal.

Communication during the planning stage is limited, due in part to Federal Trade Commission (FTC) regulations and in part to the tentative nature of the deal at this stage. This lack of communication tends to increase uncertainty, causing employees to seek any available information to use in formulating expectations for postacquisition life (Rentsch & Schneider, 1991). Two pieces of information employees use to form expectations are the initial contact between the two organizations and the tone of the negotiations. In some cases, the acquisition may be fiercely contested and the initial contact and negotiations may be hostile. In other cases, both organizations may welcome the acquisition and the negotiations may be friendly. Employees from both organizations may use the tone of the negotiations to establish expectations for how they will be treated during later stages of the acquisition.

The implementation stage consists of uniting the two organizations and may last several years. During this stage, the differences (e.g., cultural, managerial, philosophical, structural) between the two organizations must be reconciled. According to Schweiger and Walsh (1990), three questions need to be answered during this stage. First, acquiring management must determine who should make and implement decisions. Second, the decision makers must determine the organizational differences that must be addressed and the organizational functions (e.g., departments, systems) that should be combined. Third, decision makers need to determine the speed at which decisions should be implemented.

Acquired personnel often have little or no say in the instituted changes. Yet, many of these decisions will have a long-term impact on employees' jobs, careers, and personal lives. Managers may fail to understand that the procedures for implementing these changes may be more meaningful to employees than the changes themselves. Indeed, employees may react negatively to acquisitions because they believe that they are not treated fairly during the acquisition process. Perhaps, the dismal success rate of acquisitions could be improved if managers applied organizational justice principles to the acquisition process.

ORGANIZATIONAL JUSTICE

Organizational justice research has focused on distributive and procedural justice (Greenberg, 1987, 1990). Distributive justice research examines the fairness of allocation or decision outcomes. Procedural fairness research examines the rules used to make these distributions or allocations.

Distributive Justice

Employees evaluate the fairness of the distribution of outcomes based on the principle of equity. According to this principle, rewards are perceived as fair when they are distributed based on contribution. Employees judge equity by first determining the ratio of their perceived outcomes (e.g., pay benefits) to their perceived inputs (e.g., skill, effort). They then determine whether or not they receive fair rewards by comparing their equity ratios to those of comparable others (e.g., co-worker, neighbor, sibling). When employees feel inequitably treated they attempt to adjust their ratios by changing their inputs, increasing their outcomes, cognitively distorting their contributions and outcomes, and so on.

Following an acquisition, a multitude of decisions and reallocations are made. Perceptions of equity based on these reallocations may be significant determinants of employees' reactions to the acquisition. Employees may face drastically reduced outcomes while being expected to maintain steady levels of inputs or even to increase their inputs. Thus, if employees compare their current equity ratios to their equity ratios prior to the acquisition they may perceive injustice. Employees may also regard their counterparts in the "other" organization as a new reference or comparison group (Buono & Bowditch, 1989). Although many decisions may be made following an acquisition, a few examples are presented to illustrate how distributive justice may be applied to the acquisition process.

Staffing and Compensation. Changes in staffing and compensation often result from acquisitions. Some acquisitions are initiated for the purpose of economies of scale. Economies of scale are achieved by combining similar functions and eliminating redundant positions. Bohl (1989), in a survey of approximately 100 companies, found that 36% of mergers and acquisitions resulted in a reduction in force (i.e., layoff). A layoff will be perceived as inequitable if employees, who have worked for an organization for a number of years and have been performing at an acceptable level, lose their jobs. If layoffs must be made, consistent criteria should be used to determine which employees keep their jobs and which employees lose their jobs. Such criteria might include tenure or performance. Unfortunately, because performance appraisals are unique to organizations, there may be no adequate way of assessing and comparing the performance of employees from the two organizations.

With reductions in work force, surviving employees may be asked to pick up the slack and to take on more work. This means that employees are asked to increase their inputs without any comparable increase in outcomes. In fact, employees may even be required to take a pay cut. For example, following Carl Icahn's acquisition of TWA, pilots took a 30% cut in pay and machinists took a 15% cut in pay (Shleifer & Summers, 1988). Other benefits (i.e., health and dental plans, vacation time, expense accounts, tuition reimbursement programs) may also be changed.

Acquisitions can also derail employees' career opportunities. Changes in performance appraisals may mean that the track records of employees evaporate following an acquisition. DeMeuse (1986) reported that, in an acquired company, employee satisfaction with career opportunities significantly decreased following an acquisition. In contrast, in the acquiring company, employee satisfaction with career opportunities increased.

Cultural Symbols and Artifacts.   Employees attach meaning to the symbols and artifacts that represent their organization's culture. If during the acquisition, cultural symbols and artifacts are altered or removed, employees may feel distressed over this loss. Such changes in organizational culture are nearly inevitable during the implementation stage. When two organizations are united, a clash of cultures often becomes apparent (Buono & Bowditch, 1989; Buono, Bowditch, & Lewis, 1985; Marks & Mirvis, 1985, 1986). For example, Buono and Bowditch (1989) reported that, in a merger of two banks, the decoration and style of their eating facilities represented the values of the two banks. One bank had a plush, comfortable, restaurant-like facility reflecting its people orientation; whereas the other bank's facility was more cafeteria-like and reflected its task orientation. In such cases, usually, one style is selected for both organizations. Therefore, employees from one organization will experience a cultural change. Employees from the acquired organization may feel they are being unfairly treated when their cultural symbols and values are changed or eliminated, while employees of the acquiring organization retain their culture.

Furthermore, following an acquisition, cultural symbols may become status symbols. For example, space allocations may symbolize who has status and who does not. Office size and style may figure in employees' judgments of fairness. Greenberg (1988) found that equity theory predicted changes in performance due to temporary changes in workplace status (i.e., office size, number of people to an office). Employees who temporarily experienced a reduction in status (i.e., underpayment inequity) decreased their performance, whereas employees who temporarily experienced an increase in workplace status (i.e., overpayment inequity) increased their performance. The effects of overpayment inequity, however, were shortlived. If the integration process temporarily or permanently moves employees to lower status and less desirable offices, employees may view this as inequitable and reduce their performance.

Inequity can also arise when employees make comparisons to employees from the other organization in the acquisition. Company cars became a point of contention in Bank of America's acquisition of Charles Schwab & Company. Bank of America employees had modest, economical company cars (i.e., Buick LaSabres, Pontiac Phoenixes, and Chevrolet Citations), whereas Schwab employees had expensive, sporty company cars (i.e., Porsches, Saabs, and Jaguars) (Zonana, 1983). The Schwab employees did not want to give up their cars, but the Bank of America executives were displeased with this inequitable distribution. The cars were cultural artifacts that represented the two organizations' values and philosophies.

Technical Systems.   When two companies combine, different technical systems (e.g., accounting, personnel, information processing, computer, report writing) must be integrated. Which system an organization will use can have a major impact on its employees. Learning a new system is time consuming and increases workload because employees are typically expected to perform all of their normal duties, while learning the new system (Napier, Simmons, & Stratton, 1989). Furthermore, organizations may not always choose the most efficient system, instead they may choose the most economical one. For example, Napier et al. (1989) reported that employees of an acquired bank were frustrated when the acquiring company switched their state of the art banking system to an outdated system. From an economical point of view, the acquiring management believed that it was necessary for all branches of the combined organization to use the same system. Because the acquired company comprised only 26% of the combined organization's total number of branches, it was economically advantageous in the short run to switch to the obsolete system.

In summary, acquisitions require many resource allocation decisions that alter the distribution of resources. While there are more examples of the negative side of resource allocations than of the positive side, it is important to point out that employees are not always losers. Sometimes acquisitions result in gains. For example, some employees will gain job security and career opportunities that were unavailable in their original organization. Who gains and who loses usually depends on the type of acquisition.

Nevertheless, decision makers must be aware that any resource allocation decisions they make may be perceived as inequitable and therefore unfair. Following an acquisition, making changes may be unavoidable and the outcomes of these changes may not always be perceived as favorable. Although employees may disagree with the distributions resulting from acquisition decisions, they may still perceive the situation to be fair if they believe that the decisions were made using fair procedures. Procedural justice focuses on the rules used to make distribution decisions.

Procedural Justice

Management from the acquiring organization tends to dictate decisions to the employees from the acquired organization (Blake & Mouton, 1983). When acquiring managers make decisions autocratically, employees from the acquired organization may feel that the right to voice their opinion has been violated. This lack of voice can lead to perceptions of unfair treatment. Previous research has shown that situations in which individuals had an opportunity to voice their opinions were perceived as more fair than those in which individuals were mute (Greenberg & Folger, 1983; Tyler & Folger, 1980; Tyler, Rasinski, & Spodick, 1985). Furthermore, if individuals have the opportunity to voice an opinion and they believe that the decision maker ignored their input, they will feel unfairly treated. A lack of voice is commonplace for acquired employees.

For example, acquisitions may be one of the few situations in which employees have little or no say in who employs them. Typically, when job candidates seek jobs, they interview with several companies and select the best offer. They may choose to work or not to work for a particular company. In an acquisition, the employee has no voice in the matter. Moreover, an employee may have made a conscious decision *not* to work for a particular organization. For example, an employee may quit an organization (Company A) and choose to work for one of its competitors (Company B). When Company A acquires Company B, the employee finds himself or herself again working for Company A.

People also judge procedural fairness based on the quality of their interactions. Tyler (1987, 1989) presented a group-value model of procedural justice. He proposed that individuals are concerned with their long-term relationships with institutions or organizations. Individuals judge their status and membership in a group based on the treatment they receive from decision makers. When individuals belong to a group, they recognize that they will not agree with all decisions. Any particular decision may be unfavorable, but over the long run they expect a payoff from their commitment and loyalty. Therefore, employees are willing to compromise in the short run to reap long run benefits.

Tyler identified three dimensions of group-value: neutrality, trust, and standing. *Neutrality* refers to whether or not decisions are made in an unbiased way. Neutral decision makers use appropriate information honestly and openly. In acquisitions, the typical power and size differences between the acquiring and the acquired organizations make the "playing field" uneven. Decisions made unilaterally by the acquiring management may be considered suspect by acquired employees. Also, we–they conflicts are natural outgrowths of combinations

(Buono & Bowditch, 1989; Marks & Mirvis, 1986; Sales & Mirvis, 1984), causing members of both organizations to view members from the other organization as the enemy. These antagonistic perspectives will cause employees to believe that decision makers from the other organization are biased.

Trust refers to whether or not people believe that decision makers have good intentions. In acquisitions, decision makers have a great deal of discretion over decisions which profoundly affect employees' lives. Given that adversial conditions often exist during acquisitions, employees may tend to distrust decision makers. Managers must establish trust in order for employees to perceive procedural fairness. Employees must believe that the decision makers will treat them in an impartial and reasonable way.

Standing refers to the relative status individuals perceive they have based on the treatment they receive from decision makers. The treatment individuals receive informs them about their status in a group. For example, if managers treat employees impolitely or rudely, they imply that employees hold low status. Conversely, if managers treat employees in a polite and respectful manner, they imply that employees hold high status.

Research has shown that neutrality, trust, and standing have independent effects on perceptions of procedural justice and outcome fairness (Tyler, 1989, 1990). Each of the group-value components explained a significant amount of unique variance in evaluations of procedural justice. In addition, procedural fairness was shown to be significantly associated with organizational commitment, whereas distributive justice was not. If one of the goals of the acquisition is to maintain a loyal and committed work force, then procedural fairness must be addressed.

Tyler's group-value model is similar to an analysis of acquisitions proposed by Shleifer and Summers (1988). According to Shleifer and Summers, acquisitions create value because they involve a breach in trust between shareholders and stakeholders of an organization. Shareholders are the stock owners of a company. They invest their money in a company and expect a return on their investment. Stakeholders include the employees, customers, and suppliers of a company. Shleifer and Summers suggested that there is an implicit long-term contract between stakeholders and shareholders. Employees trade hard work, loyalty, and commitment for job security, advancement potential, and future payoffs. As part of this contract, employees must have faith that the organization's managers have their best interests at heart. In Tyler's terms, the employees must trust the managers of the acquiring firm. But, sometimes there is profit to be made in breaching the contract:

> Although both shareholders and stakeholders benefit ex ante from implicit long-term contracts, ex post it might pay shareholders to renege. For example, it will pay shareholders to fire old workers whose wage exceeds their marginal product in a contract that, for incentive reasons, underpaid them when they were young. (Shleifer & Summers, 1988, p. 38)

The contract implies a mutual obligation between management and employees. Managers of an ongoing organization fear breaking this implicit contract, because they do not want to risk their reputations and credibility. Acquiring managers, on the other hand, are more likely to break this contract because they do not feel obligated to acquired employees. Because acquiring managers are more indebted to the acquiring employees than to the acquired employees, biased decision making may be a natural consequence of acquisitions. In breaching the implicit contract, acquiring organizations indicate that acquired employees have low standing. In other words, the hard work employees have invested in their organization prior to the acquisition is now worthless in the eyes of the acquiring management. In the future, acquired employees may expect to be treated like second-class citizens.

Both distributive and procedural justice may play a role in employee reactions to an acquisition. To understand how these concepts apply to acquisitions it is useful to understand how they relate to different types of acquisitions. In the next section we discuss how distributive and procedural justice concepts are related to two dimensions of acquisitions.

DESCRIBING ACQUISITIONS

Acquisitions may be classified along many dimensions. We focus on two defining dimensions: the desired level of integration and the degree of friendliness. Each dimension represents a continuum. Level of integration refers to the degree to which the organizations become united and friendliness refers to the degree of hostility that exists between the organizations.

Levels of Integration

Level of integration can be characterized as a continuum ranging from completely autonomous to completely combined. At the autonomous end of the continuum, the acquired organization operates as a separate and independent entity. Such acquisitions are sometimes referred to as portfolio acquisitions. In most portfolio acquisitions, the acquired organization is successful and its management is expected to remain with the combined organization (Porter, 1987). The acquiring managers offer financial support, managerial expertise, and business guidance to the acquired organization in exchange for a share of the acquired organization's profits. The acquiring organization's influence, however, is kept to a minimum. The acquired organization retains its own identity and most of its decision making autonomy. Thus, few staffing, cultural, or technical systems changes are made.

In acquisitions at the other end of the continuum (i.e., completely combined), the two organizations blend most, if not all, organizational functions. Sharing activities commonly occurs when the acquisition strategy is to increase profitability through economies of scale. In these cases, redundancies in function, personnel, and technical systems are eliminated. Higher levels of integration may be expected to result in greater reductions in force. In general, sharing many activities requires the integration of many systems and resources. For example, employees in both organizations may be expected to use the same accounting systems, computer systems, and personnel and compensation systems.

Integration at any level will require making some decisions regarding personnel, culture, and technical systems changes, but the number and types of acquisition decisions to be made will depend on the desired level of integration. The primary challenges are to ascertain which systems can be shared and to determine how to share them most effectively. These determinations will affect perceptions of distributive fairness. Three examples of distributive fairness are presented to illustrate how perceptions of inequity might result when a high level of integration is desired.

Sweeping reductions in force are associated more frequently with high levels of integration than with low levels of integration. When employees lose their jobs due to an acquisition, they suffer hardships. Managers, however, may not realize that layoffs also affect survivors. Brockner and Greenberg (1990) reported that the perceived fairness of a layoff affected survivors' reactions. When surviving employees felt sympathetically toward the victim and the victim was uncompensated, the surviving employees reduced their performance and had lower levels of organizational commitment. Reports of low morale following acquisitions may be explained, in part, by survivor reactions to the inequitable treatment of their fellow employees.

The differences between the two organizations' cultures are likely to become apparent at high levels of integration. Also, if the goal of the acquisition is one united organization, then the acquiring organization is likely to seek uniformity in organizational symbols. For example, acquiring organizations are likely to change the name of the acquired company or its logo when high levels of integration are desired. These changes are likely to cause acquired employees to perceive inequity. Even minor changes (e.g., letterhead) might be perceived as inequitable. Acquiring management may be placed in a difficult position because inequitable differences may have existed prior to the acquisition. During the implementation stage of the acquisition, however, members of the other organization become a relevant comparison group causing previous inequities to become salient. For example, offices in one organization may be larger and more plush than in the other organization. Leaving this inequity in office size and style may be viewed negatively by those who have smaller offices. On the other hand, standardizing office size, by making some smaller and some larger will result in feelings of inequity, especially for those employees who originally had large offices.

As organizations share more activities, there are higher levels of integration of technical systems. Employees are likely to evaluate the choice of systems to be used in terms of equity. In a survey of human resource managers, Schweiger and Weber (1989) found that the most popular strategy for integrating personnel systems was to use the acquiring organization's system. Keeping separate systems was a distant second, and using the acquired organization's system occurred rarely. In general, if acquired employees are forced to adopt the acquiring organization's systems, they may perceive this distribution of outcomes as unfair. Furthermore, changes in technical systems are likely to be perceived as unfair if the selected system is inadequate or difficult to learn. Thus, there are many decisions concerning which functions and systems will be integrated.

Given these few examples it is clear that managers must evaluate the potential consequences of all decisions. Even those decisions that they consider to be minor may affect equity perceptions. They should also recognize that even when no changes are made there may still be justice implications.

Degree of Friendliness and Hostility

Pritchett (1985) outlined a degree of hostility continuum that may exist between the acquired and acquiring organizations. The adversarial nature of the negotiations prior to the acquisition determines the level of friendliness or hostility that characterizes the acquisition process.

At one end of the continuum are friendly acquisitions. Friendly acquisitions occur when management from both organizations agree that the two organizations should be united. One example of a friendly acquisition is a collaboration where both organizations agree to the acquisition and attempt to negotiate a deal. These negotiations are usually characterized by goodwill and diplomacy. The congenial and cooperative nature of the negotiations often results in mutual respect and understanding between the managers from both organizations.

At the other end of this continuum are hostile takeovers. Hostile takeovers occur when the acquired organization fights the takeover attempt. The most hostile type of takeover is a raid. Raids are characterized by high levels of anxiety and aggression. The adversarial nature of the negotiations sets the hostile tone for the entire acquisition process. The battle often lasts a long time and has long-term repercussions. Although most acquired employees find it difficult to cope with the raid, leaders from the acquired company are placed in a particularly difficult position. Once they have taken an adversarial stand against acquiring management, they cannot become "members" of the raiding organization without losing the trust of their followers. They may have no choice but to resign, leaving their followers without leadership (Pritchett, 1985). Thus, employees involved in a hostile raid may experience a loss of leadership and lose individuals who acted as their champions in attaining resources. Employees in hostile raids may find it difficult to attain rewards, support for their ideas, and funding for their projects from acquiring management. They also may lose their decision-making autonomy.

Based on Tyler's (1989) group-value model, hostile takeovers may be perceived as more procedurally unfair than friendly acquisitions. First, it will be difficult for acquired employees to perceive acquiring decision makers as neutral. In hostile takeovers, the ruthless tactics used by acquiring managers to gain control may lead acquired employees to assume that other decisions and changes will be made in the same ruthless manner. In hostile raids, arrogance is apparent in the flagrant disregard for acquired managements' objections to the takeover. The acquiring managers have the power to preempt acquired managers' control over their own organization and they exercise this power. The acquiring management's arrogance may result in expectations for biased decision making.

Second, since acquiring management has ignored acquired employees' wishes, acquired employees may find it difficult to trust them in the future. A high degree of hostility will lead to we–they mentalities (DeMeuse, 1986). Defensive tactics taken during the planning stage may create cohesion among the acquired employees and among the acquiring employees. The result is likely to be antagonism between employees from the two organizations. Negative stereotyping can add to acquired employees levels of mistrust. Due to their defensiveness, acquired employees may find it difficult to later form psychological attachments with the raiding organization.

Third, in hostile takeovers, acquired employees may perceive themselves as having low standing. As acquired employees rally to defend their organization, they become invested in its preservation. In warding off the takeover, acquired employees come to identify strongly with the symbols of their organizational culture. Unfortunately, given the power differential between the acquired and acquiring organizations, acquired employees and their cultural symbols are often perceived as having low status (i.e. standing). Therefore, the acquiring management feels justified in eliminating the acquired organization's culture. When their cultural symbols are removed, acquired employees may suffer a sense of lost organizational identity.

Hostility and Integration

As previously discussed, two dimensions are useful in describing different organizational acquisitions: the degree of friendliness and the desired level of integration. To accurately describe an acquisition, however, it is necessary to define it along both dimensions. By crossing these two dimensions, acquisitions can be defined more explicitly. Although these dimensions represent continuua, for purposes of discussion, we focus on the four extreme cases: friendly-low integration, friendly-high integration, hostile-low integration, hostile-high integration.

Using Folger's referent cognitions theory of justice (Cropanzano & Folger, 1989; Folger, 1986) we can make predictions concerning employees' perceptions of fairness for these four types of acquisitions. According to referent cognitions theory, employees will feel unfairly treated when they receive an unfavorable outcome (that could have been favorable) and the decision maker failed to use fair procedures (that should have been used). In acquisitions it can be hypothesized that feelings of resentment will be high when employees believe that they could have received a more favorable distribution than they received and that the decision makers should have used other decision-making procedures. For example, resentment will be highest when acquired employees feel that distributions favor the acquiring organization (e.g., using the acquiring organization's obsolete banking system) and fair procedures were not used (e.g., employees were not consulted). If the acquired system was adequate prior to the acquisition, then it could have been selected for use in the combined organization. Employees are likely to perceive many more "coulds" in acquisitions involving high levels of integration than in acquisitions involving low levels of integration. In hostile takeovers acquired employees are likely to perceive many more "shoulds" than employees in friendly acquisitions. For example, decision makers should be more neutral, trustworthy, and treat acquired employees with more respect than they typically do in hostile takeovers. Thus, based on referent cognitions theory we can predict that perceptions of injustice will be more prevalent as the levels of hostility and integration increase.

A friendly acquisition in which the desired level of integration is low should be the easiest type of acquisition to manage fairly. The friendly nature of the deal would influence employees to perceive decision makers as using fair decision-making procedures, and the low level of integration will result in relatively few redistribution decisions being made. A friendly acquisition with high integration may be slightly more difficult to manage. More decisions regarding redistributions must be made to accommodate the high level of desired integration. But, any difficulty resulting from perceived distributional unfairness is likely to be mitigated by the perceived procedural fairness associated with the friendly nature of the acquisition. Likewise, a hostile acquisition with a low level of desired integration is likely to be slightly more difficult to manage than a friendly-low integration acquisition due to the hostility between members from the two organizations. But, the low level of integration should moderate these difficulties. The most difficult acquisitions to manage will be hostile-high integration acquisitions. The hostility is likely to result in unfair decision-making procedures, or at least a perception that the procedures are unfair. The high level of desired integration requires many distributive changes that are likely to be perceived as unfair. Employee resentment can be hypothesized to be greatest in this case. Therefore, managers of the combined organization need to make the greatest effort to ensure fairness in hostile-high level integration acquisitions.

MANAGING ACQUISITIONS USING ORGANIZATIONAL JUSTICE

In any type of acquisition, the decisions made may be fair, but employees may perceive them as unfair. Managers should recognize that they need to take responsibility for promoting perceptions of fairness. Folger and Bies (1989) outlined seven managerial responsibilities necessary to ensure organizational justice: (a) give adequate consideration to employees' viewpoints, (b) suppress biases in decision-making, (c) apply decision-making criteria consistently across employees, (d) supply a justification for a decision, (e) communicate honestly and candidly, (f) provide timely feedback following a decision, and (g) treat employees with respect.

These responsibilities can be mapped to Tyler's group-value dimensions. To facilitate neutral decision making, managers should give adequate consideration to employees' viewpoints, suppress biases in decision making and apply decision criteria consistently across all employees. To build the trust of employees managers should supply justifications for their decisions and communicate honestly and openly. Employees' perceptions of standing can be enhanced by providing timely feedback and treating employees with respect. Thus, if managers accept these responsibilities and incorporate these activities into managing the acquisition process, perceptions of procedural justice should be enhanced.

The managerial responsibilities can be used as the basis for making prescriptions for increasing fairness in all acquisitions. Further, managers of hostile acquisitions with a high level of integration should pay particular attention to these issues. Here we offer several applications of justice concepts for managing acquisitions.

Employee Viewpoints Need to be Considered

During the acquisition process, viewpoints of all employees are not adequately considered. There is a tendency for acquiring firms to communicate solely with the top levels of the acquired firm (Schweiger & Weber, 1989). Top level personnel in the acquired organization may seclude themselves from lower level employees, and remain unaware of lower level employees' viewpoints. In addition, because acquired employees lose their champions (i.e., their leaders resign or get fired), they are further removed from the decision-making loop.

The following quote exemplifies employees' frustrations when management fails to consider employee viewpoints prior to a layoff:

> It distressed me greatly to see people's lives being literally ruined career-wise by management personnel that had little or no contact with these individuals yet had complete control over their futures. (Leana & Feldman, 1989, p. 130)

As stated earlier, the first step in the implementation process is to determine who will make acquisition decisions. Schweiger and Weber (1989) reported that the most commonly used decision-making approaches to integration were: (a) informal interactions between the managers of the acquired and acquiring organizations, (b) participation of acquired managers in executive meetings of the acquiring organization, (c) informal interactions at social functions, and (d) formal responsibility for the integration given to a top manager from the acquiring firm. Unfortunately, none of these approaches directly assess the viewpoints of employees from the acquired organization about specific decisions. A less frequently used approach, transition teams, however, were ranked high in terms of effectiveness. Transition teams are groups of employees assigned the task of integrating the two organizations. These teams often consist of members from both organizations who jointly make decisions. Thus, the viewpoints of members from both organizations can be expressed.

To ensure fairness, employees should be given an opportunity to voice their concerns before any major changes or decisions are made. Transition teams may be an effective means for assuring that acquired employees have a voice in the acquisition process.

Decisions Should be Unbiased

In hostile takeovers, the ruthless tactics used by acquiring managers to gain control lead acquired employees to assume that these managers will make unfair acquisition decisions. This assumption is based on the negative stereotyping and we–they conflicts commonly associated with acquisitions (Sales & Mirvis, 1984). Employees identify strongly with their own organization and tend to denigrate employees from the other organization. Based on social identity theory, it can be hypothesized that decision makers, will not only be perceived as biased, but are likely to make biased decisions favoring members of their original organization (Tajfel, 1982; Turner, 1987). Because hostile acquisitions are primed for biased decision making, acquiring managers must resist this reflexive favoritism to enhance fairness.

At high levels of integration choices must be made about how to combine personnel, cultural symbols, and technical systems. As stated previously, acquiring organizations tend to select their own personnel, systems, and culture. Although the decision to use the acquiring organization's systems may be partly influenced by economics and productivity, biases may also enter into the decisions. The acquiring organization is perceived as operating more effectively and its systems may be viewed as superior to the acquired organization's. Therefore, the implied "wise" managerial choice is to select the acquiring organization's systems. To avoid biased decisions, some method for assessing the efficiency of the systems should be used. As part of this assessment, the viewpoints of all employees should be considered.

Furthermore, in hostile-high level integration acquisitions there will be a tendency to make biased layoff decisions and to fill vacant positions based on prior organizational membership. Procedures can be developed to overcome these biases and to assure fair staffing decisions. For layoffs to be perceived as fair, acquiring organizations should seek to retain employees with the highest level of performance. Unfortunately, acquiring managers may find that no fair performance criteria are available. An attempt should be made to gather relevant, accurate information about the performance of every employee. For example, Baxter Healthcare Corporation used a slating process in selecting which employees they would retain (Ulrich, Cody, LaFasto, & Rucci, 1989). The first step in the slating process was to identify all of the positions to be filled. Next, all viable candidates for each position were identified and interviewed. The best candidate was then selected to fill each position. All employees were guaranteed that they would be considered for at least one or more jobs. In addition, a review and appeals board was set up to ensure that each candidate had received fair consideration.

Decisions Should be Made Consistently Across Employees

During an acquisition many decisions must be made quickly and often decisions may be made too quickly. Changes may be made before firm rules and organizational policies are established. Decisions may be made on a case to case basis and lead to the appearance of inconsistent decision making. Efforts should be made to establish policies early in the acquisition process and to apply them consistently. In hostile-high level integration acquisitions, the contentious atmosphere will aggravate employees' frustrations and make them less tolerant of inconsistencies. When managers must make decisions on a case by case basis, they may alleviate the negative reactions by making their decision process known to the employees. It is likely that decisions are being made consistently, but that employees are unaware of it.

Justifications for Decisions Should be Given

Lack of a justification exacerbates the acquired employees' natural inclination to distrust decision makers from the acquiring organization. Bies and his associates found that only adequate and sincere justifications were associated with reduced feelings of anger and fewer complaints (Bies & Shapiro, 1988; Bies, Shapiro, & Cummings, 1988). In acquisitions, justifications may be difficult to provide for routine activities because the original reasoning has become so ingrained that no one can recall it. For example, a report may be filed month after month without anyone remembering its original purpose. If employees from the acquired company ask why they should spend time and effort on this report, no adequate justification is readily available—it is simply "the way we do things here." When many activities are shared and no adequate justifications are available for why and how things are done, acquired employees may become increasingly dissatisfied. In fact, this may be a good opportunity for acquiring organizations to reevaluate the rationale behind some of their routine activities.

More specifically, justifications may reduce the negative effects of layoff decisions. When employees are not supplied with a justification, they often construct their own explanations. For example, one employee felt:

> Age and salary had a great deal to do with my job loss. My job was not eliminated—myself along with several others were replaced by people half our age. It was simple economics. (Leana & Feldman, 1989, p. 130)

Misunderstandings can be avoided by providing explanations and justifications. In justifying layoffs, the criteria used to make the decisions should be clearly communicated to the employees.

Communication Should be Honest and Forthright

Many takeovers involve a breach of trust, therefore management needs to gain the respect and trust of the acquired employees. The problem cited most commonly in acquisitions is a lack of communication (Leighton & Tod, 1969; Marks & Mirvis, 1985; Schweiger & DeNisi, 1991). The lack of communication creates ambiguity that causes employees to turn to the rumor-mill. Rumors result in some details being omitted, exaggerated or distorted by ideosyncratic viewpoints. (Ulrich et al., 1989). Reliance on rumors for information often results in the construction of worst case scenarios (Marks & Mirvis, 1986). Open and honest communication, however, can dispel rumors and build trust. Schweiger and DeNisi (1991) found that communication efforts (i.e., a merger newsletter, a telephone hotline, weekly meetings) reduced uncertainty and stress while increasing job satisfaction, commitment, and trust levels. For example, management of acquiring organizations should portray a layoff situation honestly to employees. If layoffs and changes are inevitable, this should be communicated to the employees. Assuring employees that there will be no layoffs and later cutting employees will cause survivors to distrust decision makers.

Provide Timely Feedback About Decisions

Organizations should provide employees with timely feedback about decisions. For example, giving employees advanced warning that the name of the organization or its logo will be changed may allow them time to grieve and to get over the initial shock before such decisions are actually implemented.

Advanced warning is also recommended for layoffs. Leana and Feldman (1989) reported that one-third of the employees in their study received only one day's advance notice. Managers may be reluctant to warn employees of layoffs because they fear production may drop and employees may leave before the organization can afford to lose them. By providing advanced warning of layoff decisions, acquiring organizations may buffer employees from the negative consequences of a layoff. Advanced warning helps employees line up jobs quickly, reduces financial strain on employees, and decreases their need to relocate (Leana & Feldman, 1989). Treating laid-off employees with respect can affect remaining employees' expectations for fair treatment in the future.

Treat Employees With Respect

All employees should be treated with respect. For example, layoff victims should not be maligned. Sutton, Eisenhardt and Jucker (1986) documented the following situation at Atari:

> Top management went around and spoke to everybody. What they said was, "Now we've gotten rid of all rummies and the company's strong and all the good people are left." And they never should have said that. They should have said, "Because of business problems, we have to let people go." But they said, "We've gotten rid of all the scum," and that wasn't the case at all. And everybody knew it and everybody resented it. So it just got worse and worse. (p. 23)

When employees hear their laid-off counterparts being disparaged, they may feel that this is a reflection on their status in the organization. Leana and Feldman (1989) make several recommendations for treating laid-off employees with dignity: The news should be delivered in person from someone the employee knows well, recommendations to potential employers should be fair, retraining and outplacement services should be available to employees, and severance packages should be given to employees. Severance pay not only helps employees with financial responsibilities, but also saves them from the embarrassment of applying for government financial assistance. In an examination of the justice of layoffs, Brockner and his associates (Brockner & Greenberg, 1990) found that survivors viewed lay-offs as fair when the victims were compensated.

Similarly, when the acquiring organization's technical systems are used, the replaced system should not be disparaged. Acquired employees may take this as a personal insult. Also, respect can be shown by formally training acquired employees and giving them ample time to become comfortable with the new system. Just as newly hired trainees would not be expected to perform at the same levels as experienced workers, acquired employees need time to adjust and their performance should not be criticized as they learn. In addition, when employees have questions about the new system or do not immediately comprehend its intricacies, assistance should be readily available. These employees should receive prompt assistance and be dealt with patiently. One way to deal with this problem may be to set up a "hotline" for handling employees' questions concerning the new system. Napier et al. (1989) reported that a hotline established to field acquired employees' questions regarding the new system, nearly always solved the problem and greatly relieved employees' stress.

SUMMARY AND CONCLUSION

An organizational acquisition is a long-term process involving many decisions that will result in the redistribution of outcomes. Research has shown that many acquisitions fail to meet performance expectations and acquired employees react negatively to acquisitions. We have suggested that these negative reactions may be due, in part, to the perceived unfairness of acquisition distributions. Acquisitions may require increased employee inputs (e.g., increased workload, retraining), while potentially decreasing employee outcomes (e.g., pay, job security). Furthermore, employees' perceptions of fairness will depend on the procedures used for determining the distributions. Employees will form expectations for organizational justice based in part on the amount of trust, respect, and neutrality evident in acquisition decisions. If managers become aware of their responsibilities to enhance fairness during the acquisition process and apply justice concepts to acquisition decisions, then they may be able to avoid some of the negative consequences associated with acquisitions. In the future, researchers should consider applying an organizational justice approach in studying different types of organizational acquisitions.

ACKNOWLEDGMENTS

The authors thank Eusong Blacketer, Russell Cropanzano, Laura Finfer, Chris Gasson, Gerry Gingrich, Ted Hayes, David Meder, Jonathan Selvaraj and Rosemary Stackhouse for their comments on an earlier draft.

REFERENCES

Bies, R. J., & Shapiro, D. L. (1988). Voice and justification: Their influence on procedural fairness judgments. *Academy of Management Journal, 31,* 676–685.

Bies, R. J., Shapiro, D. L., & Cummings, L. L. (1988). Causal accounts and managing organizational conflict: Is it enough to say it's not my fault? *Communications Research, 15,* 381–399.

Blake, R. R., & Mouton, J. S. (1983). The urge to merge: Tying the knot successfully. *Training and Development Journal, 37,* 41–46.

Bohl, D. L. (1989). *Tying the corporate knot: An American Management Association research report on the effects of mergers and acquisitions.* New York: American Management Association.

Brockner, J., & Greenberg, J. (1990). The impact of layoffs on survivors: An organizational justice perspective. In J. S. Carroll (Ed.), *Applied social psychology and organizational settings* (pp. 45–75). Hillsdale, NJ: Lawrence Erlbaum Associates.

Buono, A. F., & Bowditch, J. L. (1989). *The human side of mergers and acquisitions.* San Francisco: Jossey-Bass.

Buono, A. F., Bowditch, J. L., & Lewis, J. W. (1985). When cultures collide: The anatomy of a merger. *Human Relations, 38,* 477–500.

Cropanzano, R., & Folger, R. (1989). Referent cognitions and task decision autonomy: Beyond equity theory. *Journal of Applied Psychology, 74,* 293–299.

DeMeuse, K. P. (1986, August). *Merger mania: A researcher's perspective.* Paper presented at the annual convention of the American Psychological Association, Washington, DC.

Folger, R. (1986). Rethinking equity theory: A referent cognitions model. In H. W. Bierhoff, R. L. Cohen, & J. Greenberg (Eds.), *Justice in social relations* (pp. 145–162). New York: Plenum Press.

Folger, R., & Bies, R. J. (1989). Managerial responsibilities and procedural justice. *Employee Responsibilities and Rights Journal, 2,* 79–90.

Greenberg, J. (1987). A taxonomy of organizational justice theories. *Academy of Management Review, 12,* 9–22.

Greenberg, J. (1988). Equity and workplace status: A field experiment. *Journal of Applied Psychology, 74,* 293–299.

Greenberg, J. (1990). Organizational justice: Yesterday, today, and tomorrow. *Journal of Management, 16,* 399–432.

Greenberg, J., & Folger, R. (1983). Procedural justice, participation, and the fair process effect in groups and organizations. In P. B. Paulus (Ed.), *Basic group processes* (pp. 235–256). New York: Springer-Verlag.

Hayes, R. H. (1979). The human side of acquisitions. *Harvard Business Review, 58,* 41–46.

Kitching, J. (1967). Why do mergers miscarry? *Harvard Business Review, 45,* 84–100.

Leana, C. R., & Feldman, D. C. (1989). When mergers force layoffs: Some lessons about managing the human resource problems. *Human Resource Planning, 12,* 123–140.

Leighton, C. M., & Tod, G. R. (1969). After the acquisition: Continuing challenge. *Harvard Business Review, 47,* 90–102.

Levinson, H. (1970). A psychologist diagnoses merger failures. *Harvard Business Review, 48,* 138–147.

Marks, M. L., & Mirvis, P. H. (1985). Merger syndrome: Stress and uncertainty. *Mergers and Acquisitions, 20,* 50–55.

Marks, M. L., & Mirvis, P. H. (1986, October). The merger syndrome. *Psychology Today,* pp. 36–42.

Napier, N. K., Simmons, G., & Stratton, K. (1989). Communication during a merger: The experience of two banks. *Human Resource Planning, 12,* 105–122.

Porter, M. E. (1987). From competitive advantage to corporate strategy. *Harvard Business Review, 65,* 43–59.

Pritchett, P. (1985). *After the merger: Managing the shockwaves.* Homewood, IL: Dow Jones-Irwin.

Rentsch, J. R., & Schneider, B. (1991). Expectations for postcombination organizational life: A study of responses to merger and acquisition scenarios. *Journal of Applied Social Psychology, 21,* 233–252.

Rockwell, W. F. (1968). How to acquire a company. *Harvard Business Review, 46,* 121–124.

Sales, A. L., & Mirvis, P. H. (1984). When cultures collide: Issues in acquisitions. In J. R. Kimberly & R. E. Quinn (Eds.), *Managing organizational transitions* (pp. 107–133). Homewood, IL: Irwin.

Schweiger, D. M., & DeNisi, A. S. (1991). Communication with employees following a merger: A longitudinal field experiment. *Academy of Management Journal, 34,* 110–135.

Schweiger, D. M., & Walsh, J. P. (1990). Mergers and acquisitions: An interdisciplinary view. In K. M. Rowland & G. R. Ferris (Eds.), *Research in personnel and human resources management* (Vol. 8, pp. 41–107). Greenwich, CT: JAI Press.

Schweiger, D. M., & Weber, Y. (1989). Strategies for managing human resources during mergers and acquisitions: An empirical investigation. *Human Resource Planning, 12,* 69–86.

Shleifer, A., & Summers, L. H. (1988). Breach of trust in hostile takeovers. In A. J. Auerbach (Ed.), *Corporate takeovers: Causes and consequences* (pp. 33–56). Chicago: The University of Chicago Press.

Sinetar, M. (1981). Mergers, morale, and productivity. *Personnel Journal, 60,* 863–867.

Sutton, R. I., Eisenhardt, K. M., & Jucker, J. V. (1986). Managing organizational decline: Lessons from Atari. *Organizational Dynamics, 14,* 17–19.

Tajfel, H. (1982). Social psychology of intergroup relations. *Annual Review of Psychology, 33,* 1–39.

Tyler, T. R. (1987). Conditions leading to value-expressive effects in judgments of procedural justice: A test of four models. *Journal of Personality and Social Psychology, 52,* 333–344.

Tyler, T. R. (1989). The psychology of procedural justice: A test of the group-value model. *Journal of Personality and Social Psychology, 57,* 830–838.

Tyler, T. R. (1990, August). *Using procedures to justify outcomes: Testing the viability of a procedural justice strategy for managing conflict and allocating resources in work organizations.* Paper presented at the annual meeting of the Academy of Management, San Francisco.

Tyler, T. R., & Folger, R. (1980). Distributional and procedural aspects of satisfaction with citizen-police encounters. *Basic and Applied Social Psychology, 1,* 281–292.

Tyler, T. R., Rasinski, K. A., & Spodick, N. (1985). Influence of voice on satisfaction with leaders: Exploring the meaning of process control. *Journal of Personality and Social Psychology, 48,* 72–81.

Turner, J. C. (1987). *Rediscovering the social group.* New York: Basil Blackwell.

Ulrich, D., Cody, T., LaFasto, F., & Rucci, T. (1989). Human resources at Baxter Healthcare Corporation merger: A strategic partner role. *Human Resource Planning, 12,* 87–103.

Walsh, J. P. (1988). Top management turnover following mergers and acquisitions. *Strategic Management Journal, 9,* 173–183.

Walsh, J. P. (1989). Doing a deal: Merger and acquisition negotiations and their impact upon target company top management turnover. *Strategic Management Journal, 10,* 307–322.

Zonana, V. F. (1983, January 20). The Porsches and Saabs at Schwab Aggravate Some at Bank America. *The Wall Street Journal,* p. 27.

11 The Role of Interpersonal Justice in Organizational Grievance Systems

Michael E. Gordon
Rutgers University, New Brunswick

Gerald E. Fryxell
University of Tennessee, Knoxville

Grievance administration is a central aspect of collective bargaining agreements. As the most visible and prevalent mechanism for providing workers with due process, grievance systems offer research opportunities for testing behavioral propositions about justice in the workplace, an issue of long-standing and considerable interest to trade unions (Gordon & Fryxell, 1989a). Yet, there is a dearth of behavioral research on grievances, and this is particularly surprising because behavioral scientists have delved extensively into interpersonal processes that comprise union–management relations. For example, there are vast and venerable literatures on negotiations and bargaining (e.g., Magenau & Pruitt, 1979), industrial conflict (e.g., Stagner, 1956), and participative decision making (e.g., Maier, 1963). Nonetheless, there is little definitive research on the specific factors that cause individuals to lose confidence in their ability to informally resolve interpersonal differences about contract rights and, therefore, to invoke formal grievance procedures. Likewise, empirical information is scarce regarding the personal and organizational outcomes (e.g., workplace justice) that are anticipated and actually afforded by use of the grievance system.

The purpose of this chapter is to consider grievance systems as mechanisms for providing workers with justice in their jobs. To this end, we examine the structure and functioning of grievance systems in union–management relations.[1]

---

[1]Although our review is concerned with research conducted in unionized work environments, it should be noted that some nonunion companies, especially larger firms, have grievance systems. Indeed, union avoidance often is based on "union substitution" strategies that attempt to remove the incentives for joining by, among other things, implementing a formal nonunion grievance procedure, embracing an open-door policy, or installing an ombudsperson (Kochan & Katz, 1988). Despite

Important in this discussion is the union's common law obligation to provide procedural justice (i.e., the perceived fairness of the processes used to resolve disputes) when handling workers' grievances under the doctrine of Duty of Fair Representation (DFR). Next, we discuss the precepts of organizational economics that specify the salience of safeguards of employment relationships and the consequent role of grievance systems. Finally, we review behavioral research of factors that influence the level of grievance activity as well as the disposition and aftermath of a grievance. The latter discussions concentrate on distributive justice (i.e., the perceived fairness of the outcomes of grievance resolution).

BACKGROUND

Once a union and company negotiate a collective bargaining agreement, they are bound by its terms for the duration of the contract. Because the parties are likely to interpret contract provisions differently, disputes are likely to arise over the rights guaranteed to employees and employers. Such disputes are called grievances (i.e., "allegations by employees or employers of a violation of rights to which the party has been entitled by the collective bargaining agreement;" Gordon & Miller, 1984, p. 118). Contract provisions that address discipline, work assignments, hours of work, supervisors doing bargaining-unit work, working conditions, and subcontracting are the most likely to lead to grievances. The handling of grievances is a primary responsibility of local union officers and stewards. Actions taken by a representative of management (in most cases the worker's immediate supervisor) engender most grievances.

Importance of Grievance Systems

Grievance administration is an important aspect of union–management relations for a variety of reasons. First, Section 9 (a) of the National Labor Relations Act (Wagner Act) of 1935 provides that "any individual employee or a group of employees shall have the right at any time to present grievances to their employers." Given this enabling legislation, grievance and arbitration provisions were found in all 400 contracts contained in the Collective Bargaining Negotiations and Contracts (CBNC) Basic Patterns database (Bureau of National Affairs, 1989).

Second, grievance systems can reduce or eliminate work stoppages during the life of the collective bargaining agreement. Processing a grievance permits resolution of interpretive disagreements without reliance on economic threat by either

---

opposing conceptual arguments about the degree of due process that can be provided by such systems (see Epstein, 1975; Westin, 1989), Peterson and Lewin's (1990) review uncovered relatively few studies of nonunion grievance procedures (see Bosco, 1985; Lewin, 1987).

of the parties (e.g., strikes or lockouts). Compliance with the contract is effected by an orderly process that allows the parties to determine whether the labor agreement has in fact been violated.

Third, several lines of evidence suggest that grievance administration influences the way workers view unions. Kochan's (1979) survey of approximately 1,500 American workers indicated that grievance handling was considered the most important union activity. Indeed, access to a system for redressing sources of job dissatisfaction is an important basis for the initial appeal of unions among unorganized workers. The anticipation of assistance in resolving grievances is a factor that differentiates workers who voted for union certification from those who voted against representation (Montgomery, 1989).

Finally, grievance procedures are important from the perspective of society because they represent a means of providing justice in the workplace. Slichter (1947) regarded a grievance procedure as a form of checks and balances on managerial actions, one that offered workers a measure of control over their jobs. Affording workers with due process also may have useful economic outcomes. Freeman and Medoff (1984) contend that employee "voice" expressed through the grievance system provides dissatisfied employees with an alternative to turnover, thereby increasing job tenure, raising skill levels, and improving productivity.

Structure of Grievance Systems

A formal grievance system consists of a sequence of steps through which the union and management can resolve any charges of failure to comply with both written and unwritten (e.g., past practice) agreements that define the employment relationship. The scope of the grievance procedure is specified in 91% of agreements, and of these 79% permit grievances over any interpretation or application of the contract. Typically, collective bargaining agreements call for three-step procedures, although four-step procedures were found in 21% of the CBNC database (Bureau of National Affairs, 1989). Succeeding steps in the process involve higher levels of the union and management organizations.

Many complaints never reach the first formal step in the grievance procedure because they are settled informally. While informal settlement has economic advantages (viz., reduction in the costs to both parties of resolving the matter) and provides a measure of justice through quick resolution of the issue (justice delayed may be justice denied), it does not generate a paper trail of data that can be used to study grievance handling. As a result, statistics on grievance filings are assumed to present a biased picture of grievance activity because they measure only the number and type of complaints that cannot be resolved informally and, therefore, are put in writing. Gordon and Miller (1984) explored the criterion problems (i.e., deficiency and contamination) associated with the use of grievance data as dependent variables in behavioral research and concluded that the extent of grievance activity can, at best, only be estimated by researchers.

The final step in virtually all grievance procedures is arbitration, which involves the intervention of a third party when the union and management cannot settle an issue bilaterally. Section 203(d) of the Labor–Management Relations Act (Taft–Hartley Act) of 1947 encouraged grievance arbitration: "Final adjustment by a method agreed upon by the parties is hereby declared to be the desirable method for settlement of grievance disputes arising out of the application or interpretation of an existing collective-bargaining agreement." Three Supreme Court decisions rendered in 1960 (the *Steelworkers Trilogy*) protected the status of grievance arbitration by limiting the involvement of the courts in the settlement of contract disputes and insulating arbitration awards from judicial review.

Because of certain limitations on awards that arbitrators are allowed to make in disposing of a grievance, a struggle for controlling access to workplace justice has evolved between unions and tort lawyers who contend that workers should have a choice of remedies. In the case of a discharged worker, for instance, lawyers want to process the legal claims of individuals in state and federal courts, which can award compensation and punitive damages. By contrast, union representation through the grievance system typically ends with binding arbitration that, when it upholds the grievant, can only reinstate the individual with back pay. If discharged employees can be handsomely rewarded by state courts, arbitration becomes a less attractive mechanism through which to seek redress. Recent Supreme Court rulings, however, provide support for the grievance system as a way of resolving disputes that pertain to contractual rights (e.g., *Allis-Chalmers Corp. v. Lueck*, 1985). If legal challenges to union exclusivity for providing due process prevail in the future, organized labor's mandate may be substantially reduced and it could no longer assure employers that all employee grievances would be resolved through the contractual process (Gordon & Coulson, 1989).

Duty of Fair Representation (DFR)

Whereas enlightened managements may consider a variety of process issues that engender justice in resolving disputes with their employees, unions are obliged to assure a modicum of procedural justice when attempting to resolve disputes on behalf of workers they represent. And, whereas managers report that being perceived as acting fairly is a greater concern than actually using fair procedures (Greenberg, 1988), common law precepts of the DFR demand that union representational procedures are fair.

The concept of DFR was first articulated by the Supreme Court in *Steele v. Louisville & Nashville Railroad*, a 1944 verdict that addressed racial discrimination by a union that refused membership to minorities. The union negotiated contract language that would have effectively excluded blacks from positions as firemen. A black bargaining-unit member filed suit in order to void the contract.

The Court held that in return for its rights of exclusive representation, the union had the duty to represent all members of the bargaining unit "without hostile discrimination, fairly, impartially, and in good faith," even if they were not union members.

Although DFR considerations apply to a variety of union actions, DFR cases most often involve the manner in which a union handles grievances. Two avenues are open to aggrieved workers through which DFR charges can be processed: the court system as a violation of Section 301 of the Taft-Hartley Act; and, the National Labor Relations Board (NLRB) as an unfair labor practice. The criteria for determining whether union conduct constitutes a breach of its DFR obligations are generally the same for the NLRB and the courts. These criteria focus on procedural standards of justice. A breach of DFR has routinely been established only by evidence of arbitrary, perfunctory, capricious, or grossly negligent conduct on the part of the union in handling a grievance. Distributive justice is less important in DFR cases. Courts appear unconcerned about the equity of outcomes resulting from union representation. In *Vaca v. Sipes,* the Supreme Court ruled that a union's decision that a particular grievance lacks sufficient merit to justify arbitration will not constitute a breach of the DFR because a judge or jury later finds the grievance meritorious. "The Court indicated that it did not matter whether a union was right or wrong, only whether a union had acted arbitrarily, discriminatorily, or in bad faith in dropping a grievance" (Feldacker, 1990, p. 349). Further, because contract administration often involves processing grievances of employees with conflicting claims, the union may be forced to represent one worker against another. In such situations, unions are expected to investigate the facts and relevant contract language, and make a reasoned decision. By taking this approach, the union would satisfy its DFR obligations regardless of which employee it supported or whether its decision was right or wrong.[2]

GRIEVANCE SYSTEMS AS TRANSACTION GOVERNANCE MECHANISMS

In this section, we draw on organizational economics (viz., transaction cost analysis) to offer tentative explanations of how the grievance system is influenced by certain dimensions underlying specific employment relationships. By so doing, we consider a framework that offers organizational explanations for grievance-related phenomena. It is appropriate to consider employment relationships as transactions. Although there are many types of economic transactions, employment involves the fundamental exchange of work for pay or, in more general terms, the exchange of employer inducements for employee contri-

---

[2]Additional information about DFR can be found in the following: Feldacker (1990, chap. 12), McKelvey (1985), Taylor and Witney (1987), pp. 427–433.

butions (Barnard, 1938). Extrapolating from the seminal work of Williamson (1975), organizational economics suggest that the emergence of governance structures such as grievance systems stem from certain characteristics of this fundamental contributions-inducements transaction. Because people are both boundedly rational (March & Simon, 1958) and tempted toward opportunistic behavior (Cyert & March, 1963), some set of governance mechanisms is required to insure that transactions occur as anticipated by both parties. Although Williamson's work focuses on explaining the choice between market governance (i.e., subcontracting that is governed by a general set of legal rules and more specific contract provisions) versus hierarchical governance (i.e., bringing the transaction into the firm subject to rules, policies, and procedures), Ouchi (1979) and Wilkens and Ouchi (1983) extended transaction-cost principles to full-time employment relationships. They argued that, in addition to formal organizational mechanisms, employment relationships may also be subject to "clan control"— a form of governance that is associated with implicit values, assumptions, and premises which develop in a group over time and that is often currently (and loosely) referred to as "corporate culture." Thus, employment relationships are transactions that typically are embedded in a governance structure comprised of a combination of formal and informal mechanisms.

This economic interest in internal employment transactions stems from the fact that governance structures entail costs. Moreover, the predictive ability of the transaction cost framework rests on the underlying assumption that both parties typically have a stake in minimizing governance costs while simultaneously assuring the integrity of the contributions-inducements agreement. Thus, the choice of governance mechanism is quasi-rational and contingent upon certain characteristics of the transaction. According to Williamson (1975, 1985), the primary dimensions that account for the selection, importance, and purpose of various governance mechanisms are the frequency of the transaction, asset specificity, and the uncertainty of the transaction.

Transaction dimensions are useful in deriving a situational- and organizational-based explanation of the role of grievance systems. We focus on full-time employment transactions and the influence of each transaction dimension on the role of grievance systems as a particular type of transaction governance mechanism. Although discussed separately, each dimension will inevitably influence employment relationships, thereby involving multiple roles for grievance systems.

Transaction Frequency

Transaction costs are related to the number of similar transactions in the organization. Greater similarity permits standardization of governance structures across transactions with the consequent potential of reducing associated governance costs. Williamson, Wachter, and Harris (1975) reported that one of the advantages of a union contract is its efficiency in aggregating individual employment agreements, thereby making it economical to use more sophisticated governance mechanisms. It follows that larger firms with a dominant core technology (e.g., automobile production or food processing) are in a position to develop detailed contract provisions and to maintain grievance systems more efficiently than smaller or more heterogeneous firms. This prediction about the sophistication of grievance systems is borne out in the CBNC database. By comparison with nonmanufacturing firms, manufacturing firms have grievance systems that are more likely to contain special job security and pay provisions for grievance representatives, provisions for expedited arbitration, and above average numbers of steps (Bureau of National Affairs, 1989). The fact that grievance systems are universally adopted as part of collective bargaining agreements is due in part, to their flexibility in accommodating to a variety of transaction issues and the economies of scale resulting from transaction frequency.

As transaction frequency encourages standardization of employment relationships amenable to collective bargaining, it is likely that labor and management will have articulated and codified the subtleties of the transaction in the collective bargaining agreement. Thus, transaction frequency leads to an elaboration of contract provisions governing an increasing range of jurisdictional matters, rules, procedures, and contingencies. Given the limitations of contract writers in anticipating all employment circumstances affected by the contract, and given the difficulties inherent in preparing unambiguous contract language, there must be some role that procedural justice plays in contract administration. However, transaction frequency suggests that the role of a grievance system will be primarily to ensure compliance with a complex collective bargaining agreement. Thus, by emphasizing outcomes (i.e., getting everything one is entitled to by the contract), the salience of distributive justice is increased. Furthermore, the extent to which management acts in ignorance of the collective bargaining agreement or is predisposed toward contrary or opportunistic behavior will affect the importance attached to the grievance system.

Asset Specificity

One or both parties may have to invest in the employment relationship as a precondition or may acquire employment-related assets over time. Specific assets cannot be recouped should the employment relationship end (Williamson, 1975). While some of these specific assets are of value only to one of the parties (viz., unilateral asset specificity), many are mutually beneficial to both employer and employee (viz., mutual asset specificity). Unilateral asset specificity is exemplified by an employer who pays the moving expenses of a new employee or invests in worker training, some of which may be proprietary or otherwise unique to a particular job setting (e.g., a particular accounting system or unique production process). An employee may acquire nonrecoverable assets in a variety of ways. He or she may have to pay for tools, uniforms, or union dues, or acquire special knowledge about operations, technologies, or people, which are relatively nontransferable. Also, employees may acquire special benefits or other privileges through norms of reciprocity or seniority provisions.[3] Asset specific investments that are mutually beneficial to both parties are quite numerous. For example, unique knowledge of operations, the ability to function as part of an existing team, and stakeholder relations (e.g., the goodwill established by a salesperson with his or her customers) are assets of value to both employees and employers.

Ceteris paribus, with low unilateral and mutual asset specificity, grievance systems would be relatively less important in governing transactions that are relatively more amenable to forms of market governance through enhanced labor mobility. However, when unilateral and mutual asset specificity are significant, grievance systems do have important roles to play in governing employment transactions. Along with the availability of alternative employment and relative financial dependency, unilateral asset specificity contributes to the value attached by one of the parties to a particular employment relationship. If few employment options are available for other nontransactional reasons (e.g., age, race, or geographic location), the prospect of losing asset-specific investments is a cause for concern. Thus, in the case of unilateral asset specificity, grievance systems play a role in job security, especially in cases which are perceived to be unjust dismissals. The manner in which the union pursues grievances that involve discipline (e.g., suspensions and discharges) is likely to be critical in shaping employees' evaluations of, and relations with, the union.

Mutual asset specificity fosters an interest in maintaining the transaction over time among both parties and, in contrast to unilateral asset specificity, implies mutual dependence. Also, whereas unilateral asset specificity often characterizes the personal investments of employees with little bargaining power (e.g., the "Okies" in Steinbeck's, 1972, *Grapes of Wrath* who made huge personal and emotional investments to migrate to California), parity in the bargaining power of the parties is more likely with mutual asset specificity. Thus, we speculate that employment relationships characterized by high mutual asset specificity will rely more on informal mechanisms for governing employment relationships (e.g., clan control or informal settlement of disputes about rights under the collective bargaining agreement). Under these circumstances, the formal grievance procedure is, nonetheless, necessary as a last resort since asset-specific transactions "have to be embedded in a protective governance structure lest productive values be sacrificed if the employment relation is severed" (Williamson, 1985, p. 243).

---

[3]It is important to clarify that asset specificity is unrelated to educational attainment and skill level. For example, many skilled trades people (e.g., tool-and-die makers) and professionals (e.g., registered nurses) possess abilities (or credentials) that are easily transferable to a new work context and, therefore, have low asset specificity.

Transaction Uncertainty

According to Williamson (1985), uncertainty derives mostly from the employer's inability to measure an employee's output, generally as a result of teamwork or reciprocal technologies (Thompson, 1967). However, a broader view of uncertainty suggests many other possibilities in employment transactions. Hickson, Hinings, Lee, Schneck, and Pennings (1971) identified five basic dimensions of uncertainty: uncertainty regarding information availability, accuracy, and clarity; uncertainty regarding cause-effect relationships; uncertainty regarding outcome preferences; uncertainty deriving from the time span of definitive feedback; and, uncertainty stemming from the inability to assign probabilities to future events.

Employment transactions are susceptible to each of these forms of uncertainty. For example, in transactions with professional employees (e.g., engineers, teachers, or social workers), both sides often lack fundamental information about such matters as what constitutes good performance, what behaviors are related to effective functioning, what work loads will be, what new technologies will emerge, and so on. Under these conditions, all elements of a "fair" transaction cannot be determined a priori, requiring the use of ad-hoc negotiation mechanisms for dealing with information as it becomes available and events as they unfold. In addition, grievance systems can reduce uncertainty about employment relationships due to ambiguous contract language. For example, the grievance procedure provides a mechanism for dispelling uncertainty about the meaning or relevance of general contract language (e.g., firing only for "just cause") in specific situations (e.g., firing an employee whose error in judgment cost the company a valued customer). Hence, under conditions of transaction uncertainty the grievance system is used as an ad-hoc negotiation mechanism for incorporating new information into the employment transaction.

Transaction uncertainty has particular salience when workers and their unions have been asked (or forced) to adopt a variety of organizational interventions (e.g., quality of working life [QWL]) that fundamentally alter time-honored employment relationships (many unionists contend that QWL is the modern equivalent of the old-fashioned speedup or a prelude to a reduction in force). Apprehension exists that the union's representational effectiveness (i.e., ability to influence the employment relationship) will be undermined by such programs. To the extent that formal grievance procedures are still effective in negotiating employment transactions, we would expect that resistance to the adoption of measures such as QWL would be less. This notion is supported by Eaton, Gordon, and Keefe's (1992) finding that workers, who were confident in the ability of the grievance system to afford workplace justice, had fewer concerns about the continued ability of the union to regulate employment relationships.

Interaction of Uncertainty and Asset Specificity

Both Williamson (1975) and Wilkens and Ouchi (1983) discussed the interaction of asset specificity with transaction uncertainty as posing special problems for transaction governance. Some transactions require governance mechanisms which foster mutual, long-term commitment and are highly flexible in dealing with unforeseen contingencies. For example, in concert with other Research and Development (R&D) scientists, a researcher engages in long-term, idiosyncratic projects with highly uncertain outcomes. Moreover, certain transactional concerns such as covenants not to compete or royalty sharing of innovations would not be subject to consultation with a traditional union. Under these conditions, it is obviously inefficient to use a standardized approach to transaction governance (i.e., a collective bargaining agreement) nor is adequate governance possible with individual contracting. Under such circumstances, the transaction governance problems require implicit and flexible mechanisms which must be achieved through "clan control." Wilkins and Ouchi (1983) asserted that distributive justice is especially important in this type of social governance because of the shared belief that "in the long run both honest and dishonest people will be discovered and dealt with accordingly" (p. 476). Thus, a widely shared organizational value of workplace justice reduces the importance of more formal mechanisms (i.e., the grievance system) in governing employment transactions. Both the needs for flexibility and individuality, plus a smaller role for formal grievance mechanisms, could provide an explanation for occupational variation in union popularity. However, it is worth noting that even in this context some type of formal appeal procedure may be useful as a backup for lapses in trust or in adding tangible evidence of the existence of justice norms.

RESEARCH ON GRIEVANCES

Although grievance systems still do not engender a large amount of research, there have been definite signs of renewed interest in the topic over the last decade. This resurgence is the likely consequence of increased behavioral research in the domain of union–management relations (Gordon & Nurick, 1981) and more vivid societal interest in the subject of employee rights (Ewing, 1977; Gordon & Lee, 1990, pp. 304–305). Because of the fragmentary character of research on grievances, classifying existing literature is difficult. Previous reviews are organized on the basis of different categories of independent variables that have some influence on the level of grievance activity (e.g., Dalton & Todor, 1979). We believe that a clearer picture of contemporary research can be gained by using dependent variables to classify studies of grievances. Such a taxonomy highlights a shift in the research interests of investigators. Whereas earlier studies investigated factors that were related to the caseload of grievances, more recent research utilizes dependent variables that reflect an increasing interest in matters pertaining to workplace justice. This shift also indicates an interest in studying grievance-filing behavior from the perspective of the worker. Given the importance of subjective factors in perceptions of workplace justice, study of grievance systems is incomplete if it lacks the perspective of the grievants themselves. Five types of criteria used in research on grievances comprise our taxonomy.

Grievance Activity Criteria

Most research on grievances attempts to define the environmental and individual differences variables that are correlated with the level of grievance activity. Grievance activity may be operationalized in terms of grievance rates (the number of grievances filed per 100 workers per year), settlement level, and the incidence of wildcat strikes (i.e., failures of the grievance system to resolve an issue without an unauthorized work stoppage). Little of this work specifically addresses the issue of workplace justice, but it does provide information about the role of grievance systems in governing employment relationships.

Grievance-filing behavior cannot be lifted out of its industrial relations context and, therefore, researchers have investigated whether caseload is related to various facets of the work environment. Technology, and technological change in particular, has a significant relationship to caseload. Peach and Livernash's (1974) study of the steel industry found that higher grievance rates characterized task environments with high levels of worker responsibility and close supervision. Low grievance rates were observed where the task environment was relatively free from technological change. These findings suggest that grievance activity increases where technological change introduces transaction uncertainty, thereby prompting a renegotiation of employment relationships. In addition, new technology may alter the value of employee skills, thereby displacing the worker (i.e., causing him or her to accept employment in another department) or disemploying the individual (i.e., permanently separating him or her from the employer), resulting in the loss of unilateral asset specific investments. Consequently, invoking the grievance procedure as a response to technological change is a method of attempting to control unfolding events in order to reduce uncertainty and receive just consideration of worker investments in the employment relationship.

The social environment is also a source of factors related to the grievance rate. Prominent among these factors is the leadership style of first-level supervisors. Peach and Livernash (1974) reported higher grievance rates where policies were less formal and were applied less consistently. In other words, the greater the uncertainty about the employment relationship, the greater the salience of a mechanism to govern that relationship. Fleishman and Harris (1962) defined leadership style in terms of Consideration and Initiating Structure, constructs that emerged from the Ohio State studies. They found that foremen who were low on Consideration had high grievance rates regardless of their emphasis on Initiating Structure, whereas grievance rates displayed a positive (though curvilinear) relationship to Initiating Structure for foremen who were high on Consideration. These findings may be explained in two ways. First, it is important to note that Consideration is a measure of the degree to which leaders permit participation in decision making. The fact that grievance rates were high whenever Consideration was low suggests that grievants might have used the grievance system to gain more control over the employment relationship from supervisors who were inclined to dictate the terms unilaterally. Second, Consideration is also related to informal transaction governance. The increased communication, trust, and approachability associated with high Consideration suggest that disputes were settled "on the spot" and, therefore, didn't turn into formal grievances.

Two experimental studies of worker perceptions of management behavior and its potential for creating an intent to grieve support earlier findings about the effects of leadership (Gordon & Bowlby, 1989). Using large samples of bargaining-unit members from both public- and private-sector unions, the intent to grieve was examined in relation to reactance (Brehm & Brehm, 1981) and intentionality attributions (Shaver, 1985). Participants responded to a series of vignettes, each of which described a management action taken against a worker (viz., formal punishment, informal warning, promotion denial). The vignettes varied systematically in terms of the perceived threat to worker freedom posed by the action, and the degree to which the action was motivated by a dispositional rather than an environmental attribution. In both studies, the stronger the perception of threat inherent in the management action, the stronger the intent to redress the discipline by filing a grievance. Also, to the extent that the management action was judged to be motivated by personal animus toward the worker, it was considered less justifiable and was more likely to engender a grievance. Use of the grievance procedure was an attempt to restore an employment relationship unilaterally altered by management to include dispositional factors. By contrast, discipline was considered more justified if the action was perceived to be the result of environmental coercion. Such coercion could take the form of management simply implementing provisions of the labor contract (e.g., the manager was simply following rules that required punishment for specific worker behavior) which does not entail changing the employment relationship.

Analogous findings about the importance of governing employment relationships were reported in a study of union leadership by Glassman and Belasco (1975). Working in the context of public education, initial grievance filings were related to chapter chairmen's perceptions of their influence on the decision-making process. Unfulfilled teacher aspirations for greater participation in both instructional and noninstructional matters are consequences of employment relationships that were established without specifying appropriate levels of communication, consultation, and joint decision making. Hence, chapter chairmen used the grievance system as an ad-hoc negotiating mechanism to deal with these transaction uncertainties.

Finally, several studies have demonstrated a relationship between caseload criteria and the attitudinal climate between the parties. Settlement of grievances at lower steps of the procedure was more likely when the union and management had cooperative attitudes (Brett & Goldberg, 1979; Thomson & Murray, 1976; Turner & Robinson, 1972). Two studies in the automotive industry demonstrated a positive correlation between indicators of the intensity of conflict in local contract negotiations and the level of grievance activity (Kochan & Katz, 1988, p. 302).

Individual differences related to grievance-filing behavior provided the initial interest among psychologists in the study of grievances. Personality profiles of grievants created the unmistakable impression that chronically discontented employees were maladjusted rather than concerned with workplace justice (McMurry, 1944), although Stagner (1962) observed that personality factors interacted with characteristics of the shop environment (e.g., "emotional tone") to influence the level of grievance activity.

A great number of demographic variables has been investigated in order to construct a profile of the worker who invokes the grievance system (Lewin & Peterson, 1988, pp. 39–40). The findings are inconsistent and none of the studies have employed a cross validation model to demonstrate the generalizability of its results. Interestingly, researchers appeared to ignore the social implications of this stream of research which potentially could jeopardize the well-being of employees with demographic characteristics matching those of individuals with proclivities for dissent (a right they enjoy outside of the workplace). If measured in terms of published articles over the last ten years, behavioral scientists appear to have lost interest in this stream of research.

Finally, Klaas (1989a) developed an integrative theoretical framework for grievance filing behavior which encompassed both workplace and individual characteristics with, among other cognitive variables, the construct of procedural justice. When a grievance opportunity is engendered by a sense of inequity, workers were hypothesized to consider different methods for redressing their complaint. A variety of alternative responses to the perceived inequity (e.g., absenteeism, lower productivity, turnover, and disruptive behavior) were hypothesized to replace or supplement filing a grievance. Klaas surmised that perceptions of the procedural justice afforded by the grievance system will determine whether a worker who receives a negative outcome on his or her grievance will engage in alternative responses to the perceived inequity. If perceptions of procedural justice are sufficient to ameliorate feelings of inequity resulting from the denial of a grievance, no further consequences would be expected; if not, workers are predicted to seek other ways to reduce the inequity. This and many other propositions suggested by Klaas' theory require empirical verification.

Disposition of a Grievance

Justice in the workplace requires consistency in the disposition of cases. Basing decisions to grant or deny a grievance on the contractual merits of the case is an important factor in disposing of cases in a consistent manner, thereby helping to assure distributive justice. However, a few studies raise questions about whether managerial and arbitral decisions are affected by noncontractual factors such as characteristics of the grievant or political and economic considerations.

The results of three field studies that investigated gender effects on the disposition of grievances short of arbitration provide mixed results. After controlling for the severity of the issue and the settlement step, Dalton and Todor (1985a) found that female grievants were 50% more likely to have their grievance sustained than male grievants in a sample of 294 grievances at a western public utility. However, a main effect for the grievant's gender was not observed in two samples (310 grievances filed during one year at a western public utility and 222 grievances filed by employees in a large western labor union) studied by Dalton and Todor (1985b), nor in a sample of 498 grievances filed over a 1-year period by employees in a large labor union that represents a public utility (Dalton, Todor, & Owen, 1987).[4] The authors offer no explanations for the inconsistent results for the main effects of gender on managerial dispositions of grievances. "We report only a phenomenon here—the dynamics that may account for these results remain unexplored" (Dalton & Todor, 1985b, pp. 709–710). However, the disposition of the cases was found to be more consistently related to the gender composition of the individuals responsible for hearing the cases. Grievants were less likely to prevail when the supervisor was a female, especially when the union representative was a male. For example, workers received a favorable outcome in only 13% of the cases when male stewards negotiated the grievance with female supervisors, whereas male–male dyads produced favorable outcomes for the grievance in 40% of the cases (Dalton & Todor, 1985b; Dalton et al., 1987).

Two studies that investigated the effects of the grievants' gender on arbitrators' decisions offer diametrically opposite results. Rodgers and Helburn's (1985) analysis of 37 discharge cases from five petroleum refineries found that male grievants were more likely than females to be reinstated by an arbitrator. In a more elaborate study, Bemmels (1988) examined archival data for 104 disciplinary discharge cases that provided evidence of significantly more lenient arbitration rulings involving female grievants. In all cases, the arbitrators were male. After controlling for a variety of factors (e.g., type of grievance, occupation, and sector), Bemmels estimated that women were twice as likely as men to have their grievance sustained, and 2.7 times more likely than men to receive a full (as opposed to a partial) reinstatement. Finally, on average women received suspensions that were 2.1 months shorter than men.

---

[4]It is not clear from the published papers whether the samples overlap across the three studies.

Another personal characteristic that might influence the disposition of a grievance is the work history of the grievant. Klaas (1989b) analyzed 986 grievance decisions rendered in a public-sector organization. The results indicated that managers at higher steps in the process were influenced by the grievant's work record—even when that history was not pertinent to assessing the merits of the case. Greater leniency was extended toward individuals whose past performance was rated favorably, who had been disciplined fewer times, and who had more seniority. Work history, regardless of its relevance to the facts of the case, may influence the way managers decide grievances because they form attributions based upon the grievant's record of employment and/or because they believe that it is functional to treat good performers with more leniency. Transaction cost analysis offers an alternative explanation for these results. Since many aspects of an employee's work history constitute unilateral asset-specific investments (e.g., seniority), the union could be expected to fight somewhat harder when greater idiosyncratic assets are threatened by an action of management.[5]

Finally, economic and political factors affect disposition of grievances. Unions may overload the grievance system to exert pressure on management in order to win special concessions for one or more interest groups (Kuhn, 1961). Such behavior may necessitate periodic "fire sales" in which parties "horse-trade" grievances (Fossum, 1985, pp. 392–394). Meyer and Cooke (1988) estimated the impact of political and economic factors in grievance settlements over a 10-year period for a single Ford-United Automobile Workers local. The results of their analyses provided general support for the idea that these factors were more likely to influence the disposition of cases when the contractual rights and/or facts surrounding the grievance were less clear. While Meyer and Cooke (1988) conceded that "management's concerns about consistency and predictability in contract administration do, however, restrict the effect of economic interests on grievance outcomes" (p. 321), management is still moved to act in the grievant's favor where granting the grievance can be expected to reduce the potential for workplace disruptions (and thus minimize production costs).

Hence, grievances are likely to be resolved independent of their merit. In order to mitigate long-term effects on standards of workplace justice, the parties may agree to settle one or more grievances without prejudice. This means that the settlement will not establish precedent should similar grievances arise in the future. Nonetheless, the politicization of the grievance system prevents it from fulfilling its governance roles. This should be particularly demoralizing to workers as it has the dual effect of depriving workers of governance mechanisms

---

[5]Rodgers, Helburn, and Hunter's (1986) investigation of the relationship between seniority and job performance of the reinstated workers suggested the existence of a moderator variable (viz., exoneration of the worker). The correlation between seniority and performance was $-.18$ in studies which only examined workers who had not been exonerated. By contrast, this correlation was $+.20$ in mixed samples in which a portion (from 30% to 39% of the workers had been exonerated). Rodgers et al.'s rather strained interpretation of these findings suggests that the grievant's record of infractions influences the manner in which management disposes of the case.

needed for controlling transactions while simultaneously increasing the perceived need for justice mechanisms.

Aftermath of Filing a Grievance

For an individual employee, filing a grievance has potential benefits and costs. Receiving due process of a complaint about the employment relationship must be weighed against the potential cost of filing a grievance (viz. managerial retribution against grievants). The earliest interest in the aftermath of filing a grievance involved the study of reinstatement cases (i.e., what happens after an arbitrator finds for a discharged grievant and reinstates the worker). If the grievance system in fact promotes industrial justice, unfairly disciplined workers should be able to return to their jobs with expectations of receiving fair performance evaluations and opportunities for advancement within the organization. Rodgers, Helburn, and Hunter (1986) combined the results of six studies involving 277 workers who were reinstated by arbitrators. They found that only 60% of the workers performed satisfactorily after reinstatement. Two of the studies encompassed by their analysis reported that 10% of the reinstated workers did not return to work (McDermott & Newhams, 1971; Ross, 1957), whereas 20% of the reinstated workers in one of these studies left their jobs within a year of reinstatement (McDermott & Newhams, 1971).

In the first large-scale study that actually consulted workers who had used a grievance system, Gordon and Bowlby (1988) analyzed the self-reports of 324 grievants in seven unions concerning the characteristics of a grievance-filing incident and its aftermath. Participants completed a questionnaire that requested information about the "most important grievance you filed which has been settled." The coded responses were categorized into three types of grievance: staffing, nature of work assignment, and discipline. The nature of the settlement was indicated as being in the grievant's favor, in management's favor, or a compromise in which each party got a portion of what it wanted. Respondents reported the step in the grievance procedure at which the issue was finally settled. Finally, outcomes of having filed the grievance were described in terms of their effects on personal relations with management, the union and co-workers, and job satisfaction of the grievant and his or her co-workers.

Contrary to conventional wisdom about grievance systems, the settlement level was unrelated to any of the outcome measures. Resolving a grievance quickly at a low step in the process did not influence the reports of the kinds of effects experienced subsequent to the settlement. This finding may be explained by organizational limitations imposed upon management and/or union representatives that restrict the degree to which they can fashion an acceptable solution.[6]

---

[6]For example, Mullen (1954) reported that 27% of a sample of approximately 800 foremen indicated that their authority to settle grievances was sharply curtailed by higher management.

By contrast, the nature of the settlement affected both outcome criteria. Winning the grievance had a salutary effect on all the satisfaction measures, whereas losing the grievance adversely affected the different dimensions of job satisfaction. However, relations with both the immediate supervisor and higher management were reported to have worsened when the grievance was granted or denied, and a compromise settlement did not appear to change the nature of the relations with management.

The results also indicated that different outcomes of filing could be expected for each type of grievance. For example, settlements of grievances involving discipline were perceived to have the most beneficial impact on subsequent relations between the worker and the union. These findings follow from transaction cost analysis which would identify discipline as a significant threat to asset-specific investments. The vigor and skill with which the union pursues such a grievance in order to protect the worker's investment in the employment relationship is obviously critical in shaping subsequent interactions.

The most thorough examination of the aftermath of filing a grievance is the research of Lewin and Peterson (1988). Longitudinal data were collected from organizations in steel manufacturing, retail department stores, nonprofit hospitals, and local public schools. This multistage field study examined the consequences of grievance procedure usage by obtaining personnel data on pre- and post-settlement behavior of workers and supervisors/managers in terms of job performance, promotions, work attendance, and turnover. Lewin and Peterson found substantial evidence of negative outcomes for grievants in the immediate post-grievance settlement period. Compared to control groups of nongrievants, grievants had significantly lower job performance ratings, lower promotion rates, poorer work attendance, and higher turnover in the year following the settlement. These effects were even more pronounced for grievants who pursued their cases to higher levels of the procedure and those who prevailed (i.e., had their grievance sustained). The implications of these findings for workplace justice becomes clearer when one considers the fact that, immediately prior to grievance usage, grievants had slightly higher performance ratings, proportionately fewer work absences, and a higher incidence of promotions than the nongrievants.

Interestingly, supervisors/managers who were parties to the grievances had the same negative profile of aftereffects as the grievants. Relative to a comparison group of management representatives, supervisor/managers of grievants received lower performance ratings and fewer promotions, and were more likely to experience involuntary turnover.

The major implication of this stream of research is that the union and management must pay closer attention to events that transpire subsequent to the resolution of a grievance. Although most of the attention on grievance systems has focused on insuring that the procedures used to file and resolve complaints are fair and equitable, a more fundamental challenge lies in assuring that workers' careers are not jeopardized when they exercise their right to process a grievance.

Relations With Parties Who Control the
Employment Relationship

Given the high priority that members attach to their union's handling of grievances, it follows that satisfaction with and commitment to the union will be
related to perceptions of the justice afforded by the grievance system. Fryxell and
Gordon (1989) provided direct evidence about these relationships from the findings of surveys conducted in eight unions representing workers in both the public
and private sectors, and manufacturing and service industries. Approximately
2,000 usable questionnaires were received from workers in clerical, security,
custodial, technician, and engineering jobs. The surveys contained scales to
measure union commitment and satisfaction with the union, management, and
various facets of the job (e.g., pay, job security, and the amount of decision
making). Also, scales were developed to assess perceptions of justice in the
workplace (i.e., workers' beliefs about an underlying moral order in their work-
places that ensures that good workers are rewarded and poor workers are
punished) and the procedural and distributive justice afforded by the grievance
system.

The results demonstrated the important relationship between the evaluation of
institutions and confidence in the grievance system's ability to provide workplace
justice. The strongest correlates of satisfaction with the union were the measures
of procedural and distributive justice. Although a worker's satisfaction with pay
and job security were correlated with their satisfaction with the union, the influence of these factors was small in comparison to that of the grievance system.
Interestingly, the measures of justice afforded by the grievance system were
significantly better predictors of satisfaction with the union than satisfaction with
management. Apparently, the union's reputation among workers is more closely
staked to the performance of the grievance system than is management's. Given
the frequent use by union organizers of promises to settle complaints in order to
win certification, it is likely that members evaluate their union in terms of its
performance in handling grievances.

The best predictors of satisfaction with management were beliefs in a just
workplace and the various facets of job satisfaction. This finding may be explained by the fact that many aspects of the employment relationship are not
governed by the contract and fall into traditional areas of management pre-
rogatives. As a result, workers may perceive that management has greater control over employment relationships and, therefore, is more likely than the union
to be held accountable for fairness and equity in the workplace.

Because labor legislation has created different categories of membership
(e.g., in agency shops workers do not have to join the union, but they are
required to pay it a representation fee), Gordon and Fryxell (1989b) investigated
relations between the union and different types of members. They tested Tyler's
(1986) assertion that the importance attributed to procedural justice is affected by

the voluntariness of association between the individual and the social organization to whose decision making he or she is subject. It was anticipated that procedural justice would be a stronger correlate of satisfaction with the union for nonmembers than members in an agency shop since the latter have an involuntary financial association with the union. No such differences in these correlations were expected in an open shop in which nonmembers are not compelled to pay the representation fee. The results supported these predictions and were interpreted in terms of workers' requirements for control over their employment relationships. Because nonmembers had less control, transaction uncertainty was greater (the imposition of the representation fee was a potent reminder of their lack of control) and, therefore, satisfaction with the union was more closely related to their confidence that the grievance system could assist in negotiating their employment relationship. Subsequent research (Ambrose, Harland, & Kulik, 1991) affirmed that procedural justice is more important to individuals with low control.[7]

The link between attitudes toward the grievance system and commitment to the union also has been investigated. Clark and Gallagher (1989) developed measures of attitudes toward four identifiable aspects of the grievance system: effect on the workplace, process, representation, and importance. These were administered along with two of Gordon, Philpot, Burt, Thompson, and Spiller's (1980) union commitment scales (Union Loyalty and Responsibility Toward the Union) in a sample of approximately 1,000 members of the National Association of Letter Carriers. The importance (i.e., overall value associated with the availability of a grievance system) and process (i.e., the fairness and integrity of the grievance procedure itself) predicted the level of commitment. Eaton et al. (1992) replicated these results using survey data from four bargaining units within the same local of an industrial union. Member perceptions of the effectiveness of the grievance system were the strongest predictors of union commitment. The fact that the results of this study parallel those of Clark and Gallagher (1989) despite substantial methodological differences (differences in the participating unions and the scales used to measure attitudes about the grievance system) attests to the robustness of the relationship among these variables.

Although it may be easier to conceive of union commitment growing out of experiences with the grievance system that recommend its procedural and distributive justice, it is possible that the direction of the relationship is the opposite.

---

[7]In the absence of the ability to control processes and outcomes related to their employment relationships, grievance systems are particularly important correlates of workers' beliefs in workplace justice. Using five occupational samples, Fryxell and Gordon (1991) found that custodians look more strongly to the procedural justice afforded by the grievance system as evidence of a just workplace than other occupations. Interestingly, the relationship between belief in the ability to influence events (i.e., sociopolitical control) and belief in a just workplace was *in*significant only in the custodial sample.

Konovsky, Folger, and Fogel (1990) conducted a panel study that permitted longitudinal investigation of the relationship between the perceived justice in organizational decision making and organizational commitment. Their data from 123 individuals in 27 departments of a testing laboratory and 186 individuals in 52 departments of a manufacturing company suggest that organizational commitment predicts employee procedural and distributive justice perceptions rather than the reverse. These findings underscore the need for longitudinal investigation of procedural and distributive justice.

Handling of a Grievance

Another factor of interest is the behavior used by union and management representatives to resolve a grievance. Two studies suggest that stewards and grievance committeemen display greater concern about procedural and distributive justice during attempts to resolve grievances than their counterparts in management. Martin and Cusella (1986) analyzed transcripts from 10 grievance hearings held by a panel of adjudicators for a county government. The 17 tactics used by the union and management representatives to persuade the panel were coded into five influence categories including one that dealt with moral standards (i.e., a standard or principle of morality is invoked in support of the representative's position). The results revealed that union representatives relied more heavily on arguments that invoked moral standards than management representatives. In particular, both the equality (i.e., "People should be treated equally/consistently") and equity (i.e., "People should be treated fairly/justly") tactics constituted larger percentages of the influence arguments used by the union. Given its similarity to Leventhal, Karuza, and Fry's (1980) consistency principle, the equality tactic appears to be an attempt to make the grievance resolution process more procedurally just. By contrast, the equity tactic seems to call upon panel members to consider distributive justice when determining the outcome of the grievance.

Although he did not specifically examine justice issues, the results of Knight's (1986) investigation of the use of feedback by union and management representatives is consistent with the findings of Martin and Cusella. Basing his conceptual arguments on systems theory, Knight hypothesized that the observed rate of grievance resolution at any given level, or for the system as a whole short of arbitration, should improve as a consequence of returning information about the system's output to the process stage. Using questionnaire data gathered in case studies in four industries, Knight found that both parties appreciate the value of referring to previous settlements and arbitrator decisions in resolving subsequent grievances. However, stewards and grievance committeemen reported significantly more frequent reference to previous settlements during grievance negotiations than management representatives. Knight inferred that union representatives, who are principally involved in grievance handling, were more aware of previous outcomes and, therefore, more inclined to refer to them in grievance negotiations than their management counterparts. However, these results may also be explained in terms of the union's greater reliance on equity and equality tactics to promote both procedural and distributive justice.

CONCLUSION

Worker perceptions of grievance systems are closely tied to their expectations about justice in the workplace and their evaluations of organizations empowered to represent them when they attempt to exercise their rights. However, the data on the aftermath of grievance filing suggest that grievants still may pay an unfair price for using the system. Further, since the grievance system must operate in the political environments of both the union and management, it is clear that at least some cases are decided by factors other than their merits and, therefore, equal treatment under the law is threatened. Nonetheless, workers continue to view the grievance system as an important governance mechanism that provides a measure of control over employment relationships.

The retrospective reinterpretation of the research appears to strongly support a transaction-based explanation of a broad range of grievance-related phenomena. This should be welcome in the emerging field of organizational justice, which has generally relied on other disciplines for its theory base. Up to this point the field may be empirically "organizational," but lacks a legitimate theoretical framework to guide its focus. As a result, Greenberg (1990) called for "conceptualizations of organization justice that are more sensitive to organization variables" (p. 422). We assert that a transaction-based approach is a significant contribution toward this end. However, post-hoc reinterpretation is no substitute for the confirmation of theoretically guided predictions and, therefore, further conceptual development and empirical research is needed.

If there were any doubts, this research demonstrates the importance of fair grievance procedures to unions. Unions are bound by common law to act fairly when representing workers. The fact that they win 90% of DFR cases indicates that unions are cognizant of procedural justice. This awareness is reinforced by evidence that union representatives are more likely than their management counterparts to invoke standards of procedural and distributive justice in attempting to settle a grievance. Finally, a union's relations with its constituents is tied more closely to the procedural and distributive justice afforded by its representation in the grievance system than by any other type of benefit provided in the collective bargaining agreement.

POSTSCRIPT

Workers do not enjoy the same rights on the job that they do as private citizens outside of the plant or office doors. While the following quote is somewhat dated, the point it makes is true today. "The fact . . . that only the Steelworkers union has negotiated a justice and dignity clause, which presumes that a worker is innocent until proven guilty, indicates that most employees still lack basic rights on the job that are taken for granted elsewhere in civilian life" (Repas, 1984, p. xvi). Admittedly, economic factors played a role in the negotiation of this contract provision (e.g., the can companies with whom the Steelworkers negotiated became less vulnerable to back-pay claims awarded when arbitrators sustained the grievance). Nonetheless, the concept of justice and dignity can serve as an ideal that will move practitioners and scholars to reconsider traditional corporate constructions of employee/employer responsibilities and rights. In our view, research on workplace justice has an important role to play in bringing about such change by evaluating existing and yet-to-be-implemented mechanisms for providing due process in employment relations.

REFERENCES

Allis-Chalmers Corp. v. Lueck, 105 S.Ct. 1904 (1985).

Ambrose, M. L., Harland, L. K., & Kulik, C. T. (1991). Influence of social comparisons on perceptions of organizational fairness. *Journal of Applied Psychology, 76,* 239–246.

Barnard, C. I. (1938). *The functions of the executive.* Cambridge, MA: Harvard University Press.

Bemmels, B. (1988). The effect of grievant's gender on arbitrators' decisions. *Industrial and Labor Relations Review, 41,* 251–262.

Bosco, M. L. (1985). Non-union grievance procedures. *Personnel, 62*(1), 61–64.

Brehm, S. S., & Brehm, J. W. (1981). *Psychological reactance.* New York: Academic Press.

Brett, J. M., & Goldberg, S. B. (1979). Wildcat strikes in bituminous coal mining. *Industrial and Labor Relations Review, 32,* 465–483.

Bureau of National Affairs. (1989). *Basic patterns in union contracts* (12th ed.). Washington, DC: Author.

Clark, P. F., & Gallagher, D. G. (1989). Building member commitment to the union: The role of the grievance procedure. *Work Place Topics, 1*(2), 16–21.

Cyert, R. M., & March, J. G. (1963). *A behavioral theory of the firm.* Englewood Cliffs, NJ: Prentice-Hall.

Dalton, D. R., & Todor, W. D. (1979). Manifest needs of stewards: Propensity to file a grievance. *Journal of Applied Psychology, 64,* 654–659.

Dalton, D. R., & Todor, W. D. (1985a). Gender and workplace justice: A field assessment. *Personnel Psychology, 38,* 133–151.

Dalton, D. R., & Todor, W. D. (1985b). Composition of dyads as a factor in the outcomes of workplace justice: Two field assessments. *Academy of Management Journal, 28,* 704–712.

Dalton, D. R., Todor, W. D., & Owen, C. L. (1987). Sex effects in workplace justice outcomes: A field assessment. *Journal of Applied Psychology, 72,* 156–159.

Eaton, A. E., Gordon, M. E., & Keefe, J. H. (1992). The impact of quality of work life programs and grievance system effectiveness on union commitment. *Industrial and Labor Relations Review, 45,* 591–604.

Epstein, R. L. (1975). The grievance procedure in the non-union setting: Caveat employer. *Employee Relations Law Journal, 1,* 120–127.

Ewing, D. W. (1977). *Freedom inside the organization.* New York: McGraw-Hill.

Feldacker, B. S. (1990). *Labor guide to labor law* (3rd ed.). Englewood Cliffs, NJ: Prentice-Hall.

Fleishman, E. A., & Harris, E. F. (1962). Patterns of leadership behavior related to employee grievances and turnover. *Personnel Psychology, 15,* 43–56.

Fossum, J. A. (1985). *Labor relations: Development, structure, process* (3rd ed.). Plano, TX: Business Publications.

Freeman, R.B., & Medoff, J. L. (1984). *What do unions do?* New York: Basic Books.

Fryxell, G. E., & Gordon, M. E. (1989). Workplace justice and job satisfaction as predictors of satisfaction with the union and management. *Academy of Management Journal, 32,* 851–866.

Fryxell, G. E., & Gordon, M. E. (1991). Occupation as a moderator of the relationship between grievance systems and the belief in a just workplace. *Best Papers Proceedings* (pp. 321–325). 51st Annual Meeting of the Academy of Management, Miami Beach, FL.

Glassman, A. M., & Belasco, J. A. (1975). The chapter chairman and school grievances. *Industrial Relations, 14,* 233–241.

Gordon, M. E., & Bowlby, R. L. (1988). Propositions about grievance settlements: Finally, consultation with grievants. *Personnel Psychology, 41,* 107–123.

Gordon, M. E., & Bowlby, R. L. (1989). Reluctance and intentionality attributions as determinants of the intent to file a grievance. *Personnel Psychology, 42,* 309–329.

Gordon, M. E., & Coulson, R. (1989). A perspective on workplace justice for organized and unorganized workers. In C. A. B. Osigweh (Ed.), *Managing employee rights and responsibilities* (pp. 21–48). New York: Quorum Books.

Gordon, M. E., & Fryxell, G. E. (1989a). Behavioral research on grievance administration. *Work Place Topics, 1*(3), 10–15.

Gordon, M. E., & Fryxell, G. E. (1989b). Voluntariness of association as a moderator of the importance of procedural and distributive justice. *Journal of Applied Social Psychology, 19,* 993–1009.

Gordon, M. E., & Lee, B. A. (1990). Property rights in jobs: Workforce, behavioral and legal perspectives. In G. R. Ferris & K. M. Rowland (Eds.), *Research in personnel and human resources management* (pp. 303–348). Greenwich, CT: JAI Press.

Gordon, M. E., & Miller, S. J. (1984). Grievances: A review of research and practice. *Personnel Psychology, 37,* 117–146.

Gordon, M. E., & Nurick, A. J. (1981). Psychological approaches to the study of unions and union-management relations. *Psychological Bulletin, 90,* 293–306.

Gordon, M. E., Philpot, J. W., Burt, R. E., Thompson, C. A., & Spiller, W. E. (1980). Commitment to the union: Development of a measure and an examination of its correlates. *Journal of Applied Psychology, 65,* 479–499.

Greenberg, J. (1988). Cultivating an image of justice: Looking fair on the job. *Academy of Management Executive, 2,* 155–158.

Greenberg, J. (1990). Organizational justice: Yesterday, today, and tomorrow. *Journal of Management, 16,* 399–432.

Hickson, D. J., Hinings, C. R., Lee, C. A., Schneck, R. E., & Pennings, J. M. (1971). A strategic contingency theory of intraorganizational power. *Administrative Science Quarterly, 16,* 216–229.

Klaas, B. S. (1989a). Determinants of grievance activity and the grievance system's impact on employee behavior: An integrative perspective. *Academy of Management Review, 14,* 445–458.

Klaas, B. S. (1989b). Managerial decision making about employee grievances: The impact of the grievant's work history. *Personnel Psychology, 42,* 53–68.

Knight, T. R. (1986). Feedback and grievance resolution. *Industrial and Labor Relations Review, 39,* 585–598.

Kochan, T. A. (1979). How American workers view labor unions. *Monthly Labor Review, 102*(4), 23–31.

Kochan, T. A., & Katz, H. C. (1988). *Collective bargaining and industrial relations* (2nd ed.). Homewood, IL: Irwin.

Konovsky, M. A., Folger, R., & Fogel, D. S. (1990). *A panel analysis of the effects of distributive and procedural justice on employee commitment and pay satisfaction.* Working paper 90-HRMG-05, Tulane University.

Kuhn, J. W. (1961). *Bargaining in grievance settlement: The power of industrial work groups.* New York: Columbia University Press.

Leventhal, G. S., Karuza, J., & Fry, W. R. (1980). Beyond fairness: A theory of allocation preferences. In G. Mikula (Ed.), *Justice in social interaction* (pp. 167–218). New York: Springer Verlag.

Lewin, D. (1987). Dispute resolution in the nonunion firm: A theoretical and empirical analysis. *Journal of Conflict Resolution, 31,* 465–502.

Lewin, D., & Peterson, R. P. (1988). *The modern grievance procedure in the United States.* New York: Quorum Books.

Lind, E. A., & Tyler, T. R. (1988). *The social psychology of procedural justice.* New York: Plenum Press.

Maier, N. R. F. (1963). *Problem-solving discussions and conferences: Leadership methods and skills.* New York: McGraw-Hill.

Magenau, J. M., & Pruitt, D. G. (1979). The social psychology of bargaining: A theoretical synthesis. In G. M. Stephenson & C. J. Brotherton (Eds.), *Industrial relations: A social psychological approach* (pp. 181–210). New York: Wiley.

March, J. G., & Simon, H. A. (1958). *Organizations.* New York: Wiley.

Martin, E. A., & Cusella, L. P. (1986). Persuading the adjudicator: Conflict tactics in the grievance procedure. In M. L. McLaughlin (Ed.), *Communication yearbook* (Vol. 9, pp. 533–552). Beverly Hills, CA: Sage.

McDermott, T. J., & Newhams, T. H. (1971). Discharge-reinstatement: What happens thereafter? *Industrial and Labor Relations Review, 24,* 526–540.

McKelvey, J. T. (Ed.). (1985). *The changing law of fair representation.* Ithaca, NY: ILR Press.

McMurry, R. N. (1944). *Handling personality adjustment in industry.* New York: Harper.

Meyer, D., & Cooke, W. N. (1988). Economic and political factors in the resolution of formal grievances. *Industrial Relations, 27,* 318–335.

Montgomery, B. R. (1989). The influence of attitudes and normative pressures on voting decisions in a union certification election. *Industrial and Labor Relations Review, 42,* 262–279.

Mullen, J. H. (1954). The supervisor assesses his job in management. *Personnel, 31*(5), 94–108.

Ouchi, W. G. (1979). A conceptual framework for the design of organizational control mechanisms. *Management Science, 25,* 833–848.

Peach, D., & Livernash, E. R. (1974). *Grievance initiation and resolution: A study of basic steel.* Cambridge, MA: Harvard University Press.

Peterson, R. B., & Lewin, D. (1990). The nonunion grievance procedure: A viable system of due process? *Employee Responsibilities and Rights Journal, 3,* 1–18.

Repas, B. (1984). *Contract administration.* Washington, DC: Bureau of National Affairs.

Rodgers, R. C., & Helburn, I. B. (1985). The arbitrariness of arbitrators' decisions. *Proceedings of the Thirty-Seventh Annual Meeting* (pp. 442–445). Madison, WI: Industrial Relations Research Association.

Rodgers, R. C., Helburn, I. B., & Hunter, J. E. (1986). The relationship of seniority to job performance following reinstatement. *Academy of Management Journal, 29,* 101–114.

Ross, A. M. (1957). The arbitration of discharge cases: What happens after reinstatement? *Proceedings of the Tenth Annual Meeting of the National Academy of Arbitrators* (pp. 21–60). Washington, DC: Bureau of National Affairs.

Shaver, K. G. (1985). *The attribution of blame: Causality, responsibility, and blameworthiness.* New York: Springer-Verlag.

Slichter, S. H. (1947). *The challenge of industrial relations: Trade unions, management, and the public interest.* Ithaca, NY: Cornell University Press.

Stagner, R. (1956). *Psychology of industrial conflict.* New York: Wiley.

Stagner, R. (1962). Personality variables in union-management relations. *Journal of Applied Psychology, 46,* 350–357.

Steele v. Louisville & Nashville Railroad, 323 U.S. 192, 15 LRRM 708 (1944).

Steinbeck, J. (1972). *The grapes of wrath.* New York: Viking Press.

Taylor, B. J., & Witney, F. (1987). *Labor relations law* (5th ed.). Englewood Cliffs, NJ: Prentice Hall.

Thompson, J. D. (1967). *Organizations in action: Social science bases of administrative theory.* New York: McGraw-Hill.

Thomson, A. W. J., & Murray, V. V. (1976). *Grievance procedures.* Lexington, MA: Lexington Books.

Turner, J. T., & Robinson, J. W. (1972). A pilot study of the validity of grievance settlement rates as a predictor of union-management relationships. *Journal of Industrial Relations, 14,* 314–322.

Tyler, T. R. (1986). When does procedural justice matter in organizational settings? In R. J. Lewicki, B. H. Sheppard, & M. H. Bazerman (Eds.), *Research on negotiation in organizations* (Vol. 1, pp. 7–23). Greenwich, CT: JAI Press.

Vaca v. Sipes, 386 U.S. 171, 64 LRRM 2369 (1967).

Westin, A. F. (1989). Internal mechanisms for resolving employee complaints in nonunion organizations. In C. A. B. Osigweh (Ed.), *Managing employee rights and responsibilities* (pp. 151–160). New York: Quorum.

Wilkens, A., & Ouchi, W. G. (1983). Efficient cultures: Exploring the relationship between culture and organizational control. *Administrative Science Quarterly, 28,* 468–481.

Williamson, O. E. (1975). *Markets and hierarchies: Analysis and antitrust implications.* New York: Free Press.

Williamson, O. E. (1985). *The economic institutions of Capitalism.* New York: Free Press.

Williamson, O. E., Wachter, M. L., & Harris, J. (1975). Understanding the employment relationship: The analysis of idiosyncratic exchange. *Bell Journal of Economics, 6,* 250–280.

12 Justice and Pay System Satisfaction

Marcia P. Miceli
Ohio State University

Substantial portions of the budgets in most organizations are devoted to employee compensation; this is particularly true in the growing service industries, where frequently between 40¢ and 80¢ of each revenue dollar is spent for employee compensation (Henderson, 1989). In an increasingly competitive global economy, managers are concerned with designing and operating pay systems that will meet strategic objectives, such as enhancing employee commitment, retention, and loyalty to the organization. Preliminary evidence (e.g., H. Heneman, 1985; Motowidlo, 1983) suggested that the effective management of compensation will enhance satisfaction with pay, and thereby affect employee retention and other outcomes.

Most of the research has shown that pay satisfaction is multidimensional (Ash, Dreher, & Bretz, 1987; H. Heneman & Schwab, 1985; R. Heneman, Greenberger, & Strasser, 1988; Mulvey, Miceli, & Near, in press: Scarpello, Huber, & Vandenberg, 1988; Ziemak, 1988). This research has produced and examined the Pay Satisfaction Questionnaire, an 18-item instrument (H. Heneman & Schwab, 1985). A few investigations have found support for the unidimensional approach (e.g., Orpen & Bonnici, 1987), whereas still others (Carraher, in press) have found distinct but correlated components. Generally, the research has shown that an individual may react differently to the level of his or her salary than to the system that produces this salary, and his or her satisfaction with benefits may be independent of these other views. For example, an individual may believe that his or her salary level compares favorably to those of salaries of others inside and outside the organization, and therefore, he or she may be satisfied with that salary. However, the same individual may be dissatisfied with the pay system if it is designed to reward performance, but high performers are not rewarded because they won't "play politics." There is evidence that political connections and dependence on subordinates' expertise sometimes play a role in managers' pay raise decisions (Bartol & Martin, 1990).

Unfortunately, although there is an impressive body of research on the predictors of satisfaction with pay level (as reviewed by H. Heneman, 1985; Miceli & Lane, 1991), very few studies have investigated the other components of pay satisfaction. Thus, little is known about what causes employees to be satisfied or dissatisfied with pay systems; consequently, little guidance can be offered to managers who wish to design and administer pay systems effectively.

The purpose of this chapter is to help compensation specialists and line managers understand potential employee reactions to pay systems. As such, this chapter is not concerned directly with the literature on pay level satisfaction, which has been reviewed elsewhere (H. Heneman, 1985; Miceli & Lane, 1991). This chapter defines satisfaction with pay systems and describes preliminary models based on theory and research. The factors that may affect satisfaction with this variable are then discussed. Because pay satisfaction has been shown to be influenced by concerns about justice (e.g., Folger & Konovsky, 1989), factors are drawn from the literature on distributive justice (e.g., Lawler, 1971), procedural justice (e.g., Cropanzano & Folger, in press), and interactional justice (e.g., Bies, 1987) in organizations. Some authors (e.g., Greenberg, this volume) have argued that interactional justice can be considered a type of procedural justice; therefore distinctions are not drawn as these approaches are applied to pay administration. Finally, implications for practice and research are derived from these models. Readers must be cautioned, however, that these implications are quite speculative, because of the very limited research published to date specifically dealing with pay system satisfaction.

Three caveats are in order. First, it should be noted that this chapter is concerned primarily with the systems that determine wages and salaries. Benefits are an important part of the pay package, but consideration of satisfaction with benefits and benefit systems is beyond the scope of this chapter. Second, the models and implications of them are oriented toward traditional individual-based pay systems, rather than group-based pay systems, such as profit sharing, gain-sharing, or nontraditional systems, such as pay for knowledge (skill-based pay) systems. Third, the chapter deals with rather formal, complex pay systems in some but not all large organizations; some of the propositions offered may also be applicable to smaller organizations as well.

THE DEFINITION OF PAY SYSTEM SATISFACTION

Unfortunately, there is no agreed-upon definition of pay satisfaction in the current literature on pay satisfaction (Deckop, 1990). In a review of the literature, Miceli and Lane (1991) defined pay satisfaction to be the amount of overall

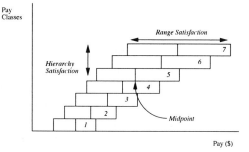

FIG. 12.1. Contrasting the two types of pay system satisfaction.

positive or negative affect (or feelings) that individuals have toward their pay. Following Mulvey (1991), they distinguished satisfaction with pay outcomes (or levels) from satisfaction with systems. The construct of pay system satisfaction was further subdivided into reactions to the process of setting pay rates within a job class and reactions to the process of setting pay rates between job classes.

To illustrate this difference, Fig. 12.1 depicts seven pay classes in a pay structure in a hypothetical organization. Each job is slotted into one pay class on the basis of value or worth; jobs judged to be of similar value by the organization are grouped together into a pay class. Jobs judged to be of higher value are paid more than are those in lower pay classes; for example, the midpoint of Pay Class 5 represents more salary or wages than does the midpoint of Pay Class 4. Within each pay class, incumbents may receive varying amounts of pay. For example, the job of employment recruiter may be slotted in Pay Class 6; an experienced, high performing recruiter may earn a salary above the midpoint for Pay Class 6, whereas a relatively inexperienced or low performing recruiter may earn a salary below the midpoint.

Figure 12.1 shows that satisfaction with the range of pay for one's job class is represented by the horizontal arrow. It is easy to generate examples of how employees may react to the system that determines pay ranges and where they "stand" in the range. A new employee may question why she or he receives a starting pay rate of $10 per hour, whereas another new hire in the same job receives $12 per hour. High performers may be much more satisfied when they believe that they and other high performers are receiving higher raises than are low performers. These examples illustrate reactions to within-job pay system operation, or range satisfaction. Obviously, systems operate to determine which employees in the same job class receive which salaries or wages, and presumably employees develop views about these systems, even though the systems may be flawed, inconsistent, communicated poorly, or incomprehensibly complex.

In contrast, Fig. 12.1 uses a vertical arrow to show that employees may react to the hierarchy of classes in the pay structure. Employees may be concerned with why a marketing research analyst job is slotted in Pay Class 5, earning at the midpoint $23,000 per year, whereas an engineering draftsperson job is slotted in

Pay Class 7, earning at the midpoint $27,500 per year. Or, they may evaluate the difference in pay they would receive if they were to accept a promotion from administrative assistant 1, to administrative assistant 2, a job in the next higher pay class. These are examples of reactions to between-job pay system operation, or hierarchy satisfaction. Again, some system must operate to determine the pay rates associated with each pay class, although the system is not guaranteed to operate logically or effectively. Employees may not fully understand it but they are likely to have opinions about it.

Hence, there are opportunities for employees to feel satisfied or dissatisfied both with the range and the hierarchy systems. The distinction is important, for three reasons. Theoretically, it is important to determine if employees can differentiate the operation of different aspects of the pay system and to identify what causes unique reactions to each. Practically, fundamentally different responses may be required to rectify problems with ranges rather than hierarchies and vice versa. For example, job evaluation (i.e., a process of determining the relative worth of jobs) may be used to correct inequities between jobs, and performance evaluation (i.e., a process of determining the relative performance of employees) may be used to correct inequities within jobs.

There are legal reasons to make this distinction as well. A female employee who alleges that a violation of the Equal Pay Act of 1963 has occurred, is expressing pay range dissatisfaction, because she believes she is paid less than a man in the same job for reasons that do not appear justified. A female employee who alleges that jobs are not paid according to "comparable worth" (Greenberg & McCarty, 1990) is expressing hierarchy dissatisfaction, because she believes that her job is classified in an unfairly low pay class relative to job worth because of a factor she believes to be illegitimate, namely the gender of most incumbents in her job. But at a given time, there may be a legal basis for only one type of complaint against the employer. Consequently, a model for each type of pay system satisfaction is developed in the following sections, although the models (earlier versions of which were developed in Miceli & Lane, 1991) are very similar with regard to their reliance on the justice literature.

WHAT CAUSES SATISFACTION WITH THE PAY RANGE SYSTEM?

In an era of increasing environmental uncertainty reflected in global competition from organizations with low labor costs, many organizations are moving away from straight salary or seniority pay systems to pay systems that place pay at risk to the employee, such as bonus systems (Brown & Huber, 1991). Despite this trend, very little attention has been devoted to the reactions of employees to the systems that may be used to determine variations in pay within a job class. Pay range satisfaction is concerned with the process of setting differences in starting

FIG. 12.2. A preliminary model of some factors that may influence pay system satisfaction—within jobs (range satisfaction).

pay among employees as well as opportunities for changes while remaining in the same job (Miceli & Lane, 1991).

A preliminary model of the factors that may influence within-job pay system satisfaction, or pay range satisfaction, appears in Fig. 12.2. This model, as well as its predecessor (Miceli & Lane, 1991), is based loosely on Lawler's (1971) original discrepancy model of pay level satisfaction. Lawler's model, as noted earlier, can be considered a distributive justice model that bears many similarities to equity theory (Lawler, 1971). His model proposed that the greater the discrepancy between what employees believe they should receive and the amount of pay they believe they do receive, the greater the pay dissatisfaction. As shown in Fig. 12.2, the model of pay range satisfaction also proposes a discrepancy process may occur; however, here individuals do not compare amounts. Rather, range satisfaction may result from a comparison between the employee's beliefs about how the system should operate and the employee's beliefs about how the system operates. The more closely these two beliefs are perceived to match, the higher the level of range satisfaction. That is, the extent to which the system appears to adhere to the rules that the employee believes should govern how the system should operate, and the employee's own pay level, will affect range satisfaction.

One proposition that is implicit in this model of range satisfaction is that both perceptions about the outcomes and perceptions about the process through which pay rates are assigned will affect range satisfaction. Although range satisfaction is concerned with reactions to the part of the pay system that determines how individuals in the same job come to be paid different amounts, the model does not propose that only procedural justice concerns will determine range satisfaction. As an example, no matter how fairly the procedures appear to operate, an employee who believes that his or her pay level or raise is unfairly low will probably be more dissatisfied with the range system than an employee who shares all of the same beliefs and perceptions except that he or she believes his or her pay is high. If this is true, then the practical implication is that an employer cannot induce range system satisfaction at low cost by operating it in a procedurally just fashion (e.g., by operating it consistently) but providing low pay. The theoretical implication is that authors must be careful not to oversimplify their views of system satisfaction by equating distributive justice with pay level satisfaction and procedural justice with pay system satisfaction. Obviously, these propositions should be tested.

Another proposition implicit in the model is that reactions to the outcomes are not simply determined by how low or high they appear to be in absolute terms, but rather by the extent to which they may conform to beliefs about how high or low they are relative to the basis that should be used to determine pay. This proposition is drawn directly from the justice literature in that the importance of comparison to social standards been demonstrated empirically in many contexts (e.g., Greenberg, 1982). That is, the model distinguishes (a) low outcomes relative to what others receive regardless of inputs or low in some absolute sense (e.g., a zero pay increase) from (b) low outcomes relative to some standard of input. In some sense, this distinction is analogous to the distinction drawn by Martin (1981) in that (a) is a relative deprivation proposition (though also a part of equity theory) and (b) is emphasized by equity theory. Both variables may affect range satisfaction, but not necessarily in the same way. In some prior articles, this distinction is not made; again the proposition should be tested.

For example, low performers in a properly functioning merit system may receive small annual increases in pay. However, they may not be dissatisfied with the range determination system, because they may view the system as providing appropriate raises relative to the contributions they have made. In this case, the outcomes are low relative to what others receive, but they are not low relative to inputs. If this is true, the implication is that range dissatisfaction (and its potential consequences, such as complaining, sabotage, or low commitment) on the part of all of the employees who receive low raises is not inevitable. In other words, proper management of the system may increase range satisfaction for employees as a group, without requiring that everyone get a pay raise.

Clearly, research is needed in this area. With these limitations in mind, attention is turned to the proposed factors that may affect the standards against which employees judge their employers' systems for setting pay rates within ranges.

Preferences for the Basis for Within-Job Pay Differences

As Fig. 12.2 implies, employees and employers may have preferences concerning the bases for initial pay differences and pay increases within job classes. This constitutes a distributive justice factor, which pertains to the allocation of pay according to acceptable standards. For example, one employee may believe that all newcomers should receive the same pay rate when they begin working as assemblers; another employee may believe that there should be differentiation based on past experience. As another example, some employers may wish to motivate performance through providing increases to high performers, while other employees prefer to reward all employees in the pay class with similar percentage increases.

Employees are likely to believe that employers should maintain systems that are consistent with employee notions of distributive justice. For example, organizations may allow individuals to negotiate for starting salaries (e.g., Gerhart & Rynes, 1991). Empirical evidence suggests that the effects of these negotiations sometimes result in lower starting salaries for women relative to men (Gerhart & Rynes, 1991). Presumably, if gender is not considered a legitimate basis for pay differentiation, then such results (if so perceived by employees) would violate distributive justice norms, resulting in lower range satisfaction.

One issue that has not been resolved is whether (a) one considers only the perceived basis for his or her own pay, or (b) one considers the perceived basis of pay of everyone. For example, if an employee believes that his or her own pay is commensurate with his or her own performance, but that certain co-workers do not get what they deserve, is the level of range satisfaction different from where the employee believes that all co-workers get what they deserve? Three studies of merit systems examined some form of this question; two of them used measures focusing on one's own pay, while the third examined more general perceptions. The first study examined pay-for-performance perceptions concerning one's own raise and found that these perceptions were unrelated to pay raise satisfaction (Folger & Konovsky, 1989); however, the extent to which the H. Heneman and Schwab (1985) measure of pay raise satisfaction used in this study captures the construct of pay range satisfaction is not clear.

In a second study, effort-reward consonance, which reflected respondents' perceptions that they would receive more pay if they worked harder in their present jobs, was associated with pay system fairness and success in merit systems (Miceli, Jung, Near, & Greenberger, 1991). A third study used a measure of pay-for-performance perceptions that tapped views of hypothetical raises and perceptions of others' raises, rather than the linkage between one's own perceived performance and pay raise (R. Heneman et al., 1988). Pay raise satisfaction was related to pay-for-performance perceptions, even after the effects of salary level, salary increases, performance ratings, job tenure, job satisfaction, and promotions were controlled, and even though merit was not the only basis for reward. These studies suggested that perceptions concerning both one's own and others' raise basis may affect pay range satisfaction, at least in merit systems. If so, managers should strive to show how pay conforms to accepted bases for pay determination.

Studies of political behavior in organizations also seem relevant here. Within a given job, individuals may perceive that certain employees receive higher pay for reasons other than merit, seniority, or other input. One factor that may be perceived to be rewarded with higher pay is organizational political behavior. Organizational politics has been defined (Ferris, Fedor, Chachere, & Pondy, 1989) as: "a social influence process in which opportunistic behavior (demonstrated by individuals, groups, or organizations) is engaged for purposes of self-interest maximization" (p. 88). Clearly, some employees may view political behavior as a means of maximizing self-interest in getting higher pay. In pay contexts, there are many opportunities for (and potentially, rewards for) political behaviors. Ferris, Russ, and Fandt (1989) cited two recent studies showing that politics influences salary attainment. First, Gould and Penley (1984) found that opinion conformity and other enhancement were significantly related to salary progression. Second, Dreher, Dougherty, and Whitely (1988) found that upward influence tactics explained a significant proportion of the variance in salaries, though different tactics worked for men and women.

Some employees may view political behaviors to be a "fact of organizational life" whereas others may believe that such behaviors are inherently wrong. To the extent that political behaviors are not seen as legitimate substitutes for inputs deserving of rewards, pay system satisfaction will be lower when political behaviors are rewarded than when they are not. Whether this would be true for most employees in the system or only for those who do not receive the rewards remains for future research. It should be remembered that studies show that even those employees who did not receive rewards were more satisfied when they saw stronger linkages between pay and performance than when they did not. Thus, it may be that views concerning political behavior and perceptions of its linkage to rewards for everyone, rather than one's own engaging in such behavior and receiving or not receiving rewards, may be critical. For example, if an employee believes that other employees are engaging in ingratiation or impression management and being rewarded for it but that this is illegitimate, he or she may be more dissatisfied with the pay system than if he or she does not believe that this is happening. It is hypothesized that this will be true regardless of whether the employee himself or herself has attempted to ingratiate.

Should employers attempt to influence employee preferences? Perhaps not; Miceli et al. (1991) found that perceptions that the system operation adhered to merit distribution rules favorably influenced reactions to the pay system whether or not the surveyed managers endorsed the concept of merit. Further, it may be difficult to affect employee preferences. For example, employees in different job categories may bring stable but diverse values to the workplace; union members may not trust managerial judgments of performance and thus may prefer seniority-based systems, while managerial employees may prefer merit (H. Heneman, 1985). Cultural values (e.g., the value that individuals who are better performers deserve more pay vs. the value that high performers should share rather than enjoy exclusively the profits from their good fortune or high ability) may affect these preferences. In both instances, employees may prefer the seniority system because they value security or because they think it is more inherently "right." These observations suggest that employers should strive to understand employee preferences and to communicate their own preferences rather than try to bring about changes in preferences, but obviously this speculation should be tested.

Mulvey (1991) completed the only known study in which a reliable measure of range satisfaction was devised and justice hypotheses were explicitly tested. He found support for this speculation. Results of a survey of social service employees showed a significant zero-order relationship between the "congruence" between an individual's preferences for reward systems and the perceived reward system operation and range satisfaction. However, once control variables (including job satisfaction) were entered in a hierarchical regression, the relationship was no longer significant. Mulvey (1991) also found that the relationship between range satisfaction and the extent of "compliance" between employers' stated intentions and system operation remained significant even after the control variables were entered. This was also true when the dependent measure was the structure/administration scale of the Pay Satisfaction Questionnaire (H. Heneman & Schwab, 1985). Interestingly, these results seem to suggest that it may be more important for the employer to play by the rules of the game that the employer chooses than to select the game that the employees prefer!

As shown in Fig. 12.2, two types of variables may moderate the relationship between preferences and employees' beliefs about how systems should operate: (a) the employee's perception of the environment, job and organizational characteristics; (b) the employer's communications about the pay system. Whereas an exhaustive speculation about the variables that could be classified into these categories is beyond the scope of this paper, we can consider some examples. One obvious example of an environmental, job, or organizational characteristic that may moderate the relationship between preferences and range satisfaction concerns the extent to which individuals have control over their work output. Employees who generally prefer individual-based merit systems may suspend this preference when task interdependence exists. The implication of this speculation for practice is that, to enhance pay system satisfaction, organizations must design systems for within-job rewards that are consistent with environmental, job, and organizational characteristics. How employees will react to individual based suggestion systems, gainsharing, or both, will likely depend on these characteristics. This also implies that the greater the fit between the strategy of the organization and the pay system characteristics, the greater the pay system satisfaction.

Another example was provided in a study by Konovsky, Folger, and Fogel

(1990). Konovsky et al. (1990) found that commitment to the employer may be a cause of pay raise satisfaction rather than merely an effect as has been proposed (H. Heneman, 1985). If employee commitment is viewed as a function of employee reactions to the environmental, job, or organizational characteristics, then this variable may have a direct effect on range satisfaction. However, it is conceivable that commitment indirectly influences pay system satisfaction; for example, the pay system satisfaction of highly committed employees may be less subject to the influence of the extent to which their own preferences in the pay system are met than is the satisfaction of less committed employees.

The level of employee understanding may also be important. In a study of a newly implemented incentive system in which base pay was reduced, Brown and Huber (1991) found that bank employees' understanding of the system was associated with pay process satisfaction. The measure of pay process satisfaction used was a slightly modified version of the structure and administration subscales of the Pay Satisfaction Questionnaire. It is not known to what extent these subscales tap the constructs of range satisfaction and hierarchy satisfaction that have been proposed.

Understanding can be brought about by effective organizational communications. Communications by company officials may indicate why pay differentials are awarded; thus, the nature of the communication may be important. An organization may have an excellent reason for paying certain individuals more than others, but if this reason—or the pay philosophy in general—is not communicated to employees, then beliefs about the pay system will be adversely affected. Formal communications may be accomplished through a variety of means, such as organizational memos or performance appraisal forms. Informal communications also may vary in form, occurring during coaching or the performance interview, in response to employee questions directed to human resource professionals, or "the grapevine." Mulvey (1991) found that perceived communication enhanced pay range satisfaction; thus, there is evidence of a direct effect. He did not examine the moderator role of communications hypothesized by the present model.

The content of the communication may be critically important. According to Bies (1987), organizations may·provide information to members about the propriety of a decision maker's behavior. The impression management process may affect employee reactions (Greenberg, 1990). Excuses (attempts to reduce the apparent unfairness of a situation), and justifications (attempts to reduce the apparent harm caused by an injustice) (Greenberg & McCarty, 1990) may affect fairness perceptions. This information may provide a basis on which people can evaluate procedural fairness. Consistent with this reasoning, Bies and Shapiro (1988) found that a justification that claimed mitigating circumstances in the external environment for an unfavorable decision led to higher levels of perceived procedural fairness. Greenberg (1990) found that an explanation/justification provided by the chief executive officer (CEO) reduced theft during a temporary pay cut, compared to a group that didn't receive an explanation/ justification. These findings suggested that organizations that provide justification for pay decisions may also influence pay system satisfaction.

Mulvey (1991) found that the extent to which social service workers believed that their employers had provided a justification for pay decisions was correlated with pay range satisfaction, but this relationship was not significant after the effects of control variables, including job satisfaction, were removed in a hierarchical regression analysis. Mulvey (1991) predicted that the relationship between justification and pay system satisfaction would be moderated by belief in the justification, but instead he found that the stronger the belief, the higher the pay system satisfaction. Because hierarchical regression analysis provides a very conservative test of hypotheses involving interaction (because the main effect is entered first), it may be premature to reject the interaction hypothesis.

Future research might examine different types of pay secrecy. For example, some organizations inform employees only about their own salaries and possibly the salary range for their pay class. In addition to notifying each employee about his or her salary, other organizations share information only about the minima, midpoints, and maxima of all ranges. Some organizations maintain secrecy with respect to outsiders but share information with employees, while others, such as public universities, may maintain secrecy only until the salaries are recorded in the public documents. Thus, there may be a continuum of secrecy. There may also be various dimensions of secrecy besides secrecy about levels, such as secrecy about how individual raises were determined, how the budget pool for raises was determined, how much other groups receive, and so on. This may account for some of the equivocal findings from pay secrecy studies (H. Heneman, 1985).

Interestingly, the implications of procedural justice research stand in stark contrast to the widespread practice of various forms of pay secrecy. That is, the findings described earlier and the model suggest that communication of a certain nature can have an important, positive impact on pay satisfaction. So why would employers maintain secrecy policies?

One possibility is that employers may believe that the more detail given to employees, the more likely at least one employee will find some basis for complaint. Another possibility is that some employers may view pay discussions as raising employee privacy issues. Or, perhaps, the most secretive employers may in fact maintain the most unjust systems. Their policy of hiding information may serve temporarily to reduce employee dissatisfaction that would come with awareness. In the long-term, however, employees may be more resentful that they have not been informed of inequities than if they had been given more information originally. Finally, research has failed to consider the effects of misinformation, whether deliberate or unintentional. For example, if employees in one group are told that all groups were eligible for an average of 5% increases, but they later learn that in fact some groups were given 10%, then dissatisfaction with the system may result. Because there seem to be reasonable but opposing hypotheses about the effects of pay secrecy policies, and because these hypotheses may require delineation based on the context (e.g., how secret are the pay policies?), studies testing these competing hypotheses would be very useful.

Employees' Knowledge of Other Pay Systems

Employees' knowledge of other pay systems may influence their beliefs about how the pay system should operate. Conceivably, when a pay plan using a new basis for reward is implemented, employees will compare their new pay rates to those that they would have received under the old plan. As referent cognition theory (Folger, 1986) would predict, Miceli et al. (1991) found that employees who believed they fared better under a seniority system than under a newly adopted merit system also believed the merit system was less fair and successful than were employees who believed they were better paid under the new system. In this sense, knowledge or history serves as a distributive justice factor.

The variables that moderate the effects of distribution preferences may also moderate the effects of knowledge of other pay systems. For example, if employers communicate clearly who is better off under a new system, there may be greater differences in these individuals' reactions than if employers' communications are vague.

The Employee's Views Concerning Participation in Range Decision Making

The variables involving the basis for within-job pay differences and knowledge of other systems represent distributive justice influences on pay system satisfaction. The literature on procedural justice also suggests additional variables that may play a role. One of these is participation in the process of setting ranges or policies for determining how individuals will be treated with respect to within job pay differences. Greenberg and McCarty (1990, citing Renwick & Lawler, 1978) indicated that although employees believe they exercise little influence in the determination of pay, they want greater control in pay decisions. For example, the performance appraisal process is an important component in merit pay systems (Henderson, 1989). The opportunity for employees to provide input in selecting and defining the dimensions on which performance will be evaluated conceivably may affect employees' range satisfaction.

Two studies involving pay level satisfaction and participation have been published. Jenkins and Lawler (1981) found that pay satisfaction increased after employees participated in the development of a new pay system; however, this may have resulted from the confounding of participation with pay increases (H. Heneman, 1985). Capelli and Sherer (1988) found a strong positive relationship between pay satisfaction and (a) workers' sense of participation in the organization, and (b) workers' sense of control over issues. Other studies have examined job satisfaction. According to Florkowski (1990), prior research indicates that profit sharing and gainsharing positively influence job satisfaction. He proposed that structured participation in decision making, an inherent feature of gainsharing plans, generates more enthusiasm than would profit sharing alone. However, no published studies examined the relationship between participation and system satisfaction.

It is reasonable to propose that the greater the level of participation, the more likely that employees will believe that the pay system is fair and satisfying. Although much of the procedural justice research supporting this proposition has been conducted in the laboratory, relationships between pay system satisfaction and the use of certain procedures may be stronger in the field. Employees are in a continuing relationship with their organizations to a greater extent than are laboratory participants; individuals are more likely to be concerned with procedural justice when the relationship is expected to continue (Cropanzano & Folger, in press).

Employees may wish to participate in the process of determining merit increases or in gainsharing plan administration; employers who encourage this participation may experience higher levels of range satisfaction, for several reasons. First, this may occur because employees believe that systems should be changed in response to employee needs and wishes. Participation may enhance self-efficacy; employees who feel they have more control over their environments tend to be more satisfied (Magjuka, 1989). A second reason is suggested by referent cognition theory (Folger, 1986). Individuals become resentful if they received worse outcomes than they would have received if the allocator used an alternative procedure that should have been used. As Cropanzano and Folger (1989) found, this occurs only when individuals have no choice of procedure used; individuals have no basis for complaining that another procedure should have been used if they have in fact controlled the choice of procedure.

As was the case with secrecy, multiple forms of participation in range decision-making can be identified. For example, as noted earlier employees may generate critical incidents for constructing performance appraisal instruments (Henderson, 1989). They may serve on committees to award merit increases or participate in other forms of peer review. Their union representatives may work together with management to establish ranges. Determining the effects of these and other forms of participation, which likely will depend on how skillfully participation is utilized, is obviously an issue of practical importance. Also, it seems important to determine employees' views concerning participation. In some organizations, employees may welcome the opportunity for participation in various forms. In others, employees may prefer to let management or union officials make decisions.

As before, perceptions of certain characteristics related to the workplace and employer communications may moderate the impact of views concerning participation. For example, if employees spend much time participating on committees and the results never appear to be incorporated or considered by management, opportunities for "participation" may be negatively related to range satisfaction.

The Employee's Endorsement of Procedural Rules in Range Decision Making

Allocation preference theory (Leventhal, Karuza, & Fry, 1980) states that people compare procedures to a fairness standard that is based on procedural justice rules (Mulvey, 1991). Consistent with this perspective, Folger and Konovsky (1989) found that procedural justice, particularly in providing feedback, was related to pay raise satisfaction. Leventhal et al. (1980) identified six rules, which can be applied to pay system satisfaction (Miceli & Lane, 1991); three others were identified by Miceli and Lane (1991). These are briefly summarized.

Consistency. One example of an application of the consistency rule is that the same basis should be used to determine pay raises for all employees in the same job; this rule would clearly apply to both individual-based rewards and group-based rewards. Miceli et al. (1991) found that adherence to performance appraisal standards, which may have been viewed as an application of the consistency rule, was associated with merit pay system fairness and success.

As noted earlier, perceived environmental factors and organizational communications may moderate the relationship between the application of the consistency rule and the manner in which the system should operate. The employer can enhance perceived consistency through communications. For example, newcomers in the same job may exchange information and learn that several are paid substantially more than the others. If the employer communicates that extra pay is consistently given to those with relevant prior experience, then all employees may perceive the system favorably, but if no explanation is given, dissatisfaction may result.

Bias Suppression. One illustration of the bias suppression rule is that there should be no opportunities for the size of the merit pay increase to be contaminated by personal bias, pity for a low effort employee, perceived family needs, or other factors that have little to do with job performance. Opportunities to earn bonuses or overtime should be made available without regard to irrelevant factors.

Accuracy. Adjustments for market increases should be made on the basis of accurate pay survey information. If supervisors have spent little time observing performance, it is likely that pertinent information has been omitted and that performance ratings will be inaccurate.

Correctability.   Employees should have the opportunity to provide information, such as evidence of achievements that may have been overlooked, that is used by the supervisor to adjust pay rates. If range satisfaction is related to the opportunity to appeal and obtain a correction in the system, then systems should allow for the introduction of new information. Mulvey (1991) found that the opportunity to appeal was significantly correlated with range satisfaction, although no significant relationship remained when other variables were entered in a multivariate regression.

Representation.   Here representation may refer to the extent to which the information used to make decisions is representative of the domain of performance or other input factors. The definition of performance should reflect the variety of contributions made by incumbents in the same job. For example, some faculty members may make significant contributions in teaching and service, while others excel at research.

Ethics.   One example of an ethical standard that may pertain to within-job pay rates is that employers should not reveal performance and pay rates without the permission of the employee. It seems particularly likely that perceived environmental factors, such as competitive pressures, and organizational communications would affect the extent to which ethical standards are perceived as being upheld in the system.

In addition to these general rules of procedural justice, at least three other rules dealing particularly with pay system administration have been identified (Miceli & Lane, 1991). First, proactivity appears to be valued by many employees. Some organizations strive to maintain equity by seeking information and making appropriate adjustments, for example, through pay surveys. Their pay systems may be viewed more favorably than more reactive organizations, which make pay changes only when forced to do so by high employee turnover, impending unionization, or threats of lawsuits. Similarly, organizations that adjust pay rates within a pay class only to those who present competing offers but do not make equity adjustments for similar employees who could obtain such offers may be viewed less favorably than the organization that devotes adequate resources to rewarding individuals competitively. Controlled research testing this proposition has not been published.

Another rule may concern the sufficiency of funding for pay increases. Miceli et al. (1991) found that when the amount of money budgeted for pay increases was viewed as sufficient to provide adequate increases to all deserving employees, higher pay system fairness and success resulted than where it was insufficient. Where organizations budget insufficient amounts to support systems that they have implemented, high performers in particular may view the employer as having not fulfilled its promises. This seems likely if the employer had promised to pay "competitively."

A third rule was identified by Dyer and Theriault (1976). In merit systems, employees may be more satisfied when supervisors are highly influential, rather than uninfluential, over pay decisions. This may be true because generally, supervisors rate performance (Henderson, 1989). If supervisory recommendations appear to matter little in determining pay rates, the system may be viewed less favorably than where supervisors play a key role. Contrary to prediction, Dyer and Theriault (1976) found no relationship between supervisor influence and pay satisfaction, but the measure of pay satisfaction likely did not capture the concept of system satisfaction. Two other possibilities come to mind. First, if a supervisor is an unreliable performance rater, in other words, he or she violates many procedural or distributive justice rules, then the greater the influence, presumably the more negatively the system is viewed. This is especially likely for the high performers who receive low raises. One other issue is that there is a question of alternatives to supervisors as raters and as determiners of raises. If, for example, most employees prefer a peer review or that someone above their supervisors make decisions, then supervisor influence would have no impact or a negative impact.

Employees may use other rules in considering the manner in which the system should operate. There may be individual differences in the extent to which employees endorse each rule or believe that it is important to them. For example, to one employee the size of the raise pool may be very important, whereas to others, consistent in application of rules is critical. Researchers are encouraged to explore these possibilities. Practitioners are encouraged to consider the extent to which their current procedures for determining ranges and the relative placement of employees' salaries in the ranges are consistent with these rules and to which rules employees are most sensitive.

In summary, employees consider their beliefs about how the system operates by evaluating the extent to which the system for determining pay differences within jobs adheres to the rules and standards described earlier. Their range satisfaction is determined in part by these evaluations. Employee pay levels may also influence range satisfaction, although this variable is not anticipated to play an important role. Higher paid employees may be somewhat more satisfied with the system because they have reaped higher rewards from the system than have lower paid employees.

WHAT CAUSES SATISFACTION WITH THE HIERARCHY SYSTEM?

A preliminary model of the factors that may influence satisfaction with the determination of pay for the hierarchy of jobs within the organization—hierarchy satisfaction—appears in Fig. 12.3. Hierarchy satisfaction is concerned with the process of setting the mean or median pay rates for each job in the pay structure;

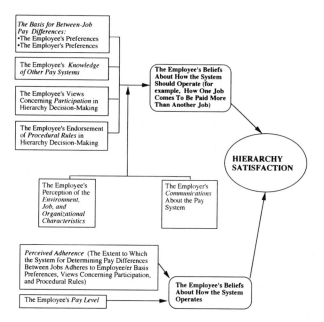

FIG. 12.3.   A preliminary model of some factors that may influence pay system—between jobs (hierarchy satisfaction).

jobs typically are grouped into classes along with jobs of similar value as determined by the pay system (i.e., through job evaluation or pay surveys). It is not clear whether the determination of the formal (as opposed to the actual) ranges for each pay class would be perceived by employees to be part of this system, or part of the system of determining pay within a class (previously discussed). Therefore, research is needed to examine this question; here only the setting of average pay rates for each job is considered.

Not surprisingly, this model, as well as its predecessor (Miceli & Lane, 1991), is very similar to the model of pay range satisfaction with respect to the general rules and categories of variables that are likely to affect satisfaction. However, the specific variables in the categories and the application of the rules differ. Because of the general similarity, the description of the model will be abbreviated. As shown in Fig. 12.3, hierarchy satisfaction may result from a comparison between the employee's beliefs about how the system should operate and the employee's beliefs about how the system operates. The extent to which the system appears to adhere to the rules that the employee believes should govern how the system should operate, and the employee's own pay level, will affect hierarchy satisfaction. For example, individuals consider whether a system that is supposed to be internally equitable through reliance on a well-functioning job evaluation system actually is internally equitable. They examine the process through which the job evaluation system is chosen and implemented, and compare it to their standards for the process.

A fundamental question that remains for future research should be mentioned here. Given the level of pay secrecy and complexity of pay system functioning existing in many organizations, readers may wonder whether employees have sufficient knowledge in order to evaluate the hierarchical pay system. Although this point was raised with respect to range satisfaction, it is probably even more salient in the case of hierarchy satisfaction. This is because individuals may be much more familiar with their own pay class than with the classes of others both above and below and the rules governing advancement. Further, how the hierarchy is established may be of little concern to participants, in part because of the same factors. If so, readers may question whether hierarchy satisfaction is a meaningful concept. The literature on pay secrecy and pay satisfaction suggests that employees form hypotheses about many phenomena about which they have little understanding, and they may develop attitudes and act on this misunderstanding. Further, with increasing attention to comparable worth (Greenberg & McCarty, 1990), its obvious relevancy to hierarchy satisfaction, and the implications that comparable worth has for employee behavior such as unionization, lawsuits, or employee withdrawal, hierarchy satisfaction is deserving of research attention. Therefore, variables and processes potentially affecting each of the primary determinants of hierarchy satisfaction are discussed.

Preferences for the Basis for Between-Job Pay Differences

As Fig. 12.3 shows, employees may have preferences concerning a philosophy underlying the operation of the system that creates and maintains the hierarchy. Employees are likely to believe that the organization should be guided by a similar philosophy and consequently, employers who maintain systems that operate consistent with these preferences will produce higher levels of hierarchy satisfaction.

For example, employees may believe that the organization should rely heavily on pay surveys to set pay rates. Other employees may believe that the focus is more properly placed on internal rather than external equity. Conceivably, employees in organizations that promote from within (in other words, internal labor markets; Doeringer & Piore, 1971) may be more inclined toward this pay philosophy. It is likely that certain subgroups of employees will have different preferences, for example, incumbents in female-dominated jobs are likely to favor internal equity approaches. As discussed earlier, it is not known whether influencing employee preferences is possible or desirable. In some sense, individuals' preferences concerning philosophy here refer to distributive justice factors (e.g., Greenberg, 1987) (in other words, the inputs that can be used as a basis for reward allocation, such as job complexity), as well as the non-input factors, such as perceived "market value" of a job.

Similarly, the organization may indicate that it intends to compensate individuals on the basis of external equity, internal equity, some combination of both, or some alternative basis. Logically, there are at least four links that should be in place in order for differences in the intended organizational pay philosophy or strategy to affect satisfaction. First, organizational leaders must develop a strategy for determining pay levels and differences between jobs, such as a "market-leading" or "internally oriented" strategy (Weber & Rynes, 1991, p. 86). Research (Weber & Rynes, 1991) showed that managers in organizations employing "market-leading" and "internally oriented" pay strategies recommended higher pay levels than did other managers, when asked to assign pay levels to jobs. Second, pay strategy presumably should be related to the objectives the organization intends to accomplish, though there is very little evidence on this point. Weber and Rynes (1991) found that, in assigning pay rates to hypothetical jobs, managers from externally oriented firms placed significantly greater weight on market survey data than did those from internally oriented firms (although both also used the job evaluation data); however, managers from internally oriented firms did not place significantly greater weight on job evaluation data than did externally oriented managers.

Third, the philosophy or strategy should be communicated to employees. Fourth, it should be possible for employees to determine the extent to which the philosophy or strategy was actually carried out; if employees cannot determine this, obviously they may base their assessment of adherence on misperceptions. Conceivably, organizations that pay in a manner consistent with the stated philosophy would induce higher levels of hierarchy satisfaction. For example, if employees believe that the organization characterizes itself as paying "market-leading" rates but they believe that few if any jobs are paid at rates that the employees believe to be comparable to the highest market rates, they will not believe that there is much adherence to the "market-leading" approach. As was the case with individuals' preferences, the organization's stated pay philosophy here refers to distributive justice factors as well as the non-input factors.

Mulvey (1991) found that both (a) congruence between an individual's preferences for reward systems and the perceived reward system and (b) compliance between the stated and perceived reward systems were significantly related to hierarchy satisfaction. This was true even after the effects of other variables (negative affinity, pay level, raise amount, tenure, performance, and job satisfaction) were held constant.

As before, two moderators—perceived environmental, job, and organizational characteristics and employer communications—may be important. For example, engineers may be slotted in Pay Class 8, while human resources specialists are in Pay Class 6, and the difference may not be attributable to differences in job inputs. The jobs may be equally demanding overall. Human resources specialists may believe that they should receive the higher pay if the difference does not appear to be justified by market operation. Whether the human resources specialist views the reason for the difference to be justified will depend in part on the employer's statements concerning the reasons for the difference. But we propose that the human resources specialist also will consider the environment, in this case possibly pay survey results or information from friends and colleagues in other organizations, in weighing the credibility of the explanations given. Mulvey (1991) found that communications were significantly related to hierarchy satisfaction; he did not examine the interactions proposed here.

Employees' Knowledge of Other Pay Systems

Employees' knowledge of other pay systems may influence their beliefs about how the hierarchy system should operate. Conceivably, when a pay plan using a new basis for reward is implemented, employees will compare their new pay rates and potential for advancement to higher pay classes to the opportunities that they would have received under the old plan. Referent cognition theory (Folger, 1986) might predict that if the system implements new restrictions in movement or classifications that do not seem reasonable, employees will be less satisfied than if these conditions are not present. Unlike this factor's counterpart in range satisfaction, it is difficult to determine without more research whether variables pertaining to familiarity with other systems would be a distributive or a procedural justice factor.

The variables that moderate the effects of distribution preferences may also moderate the effects of knowledge of other pay systems. For example, if employers communicate clearly how the new system operates to benefit employees, it may not matter whether employees participated in a prior system.

The Employee's Views Concerning Participation in Hierarchy Decision Making

The research on procedural justice suggests that opportunities for participation in the formation and maintenance of the hierarchy may be relevant to satisfaction—with the hierarchy. Employees may wish to participate in the job evaluation process; organizations that permit them this voice may experience higher levels of hierarchy satisfaction. Because of the time demanded of participants and the skills that may be required, however, employees' wish to participate may be satisfied through appropriate representation. Clearly, this issue deserves research attention. Practitioners may wish to track experiences with this and other issues and share them with other professionals.

The Employee's Endorsement of Procedural Rules in Range Decision Making

It should be apparent that the operation of the pay system that determines the hierarchy is amenable to examination using the procedural justice literature, as discussed earlier. An excellent, in-depth discussion of procedural justice within the hierarchy (specifically with reference to comparable worth) has appeared elsewhere (Greenberg & McCarty, 1990). Similarly, many of the perceived environmental factors and job and organizational characteristics discussed in the range satisfaction model (e.g., organizational size) would also apply in this model. Therefore, the rules and moderators are merely illustrated here. As before, the first six rules are derived from Leventhal et al. (1980) followed by other rules; this discussion draws heavily from Miceli and Lane (1991).

Consistency. An organization may generally follow the results of a factor-based job evaluation, but deviate from it where pay surveys indicate a clear need to do so. If the organization explains how it is consistent in following what may appear at first to be an inconsistent policy, employees may accept and be satisfied with this operation. For example, the organization may explain that it is deviating from policy based on job evaluation, because turnover has been high (or would have been high, at the pay rate determined by the job evaluation) in the job categories in which the policy was (would have been) followed. Employees may believe that other organizations tend to do the same thing, and they may believe that "supply and demand" sets pay rates for jobs. They may be aware that other organizations are hiring workers in the given job category. If all of these conditions are present, then the system may be perceived as operating "consistently" and appropriately, fulfilling employer promises.

Bias Suppression. An example of the application of the bias suppression rule is that members of the compensation committee, which is appointed to undertake a new job evaluation system, should be free from bias favoring jobs in their divisions or disfavoring certain types of workers, such as minorities who may be overrepresented in certain types of jobs.

Schwab and H. Heneman (1986) found that multiple raters who used multiple sources of information to rate jobs independently, then arrived at a consensus concerning job value, produced highly reliable results. This suggests that the use of certain procedures in performing job evaluation should be more readily accepted as fair and satisfying, perhaps because multiple (vs. single) raters may be viewed as less biased. However, there has been little controlled research on the satisfaction of participants in the job evaluation process, or of employees who observe the process or its outcomes.

It may be that organization characteristics, such as size, age, or resources, will affect the perceptions of adherence to this (and other) rules. Organizations such as General Motors would likely have experienced professionals and support available to maintain and change reward systems. In contrast, employees may not expect a locally owned small organization to have a sophisticated system, and employees may take this factor into consideration when determining the manner in which the system should operate.

Accuracy.   When pay surveys are used to set pay rates, data should be complete, representative, and up to date in reflecting other organizations' pay rates. This practice would likely be viewed as promise fulfillment.

Correctability.   Employees should have the opportunity to provide information that is used by the supervisor to adjust pay rates. In this case, an employee who believes that his or her job has been slotted incorrectly may wish to have a "job audit" in which the job analysis process is undertaken or reviewed. A system that encourages correctability will probably be viewed as responsive to employee needs and wishes. As was the case with range satisfaction, Mulvey (1991) found that the opportunity to appeal was significantly correlated with hierarchy satisfaction, though no significant relationship remained when other variables were entered in a multivariate regression.

Representation.   Members of the compensation committee should be selected from a variety of locations and functional areas. This may enhance perceptions of flexibility and consistency.

Ethics.   Organizations should be truthful in indicating the strengths and weaknesses of the pay setting process that is being utilized, or they should indicate why information cannot be shared. Again, ethical systems may be viewed as more responsive, and that employers are fulfilling promises. It seems particularly likely that perceived environmental factors, such as competitive pressures, employee views and values, and organizational communications, would affect the extent to which ethical standards are perceived as being upheld in the system.

Three other additional rules have been identified. As was the case with range satisfaction, the first concerns proactivity. For example, organizations that adjust pay rates only when employees initiate job audits may be viewed less favorably than organizations that devote adequate resources to maintaining a competitive pay structure. Another rule may concern the sufficiency of funding for the pay structure as a whole. This rule is derived from Miceli et al. (1991) who, as noted earlier, proposed that the amount of money budgeted for pay increases must be viewed as sufficient to provide adequate increases to all deserving employees. Here, if pay rates in general are seen as substantially below the market, particularly where there are no extenuating circumstances, such as a high level of funding for benefits, plentiful intrinsic rewards, or a stimulating climate, employees may view the organization as having not "held up its end of the bargain." This would seem particularly true if the organization had promised to pay "competitively."

Third, the number of pay structures may imply a rule. The appropriateness of the number of systems that may be in existence in the organization may depend on a variety of factors (Henderson, 1989). For example, having several geographical locations that may require cost of living differentials may cause some organizations to establish different pay structures. Separate structures may be established for unionized and non-unionized employees. In this case, some employees may believe that the maintenance of multiple structures masks discrimination, because jobs that employees believe to be of comparable value may not be compared by the organization.

There is essentially no research in these areas; hence, it is not known whether any of these rules—or other rules—affects hierarchy satisfaction. It is not known whether individual differences in rule endorsement is a significant factor. Researchers are encouraged to explore these possibilities.

As was the case in range satisfaction, employees compare their standards against perceptions of the operation of the hierarchy. Hierarchy satisfaction may also be influenced by pay level; again, positive attributions may be made about the system as one ascends, but it is unlikely that this variable will be highly influential.

SUMMARY AND SUGGESTIONS FOR FUTURE RESEARCH AND PRACTICE

This chapter presented revisions of two preliminary models of pay system satisfaction originally proposed by Miceli and Lane (1991) and attempted to provide some guidance as to practical and research implications. A number of potential influences on range and hierarchy satisfaction were identified. The justice literature was shown to play a critical role in the development of theory and research on satisfaction with pay systems.

The models presented here follow previous literature on pay satisfaction in drawing on Lawler's (1971) original discrepancy model, with modifications as believed to be appropriate to predict satisfaction with pay systems. Lawler's model (1971) draws substantially on equity theory. Contributions of other theoretical perspectives should be considered. Recent research on pay level satisfaction (Sweeney, McFarlin, & Inderrieden, 1990) has shown that it is influenced by comparisons to standards other than those predicted by equity theory, namely those predicted by relative deprivation theory (Martin, 1981). In this chapter there was some attempt to show how relative deprivation theory may contribute to pay system satisfaction, but further empirical research is needed to more fully develop the model.

Brown and Huber (1991) found that reward-effort ratios in comparison with those of a referent other were associated with pay process satisfaction (i.e., scores on a slightly modified version of the structure-administration scale of the Pay Satisfaction Questionnaire). It would be interesting to determine whether this variable also related to range and hierarchy satisfaction as described here; if so the variable should be added to one or both of the models.

This chapter is highly speculative simply because there has been a dearth of theory development in the pay satisfaction arena, particularly with regard to facets of pay satisfaction other than pay level satisfaction. Researchers have not published many empirical studies examining pay system satisfaction. Given the obvious practical and importance of the topic, and considerable academic interest for an extended period of time, why is this true?

One very important reason why may be that pay system data is in many cases secret, particularly with regard to outsiders. Because of the need to protect employee privacy and the wish to maintain confidentiality for competitive reasons, many employers are understandably very reluctant to allow outside researchers to examine their practices and publish results. One solution might be to ask organizations to remove identification from internal studies and share them as appropriate. However, the obvious shortcoming of this approach is that the usefulness of such studies for others depends on the choice of questions and design of the study. In many cases, the employer does not have a staff member who is familiar with sophisticated survey design techniques. Further, the purpose for which the employer may undertake the study may be quite different from the needs that others would like to see addressed. Another alternative would require a long time horizon. Researchers would have to developing trusting relationships with employers over a period of time, perhaps doing work that is less sensitive, and then cooperate with employers to examine pay systems.

But there are other factors that probably have inhibited the development of literature as well. Employee surveys and studies often are threatening to employees; in the case of pay, they may fear that their own pay may be reduced as a result of their responses. Employers may fear that undertaking a survey signals to employees that something is wrong with the pay system. It may generate beliefs that the pay rates will be increased or the system will be changed for good or ill. The person who may grant access in studies of this type is often a compensation manager. He or she may fear that the survey will produce data that suggest he or she is not doing the job well. So the compensation manager understandably may be reluctant to allow entrée!

Another factor is that many employers rely on consulting firms to design and maintain their pay structures, and these firms will have proprietary privileges that may serve to exclude academicians. It is difficult for academicians to compete with consultants because in the pay area it is helpful to have large data banks for comparative analyses. Such banks are very difficult to accumulate by any individual.

Finally, most of the existing research is cross-sectional (e.g., based on a one-time survey). Studies using longitudinal or experimental data are very valuable. But longitudinal data are very rare in the pay area because longitudinal studies require some way of identifying individual participants and this raises fears of the breach of confidentiality, depressing response rates. Experimental data are virtually non-existent in the field (with the exception of Greenberg, 1990a), but this is not hard to understand. It is difficult to imagine an employer (or its employees) who would be willing to allow a researcher to make changes in the pay system in order to trace the effects of the change!

The unfortunate consequence of all of these factors is that we have speculative advice rather than more definitive prescriptions about the best ways to manage pay systems. It is hoped that through better understanding of the practical realities of conducting research in the area, greater cooperation can take place in the future to overcome some of these barriers.

ACKNOWLEDGMENTS

The contributions of Matthew C. Lane to this chapter are acknowledged.

REFERENCES

Ash, R. A., Dreher, G. F., & Bretz, R. D. (1987, April). *Dimensionality and stability of the Pay Satisfaction Questionnaire (PSQ)*. Paper presented at the second annual conference of the Society of Industrial/Organizational Psychology, Atlanta, GA.

Bartol, K. M., & Martin, D. C. (1990). When politics pays: Factors influencing managerial compensation decisions. *Personnel Psychology, 43*, 599–615.

Bies, R. J. (1987). The predicament of injustice: The management of moral outrage. In L. L. Cummings & B. M. Staw (Eds.), *Research in organizational behavior* (Vol. 9, pp. 289–320). Greenwich, CT: JAI Press.

Bies, R. J., & Shapiro, D. L. (1988). Voice and justification: Their influence on procedural fairness judgments. *Academy of Management Journal, 31*, 676–685.

Brown, K. A., & Huber, V. L. (1991). *Lowering floors and raising ceilings: Effects on pay satisfaction*. Manuscript submitted for publication.

Capelli, P., & Sherer, P. D. (1988). Satisfaction, market wages, and labor relations: An airline study. *Industrial Relations, 27*, 56–73.

Carraher, S. M. (in press). A validity study of the pay satisfaction questionnaire (PSQ). *Educational and Psychological Measurement*.

Cropanzano, R., & Folger, R. (1989). Referent cognitions and task decision autonomy: Beyond equity theory. *Journal of Applied Psychology, 74*, 293–299.

Cropanzano, R., & Folger, R. (in press). Procedural justice and worker motivation. In R. M. Steers & L. W. Porter (Eds.), *Motivation and work behavior*. New York: McGraw-Hill.

Deckop, J. R. (1990). *A general model of pay satisfaction*. Manuscript submitted for publication.

Doeringer, P. B., & Piore, M. J. (1971). *Internal labor markets and manpower analysis*. Lexington, MA: Heath.

Dreher, G. F., Dougherty, T. W., & Whitely, W. (1988, August). *Influence tactics and salary attainment: A study of sex-based salary differentials*. Paper presented at the 48th annual meeting of the Academy of Management, Anaheim, CA.

Dyer, L., & Theriault, R. (1976). The determinants of pay satisfaction. *Journal of Applied Psychology, 61*, 596–604.

Ferris, G. R., Fedor, D. B., Chachere, J. G., & Pondy, L. R. (1989). Myths and politics in organizational contexts. *Group and Organization Studies, 14*, 83–103.

Ferris, G. R., Russ, G. S., & Fandt, P. M. (1989). Politics in organizations. In R. A. Giacalone &

P. Rosenfeld (Eds.), *Impression management in the organization* (pp. 143–170). Hillsdale, NJ: Lawrence Erlbaum Associates.

Florkowski, G. W. (1990, January). Analyzing group incentive plans. *HRMagazine,* pp. 36–38.

Folger, R. (1986). A referent cognitions theory of relative deprivation. In J. M. Olson, C. P. Herman, & M. P. Zanna (Eds.), *Relative deprivation and social comparison: The Ontario symposium* (Vol. 4, pp. 33–54). Hillsdale, NJ: Lawrence Erlbaum Associates.

Folger, R., & Konovsky, M. A. (1989). Effects of procedural and distributive justice on reactions to pay raise decisions. *Academy of Management Journal, 32,* 115–130.

Gerhart, B., & Rynes, S. (1991). Determinants and consequences of salary negotiations by male and female MBA graduates. *Journal of Applied Psychology, 76,* 256–262.

Gould, S., & Penley, L. E. (1984). Career strategies and salary progression: A study of their relationships in a municipal bureaucracy. *Organizational Behavior and Human Performance, 34,* 244–265.

Greenberg, J. (1982). Approaching equity and avoiding inequity in groups and organizations. In J. Greenberg & R. L. Cohen (Eds.), *Equity and justice in social behavior* (pp. 389–434). New York: Academic Press.

Greenberg, J. (1987). A taxonomy of organizational justice theories. *Academy of Management Review, 12,* 9–22.

Greenberg, J. (1990). Employee theft as a reaction to underpayment inequity: The hidden cost of pay cuts. *Journal of Applied Psychology, 75,* 561–568.

Greenberg, J., & McCarty, C. L. (1990). Comparable worth: A matter of justice. In G. R. Ferris & K. M. Rowland (Eds.), *Research in personnel and human resources management* (Vol. 8, pp. 111–157). Greenwich, CT: JAI Press.

Henderson, R. L. (1989). *Compensation management: Rewarding performance* (5th ed.). Reston, VA: Reston.

Heneman, H. G., III. (1985). Pay satisfaction. In K. M. Rowland & G. R. Ferris (Eds.), *Research in personnel and human resources management* (Vol. 3, pp. 115–139). Greenwich, CT: JAI Press.

Heneman, H. G., III, & Schwab, D. P. (1985). Pay satisfaction: Its multidimensional nature and measurement. *International Journal of Psychology, 20,* 129–141.

Heneman, R. L., Greenberger, D. B., & Strasser, S. (1988). The relationship between pay-for-performance perceptions and pay satisfaction. *Personnel Psychology, 41,* 745–761.

Jenkins, D. G., Jr., & Lawler, E. E., III. (1981). Impact of employee participation in pay plan development. *Organizational Behavior and Human Performance, 28,* 111–128.

Konovsky, M. A., Folger, R., & Fogel, D. S. (1990). *A panel analysis of the effects of distributive and procedural justice on employee commitment and pay satisfaction.* Manuscript submitted for publication.

Lawler, E. E. (1971). *Pay and organizational effectiveness: A psychological view.* New York: McGraw-Hill.

Leventhal, G. S., Karuza, J., & Fry, W. R. (1980). Beyond fairness: A theory of allocation preferences. In J. Mikula (Ed.), *Justice and social interaction* (pp. 127–218). New York: Springer-Verlag.

Magjuka, R. (1989, August). *Issues in the design of effective participative systems.* Paper presented at the 49th annual meeting of the Academy of Management, Washington, DC.

Martin, J. (1981). Relative deprivation: A theory of distributive justice for an era of shrinking resources. In L. L. Cummings & B. M. Staw (Eds.), *Research in organizational behavior* (Vol. 3, pp. 53–107). Greenwich, CT: JAI Press.

Miceli, M. P., Jung, I. J., Near, J. P., & Greenberger, D. B. (1991). Predictors and outcomes of reactions to pay-for-performance plans. *Journal of Applied Psychology, 76,* 508–521.

Miceli, M. P., & Lane, M. C. (1991). Antecedents of pay satisfaction: A review and extension. In K. Rowland & G. R. Ferris (Eds.), *Research in personnel and human resource management* (Vol. 9, pp. 235–309). Greenwich, CT: JAI Press.

Motowidlo, S. J. (1983). Predicting sales turnover from pay satisfaction and expectation. *Journal of Applied Psychology, 68,* 484–490.

Mulvey, P. (1991). *Pay system satisfaction: An exploration of the construct and its predictors.* Unpublished doctoral dissertation, The Ohio State University, School of Business, Columbus.

Mulvey, P. W., Miceli, M. P., & Near, J. P. (in press). The Pay Satisfaction Questionnaire: A confirmatory factor analysis. *Journal of Social Psychology.*

Orpen, C., & Bonnici, J. (1987). A factor analytic investigation of the Pay Satisfaction Questionnaire. *Journal of Social Psychology, 127,* 391–392.

Renwick, P. A., & Lawler, E. E. (1978, December). What do you really want from your job? *Psychology Today,* pp. 53–66.

Scarpello, V., Huber, V., & Vandenberg, R. J. (1988). Compensation satisfaction: Its measurement and dimensionality. *Journal of Applied Psychology, 73,* 163–171.

Schwab, D. P., & Heneman, H. G., III. (1986). Assessment of a consensus-based multiple information source job evaluation system. *Journal of Applied Psychology, 71,* 354–356.

Sweeney, P., & McFarlin, D., & Inderrieden, E. J. (1990). Using relative deprivation theory to explain satisfaction with income and pay level: A multistudy examination. *Academy of Management Journal, 33,* 423–436.

Weber, C. L., & Rynes, S. L. (1991). Effects of compensation strategy on job pay decisions. *Academy of Management Journal, 34,* 86–109.

Ziemak, J. P. (1988). *Personal, internal, and external equity: Multiple facets of pay fairness.* Unpublished doctoral dissertation, The Ohio State University, Department of Psychology, Columbus.

Author Index

Subject Index